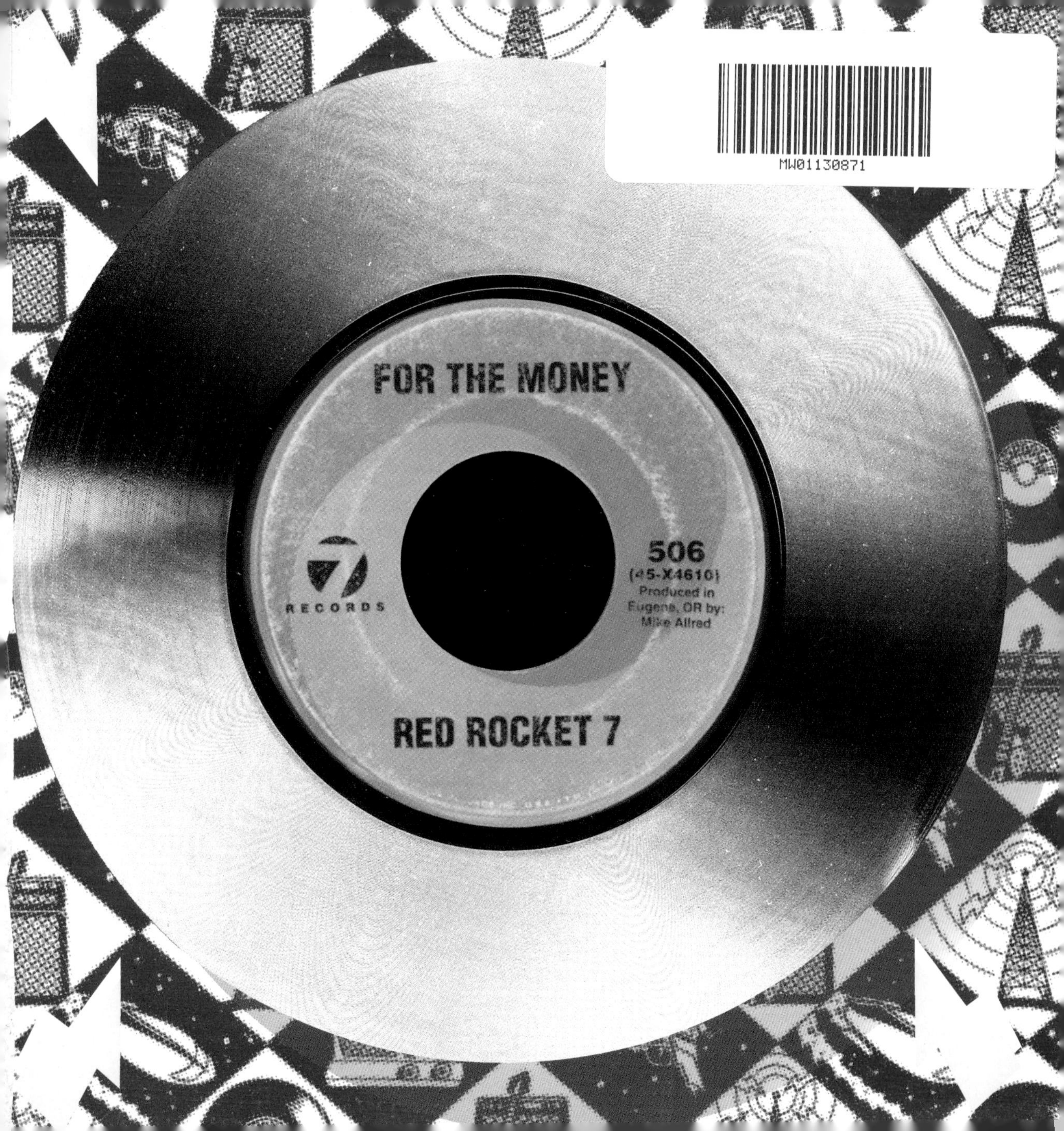
FOR THE MONEY
RECORDS
506
(45-X4610)
Produced in
Eugene, OR by:
Mike Allred
RED ROCKET 7

WRITTEN AND ILLUSTRATED BY
MICHAEL ALLRED

COLORS AND SEPARATIONS	EDITED BY	INTRO BY	OUTRO BY
LAURA ALLRED	**JAMIE S. RICH**	**ROBERT RODRIGUEZ**	**GERARD WAY**

IMAGE COMICS, INC.

Erik Larsen - *CFO*
Todd McFarlane - *President*
Marc Silvestri - *CEO*
Jim Valentino - *Vice-President*

Eric Stephenson - *Publisher*
Joe Keatinge - *PR & Marketing Coordinator*
Branwyn Bigglestone - *Accounts Manager*
Tyler Shainline - *Administrative Assistant*
Traci Hui - *Traffic Manager*
Allen Hui - *Production Manager*
Drew Gill - *Production Artist*
Jonathan Chan - *Production Artist*
Monica Garcia - *Production Artist*

www.imagecomics.com

International Rights Representative: Christine Jensen (christine@gfloystudio.com)

RED ROCKET 7. First Printing. Published by Image Comics, Inc. Office of publication: 1942 University Avenue, Suite 305, Berkeley, California 94704. Copyright © 2008 MICHAEL ALLRED. Originally published in single magazine form as RED ROCKET 7 #1-7 by DARK HORSE COMICS, INC. All rights reserved. RED ROCKET 7 (including all prominent characters featured herein), its logo and all character likenesses are trademarks of MICHAEL ALLRED, unless otherwise noted. Image Comics is a trademark of Image Comics, Inc. All rights reserved. No part of this publication may be reproduced or transmitted, in any form or by any means (except for short excerpts for review purposes) without the express written permission of Image Comics, Inc. All names, characters, events and locales in this publication are entirely fictional. Any resemblance to actual persons (living or dead), events or places, without satiric intent, is coincidental. PRINTED IN CANADA. ISBN: 978-1-58240-998-6 (TPB) - ISBN: 978-1-58240-997-9 (HC)

CONTENTS

INTRODUCTION

By ROBERT RODRIGUEZ

I guess for me this all started the day I received a script for a proposed *Madman* movie. It came in the mail from a representative of Mike Allred. Mike had made sure that along with the script came a box full of Madman toys, comics, model kits, yo-yo's, and playing cards.

Now, for me personally, there's nothing on this earth greater than receiving cool shit in the mail, especially when it's unexpected. I was so impressed not just by the script, but by the sheer volume of cool stuff Mike was putting out, that I had to call him later that evening and meet him for the first time over the phone.

He asked if I had seen *Red Rocket 7*, and the odd thing was that I had, in fact, just picked up the first issue not two days earlier, and at the time I hadn't even noticed it was Mike's. I had bought it because I collect everything and anything that has to do with rockets, that being my son's first name.

When he explained the Red Rocket 7 project to me, I got real excited by it. For one, I knew how successful he'd been with the *Madman* series and was impressed that he'd put that aside to do something else. Because one, that's really ballsy, and two, that's really cool.

We talked a long time about Red Rocket, about Madman, about having kids with cool names, about how he'd been inspired by independent filmmakers to make films of his own, about his music he was recording...on and on.

You meet people now and again that are truly brothers. Quentin Tarantino, for example, is a brother to me. We hit it off when we met, we were into the same stuff, and we could talk about the cool shit we were into for hours. Same with Mike. Mike's a brother. Mike does all the cool shit I'd love to be doing. We'd have been best friends if we had gone to junior high together. We'd have been drawing in class, making movies on the weekends, and recording music all the time. If I could go back to junior high and do anything different, then, besides kissing Catalina, I would probably populate my class with people like Mike and Quentin. That way I could make cool shit all day long, having cool people to bounce ideas off of and to glean inspiration from.

So when Mike asked me if I'd write the intro to the *Red Rocket 7* collection (realize this all happened in that same first telephone conversation, that's what I mean by brothers...), I said, "Sure!"

Issue one was barely out by a few days and Mike had already mapped out the collection! I was starting to realize that Mike was a lot more ambitious than I was. He's also better at setting and then hitting goals. But there was no jealousy, just admiration. Again, we're brothers.

Then he went into how he had a dream one night, an incredibly detailed and inspiring dream. I got really interested because I believe in the inspiration one gets from dreams. He told me that he woke up from this dream, wrote it down, and there it was--a dream so intense it fueled a year's worth of inspiration that included: the comic series *Red Rocket 7*, a full length movie idea which he had already shot and edited and was sending me a copy called *Astroesque*, and a record album titled, what else, *Son of Red Rocket 7*.

Whoa! I, too, used to keep a tablet by my bed hoping for the day that a fevered, inspiring dream would strike. Only to be disappointed that my nocturnal scribblings conjured up nothing more than "A guy in a room. Two fish walk in and start talking. The End." But Mike goes to sleep and has a dream that brings a year's worth of projects. I could feel my eyes narrowing as he told me this. I looked at my skin and it was turning green. That bastard!

I have to say that meeting Mike on the phone was turning into a humbling experience. I like to think I'm a hard working guy, that I create and work at my different arts and hobbies with insatiable glee. But the truth is, Mike is the master! I realized that had I really gone to junior high with Mike, I'd have been left in his dust.

He then told me he'd sent a package of his latest works. A few days later, a huge box arrived with even more comics, T-shirts, cards, magnets (is there anything this guy doesn't make?), Madman dolls, model kits, fake tattoos, even little balsa wood Madman planes, not to mention works in progress like his record and a trailer for yet another film he was working on (the horror movie, *Eyes to Heaven*). He even sent me some Spanish versions of *Madman*. It was amazing. It was as if someone had sent me their life's work in one really big box. Then I noticed a handwritten note on the side of the box that read: One of three.

Damn.

I was starting to feel like Cain to his Abel. It was more than humbling. But by the time I'd finished scouring through all his stuff, I was truly inspired...And to get inspired by another artist is almost as great as receiving cool shit in the mail. It sends you out on a mission...it makes you want to work harder, and it gives you a glimpse at the possibilities. I am one that thrives on inspiration, trying hard to give it back as well as receive. Mike is an inspiration. He's a cool as shit dude that creates because he has to, and he's damn good at it. He's an endless stream of ideas, and he works around the clock to deliver them.

And I know how Mike's story ends. Quite simply, it doesn't. This guy is gonna keep going onward and upward.

Like a rocket.

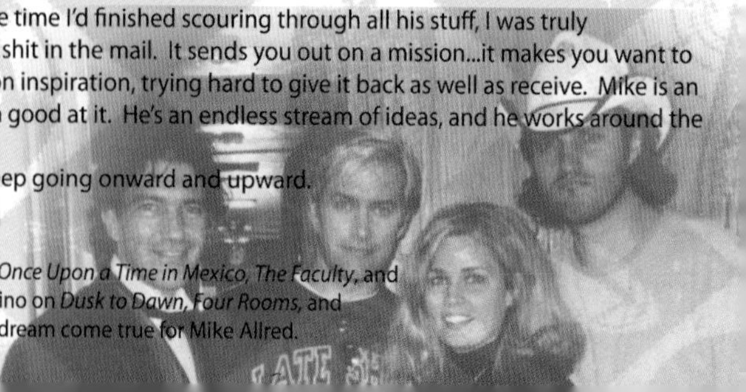

Robert Rodriguez is doing just fine as the filmmaker responsible for *El Mariachi, Desperado, Once Upon a Time in Mexico, The Faculty*, and the *Spy Kids* Trilogy, among countless other projects. And has worked with Quentin Tarantino on *Dusk to Dawn, Four Rooms*, and *Grindhouse*. He is currently developing a live action *Madman* movie to help make another dream come true for Mike Allred.

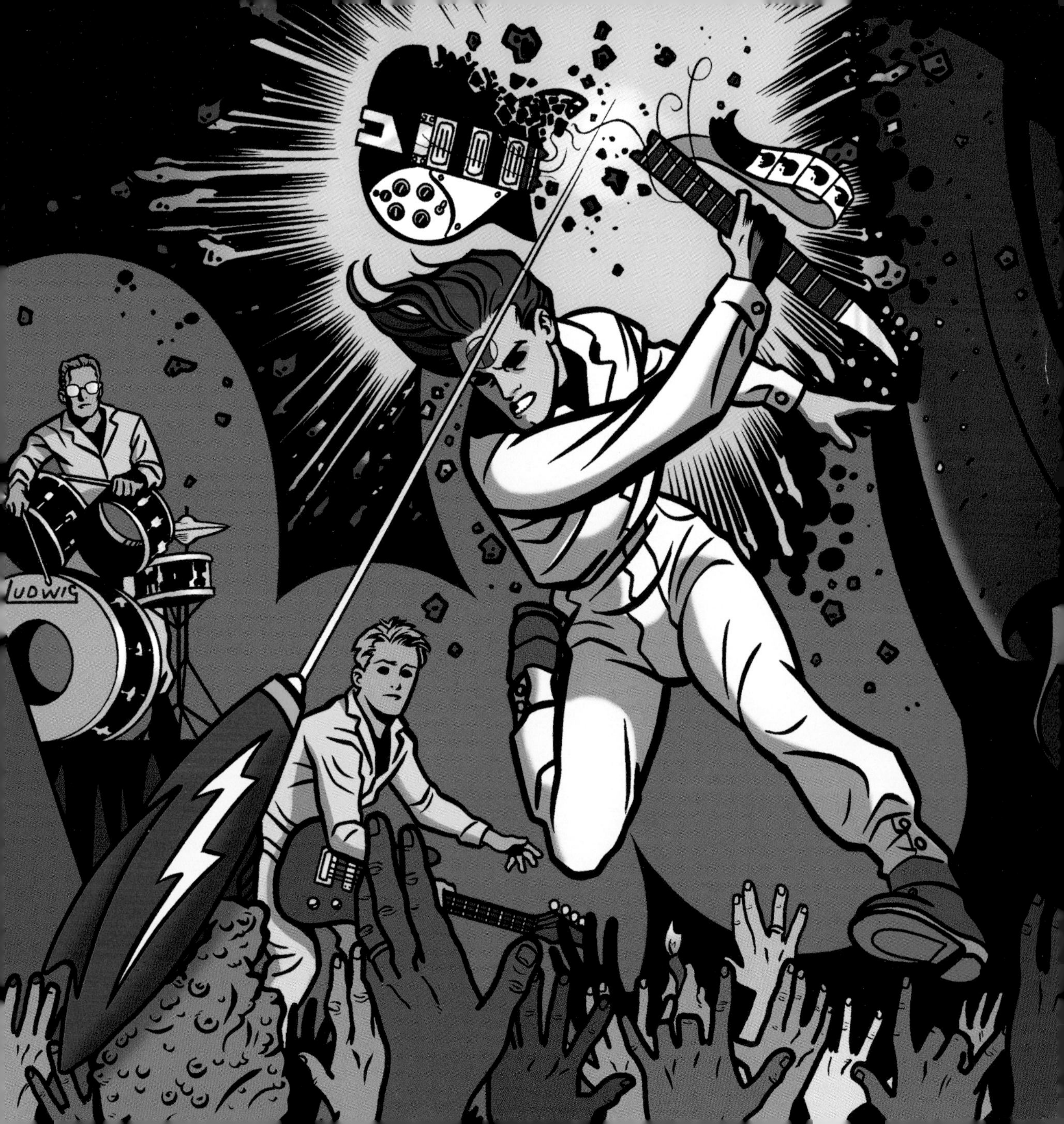

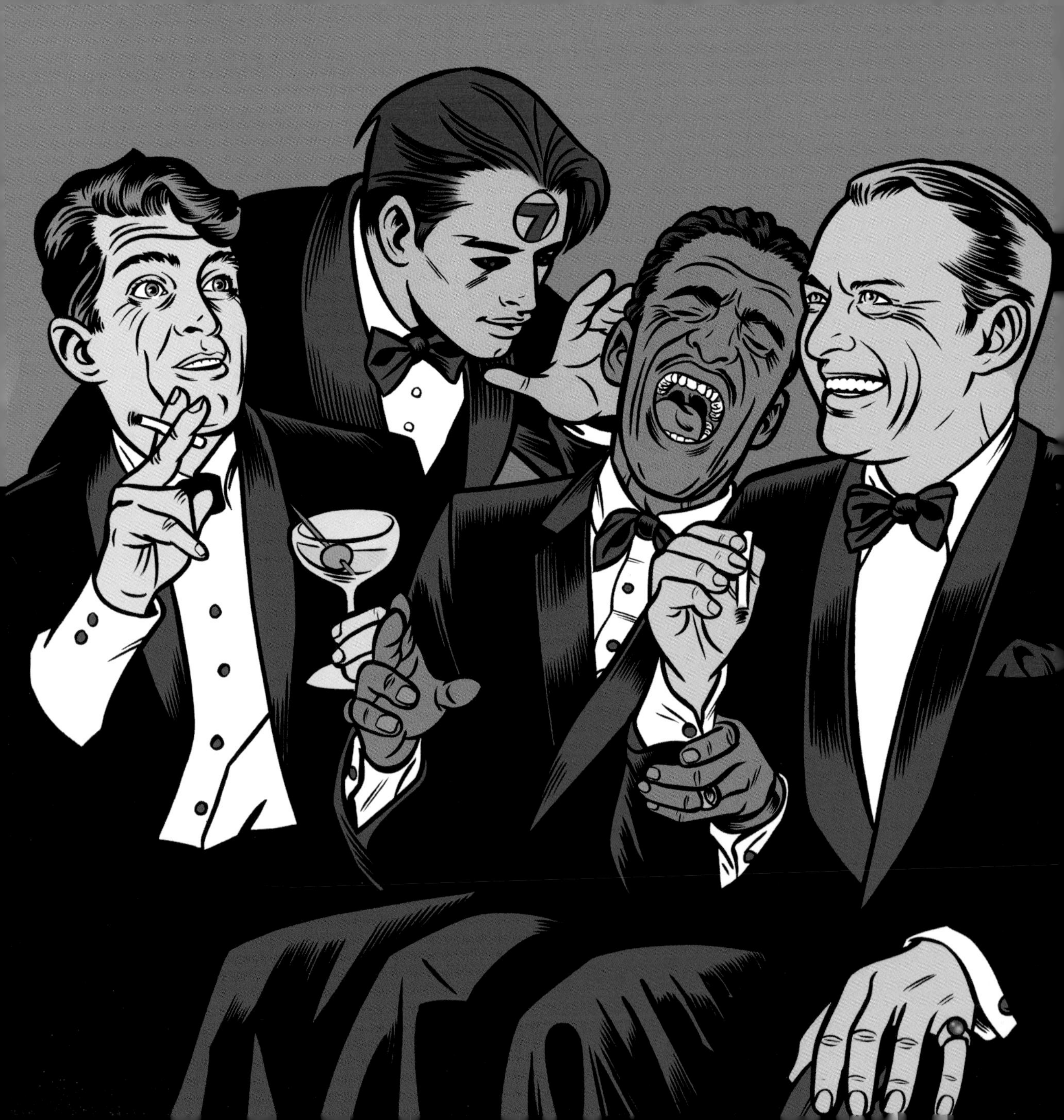

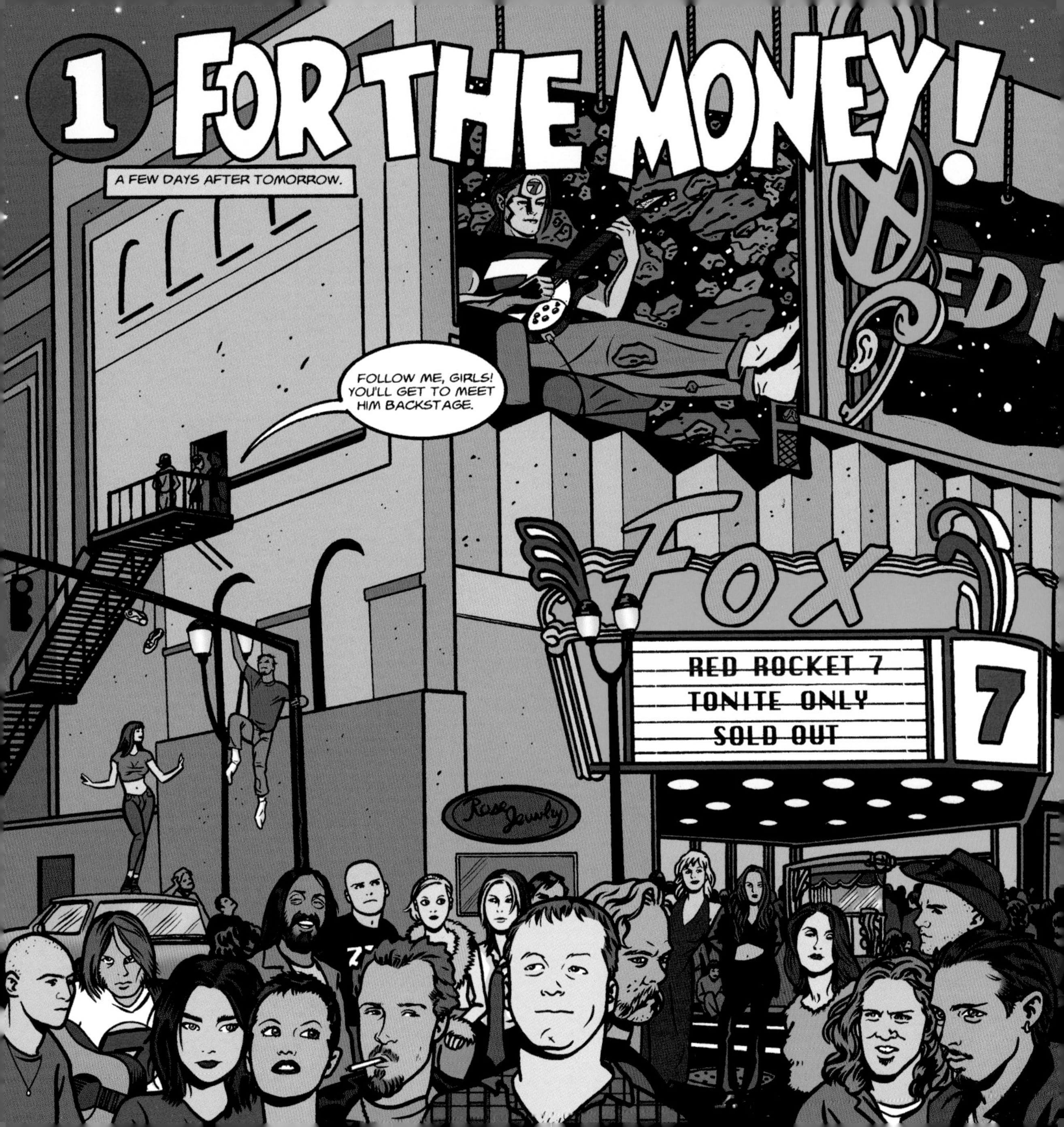
1 FOR THE MONEY!
A FEW DAYS AFTER TOMORROW.
FOLLOW ME, GIRLS! YOU'LL GET TO MEET HIM BACKSTAGE.
FOX
RED ROCKET 7
TONITE ONLY
SOLD OUT
7

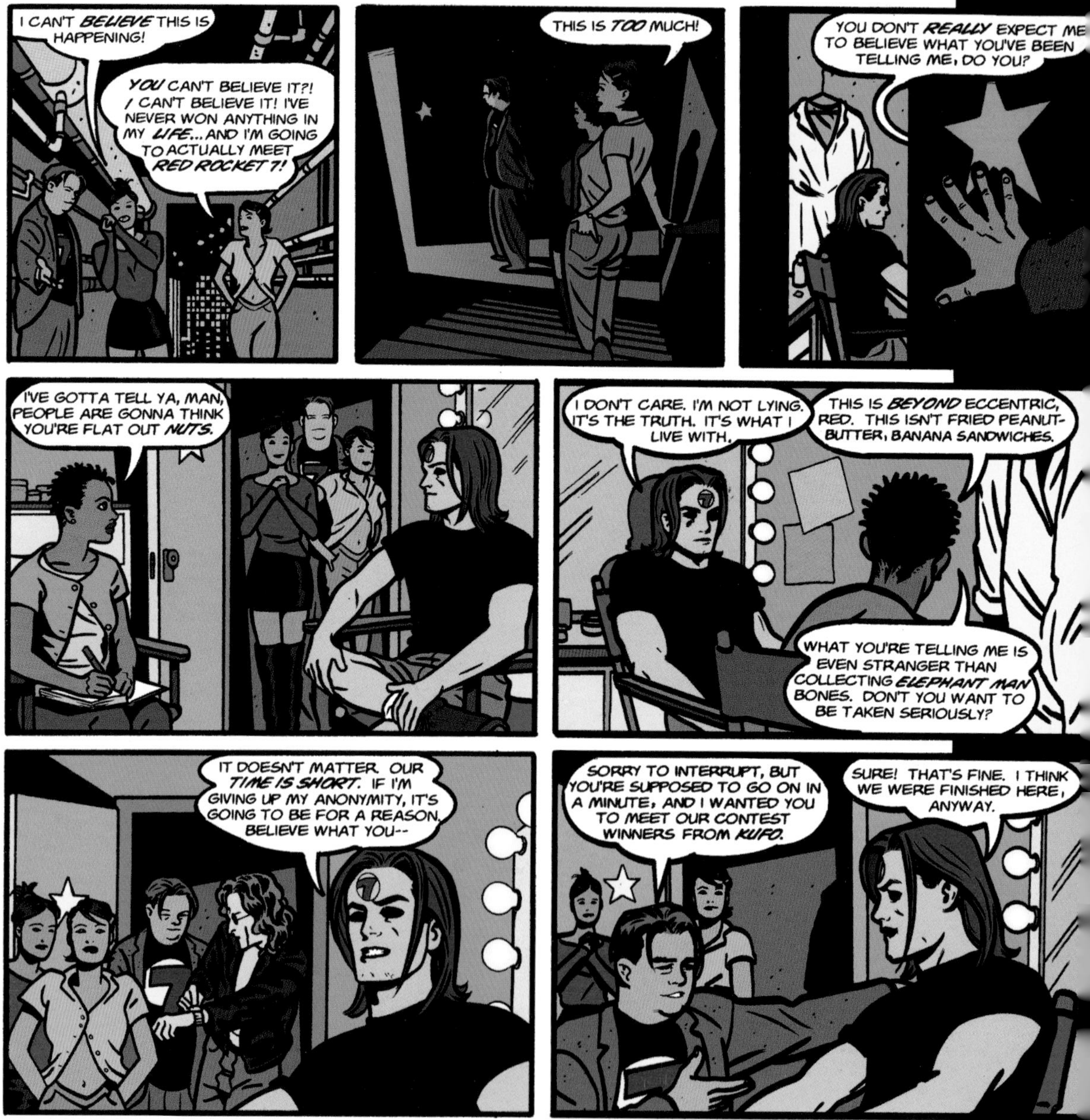

I CAN'T BELIEVE THIS IS HAPPENING!
YOU CAN'T BELIEVE IT?! I CAN'T BELIEVE IT! I'VE NEVER WON ANYTHING IN MY LIFE... AND I'M GOING TO ACTUALLY MEET RED ROCKET 7!
THIS IS TOO MUCH!
YOU DON'T REALLY EXPECT ME TO BELIEVE WHAT YOU'VE BEEN TELLING ME, DO YOU?
I'VE GOTTA TELL YA, MAN, PEOPLE ARE GONNA THINK YOU'RE FLAT OUT NUTS.
I DON'T CARE. I'M NOT LYING. IT'S THE TRUTH. IT'S WHAT I LIVE WITH.
THIS IS BEYOND ECCENTRIC, RED. THIS ISN'T FRIED PEANUT-BUTTER, BANANA SANDWICHES.
WHAT YOU'RE TELLING ME IS EVEN STRANGER THAN COLLECTING ELEPHANT MAN BONES. DON'T YOU WANT TO BE TAKEN SERIOUSLY?
IT DOESN'T MATTER. OUR TIME IS SHORT. IF I'M GIVING UP MY ANONYMITY, IT'S GOING TO BE FOR A REASON. BELIEVE WHAT YOU--
SORRY TO INTERRUPT, BUT YOU'RE SUPPOSED TO GO ON IN A MINUTE, AND I WANTED YOU TO MEET OUR CONTEST WINNERS FROM KUFO.
SURE! THAT'S FINE. I THINK WE WERE FINISHED HERE, ANYWAY.

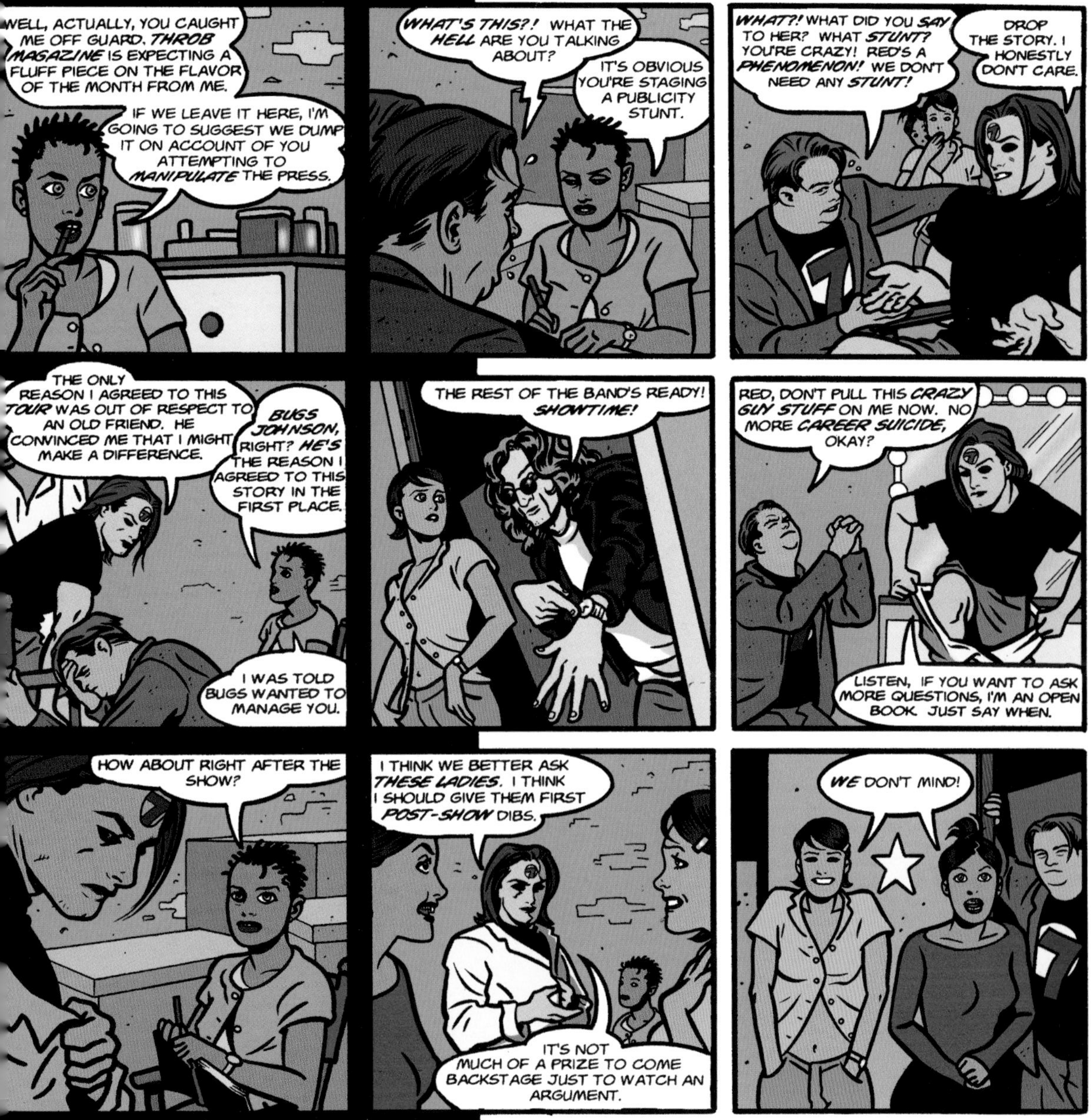
WELL, ACTUALLY, YOU CAUGHT ME OFF GUARD. THROB MAGAZINE IS EXPECTING A FLUFF PIECE ON THE FLAVOR OF THE MONTH FROM ME.
IF WE LEAVE IT HERE, I'M GOING TO SUGGEST WE DUMP IT ON ACCOUNT OF YOU ATTEMPTING TO MANIPULATE THE PRESS.
WHAT'S THIS?! WHAT THE HELL ARE YOU TALKING ABOUT?
IT'S OBVIOUS YOU'RE STAGING A PUBLICITY STUNT.
WHAT?! WHAT DID YOU SAY TO HER? WHAT STUNT? YOU'RE CRAZY! RED'S A PHENOMENON! WE DON'T NEED ANY STUNT!
DROP THE STORY. I HONESTLY DON'T CARE.
THE ONLY REASON I AGREED TO THIS TOUR WAS OUT OF RESPECT TO AN OLD FRIEND. HE CONVINCED ME THAT I MIGHT MAKE A DIFFERENCE.
BUGS JOHNSON, RIGHT? HE'S THE REASON I AGREED TO THIS STORY IN THE FIRST PLACE.
I WAS TOLD BUGS WANTED TO MANAGE YOU.
THE REST OF THE BAND'S READY! SHOWTIME!
RED, DON'T PULL THIS CRAZY GUY STUFF ON ME NOW. NO MORE CAREER SUICIDE, OKAY?
LISTEN, IF YOU WANT TO ASK MORE QUESTIONS, I'M AN OPEN BOOK. JUST SAY WHEN.
HOW ABOUT RIGHT AFTER THE SHOW?
I THINK WE BETTER ASK THESE LADIES. I THINK I SHOULD GIVE THEM FIRST POST-SHOW DIBS.
IT'S NOT MUCH OF A PRIZE TO COME BACKSTAGE JUST TO WATCH AN ARGUMENT.
WE DON'T MIND!

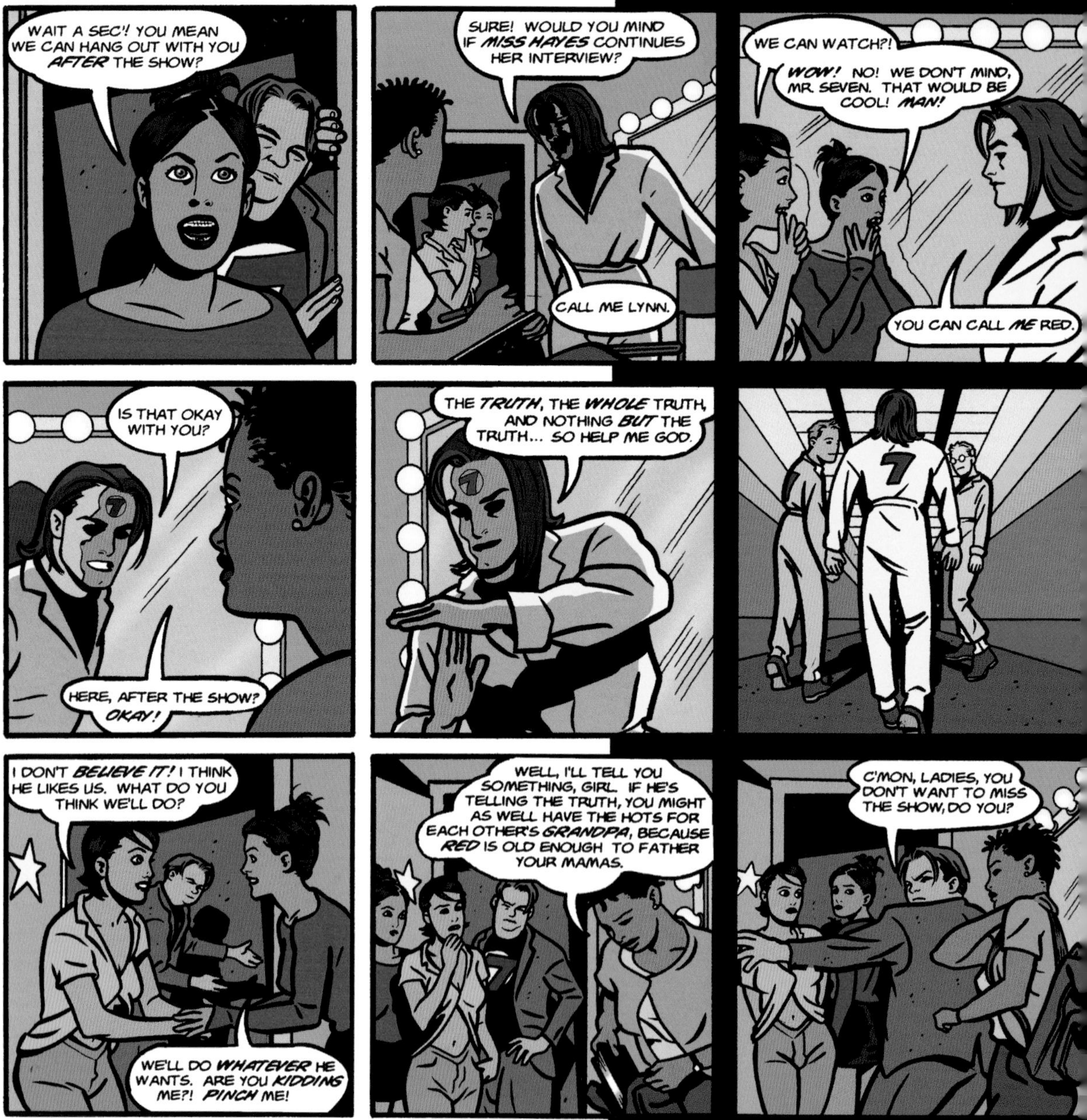
WAIT A SEC'! YOU MEAN WE CAN HANG OUT WITH YOU AFTER THE SHOW?
SURE! WOULD YOU MIND IF MISS HAYES CONTINUES HER INTERVIEW?
CALL ME LYNN.
WE CAN WATCH?!
WOW! NO! WE DON'T MIND, MR. SEVEN. THAT WOULD BE COOL! MAN!
YOU CAN CALL ME RED.
IS THAT OKAY WITH YOU?
HERE, AFTER THE SHOW? OKAY!
THE TRUTH, THE WHOLE TRUTH, AND NOTHING BUT THE TRUTH... SO HELP ME GOD.
I DON'T BELIEVE IT! I THINK HE LIKES US. WHAT DO YOU THINK WE'LL DO?
WE'LL DO WHATEVER HE WANTS. ARE YOU KIDDING ME?! PINCH ME!
WELL, I'LL TELL YOU SOMETHING, GIRL. IF HE'S TELLING THE TRUTH, YOU MIGHT AS WELL HAVE THE HOTS FOR EACH OTHER'S GRANDPA, BECAUSE RED IS OLD ENOUGH TO FATHER YOUR MAMAS.
C'MON, LADIES, YOU DON'T WANT TO MISS THE SHOW, DO YOU?

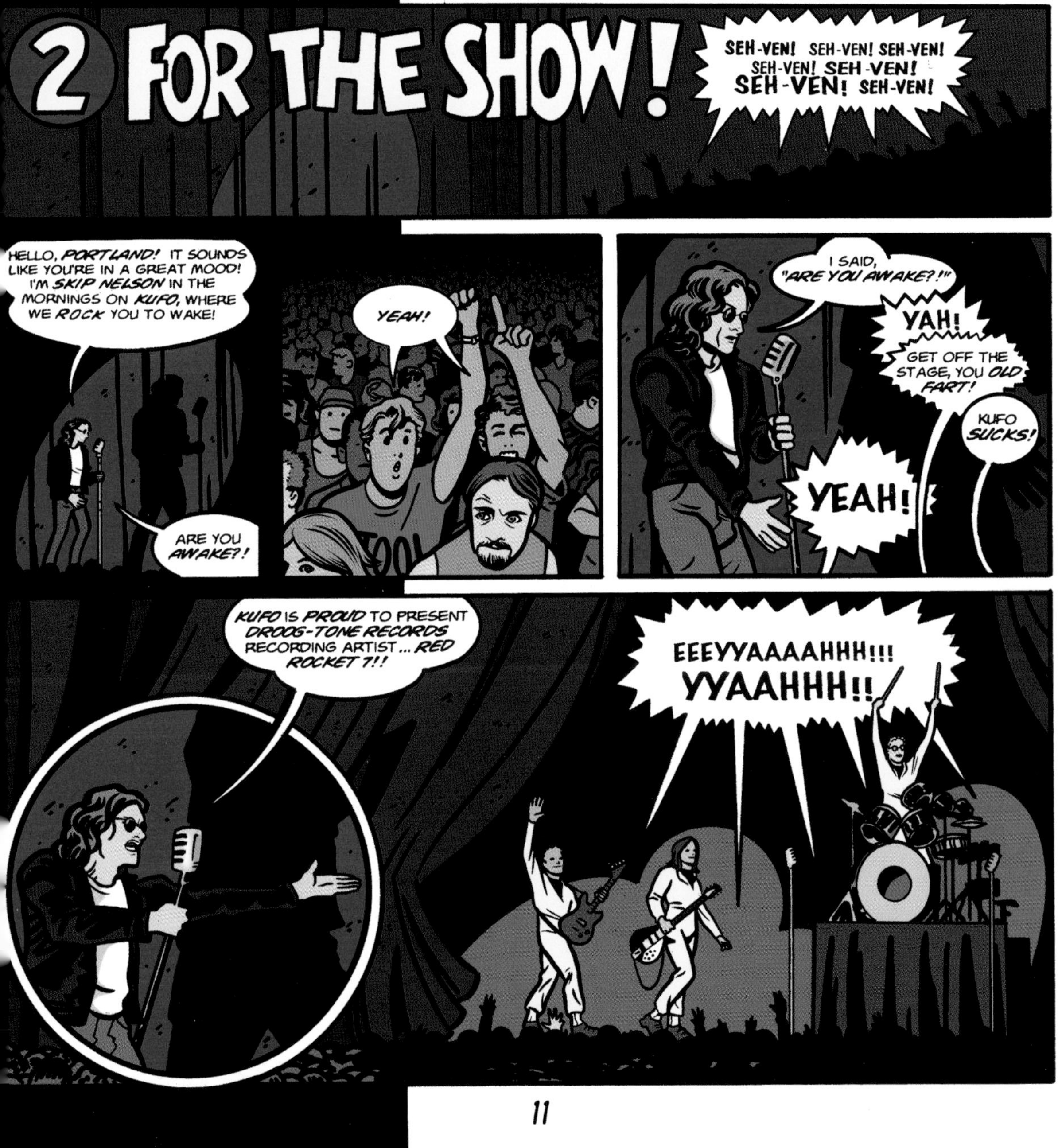

2 FOR THE SHOW!
SEH-VEN! SEH-VEN! SEH-VEN! SEH-VEN! SEH-VEN! SEH-VEN! SEH-VEN!
HELLO, PORTLAND! IT SOUNDS LIKE YOU'RE IN A GREAT MOOD! I'M SKIP NELSON IN THE MORNINGS ON KUFO, WHERE WE ROCK YOU TO WAKE!
ARE YOU AWAKE?!
YEAH!
I SAID, "ARE YOU AWAKE?!"
YAH!
GET OFF THE STAGE, YOU OLD FART!
KUFO SUCKS!
YEAH!
KUFO IS PROUD TO PRESENT DROOG-TONE RECORDS RECORDING ARTIST... RED ROCKET 7!!
EEEYYAAAAAHHH!!! YYAAHHH!!

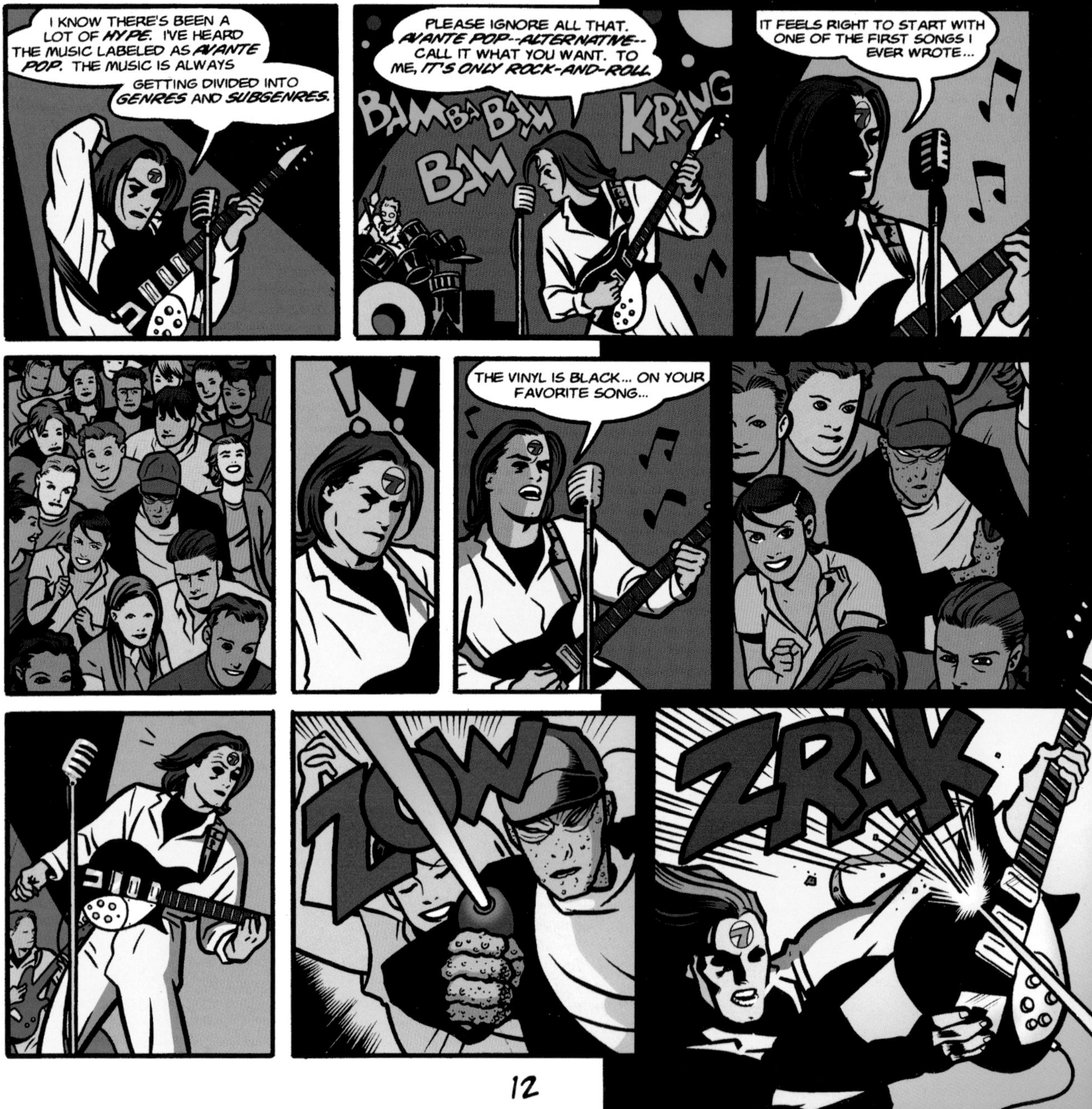
I KNOW THERE'S BEEN A LOT OF HYPE. I'VE HEARD THE MUSIC LABELED AS AVANTE POP. THE MUSIC IS ALWAYS GETTING DIVIDED INTO GENRES AND SUBGENRES.
PLEASE IGNORE ALL THAT. AVANTE POP--ALTERNATIVE-- CALL IT WHAT YOU WANT. TO ME, IT'S ONLY ROCK-AND-ROLL.
BAMBABAM
BAM
KRANG
IT FEELS RIGHT TO START WITH ONE OF THE FIRST SONGS I EVER WROTE...
!!
THE VINYL IS BLACK... ON YOUR FAVORITE SONG...
ZOW
ZRAK

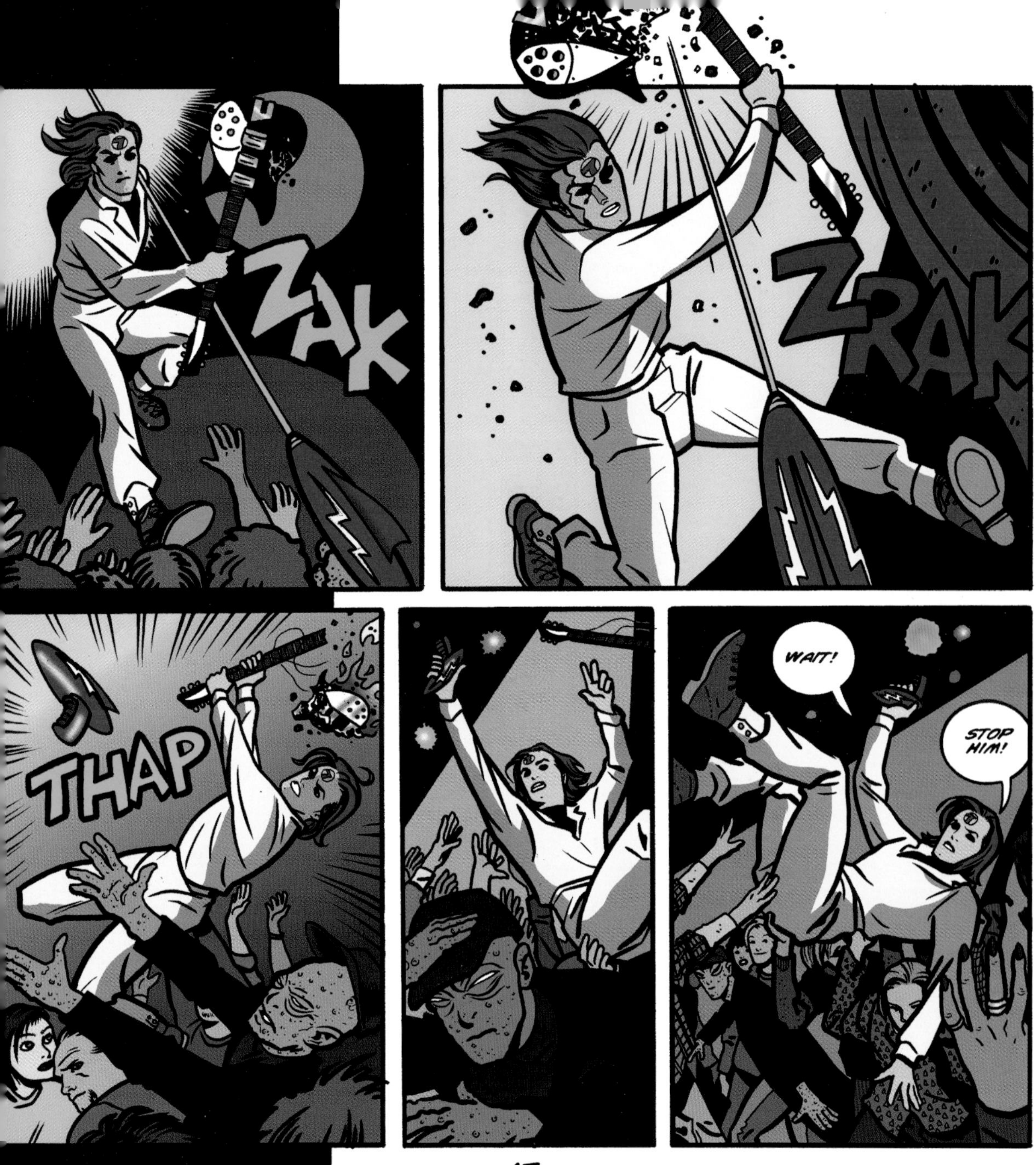
ZAK
ZRAK
THAP
WAIT!
STOP HIM!

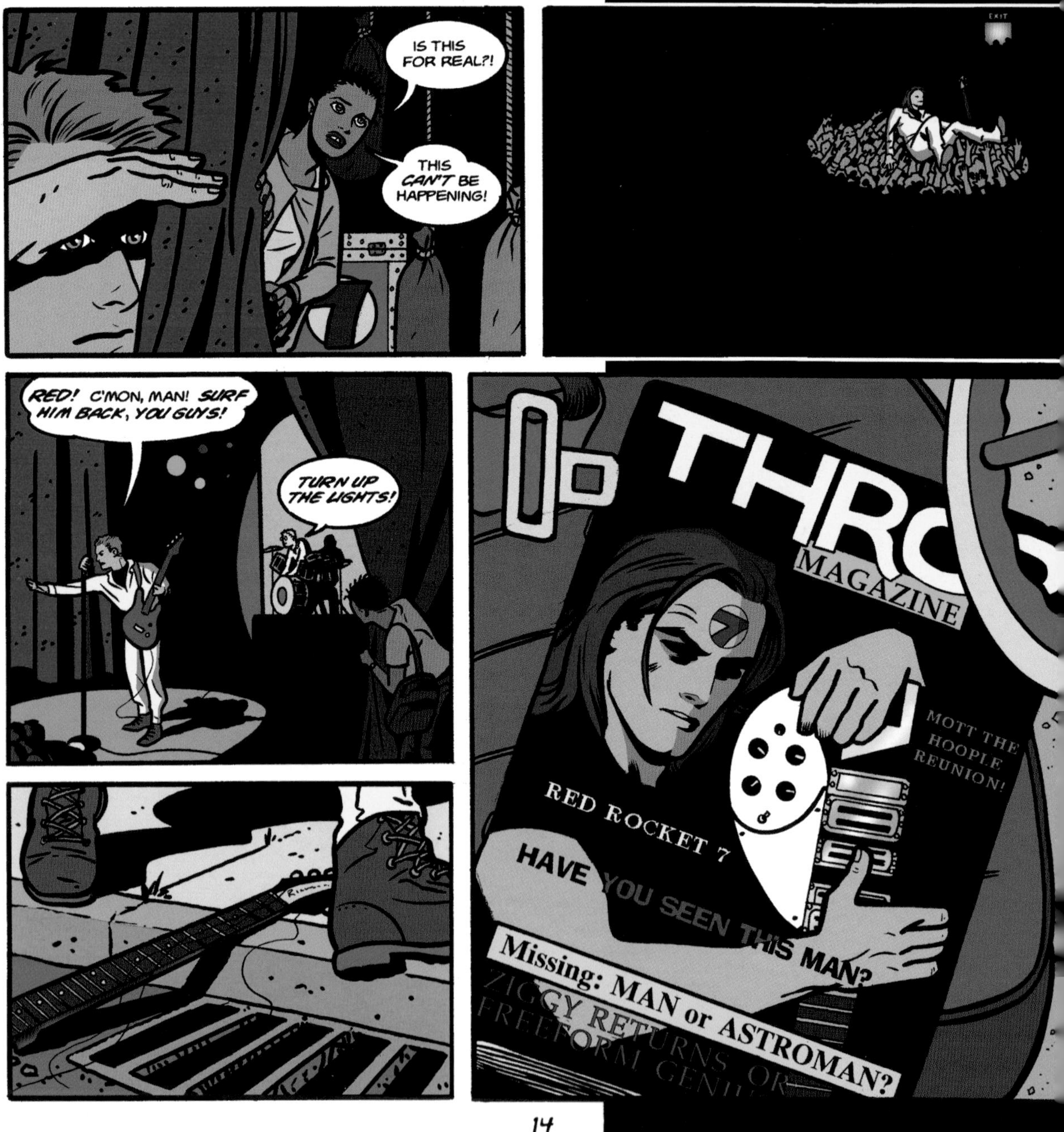
IS THIS FOR REAL?!
THIS *CAN'T* BE HAPPENING!
RED! C'MON, MAN! *SURF HIM BACK, YOU GUYS!*
TURN UP THE LIGHTS!
MAGAZINE
MOTT THE HOOPLE REUNION!
RED ROCKET 7
HAVE YOU SEEN THIS MAN?
Missing: MAN or ASTROMAN?
ZIGGY RETURNS OR

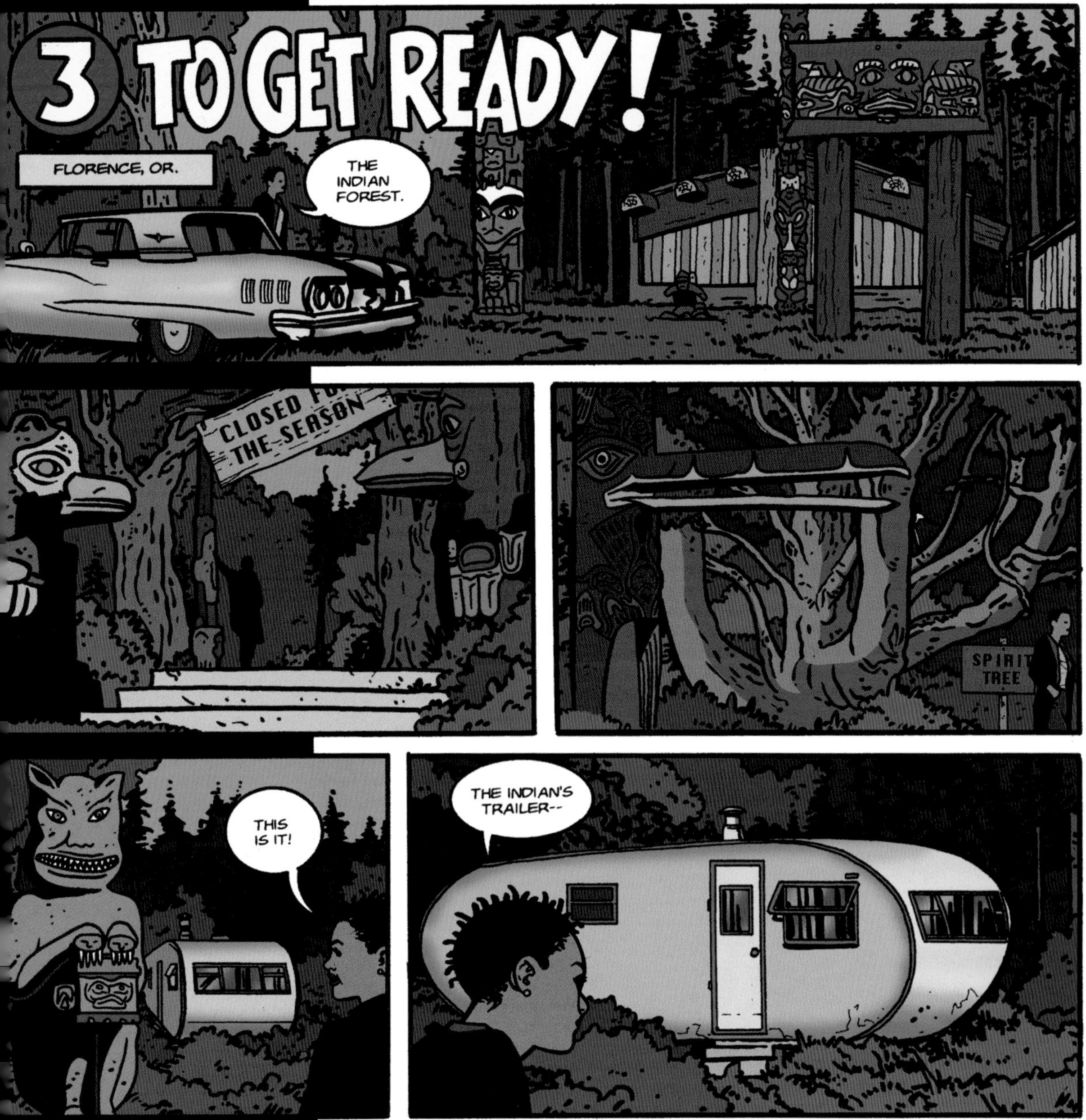

3 TO GET READY!
FLORENCE, OR.
THE INDIAN FOREST.
CLOSED FOR THE SEASON
SPIRIT TREE
THIS IS IT!
THE INDIAN'S TRAILER--

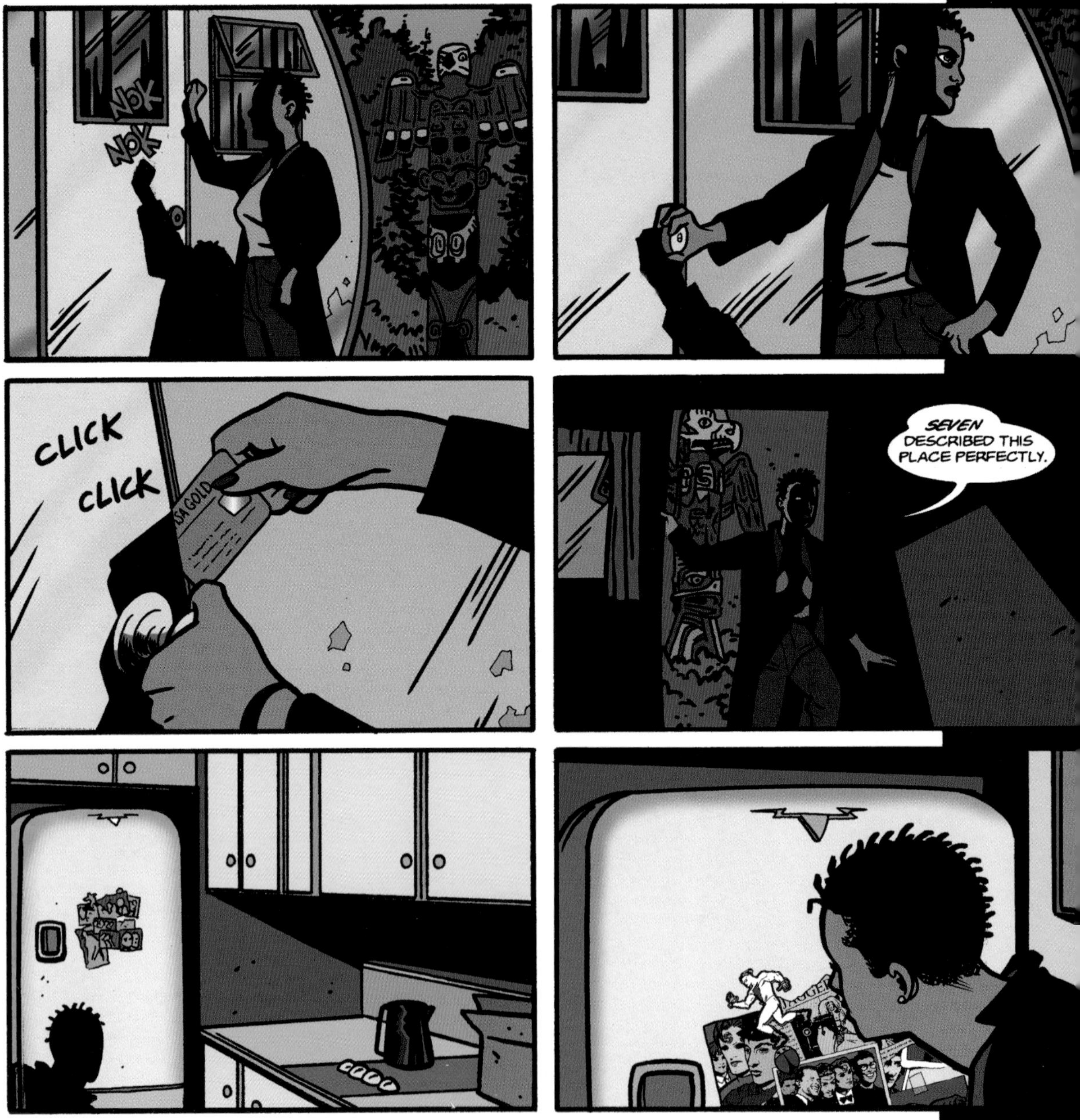
NOK
NOK
CLICK
CLICK
SEVEN DESCRIBED THIS PLACE PERFECTLY.

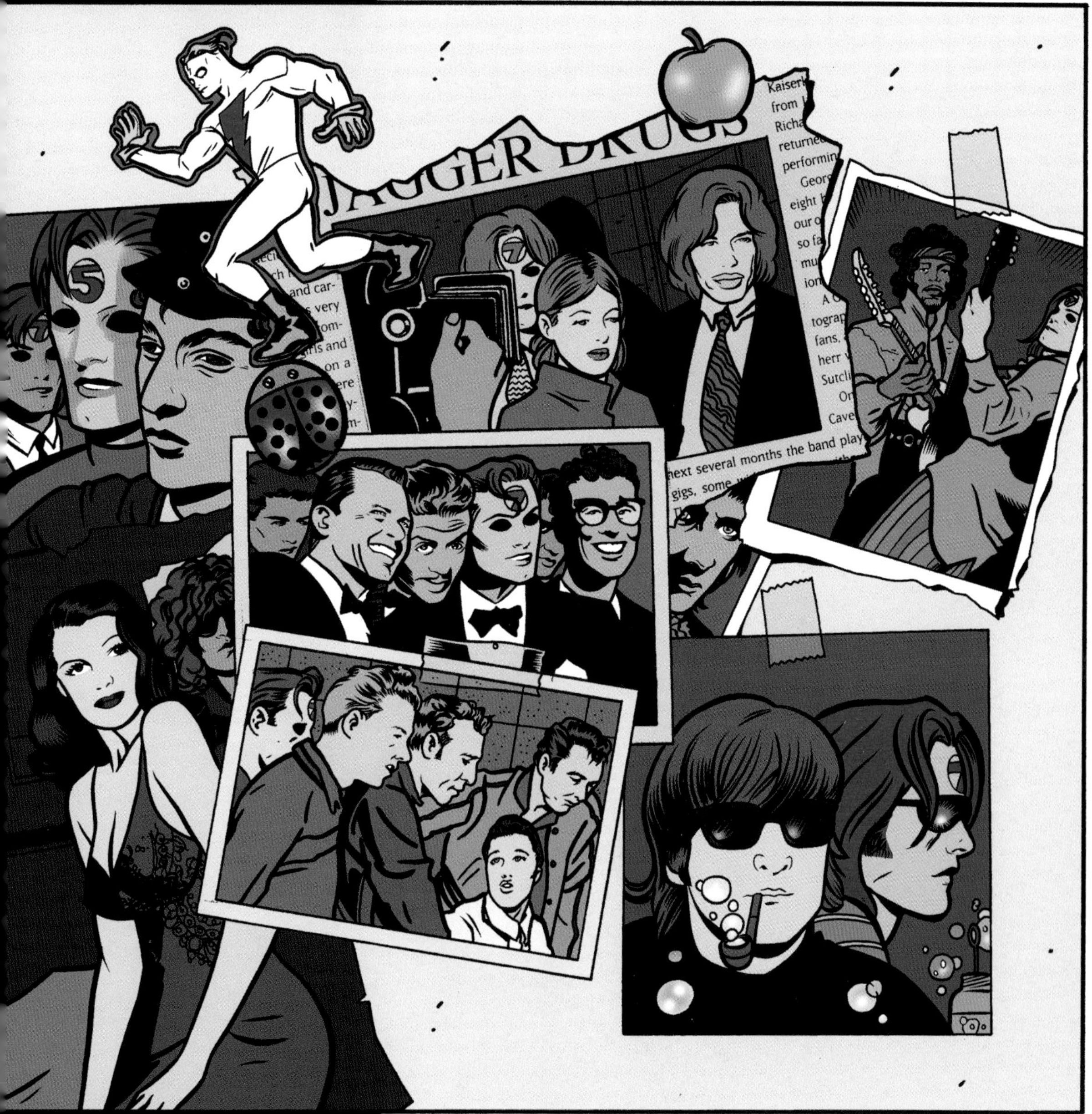
JAGGER DRUGS
next several months the band play
gigs, some

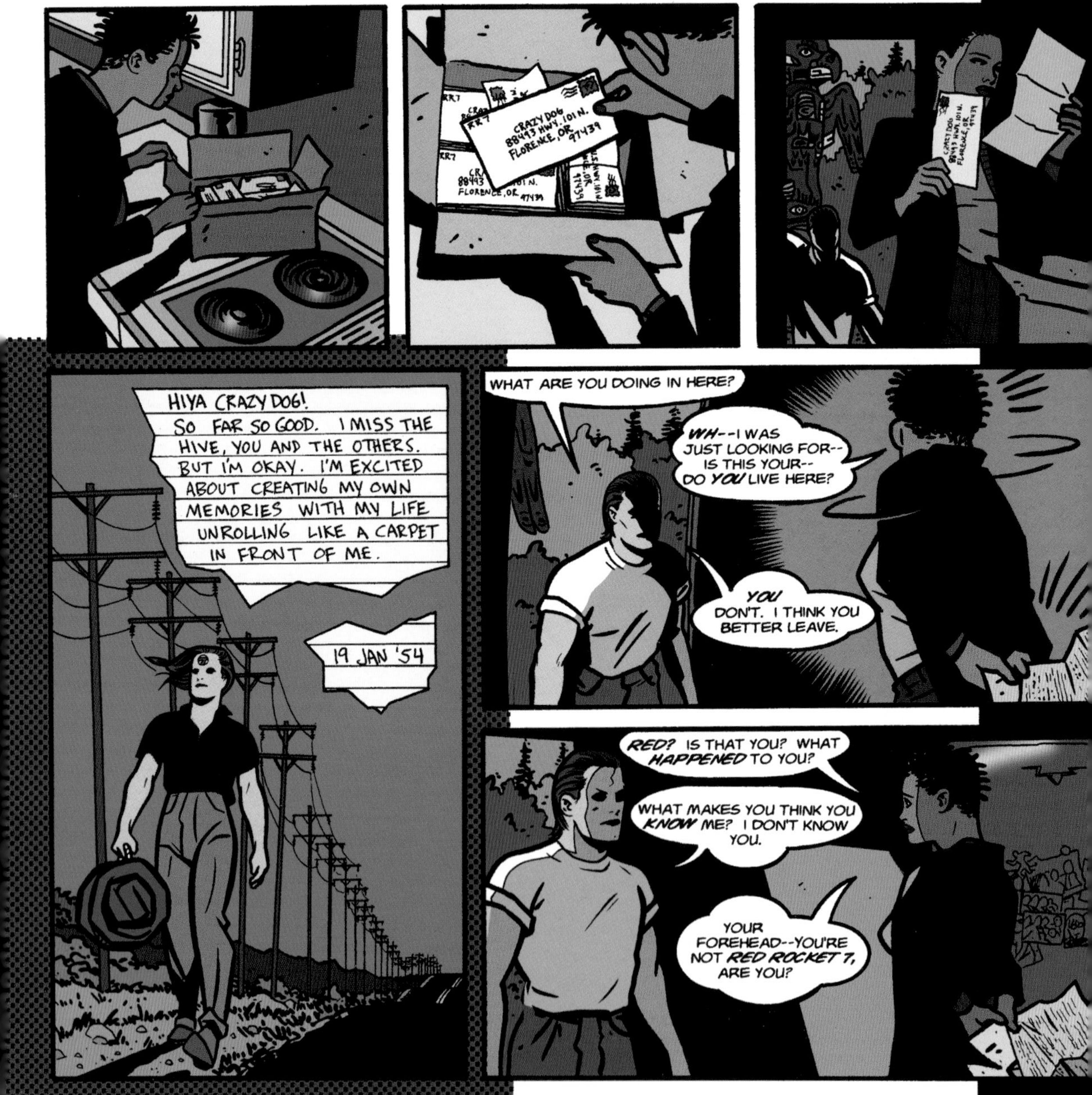
CRAZY DOG
88493 HWY. 101 N.
FLORENCE, OR 97439
HIYA CRAZY DOG!
SO FAR SO GOOD. I MISS THE HIVE, YOU AND THE OTHERS. BUT I'M OKAY. I'M EXCITED ABOUT CREATING MY OWN MEMORIES WITH MY LIFE UNROLLING LIKE A CARPET IN FRONT OF ME.
19 JAN '54
WHAT ARE YOU DOING IN HERE?
WH--I WAS JUST LOOKING FOR-- IS THIS YOUR-- DO YOU LIVE HERE?
YOU DON'T. I THINK YOU BETTER LEAVE.
RED? IS THAT YOU? WHAT HAPPENED TO YOU?
WHAT MAKES YOU THINK YOU KNOW ME? I DON'T KNOW YOU.
YOUR FOREHEAD--YOU'RE NOT RED ROCKET 7, ARE YOU?

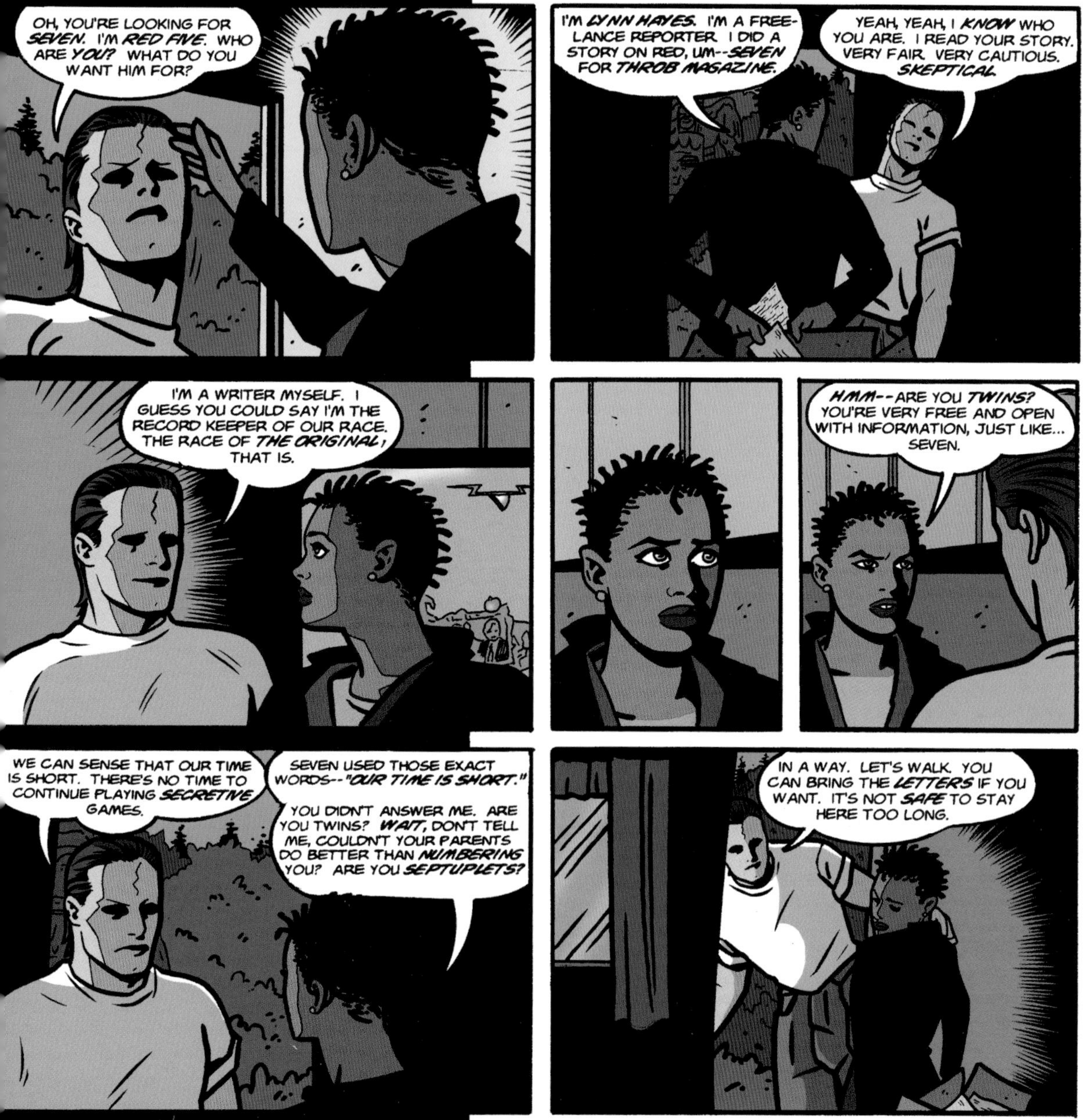
OH, YOU'RE LOOKING FOR SEVEN. I'M RED FIVE. WHO ARE YOU? WHAT DO YOU WANT HIM FOR?
I'M LYNN HAYES. I'M A FREE-LANCE REPORTER. I DID A STORY ON RED, UM--SEVEN FOR THROB MAGAZINE.
YEAH, YEAH, I KNOW WHO YOU ARE. I READ YOUR STORY. VERY FAIR. VERY CAUTIOUS. SKEPTICAL.
I'M A WRITER MYSELF. I GUESS YOU COULD SAY I'M THE RECORD KEEPER OF OUR RACE. THE RACE OF THE ORIGINAL, THAT IS.
HMM--ARE YOU TWINS? YOU'RE VERY FREE AND OPEN WITH INFORMATION, JUST LIKE... SEVEN.
WE CAN SENSE THAT OUR TIME IS SHORT. THERE'S NO TIME TO CONTINUE PLAYING SECRETIVE GAMES.
SEVEN USED THOSE EXACT WORDS--"OUR TIME IS SHORT."
YOU DIDN'T ANSWER ME. ARE YOU TWINS? WAIT, DON'T TELL ME, COULDN'T YOUR PARENTS DO BETTER THAN NUMBERING YOU? ARE YOU SEPTUPLETS?
IN A WAY. LET'S WALK. YOU CAN BRING THE LETTERS IF YOU WANT. IT'S NOT SAFE TO STAY HERE TOO LONG.

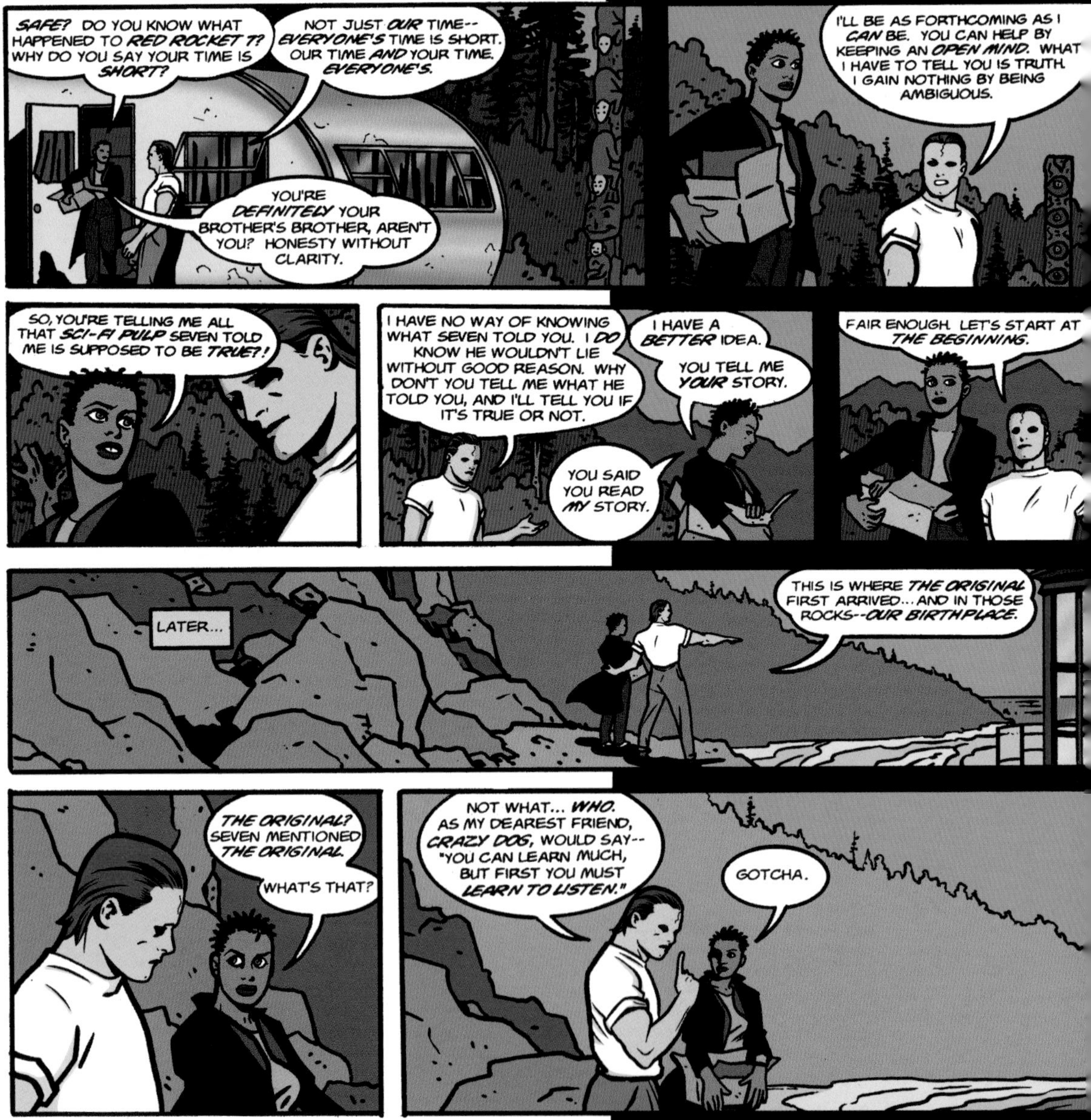
SAFE? DO YOU KNOW WHAT HAPPENED TO RED ROCKET 7? WHY DO YOU SAY YOUR TIME IS SHORT?
NOT JUST OUR TIME-- EVERYONE'S TIME IS SHORT. OUR TIME AND YOUR TIME. EVERYONE'S.
YOU'RE DEFINITELY YOUR BROTHER'S BROTHER, AREN'T YOU? HONESTY WITHOUT CLARITY.
I'LL BE AS FORTHCOMING AS I CAN BE. YOU CAN HELP BY KEEPING AN OPEN MIND. WHAT I HAVE TO TELL YOU IS TRUTH. I GAIN NOTHING BY BEING AMBIGUOUS.
SO, YOU'RE TELLING ME ALL THAT SCI-FI PULP SEVEN TOLD ME IS SUPPOSED TO BE TRUE?!
I HAVE NO WAY OF KNOWING WHAT SEVEN TOLD YOU. I DO KNOW HE WOULDN'T LIE WITHOUT GOOD REASON. WHY DON'T YOU TELL ME WHAT HE TOLD YOU, AND I'LL TELL YOU IF IT'S TRUE OR NOT.
I HAVE A BETTER IDEA.
YOU TELL ME YOUR STORY.
YOU SAID YOU READ MY STORY.
FAIR ENOUGH. LET'S START AT THE BEGINNING.
LATER...
THIS IS WHERE THE ORIGINAL FIRST ARRIVED... AND IN THOSE ROCKS--OUR BIRTHPLACE.
THE ORIGINAL? SEVEN MENTIONED THE ORIGINAL.
WHAT'S THAT?
NOT WHAT... WHO. AS MY DEAREST FRIEND, CRAZY DOG, WOULD SAY-- "YOU CAN LEARN MUCH, BUT FIRST YOU MUST LEARN TO LISTEN."
GOTCHA.

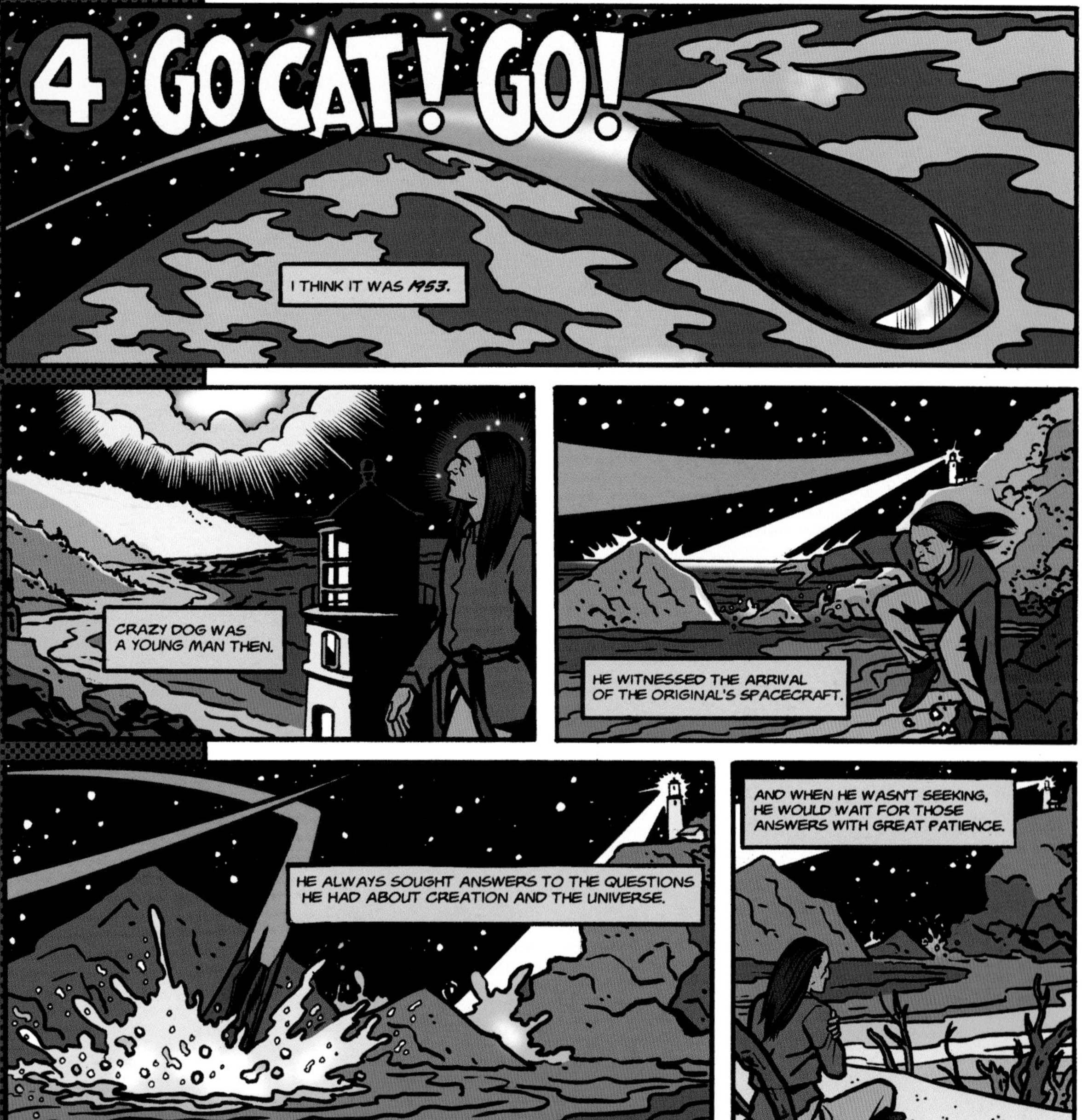
4 GO CAT! GO!
I THINK IT WAS 1953.
CRAZY DOG WAS A YOUNG MAN THEN.
HE WITNESSED THE ARRIVAL OF THE ORIGINAL'S SPACECRAFT.
HE ALWAYS SOUGHT ANSWERS TO THE QUESTIONS HE HAD ABOUT CREATION AND THE UNIVERSE.
AND WHEN HE WASN'T SEEKING, HE WOULD WAIT FOR THOSE ANSWERS WITH GREAT PATIENCE.

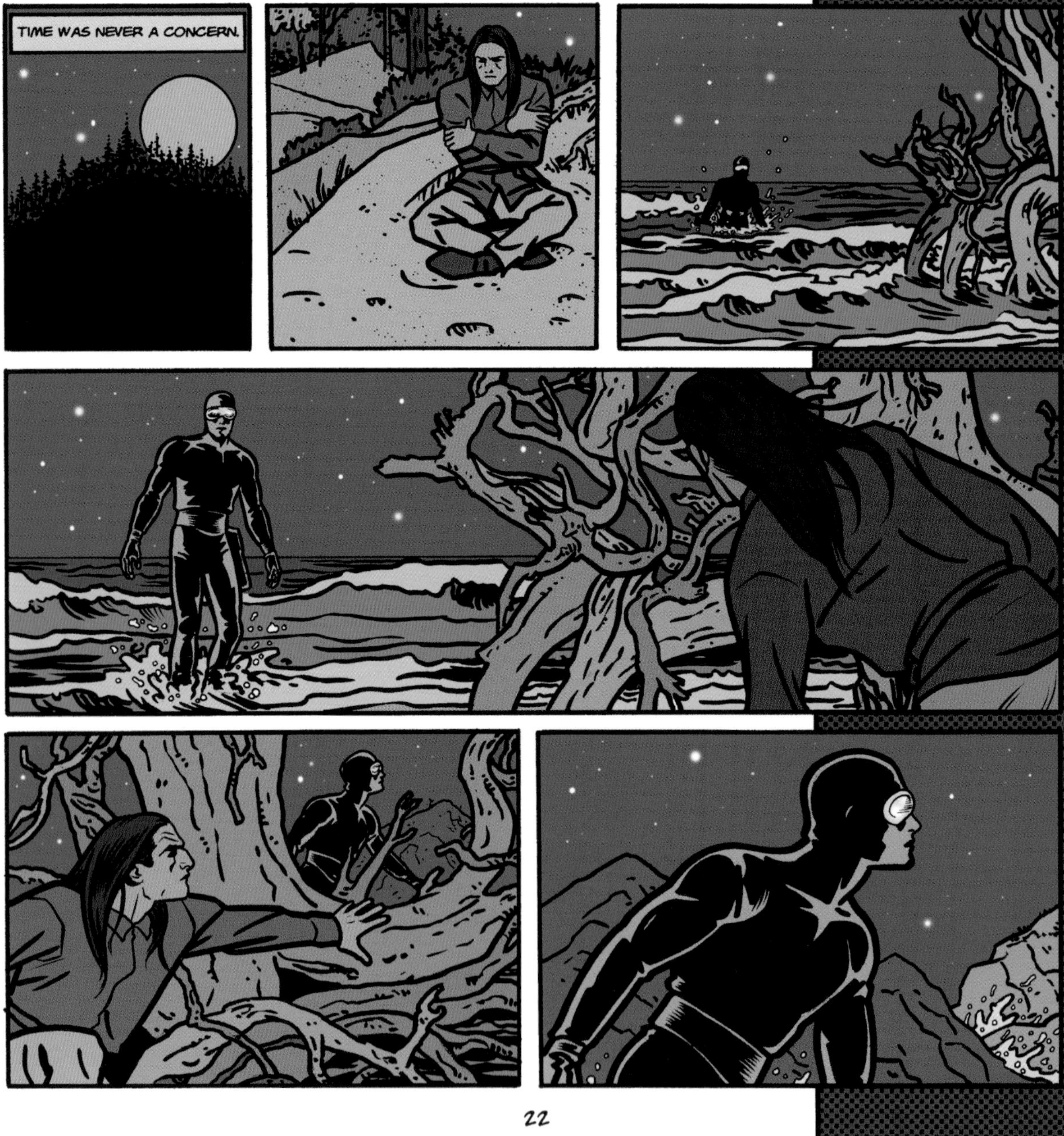
TIME WAS NEVER A CONCERN.

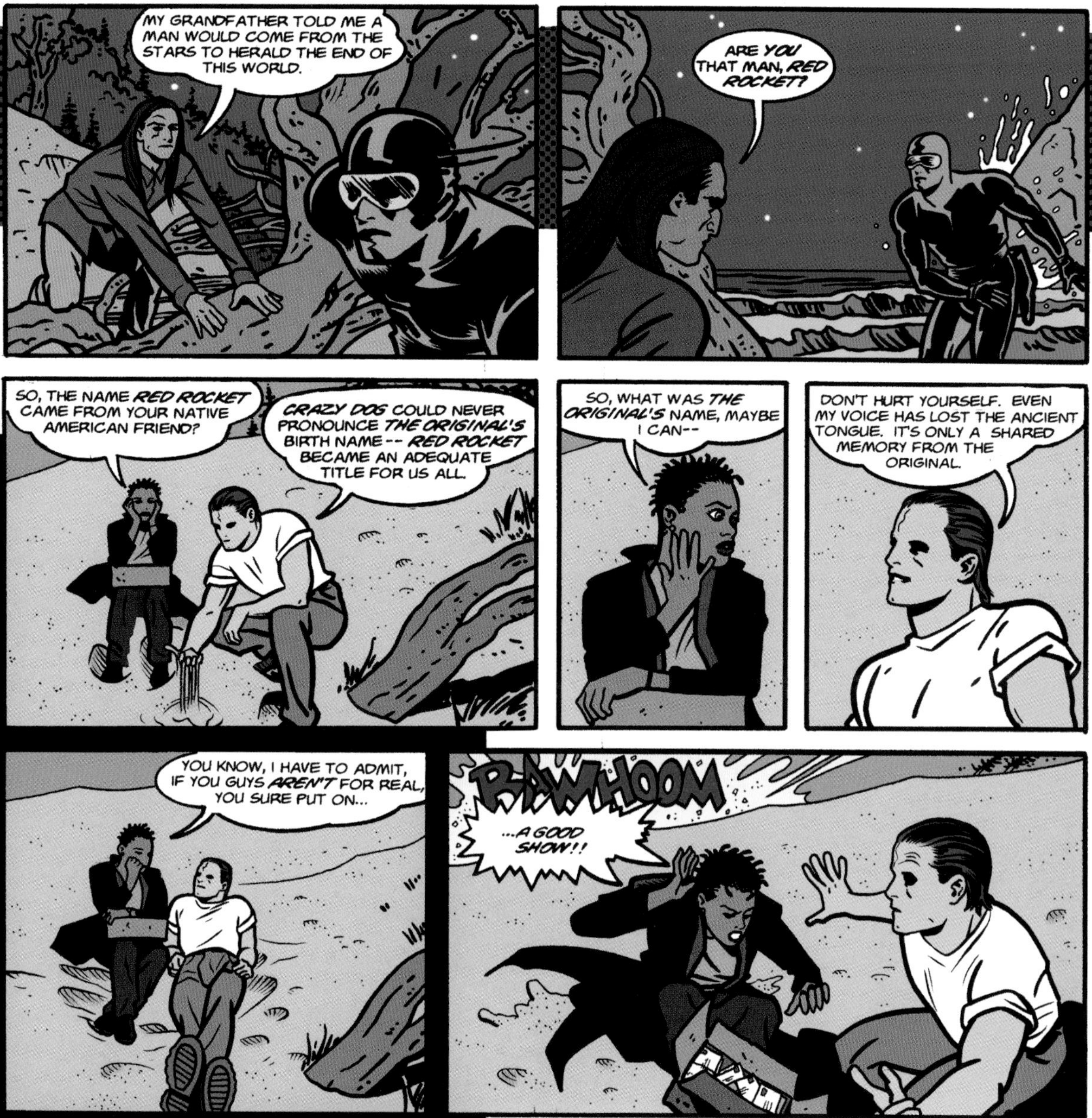

MY GRANDFATHER TOLD ME A MAN WOULD COME FROM THE STARS TO HERALD THE END OF THIS WORLD.
ARE YOU THAT MAN, RED ROCKET?
SO, THE NAME RED ROCKET CAME FROM YOUR NATIVE AMERICAN FRIEND?
CRAZY DOG COULD NEVER PRONOUNCE THE ORIGINAL'S BIRTH NAME-- RED ROCKET BECAME AN ADEQUATE TITLE FOR US ALL.
SO, WHAT WAS THE ORIGINAL'S NAME, MAYBE I CAN--
DON'T HURT YOURSELF. EVEN MY VOICE HAS LOST THE ANCIENT TONGUE. IT'S ONLY A SHARED MEMORY FROM THE ORIGINAL.
YOU KNOW, I HAVE TO ADMIT, IF YOU GUYS AREN'T FOR REAL, YOU SURE PUT ON...
BAWHOOM
...A GOOD SHOW!!

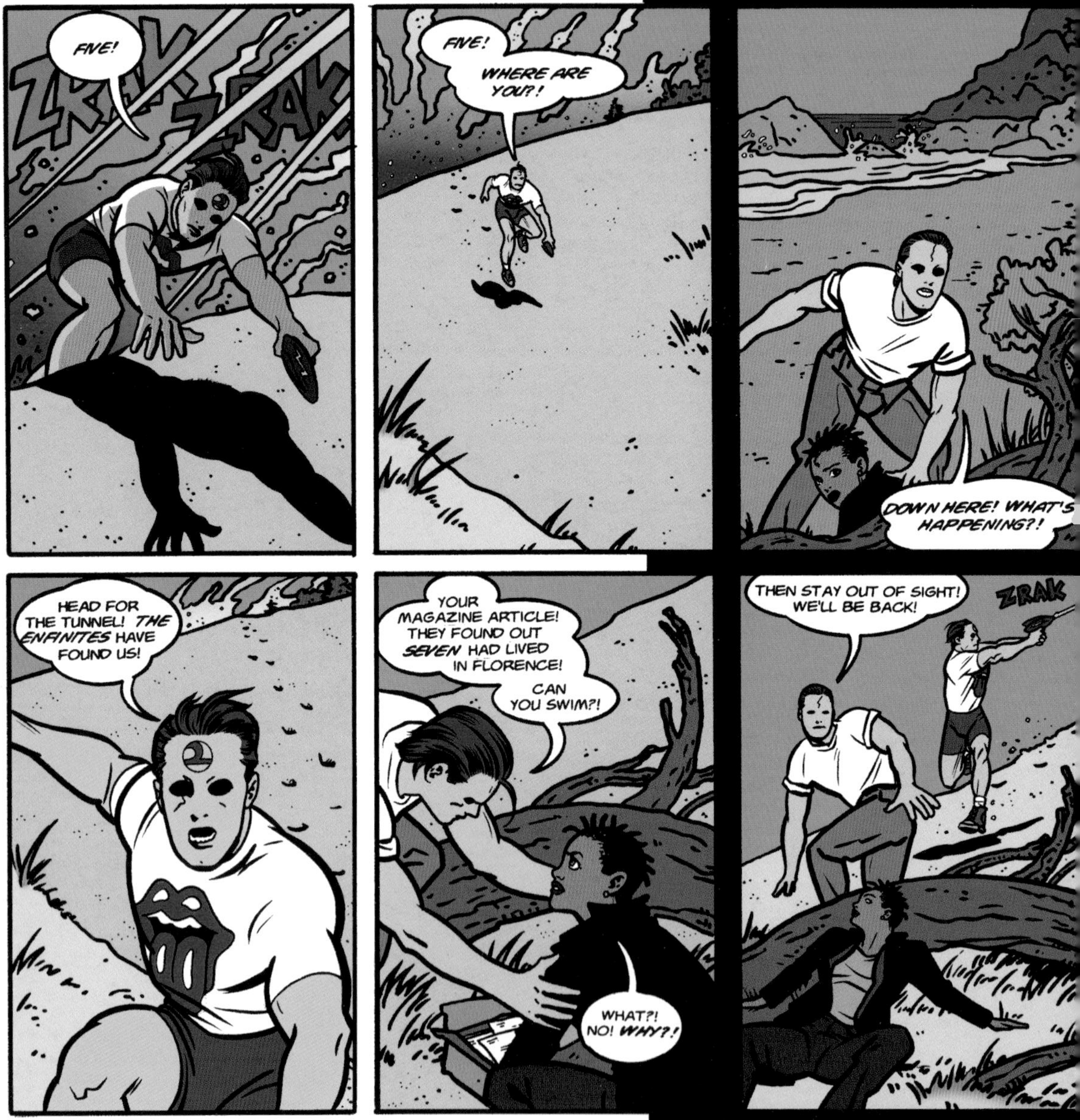
FIVE!
ZRAK ZRAK
FIVE!
WHERE ARE YOU?!
DOWN HERE! WHAT'S HAPPENING?!
HEAD FOR THE TUNNEL! THE ENFINITES HAVE FOUND US!
YOUR MAGAZINE ARTICLE! THEY FOUND OUT SEVEN HAD LIVED IN FLORENCE!
CAN YOU SWIM?!
WHAT?! NO! WHY?!
THEN STAY OUT OF SIGHT! WE'LL BE BACK!
ZRAK

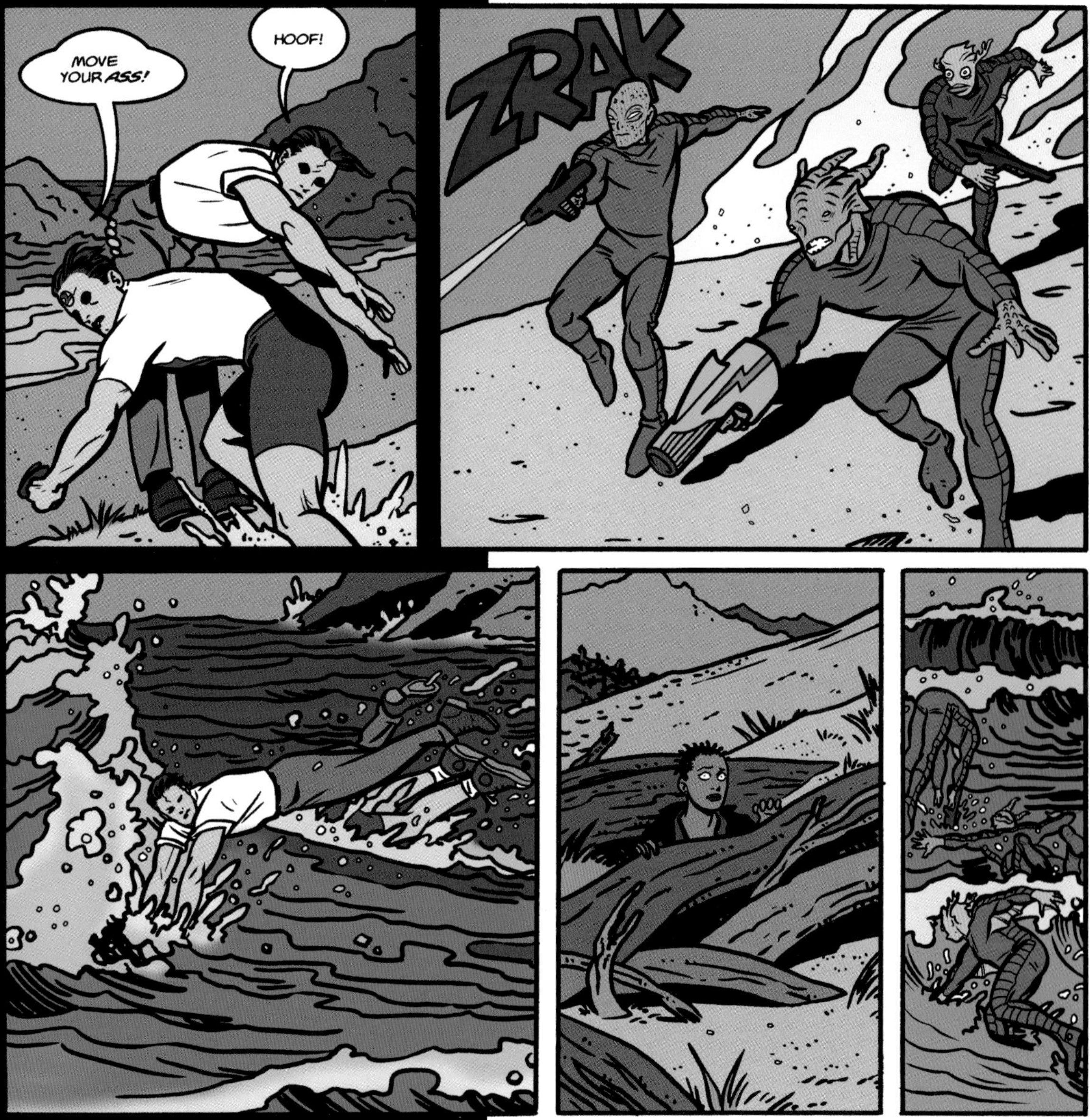
MOVE YOUR ASS!
HOOF!
ZRAK

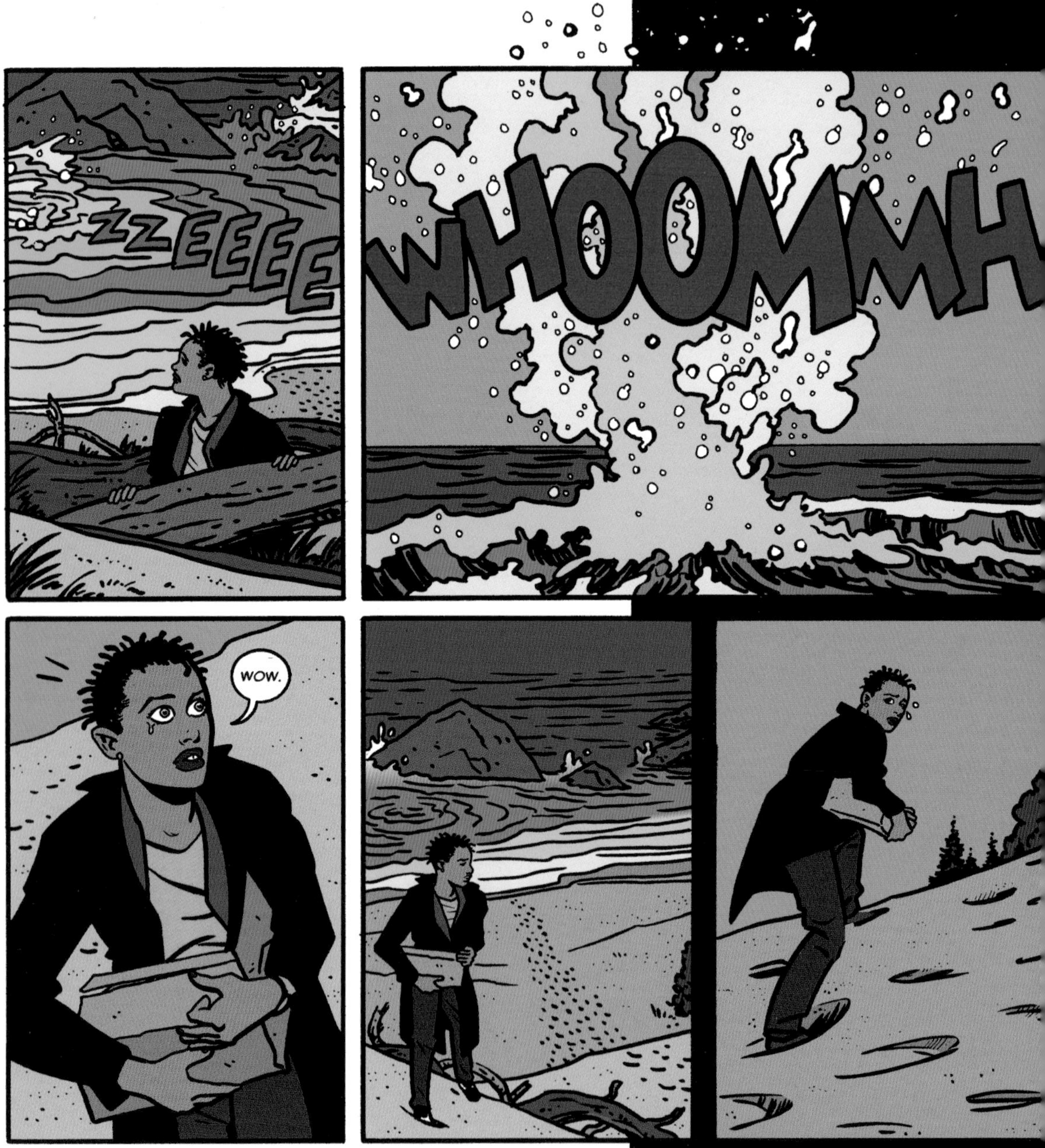
ZZEEEEE
WHOOMMH
WOW.

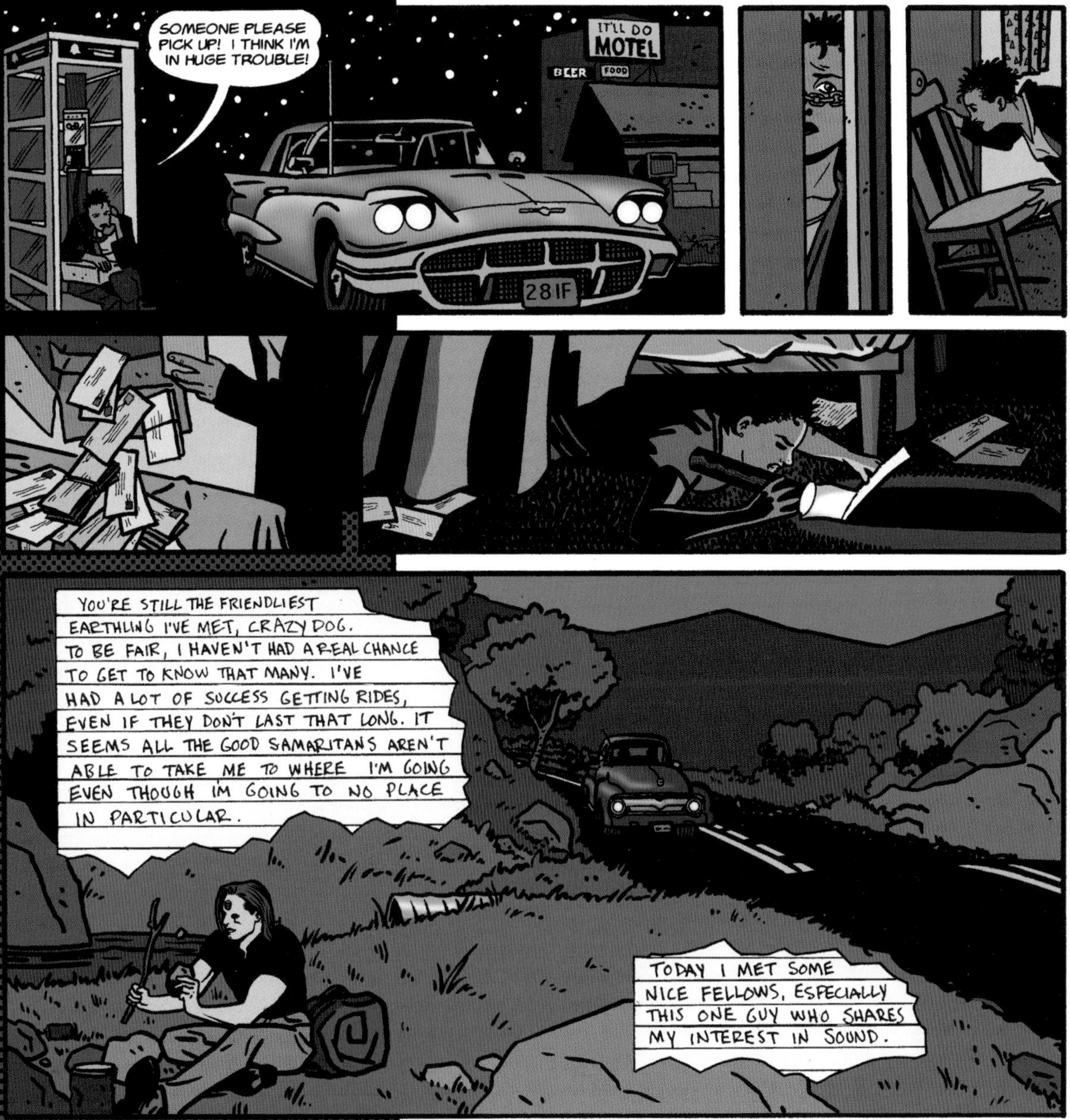
SOMEONE PLEASE PICK UP! I THINK I'M IN HUGE TROUBLE!
IT'LL DO MOTEL
BEER
FOOD
28IF
YOU'RE STILL THE FRIENDLIEST EARTHLING I'VE MET, CRAZY DOG. TO BE FAIR, I HAVEN'T HAD A REAL CHANCE TO GET TO KNOW THAT MANY. I'VE HAD A LOT OF SUCCESS GETTING RIDES, EVEN IF THEY DON'T LAST THAT LONG. IT SEEMS ALL THE GOOD SAMARITANS AREN'T ABLE TO TAKE ME TO WHERE I'M GOING EVEN THOUGH I'M GOING TO NO PLACE IN PARTICULAR.
TODAY I MET SOME NICE FELLOWS, ESPECIALLY THIS ONE GUY WHO SHARES MY INTEREST IN SOUND.

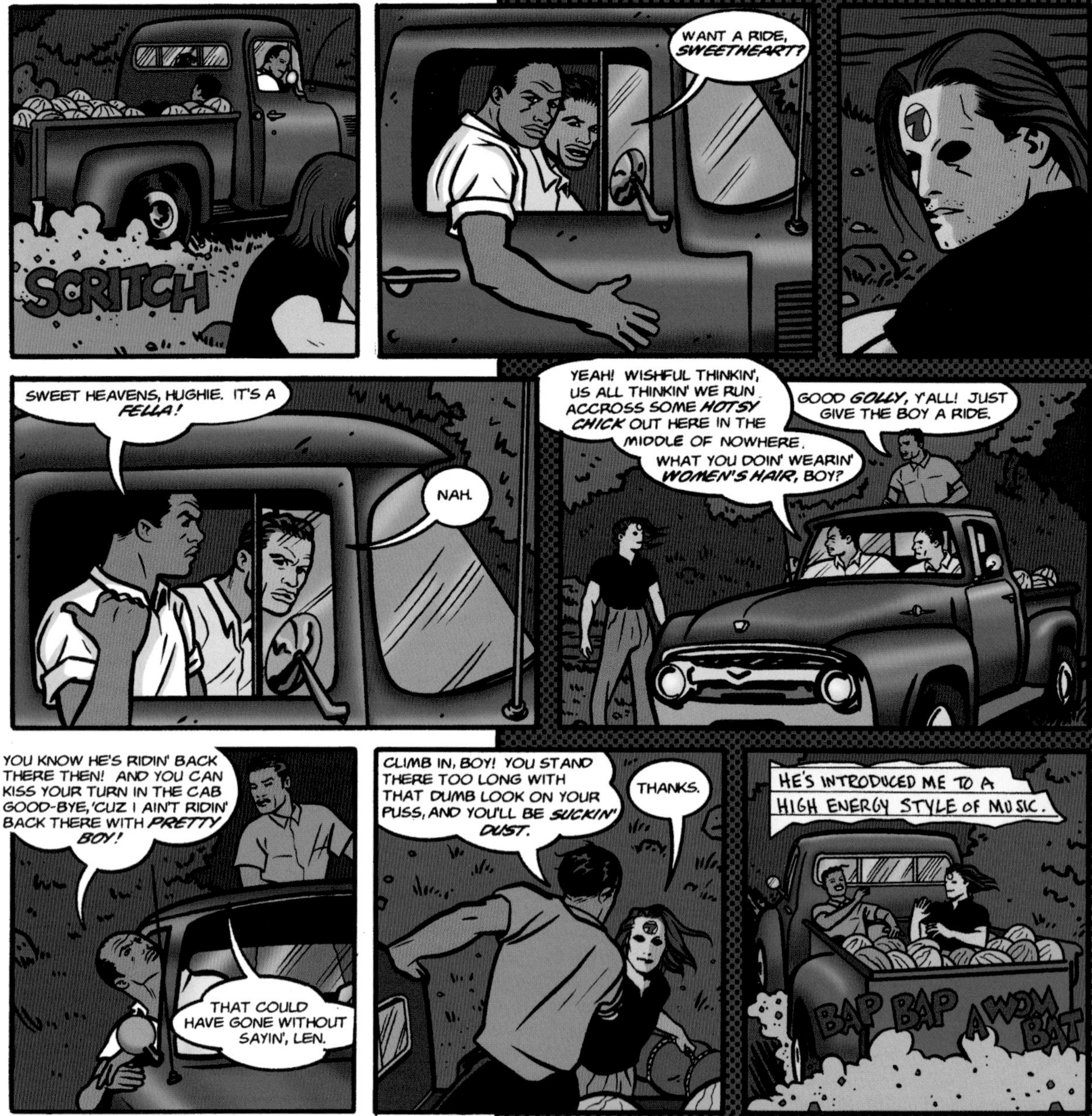
SCRITCH
WANT A RIDE, SWEETHEART?
SWEET HEAVENS, HUGHIE. IT'S A FELLA!
NAH.
YEAH! WISHFUL THINKIN', US ALL THINKIN' WE RUN ACCROSS SOME HOTSY CHICK OUT HERE IN THE MIDDLE OF NOWHERE.
WHAT YOU DOIN' WEARIN' WOMEN'S HAIR, BOY?
GOOD GOLLY, Y'ALL! JUST GIVE THE BOY A RIDE.
YOU KNOW HE'S RIDIN' BACK THERE THEN! AND YOU CAN KISS YOUR TURN IN THE CAB GOOD-BYE, 'CUZ I AIN'T RIDIN' BACK THERE WITH PRETTY BOY!
THAT COULD HAVE GONE WITHOUT SAYIN', LEN.
CLIMB IN, BOY! YOU STAND THERE TOO LONG WITH THAT DUMB LOOK ON YOUR PUSS, AND YOU'LL BE SUCKIN' DUST.
THANKS.
HE'S INTRODUCED ME TO A HIGH ENERGY STYLE OF MUSIC.
BAP BAP A WOM BAT

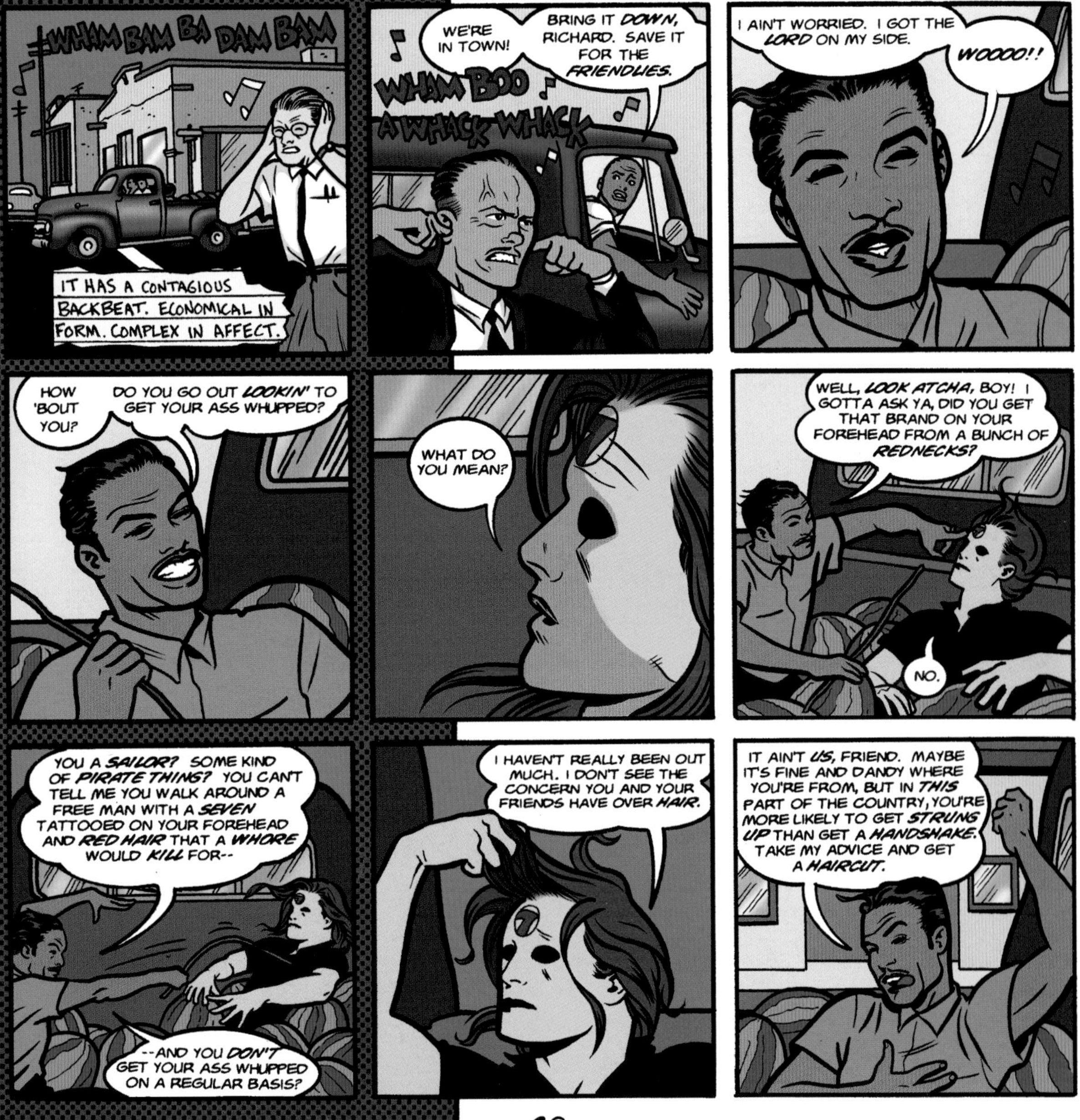
WHAM BAM BA DAM BAM
IT HAS A CONTAGIOUS BACKBEAT. ECONOMICAL IN FORM. COMPLEX IN AFFECT.
WE'RE IN TOWN!
BRING IT DOWN, RICHARD. SAVE IT FOR THE FRIENDLIES.
WHAM BOO A WHACK WHACK
I AIN'T WORRIED. I GOT THE LORD ON MY SIDE.
WOOOO!!
HOW 'BOUT YOU?
DO YOU GO OUT LOOKIN' TO GET YOUR ASS WHUPPED?
WHAT DO YOU MEAN?
WELL, LOOK ATCHA, BOY! I GOTTA ASK YA, DID YOU GET THAT BRAND ON YOUR FOREHEAD FROM A BUNCH OF REDNECKS?
NO.
YOU A SAILOR? SOME KIND OF PIRATE THING? YOU CAN'T TELL ME YOU WALK AROUND A FREE MAN WITH A SEVEN TATTOOED ON YOUR FOREHEAD AND RED HAIR THAT A WHORE WOULD KILL FOR--
--AND YOU DON'T GET YOUR ASS WHUPPED ON A REGULAR BASIS?
I HAVEN'T REALLY BEEN OUT MUCH. I DON'T SEE THE CONCERN YOU AND YOUR FRIENDS HAVE OVER HAIR.
IT AIN'T US, FRIEND. MAYBE IT'S FINE AND DANDY WHERE YOU'RE FROM, BUT IN THIS PART OF THE COUNTRY, YOU'RE MORE LIKELY TO GET STRUNG UP THAN GET A HANDSHAKE. TAKE MY ADVICE AND GET A HAIRCUT.

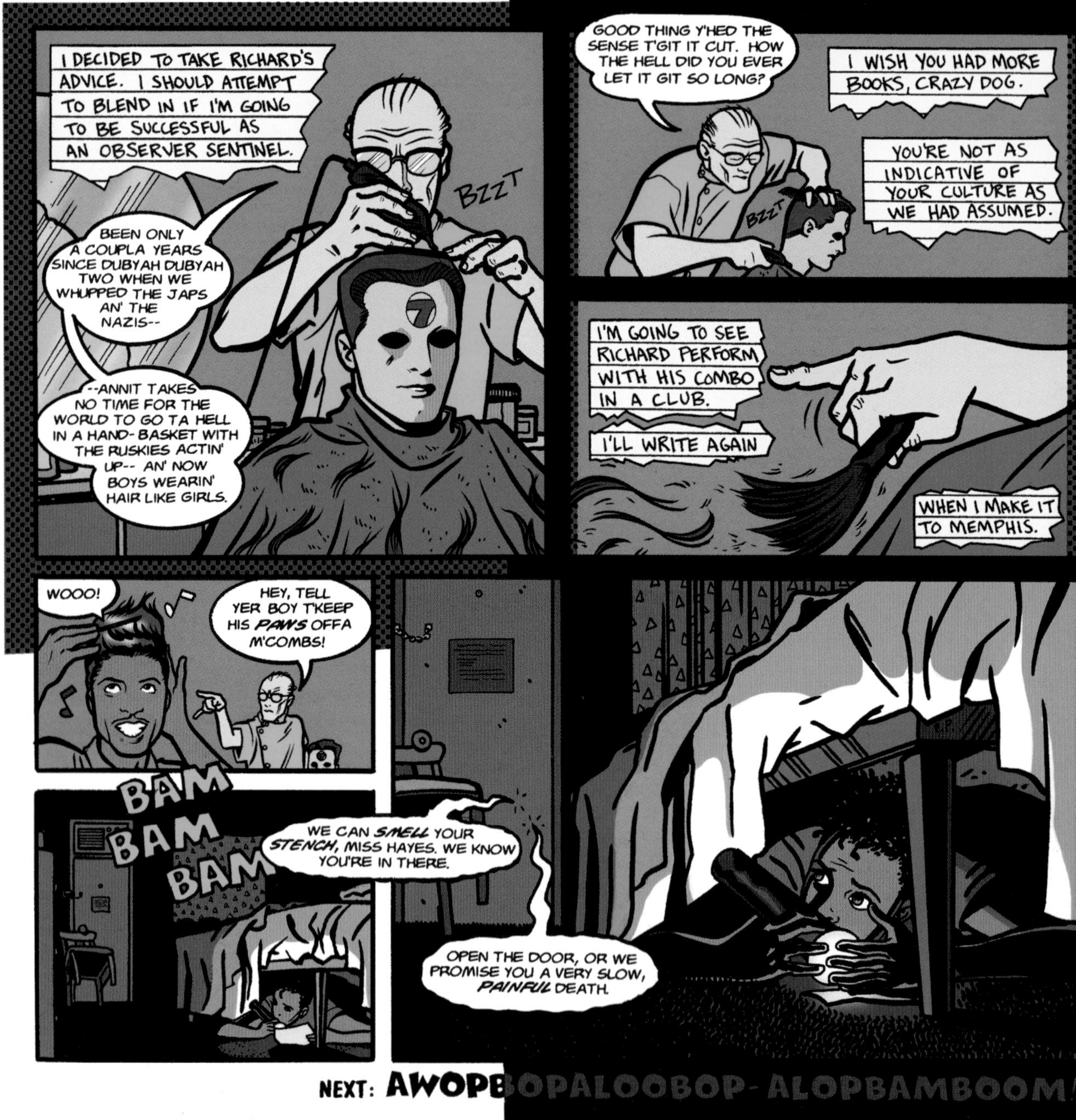
I DECIDED TO TAKE RICHARD'S ADVICE. I SHOULD ATTEMPT TO BLEND IN IF I'M GOING TO BE SUCCESSFUL AS AN OBSERVER SENTINEL.
BZZT
BEEN ONLY A COUPLA YEARS SINCE DUBYAH DUBYAH TWO WHEN WE WHUPPED THE JAPS AN' THE NAZIS--
--ANNIT TAKES NO TIME FOR THE WORLD TO GO TA HELL IN A HAND-BASKET WITH THE RUSKIES ACTIN' UP-- AN' NOW BOYS WEARIN' HAIR LIKE GIRLS.
GOOD THING Y'HED THE SENSE T'GIT IT CUT. HOW THE HELL DID YOU EVER LET IT GIT SO LONG?
I WISH YOU HAD MORE BOOKS, CRAZY DOG.
YOU'RE NOT AS INDICATIVE OF YOUR CULTURE AS WE HAD ASSUMED.
BZZT
I'M GOING TO SEE RICHARD PERFORM WITH HIS COMBO IN A CLUB.
I'LL WRITE AGAIN
WHEN I MAKE IT TO MEMPHIS.
WOOO!
HEY, TELL YER BOY T'KEEP HIS *PAWS* OFFA M'COMBS!
BAM BAM BAM
WE CAN *SMELL* YOUR *STENCH*, MISS HAYES. WE KNOW YOU'RE IN THERE.
OPEN THE DOOR, OR WE PROMISE YOU A VERY SLOW, *PAINFUL* DEATH.
NEXT: AWOPBOPALOOBOP-ALOPBAMBOOM!

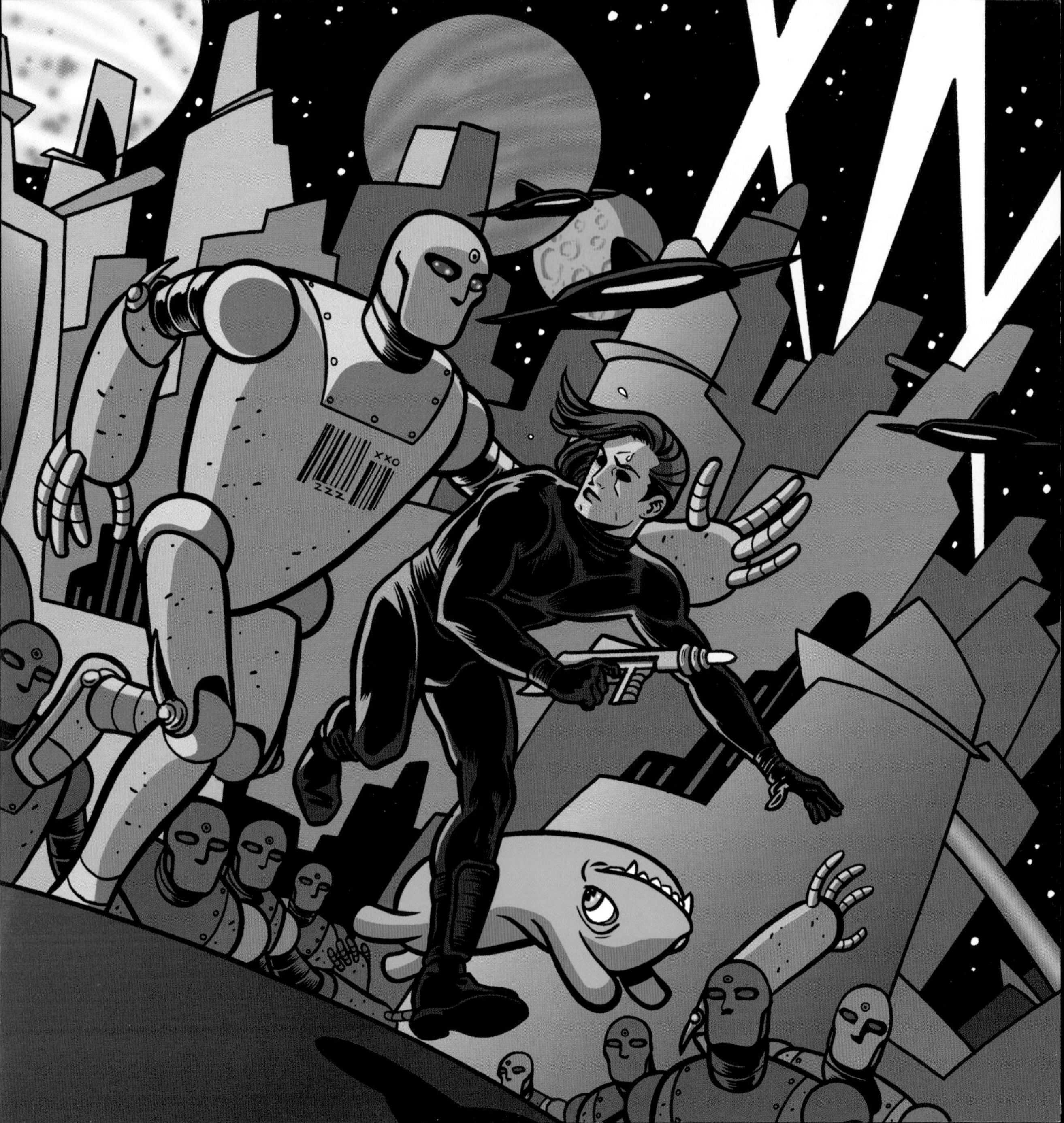

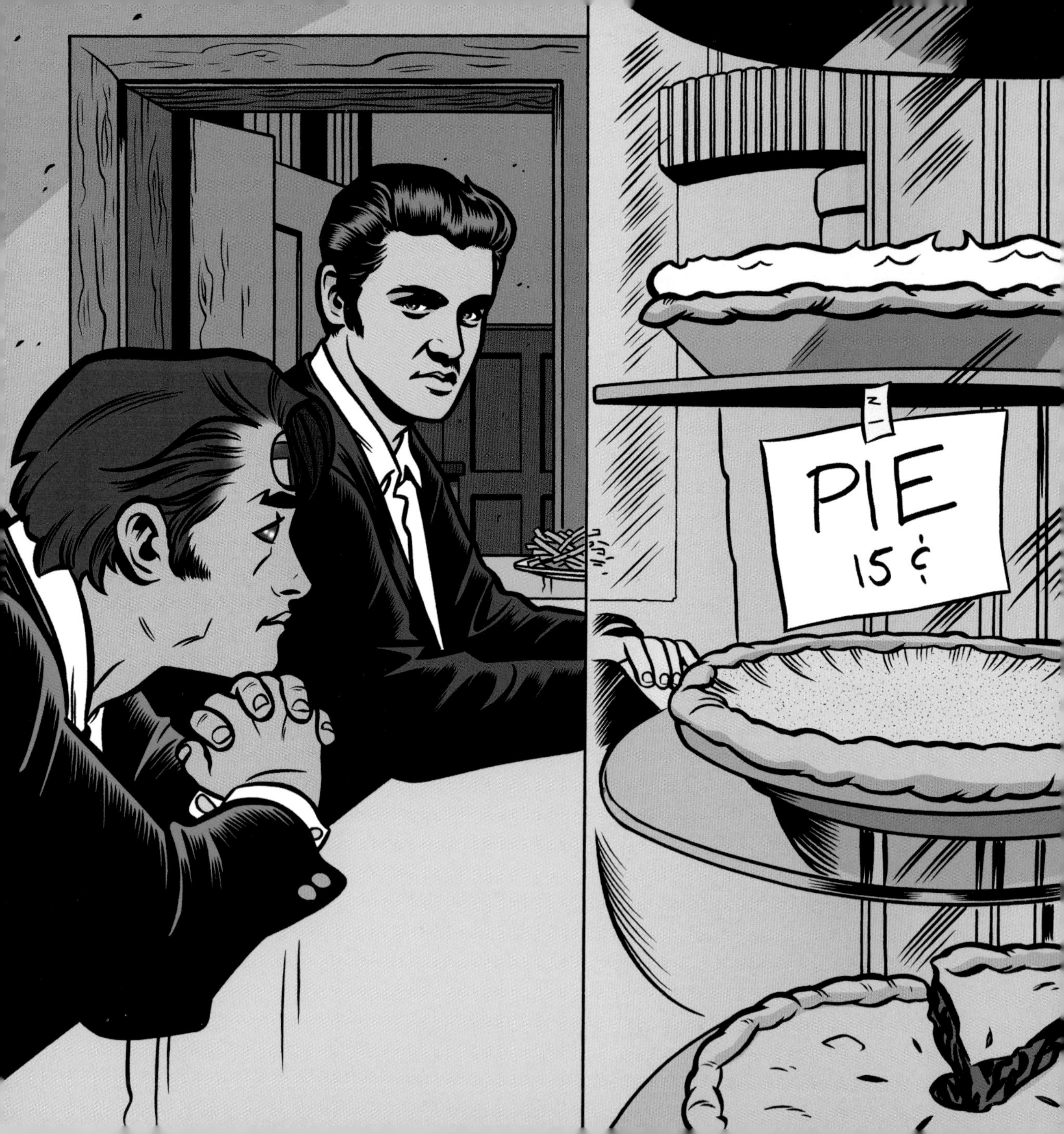
PIE
15 ¢

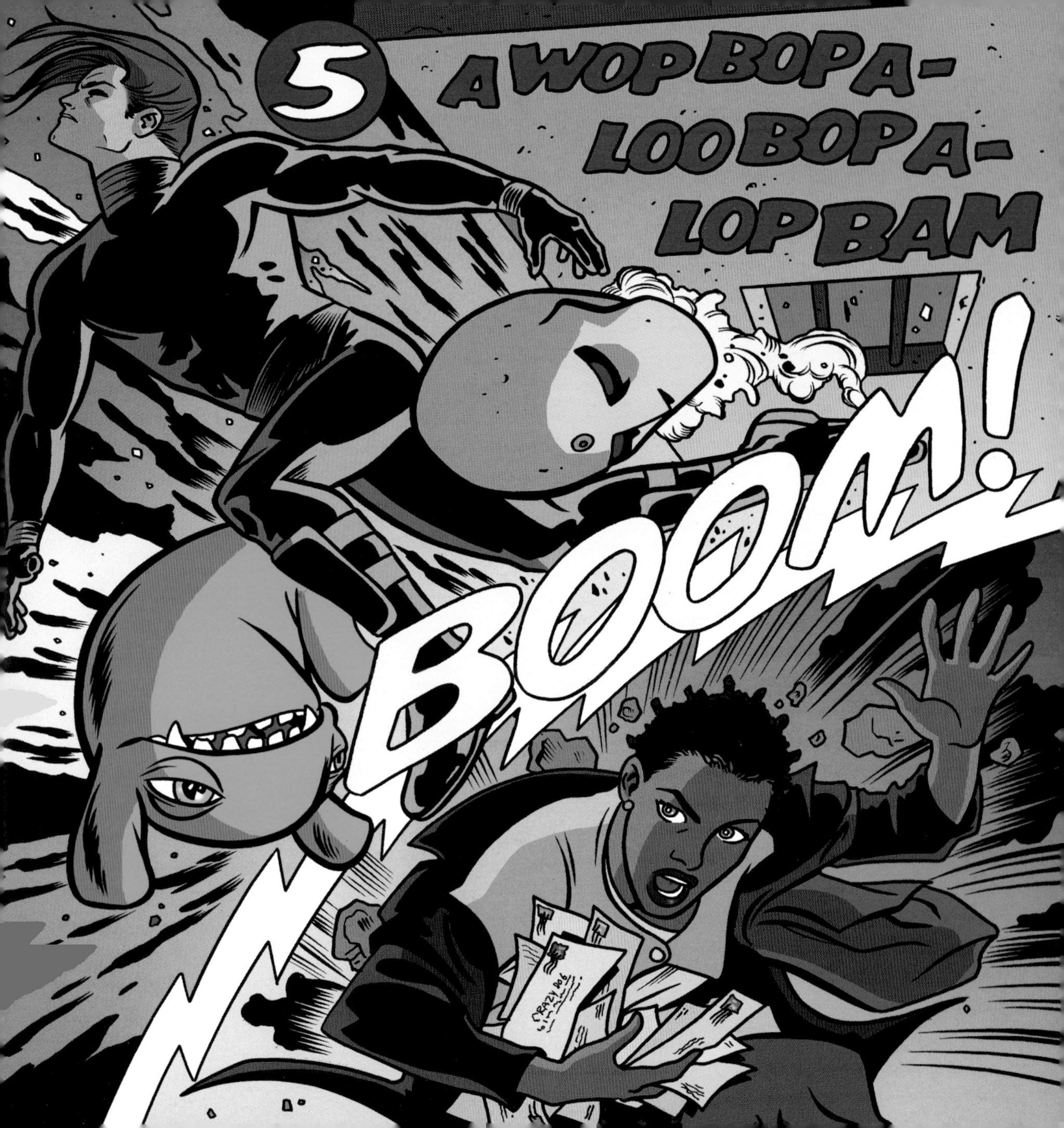
5
A WOP BOP A-
LOO BOP A-
LOP BAM
BOOM!
CRAZY DOG

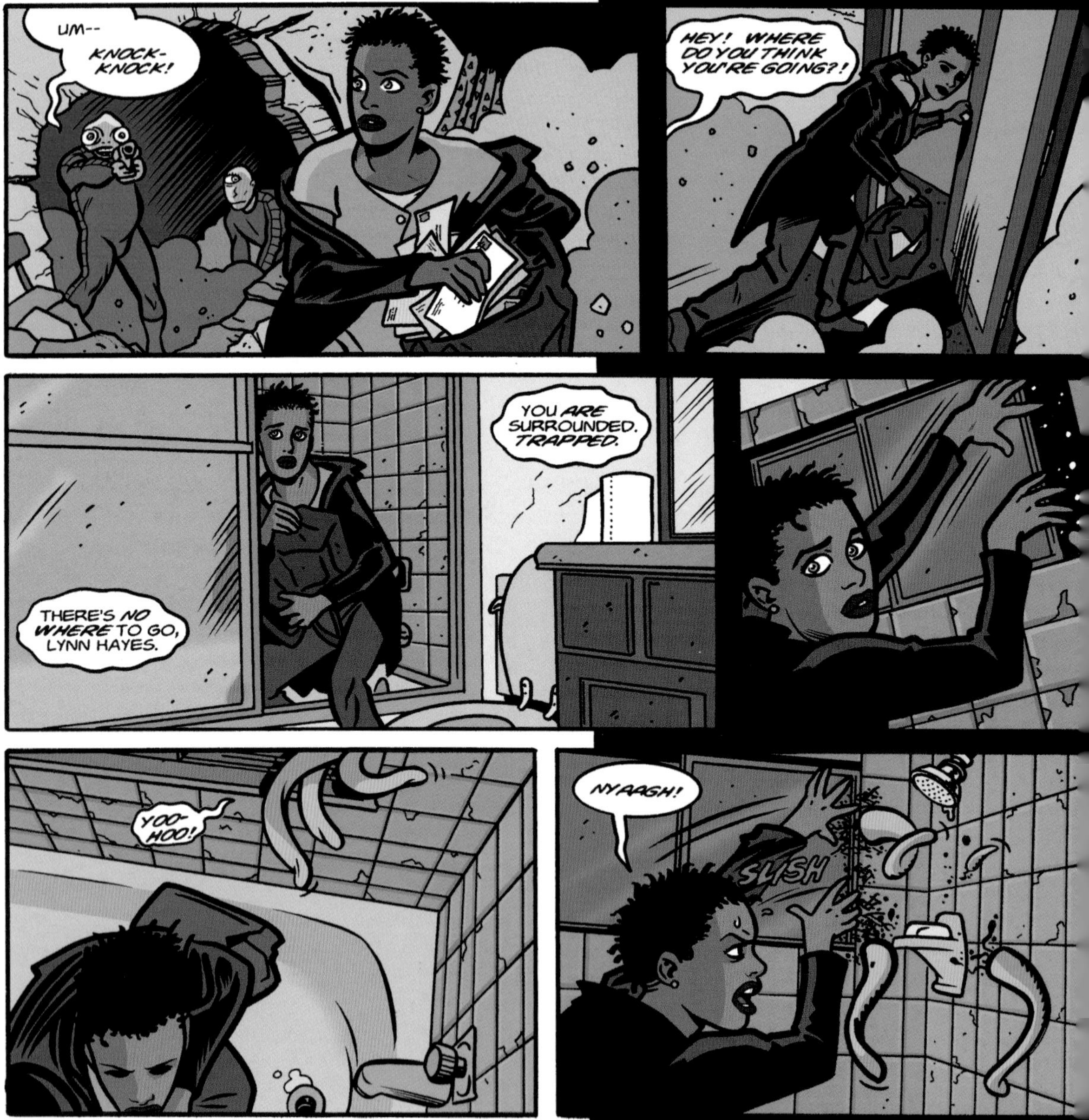
UM--
KNOCK-KNOCK!
HEY! WHERE DO YOU THINK YOU'RE GOING?!
YOU ARE SURROUNDED. TRAPPED.
THERE'S NO WHERE TO GO, LYNN HAYES.
YOO-HOO!
NYAAGH!
SLISH

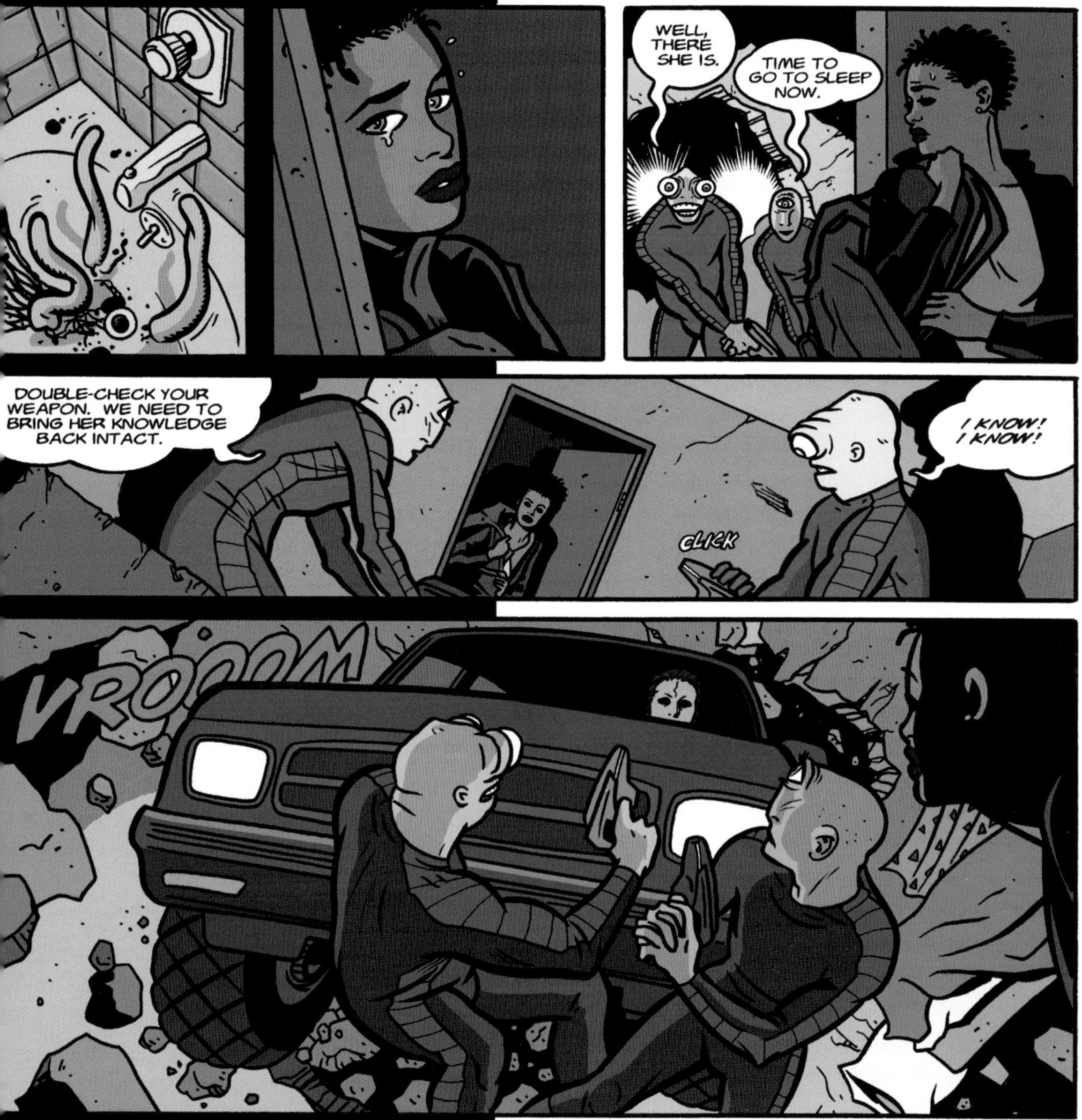
WELL, THERE SHE IS.
TIME TO GO TO SLEEP NOW.
DOUBLE-CHECK YOUR WEAPON. WE NEED TO BRING HER KNOWLEDGE BACK INTACT.
I KNOW! I KNOW!
CLICK
VROOOOM

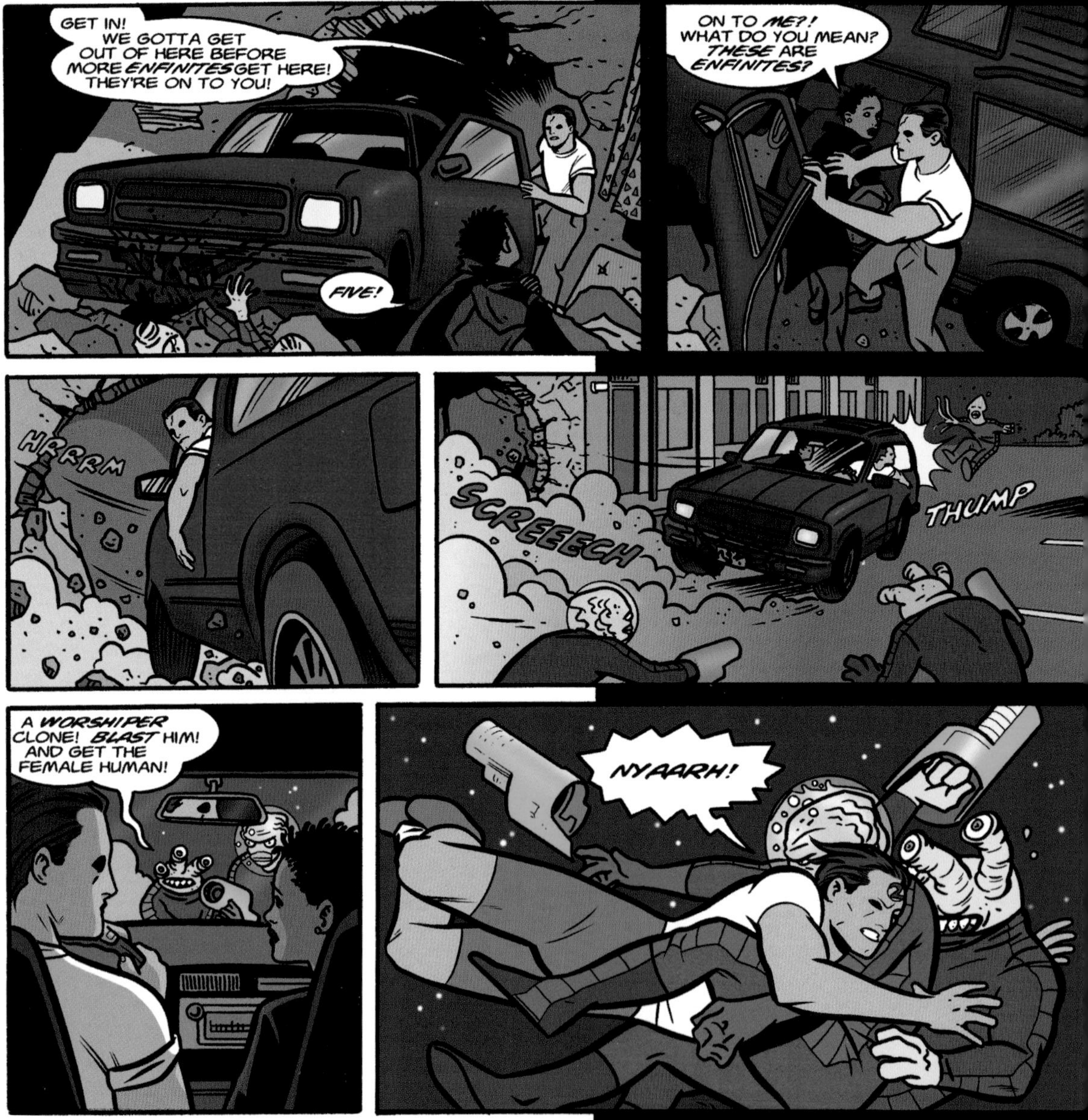
GET IN! WE GOTTA GET OUT OF HERE BEFORE MORE ENFINITES GET HERE! THEY'RE ON TO YOU!
FIVE!
ON TO ME?! WHAT DO YOU MEAN? THESE ARE ENFINITES?
HRRRM
SCREEECH
THUMP
A WORSHIPER CLONE! BLAST HIM! AND GET THE FEMALE HUMAN!
NYAARH!

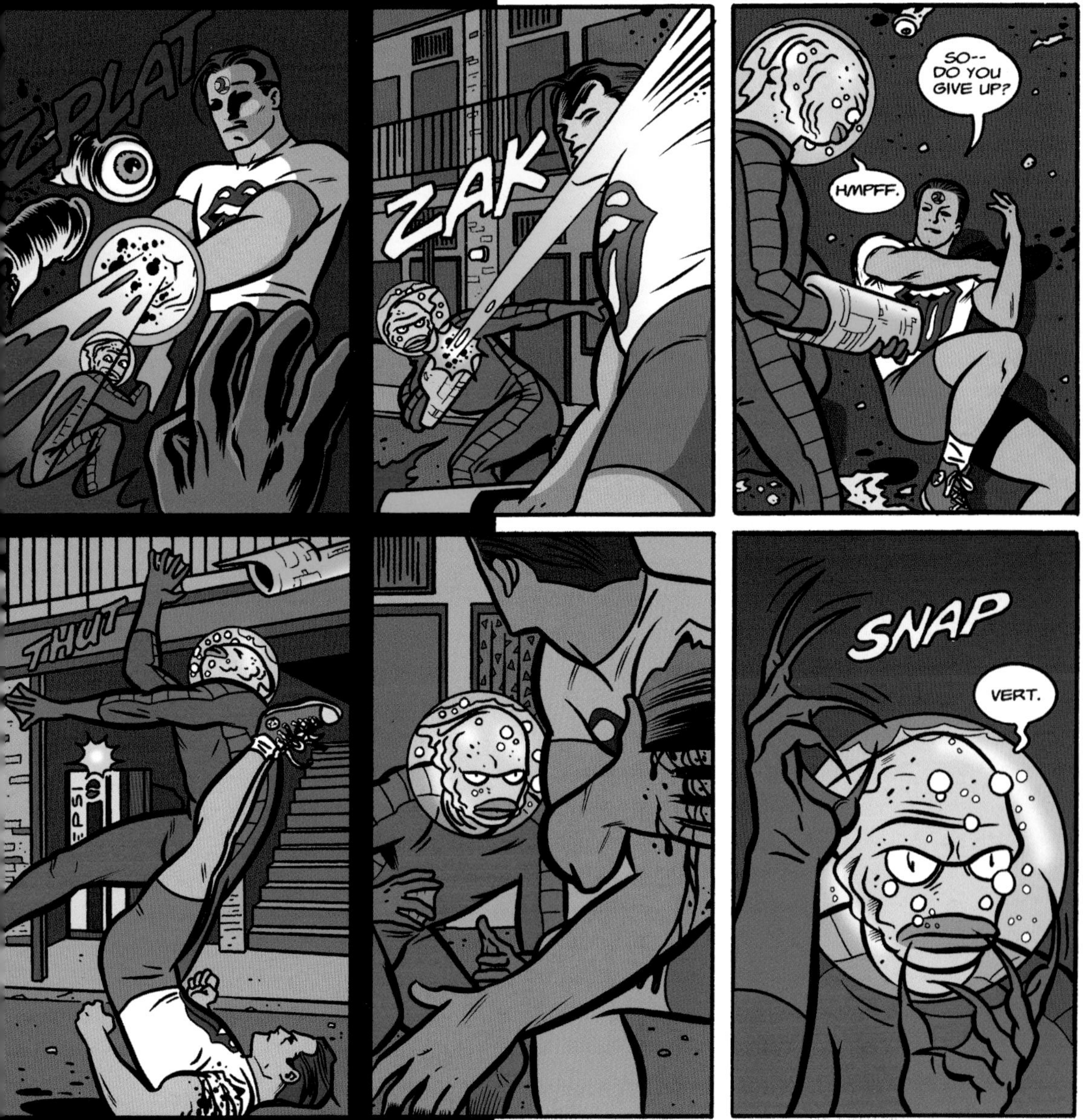
ZPLAT
ZAK
SO-- DO YOU GIVE UP?
HMPFF.
THUT
EPSI
SNAP
VERT.

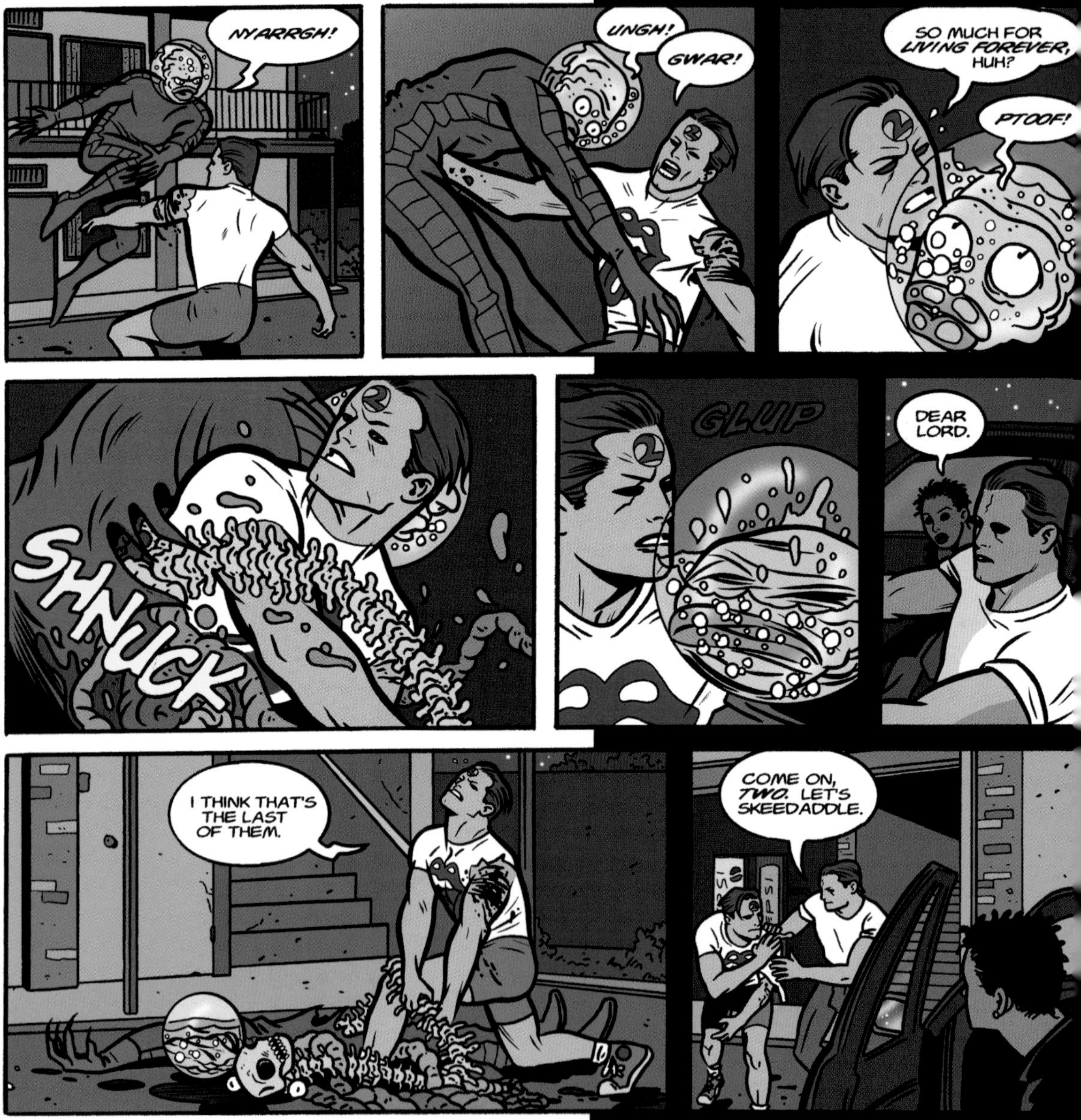
NYARRGH!
UNGH!
GWAR!
SO MUCH FOR LIVING FOREVER, HUH?
PTOOF!
SHNUCK
GLUP
DEAR LORD.
I THINK THAT'S THE LAST OF THEM.
COME ON, TWO. LET'S SKEEDADDLE.

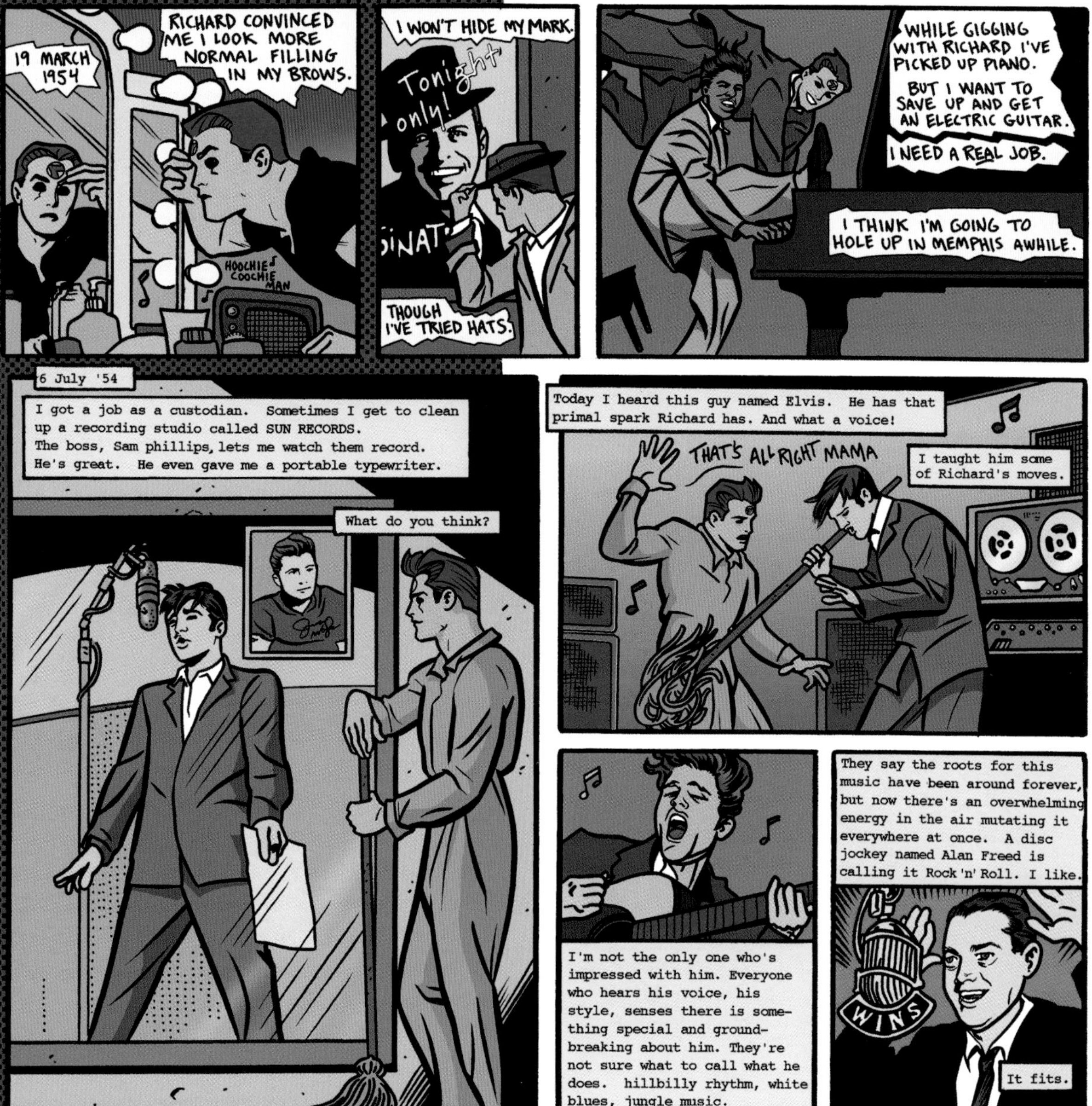
19 MARCH 1954
RICHARD CONVINCED ME I LOOK MORE NORMAL FILLING IN MY BROWS.
HOOCHIE COOCHIE MAN
I WON'T HIDE MY MARK.
Tonight only!
THOUGH I'VE TRIED HATS.
WHILE GIGGING WITH RICHARD I'VE PICKED UP PIANO.
BUT I WANT TO SAVE UP AND GET AN ELECTRIC GUITAR.
I NEED A REAL JOB.
I THINK I'M GOING TO HOLE UP IN MEMPHIS AWHILE.
6 July '54
I got a job as a custodian. Sometimes I get to clean up a recording studio called SUN RECORDS.
The boss, Sam phillips, lets me watch them record.
He's great. He even gave me a portable typewriter.
What do you think?
Today I heard this guy named Elvis. He has that primal spark Richard has. And what a voice!
THAT'S ALL RIGHT MAMA
I taught him some of Richard's moves.
I'm not the only one who's impressed with him. Everyone who hears his voice, his style, senses there is something special and groundbreaking about him. They're not sure what to call what he does. hillbilly rhythm, white blues, jungle music.
They say the roots for this music have been around forever, but now there's an overwhelming energy in the air mutating it everywhere at once. A disc jockey named Alan Freed is calling it Rock 'n' Roll. I like.
WINS
It fits.

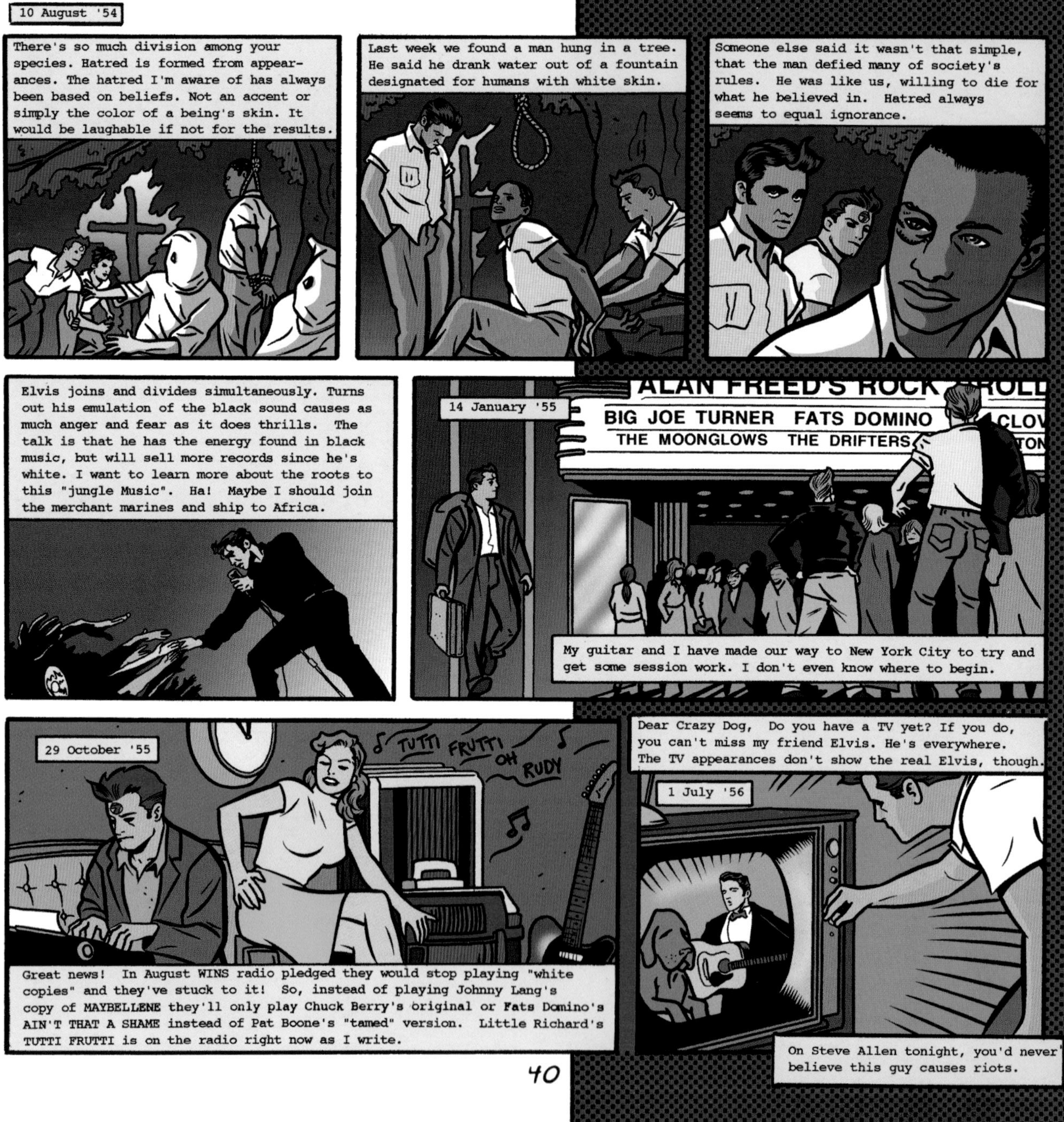
10 August '54
There's so much division among your species. Hatred is formed from appearances. The hatred I'm aware of has always been based on beliefs. Not an accent or simply the color of a being's skin. It would be laughable if not for the results.
Last week we found a man hung in a tree. He said he drank water out of a fountain designated for humans with white skin.
Someone else said it wasn't that simple, that the man defied many of society's rules. He was like us, willing to die for what he believed in. Hatred always seems to equal ignorance.
Elvis joins and divides simultaneously. Turns out his emulation of the black sound causes as much anger and fear as it does thrills. The talk is that he has the energy found in black music, but will sell more records since he's white. I want to learn more about the roots to this "jungle Music". Ha! Maybe I should join the merchant marines and ship to Africa.
14 January '55
ALAN FREED'S ROCK
BIG JOE TURNER FATS DOMINO
THE MOONGLOWS THE DRIFTERS
My guitar and I have made our way to New York City to try and get some session work. I don't even know where to begin.
29 October '55
TUTTI FRUTTI OH RUDY
Great news! In August WINS radio pledged they would stop playing "white copies" and they've stuck to it! So, instead of playing Johnny Lang's copy of MAYBELLENE they'll only play Chuck Berry's original or Fats Domino's AIN'T THAT A SHAME instead of Pat Boone's "tamed" version. Little Richard's TUTTI FRUTTI is on the radio right now as I write.
Dear Crazy Dog, Do you have a TV yet? If you do, you can't miss my friend Elvis. He's everywhere. The TV appearances don't show the real Elvis, though.
1 July '56
On Steve Allen tonight, you'd never believe this guy causes riots.

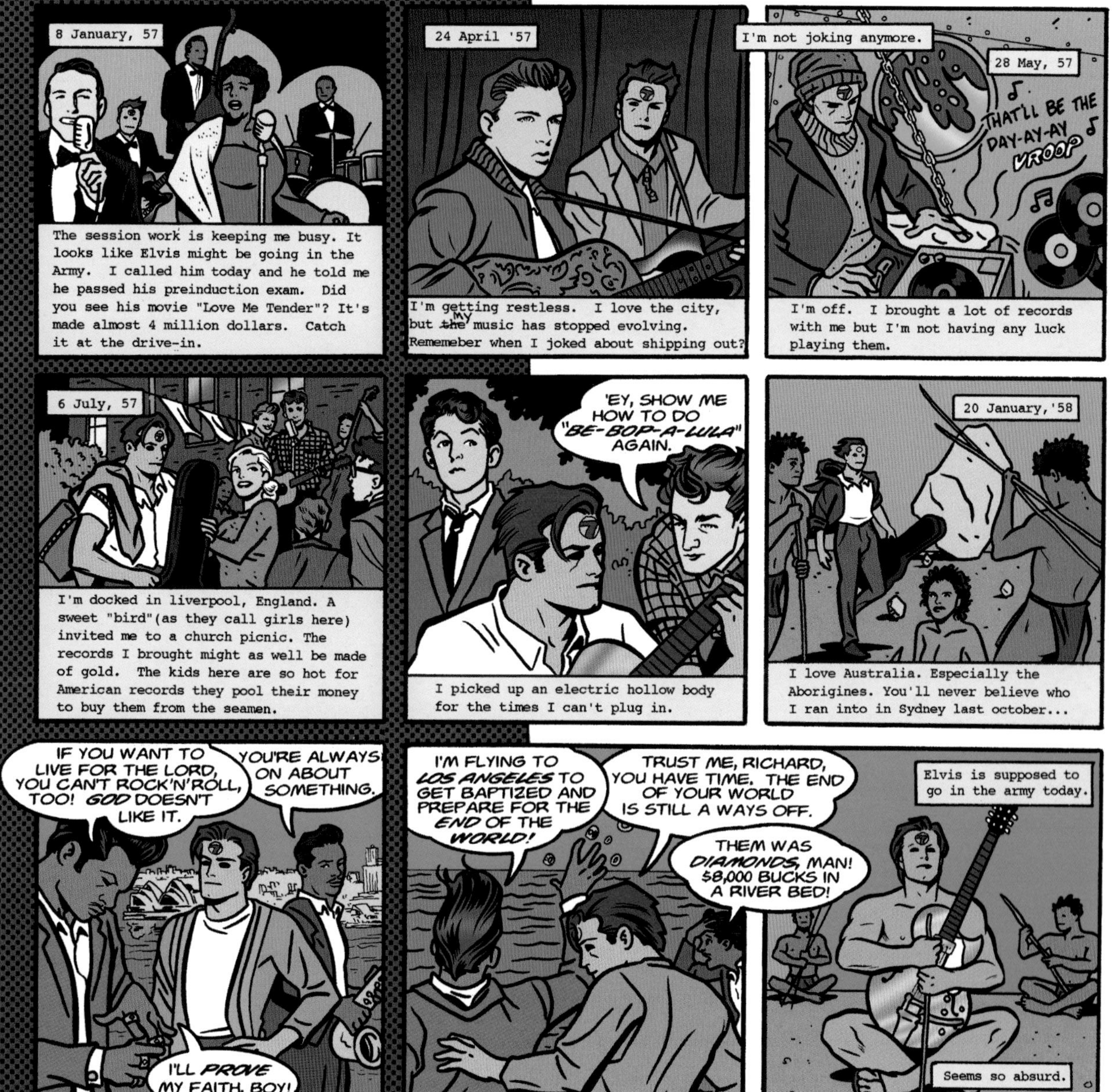
8 January, 57
The session work is keeping me busy. It looks like Elvis might be going in the Army. I called him today and he told me he passed his preinduction exam. Did you see his movie "Love Me Tender"? It's made almost 4 million dollars. Catch it at the drive-in.
24 April '57
I'm getting restless. I love the city, but ~~the~~ my music has stopped evolving. Rememeber when I joked about shipping out?
I'm not joking anymore.
28 May, 57
THAT'LL BE THE DAY-AY-AY
VROOP
I'm off. I brought a lot of records with me but I'm not having any luck playing them.
6 July, 57
I'm docked in liverpool, England. A sweet "bird"(as they call girls here) invited me to a church picnic. The records I brought might as well be made of gold. The kids here are so hot for American records they pool their money to buy them from the seamen.
'EY, SHOW ME HOW TO DO "BE-BOP-A-LULA" AGAIN.
I picked up an electric hollow body for the times I can't plug in.
20 January,'58
I love Australia. Especially the Aborigines. You'll never believe who I ran into in Sydney last october...
IF YOU WANT TO LIVE FOR THE LORD, YOU CAN'T ROCK'N'ROLL, TOO! GOD DOESN'T LIKE IT.
YOU'RE ALWAYS ON ABOUT SOMETHING.
I'LL PROVE MY FAITH, BOY!
I'M FLYING TO LOS ANGELES TO GET BAPTIZED AND PREPARE FOR THE END OF THE WORLD!
TRUST ME, RICHARD, YOU HAVE TIME. THE END OF YOUR WORLD IS STILL A WAYS OFF.
THEM WAS DIAMONDS, MAN! $8,000 BUCKS IN A RIVER BED!
Elvis is supposed to go in the army today.
Seems so absurd.

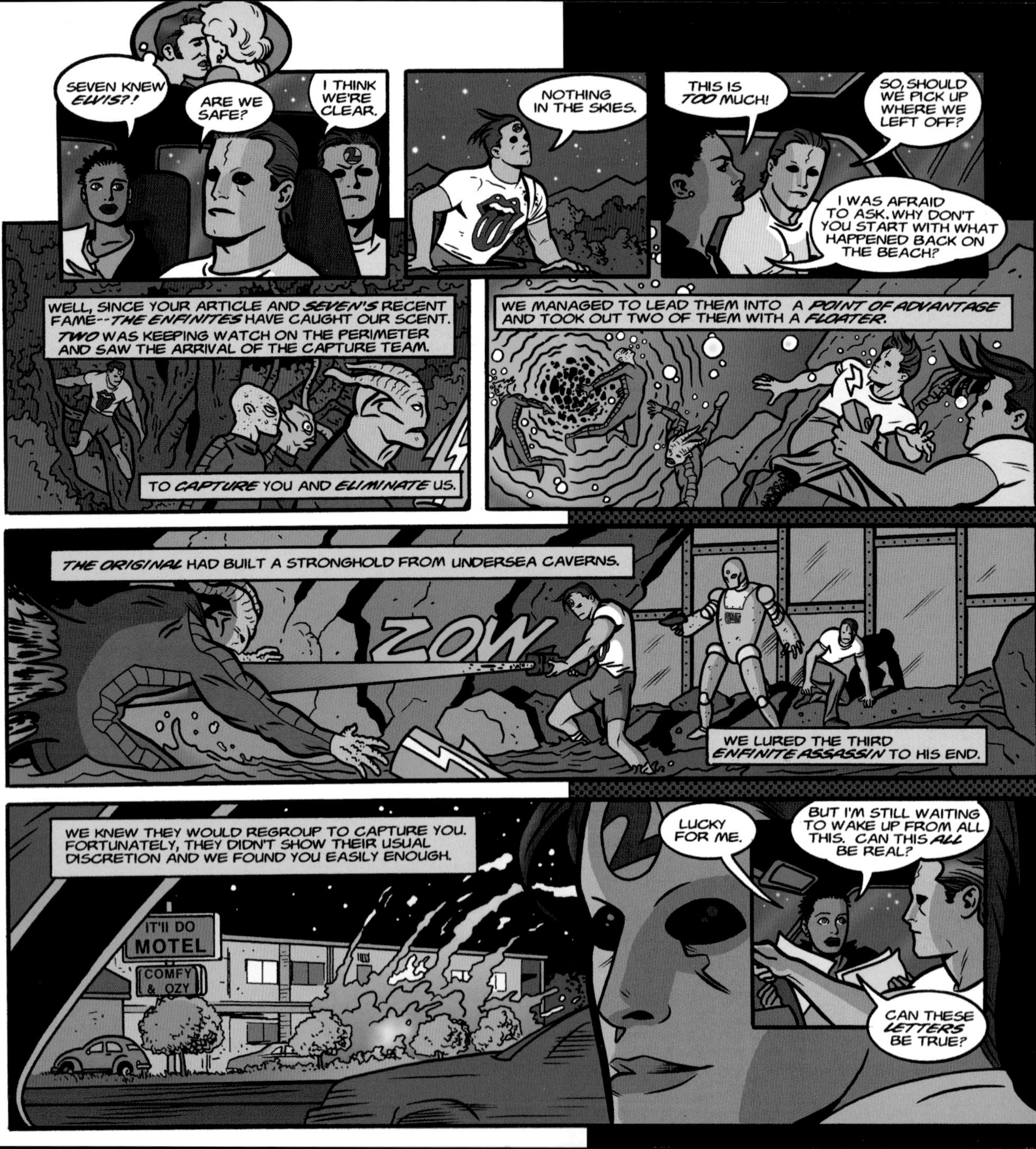
SEVEN KNEW ELVIS?!
ARE WE SAFE?
I THINK WE'RE CLEAR.
NOTHING IN THE SKIES.
THIS IS TOO MUCH!
SO, SHOULD WE PICK UP WHERE WE LEFT OFF?
I WAS AFRAID TO ASK. WHY DON'T YOU START WITH WHAT HAPPENED BACK ON THE BEACH?
WELL, SINCE YOUR ARTICLE AND SEVEN'S RECENT FAME--THE ENFINITES HAVE CAUGHT OUR SCENT. TWO WAS KEEPING WATCH ON THE PERIMETER AND SAW THE ARRIVAL OF THE CAPTURE TEAM.
TO CAPTURE YOU AND ELIMINATE US.
WE MANAGED TO LEAD THEM INTO A POINT OF ADVANTAGE AND TOOK OUT TWO OF THEM WITH A FLOATER.
THE ORIGINAL HAD BUILT A STRONGHOLD FROM UNDERSEA CAVERNS.
ZOW
WE LURED THE THIRD ENFINITE ASSASSIN TO HIS END.
WE KNEW THEY WOULD REGROUP TO CAPTURE YOU. FORTUNATELY, THEY DIDN'T SHOW THEIR USUAL DISCRETION AND WE FOUND YOU EASILY ENOUGH.
IT'll DO
MOTEL
COMFY & OZY
LUCKY FOR ME.
BUT I'M STILL WAITING TO WAKE UP FROM ALL THIS. CAN THIS ALL BE REAL?
CAN THESE LETTERS BE TRUE?

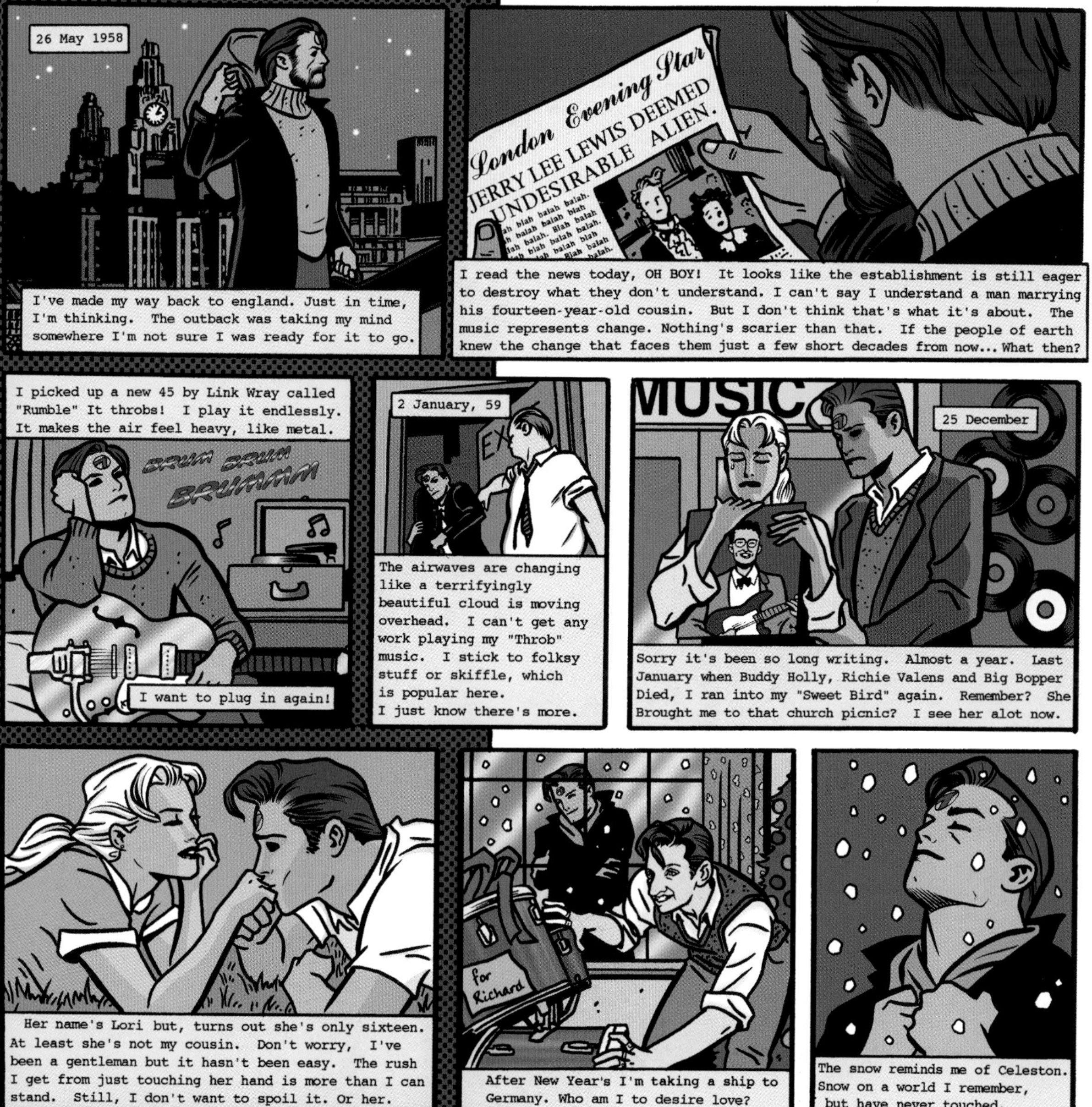
26 May 1958
I've made my way back to england. Just in time, I'm thinking. The outback was taking my mind somewhere I'm not sure I was ready for it to go.
London Evening Star
JERRY LEE LEWIS DEEMED UNDESIRABLE ALIEN.
I read the news today, OH BOY! It looks like the establishment is still eager to destroy what they don't understand. I can't say I understand a man marrying his fourteen-year-old cousin. But I don't think that's what it's about. The music represents change. Nothing's scarier than that. If the people of earth knew the change that faces them just a few short decades from now... What then?
I picked up a new 45 by Link Wray called "Rumble" It throbs! I play it endlessly. It makes the air feel heavy, like metal.
BRUM BRUM BRUMMM
I want to plug in again!
2 January, 59
The airwaves are changing like a terrifyingly beautiful cloud is moving overhead. I can't get any work playing my "Throb" music. I stick to folksy stuff or skiffle, which is popular here. I just know there's more.
MUSIC
25 December
Sorry it's been so long writing. Almost a year. Last January when Buddy Holly, Richie Valens and Big Bopper Died, I ran into my "Sweet Bird" again. Remember? She Brought me to that church picnic? I see her alot now.
Her name's Lori but, turns out she's only sixteen. At least she's not my cousin. Don't worry, I've been a gentleman but it hasn't been easy. The rush I get from just touching her hand is more than I can stand. Still, I don't want to spoil it. Or her.
for Richard
After New Year's I'm taking a ship to Germany. Who am I to desire love?
The snow reminds me of Celeston. Snow on a world I remember, but have never touched.

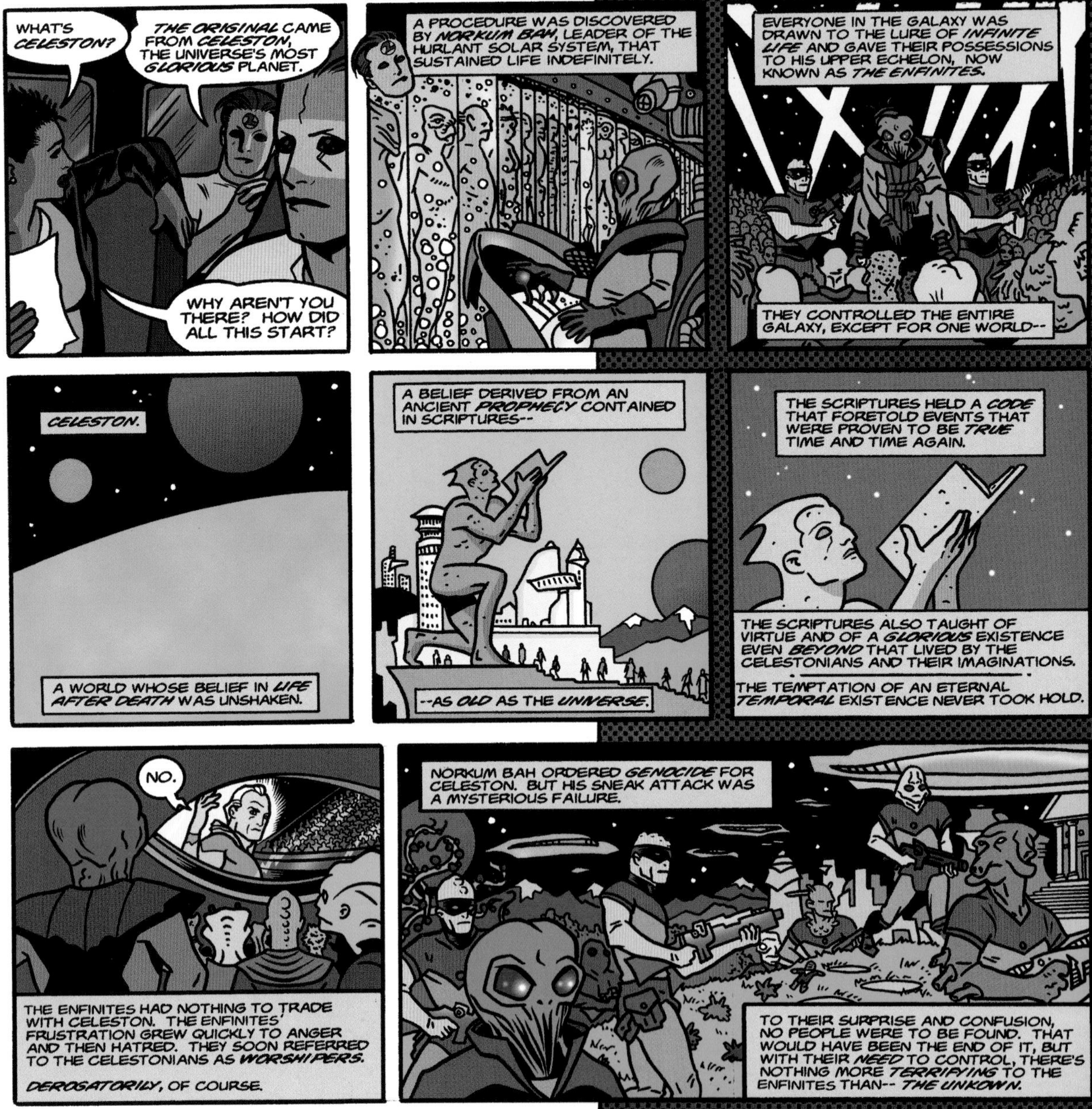
WHAT'S CELESTON?
THE ORIGINAL CAME FROM CELESTON, THE UNIVERSE'S MOST GLORIOUS PLANET.
WHY AREN'T YOU THERE? HOW DID ALL THIS START?
A PROCEDURE WAS DISCOVERED BY NORKUM BAH, LEADER OF THE HURLANT SOLAR SYSTEM, THAT SUSTAINED LIFE INDEFINITELY.
EVERYONE IN THE GALAXY WAS DRAWN TO THE LURE OF INFINITE LIFE AND GAVE THEIR POSSESSIONS TO HIS UPPER ECHELON, NOW KNOWN AS THE ENFINITES.
THEY CONTROLLED THE ENTIRE GALAXY, EXCEPT FOR ONE WORLD--
CELESTON.
A WORLD WHOSE BELIEF IN LIFE AFTER DEATH WAS UNSHAKEN.
A BELIEF DERIVED FROM AN ANCIENT PROPHECY CONTAINED IN SCRIPTURES--
--AS OLD AS THE UNIVERSE.
THE SCRIPTURES HELD A CODE THAT FORETOLD EVENTS THAT WERE PROVEN TO BE TRUE TIME AND TIME AGAIN.
THE SCRIPTURES ALSO TAUGHT OF VIRTUE AND OF A GLORIOUS EXISTENCE EVEN BEYOND THAT LIVED BY THE CELESTONIANS AND THEIR IMAGINATIONS.
THE TEMPTATION OF AN ETERNAL TEMPORAL EXISTENCE NEVER TOOK HOLD.
NO.
THE ENFINITES HAD NOTHING TO TRADE WITH CELESTON. THE ENFINITES' FRUSTRATION GREW QUICKLY TO ANGER AND THEN HATRED. THEY SOON REFERRED TO THE CELESTONIANS AS WORSHIPERS.
DEROGATORILY, OF COURSE.
NORKUM BAH ORDERED GENOCIDE FOR CELESTON. BUT HIS SNEAK ATTACK WAS A MYSTERIOUS FAILURE.
TO THEIR SURPRISE AND CONFUSION, NO PEOPLE WERE TO BE FOUND. THAT WOULD HAVE BEEN THE END OF IT, BUT WITH THEIR NEED TO CONTROL, THERE'S NOTHING MORE TERRIFYING TO THE ENFINITES THAN-- THE UNKOWN.

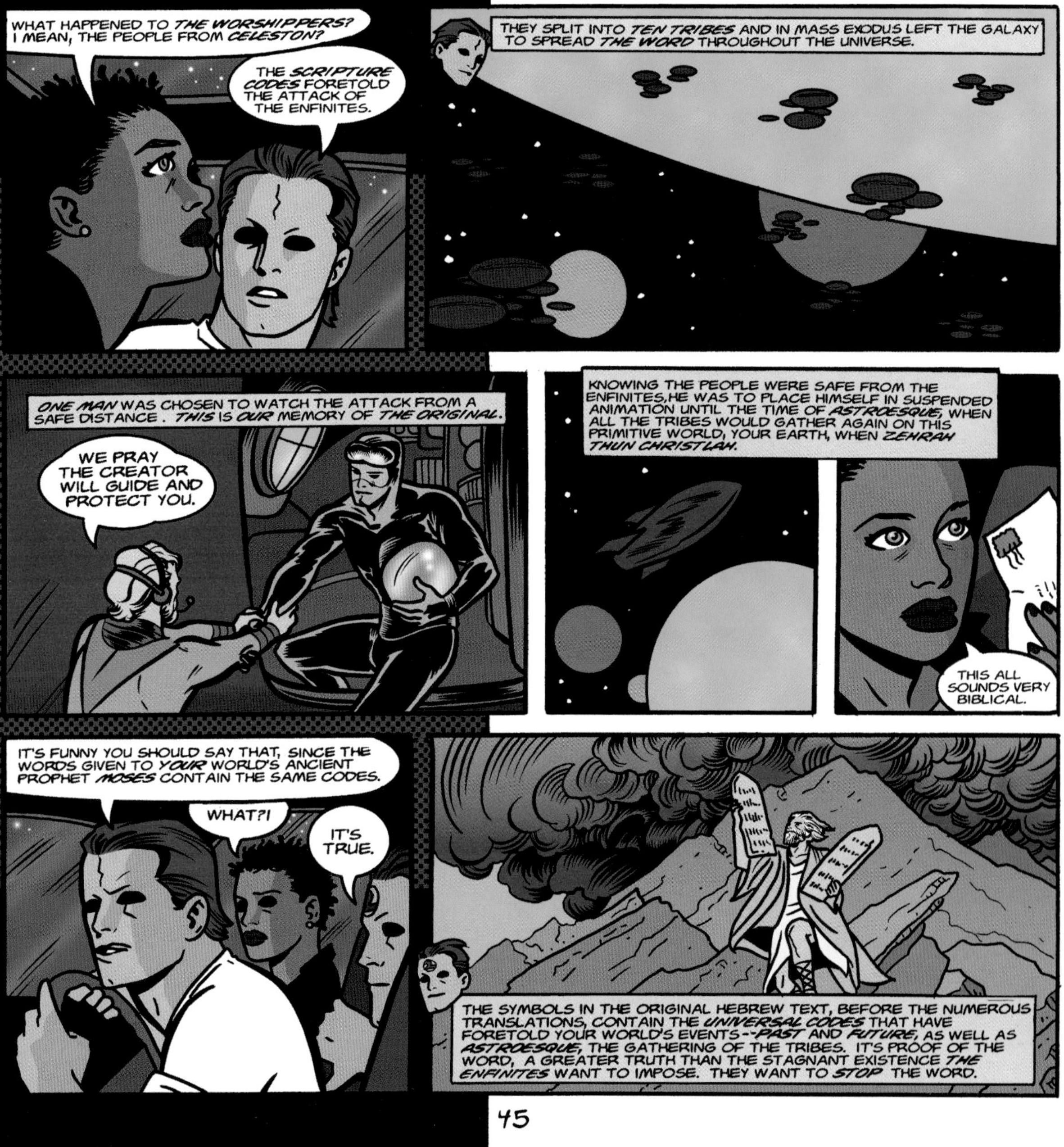
WHAT HAPPENED TO *THE WORSHIPPERS?* I MEAN, THE PEOPLE FROM *CELESTON?*
THE *SCRIPTURE CODES* FORETOLD THE ATTACK OF THE ENFINITES.
THEY SPLIT INTO *TEN TRIBES* AND IN MASS EXODUS LEFT THE GALAXY TO SPREAD *THE WORD* THROUGHOUT THE UNIVERSE.
ONE MAN WAS CHOSEN TO WATCH THE ATTACK FROM A SAFE DISTANCE. *THIS* IS *OUR* MEMORY OF *THE ORIGINAL.*
WE PRAY THE CREATOR WILL GUIDE AND PROTECT YOU.
KNOWING THE PEOPLE WERE SAFE FROM THE ENFINITES, HE WAS TO PLACE HIMSELF IN SUSPENDED ANIMATION UNTIL THE TIME OF *ASTROESQUE,* WHEN ALL THE TRIBES WOULD GATHER AGAIN ON THIS PRIMITIVE WORLD, YOUR EARTH, WHEN *ZEHRAH THUN CHRISTLAH.*
THIS ALL SOUNDS VERY BIBLICAL.
IT'S FUNNY YOU SHOULD SAY THAT, SINCE THE WORDS GIVEN TO *YOUR* WORLD'S ANCIENT PROPHET *MOSES* CONTAIN THE SAME CODES.
WHAT?!
IT'S TRUE.
THE SYMBOLS IN THE ORIGINAL HEBREW TEXT, BEFORE THE NUMEROUS TRANSLATIONS, CONTAIN THE *UNIVERSAL CODES* THAT HAVE FORETOLD YOUR WORLD'S EVENTS--*PAST* AND *FUTURE,* AS WELL AS *ASTROESQUE,* THE GATHERING OF THE TRIBES. IT'S PROOF OF THE WORD, A GREATER TRUTH THAN THE STAGNANT EXISTENCE *THE ENFINITES* WANT TO IMPOSE. THEY WANT TO *STOP* THE WORD.

HOW DID THE *ENFINITES* FIND OUT ABOUT *THE ORIGINAL* COMING HERE?

DUMB LUCK. AN ENFINITE PATROL GROUP STUMBLED ACCROSS *THE ORIGINAL'S* SPACESHIP.

WHEN THE ORIGINAL WAS REVIVED, I WAS...

I MEAN, *HE* WAS IN A CELL--

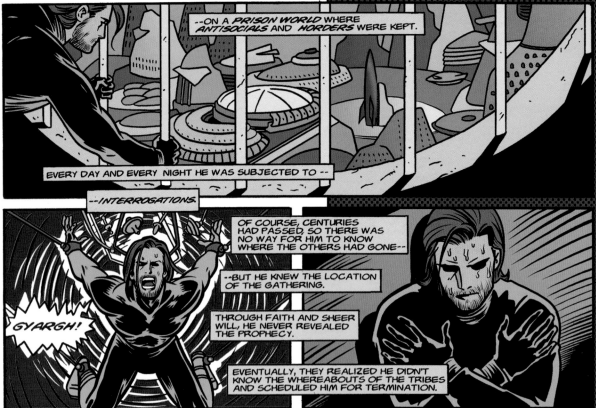

--ON A *PRISON WORLD* WHERE *ANTISOCIALS* AND *HORDERS* WERE KEPT.

EVERY DAY AND EVERY NIGHT HE WAS SUBJECTED TO --

--INTERROGATIONS.

OF COURSE, CENTURIES HAD PASSED, SO THERE WAS NO WAY FOR HIM TO KNOW WHERE THE OTHERS HAD GONE--

--BUT HE KNEW THE LOCATION OF THE GATHERING.

THROUGH FAITH AND SHEER WILL, HE NEVER REVEALED THE PROPHECY.

EVENTUALLY, THEY REALIZED HE DIDN'T KNOW THE WHEREABOUTS OF THE TRIBES AND SCHEDULED HIM FOR TERMINATION.

GYARGH!

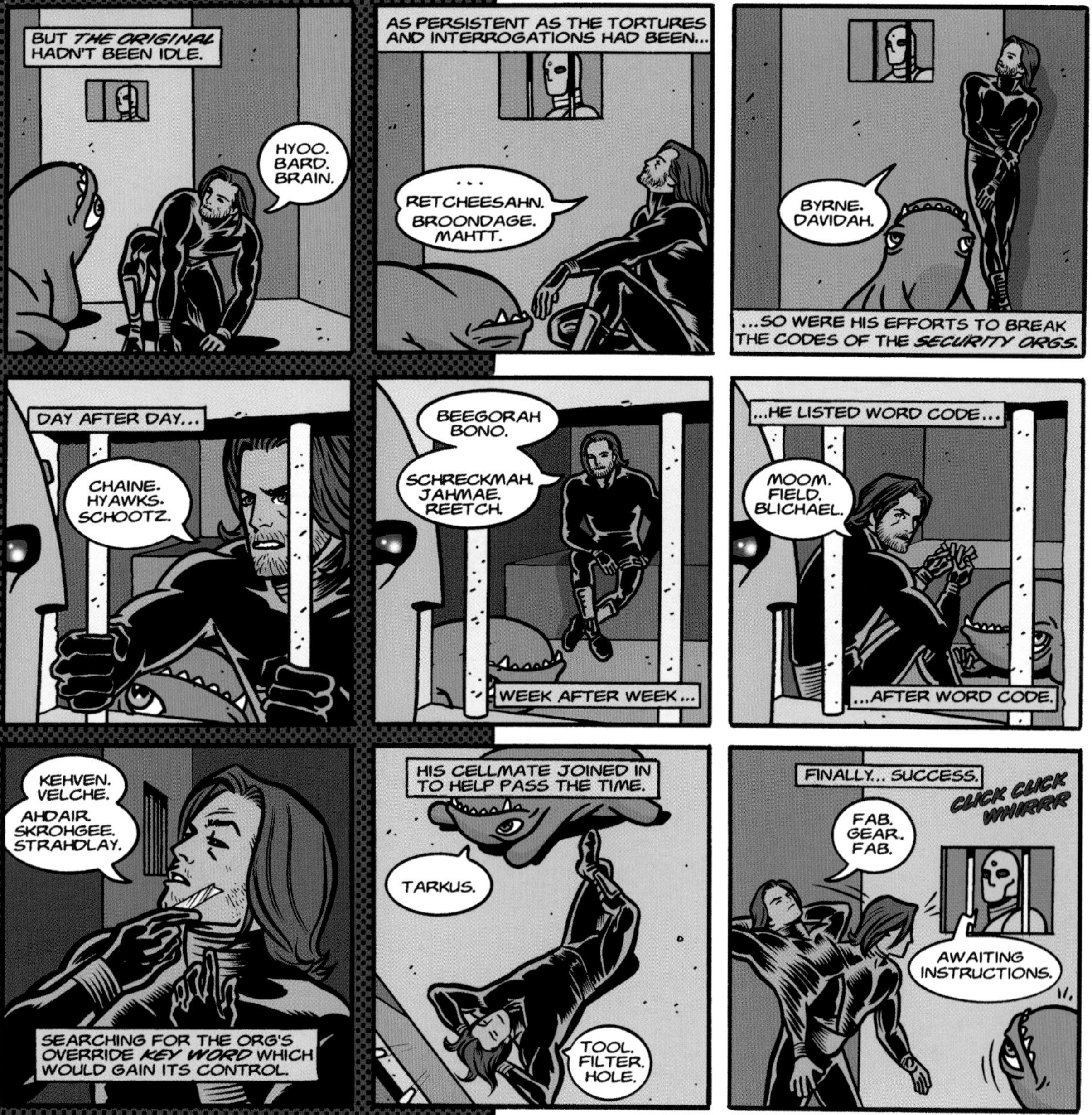

BUT THE ORIGINAL HADN'T BEEN IDLE.
HYOO. BARD. BRAIN.
AS PERSISTENT AS THE TORTURES AND INTERROGATIONS HAD BEEN...
... RETCHEESAHN. BROONDAGE. MAHTT.
BYRNE. DAVIDAH.
...SO WERE HIS EFFORTS TO BREAK THE CODES OF THE SECURITY ORGS.
DAY AFTER DAY...
CHAINE. HYAWKS. SCHOOTZ.
BEEGORAH BONO.
SCHRECKMAH. JAHMAE. REETCH.
WEEK AFTER WEEK...
...HE LISTED WORD CODE...
MOOM. FIELD. BLICHAEL.
...AFTER WORD CODE.
KEHVEN. VELCHE.
AHDAIR. SKROHGEE. STRAHDLAY.
SEARCHING FOR THE ORG'S OVERRIDE KEY WORD WHICH WOULD GAIN ITS CONTROL.
HIS CELLMATE JOINED IN TO HELP PASS THE TIME.
TARKUS.
TOOL. FILTER. HOLE.
FINALLY... SUCCESS.
CLICK CLICK WHIRRR
FAB. GEAR. FAB.
AWAITING INSTRUCTIONS.

SHUT DOWN.
DOOP
PLEASE FIND SHELTER.
WHAT-- NO KEY?
DESTRUCT 53310761.
BLAM

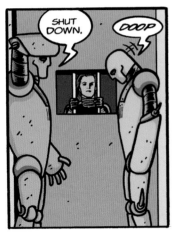

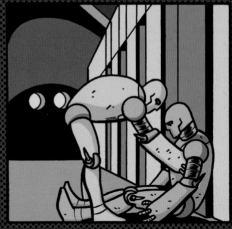

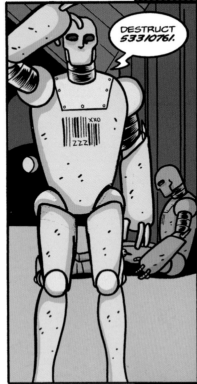

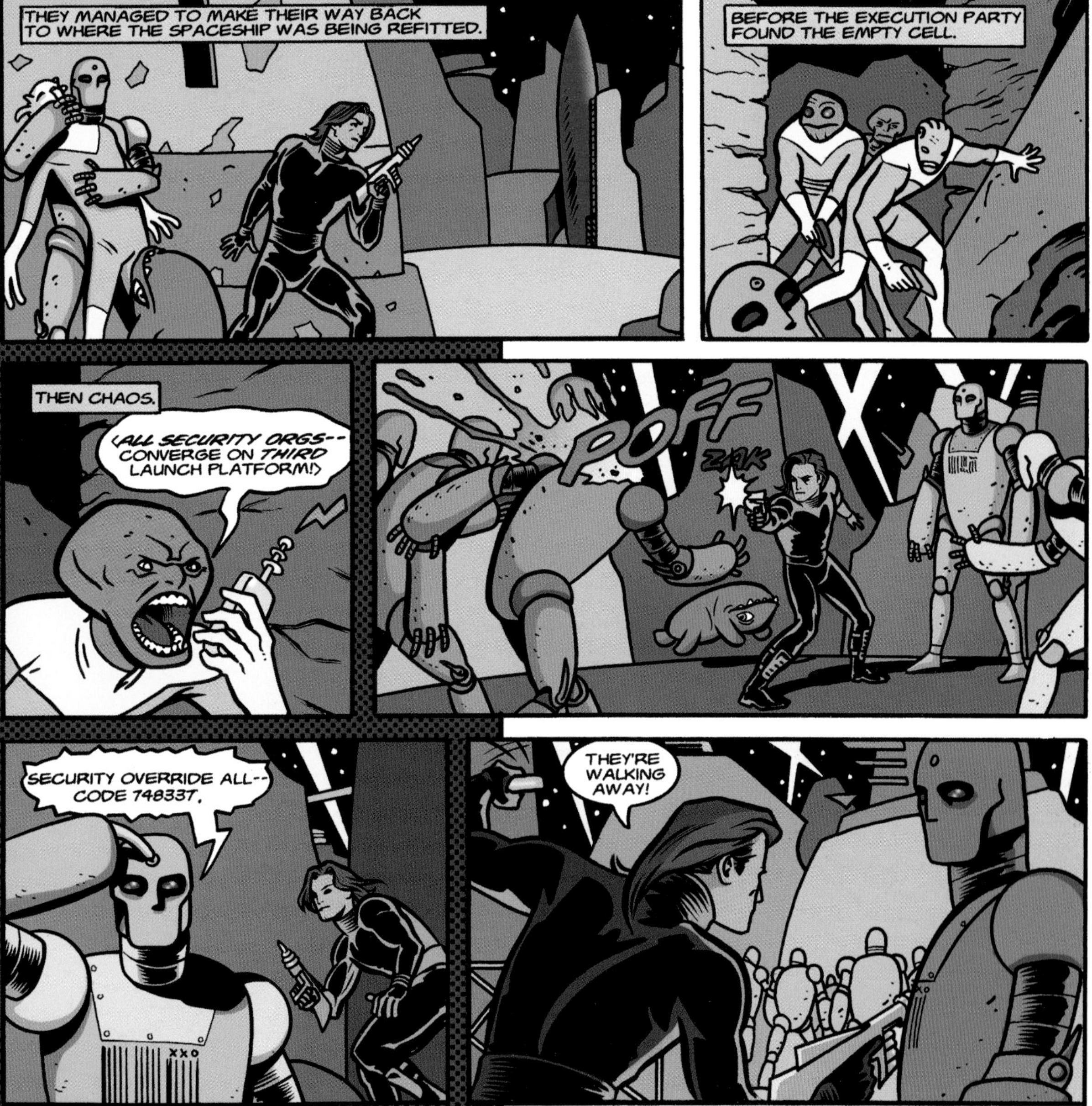
THEY MANAGED TO MAKE THEIR WAY BACK TO WHERE THE SPACESHIP WAS BEING REFITTED.
BEFORE THE EXECUTION PARTY FOUND THE EMPTY CELL.
THEN CHAOS.
‹ALL SECURITY ORGS-- CONVERGE ON THIRD LAUNCH PLATFORM!›
POFF
ZAK
SECURITY OVERRIDE ALL-- CODE 748337.
THEY'RE WALKING AWAY!

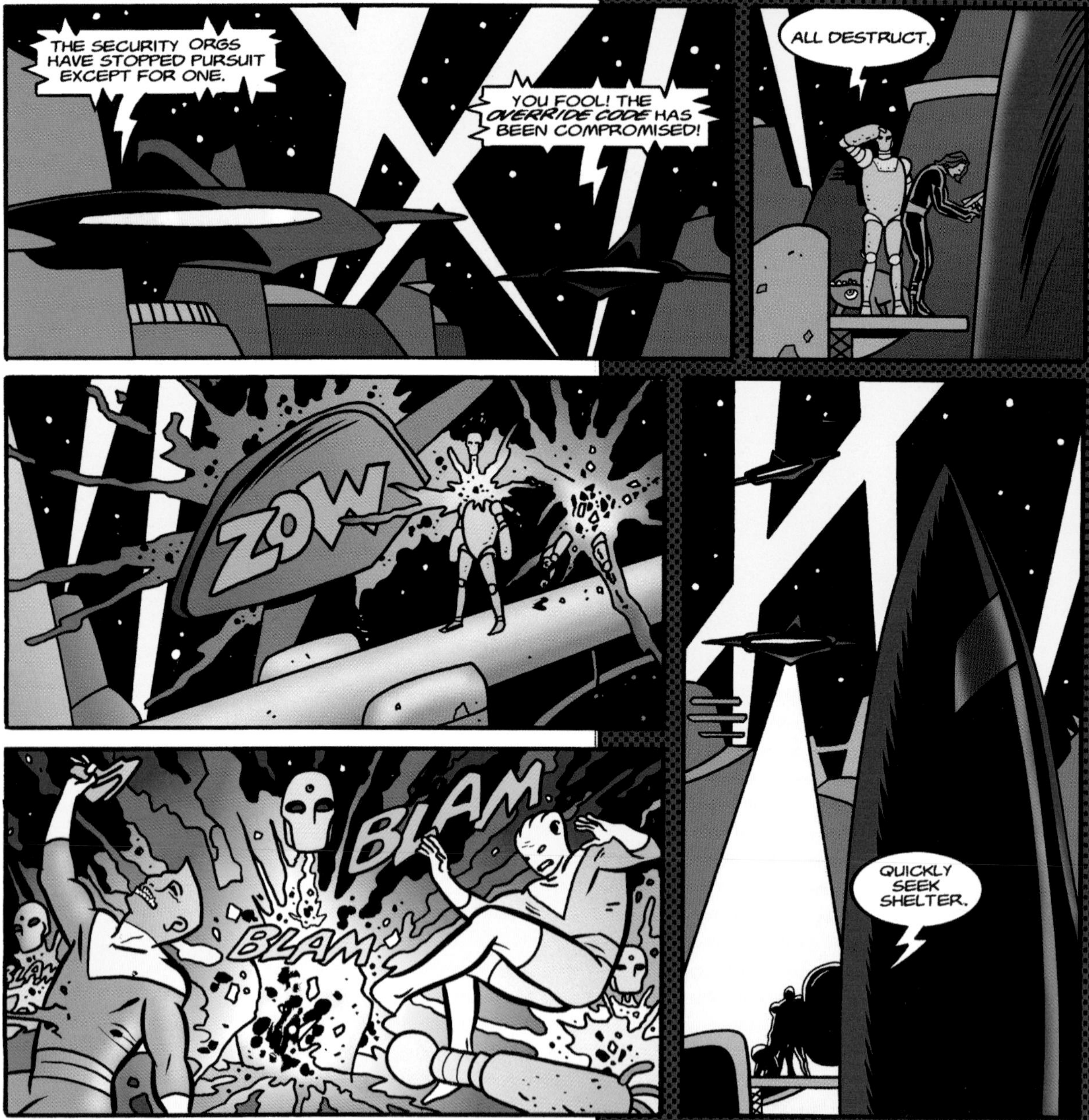
THE SECURITY ORGS HAVE STOPPED PURSUIT EXCEPT FOR ONE.
YOU FOOL! THE OVERRIDE CODE HAS BEEN COMPROMISED!
ALL DESTRUCT.
ZOW
BLAM
BLAM
QUICKLY SEEK SHELTER.

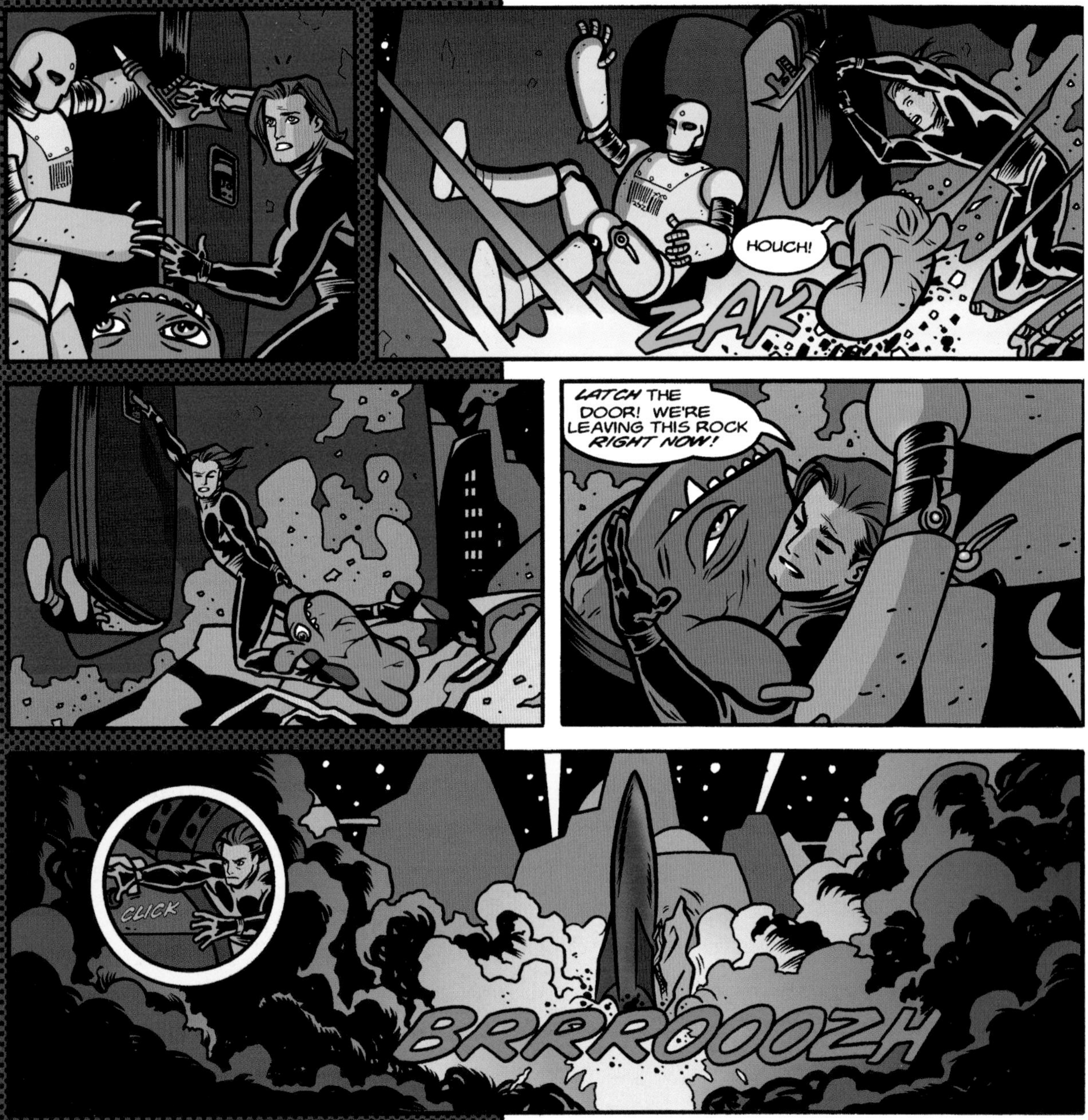
HOUCH!
ZAK
LATCH THE DOOR! WE'RE LEAVING THIS ROCK RIGHT NOW!
CLICK
BRRROOOZH

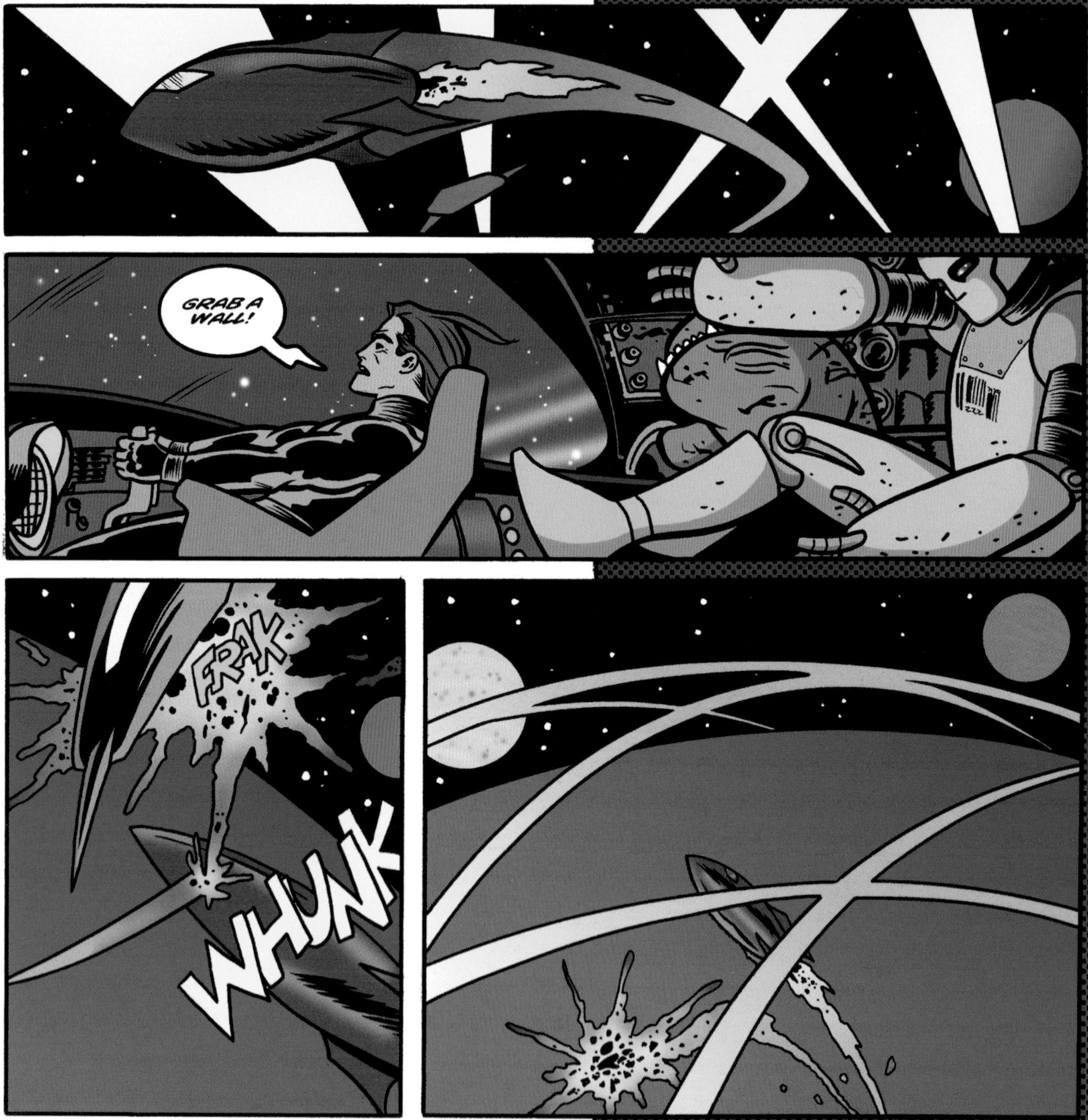
GRAB A WALL!
FRAK
WHUNK

CODE 6721863--SHUT DOWN ORBITAL SECURITY SHIELD.

I HADN'T FIGURED ON THAT. I'M GLAD YOU CAME ALONG. CAN YOU CHECK ON *TONG*? HE'S HURT REAL BAD. HE TOOK A LOT OF SHRAPNEL.

THERE WILL BE ASSASSIN SHIPS IN OUTER ORBIT. THERE ARE TWO PLOTTING AN INTERCEPT. CONTACT IN 30 SECONDS.

I CAN'T FIGHT THEM! MY ROCKET'S NOT ARMED!

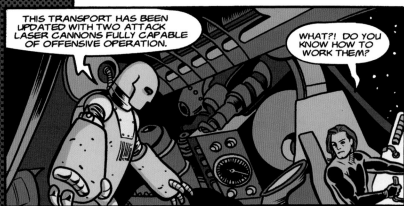

THIS TRANSPORT HAS BEEN UPDATED WITH TWO ATTACK LASER CANNONS FULLY CAPABLE OF OFFENSIVE OPERATION.

WHAT?! DO YOU KNOW HOW TO WORK THEM?

YES. WITH 99.9 PERCENT ACCURACY.

I'LL TAKE THE OTHER LASER. YOU JUST FLY US OUT OF HERE.

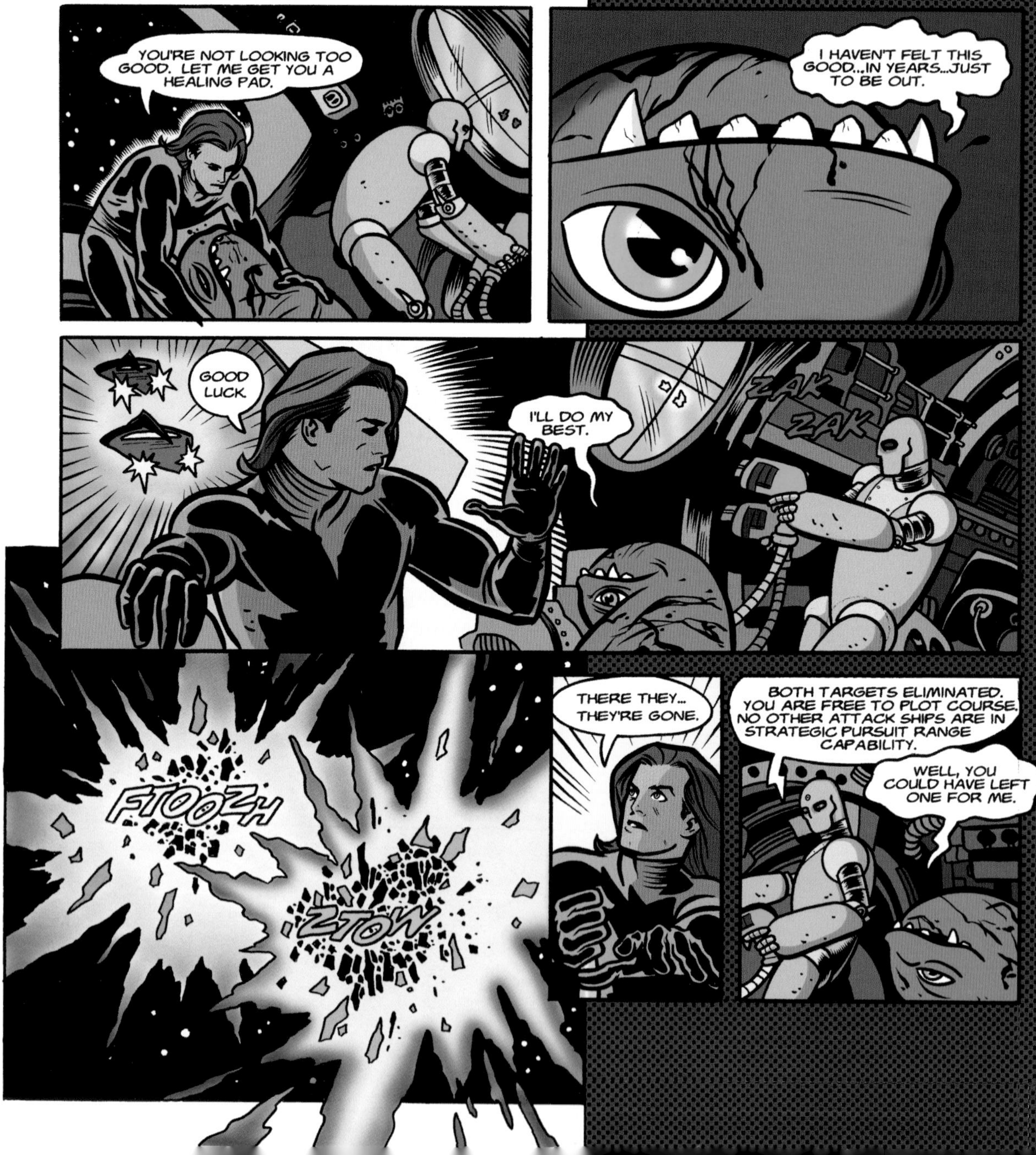
YOU'RE NOT LOOKING TOO GOOD. LET ME GET YOU A HEALING PAD.
I HAVEN'T FELT THIS GOOD...IN YEARS...JUST TO BE OUT.
GOOD LUCK.
I'LL DO MY BEST.
ZAK
ZAK
FTOOZH
ZTOW
THERE THEY... THEY'RE GONE.
BOTH TARGETS ELIMINATED. YOU ARE FREE TO PLOT COURSE. NO OTHER ATTACK SHIPS ARE IN STRATEGIC PURSUIT RANGE CAPABILITY.
WELL, YOU COULD HAVE LEFT ONE FOR ME.

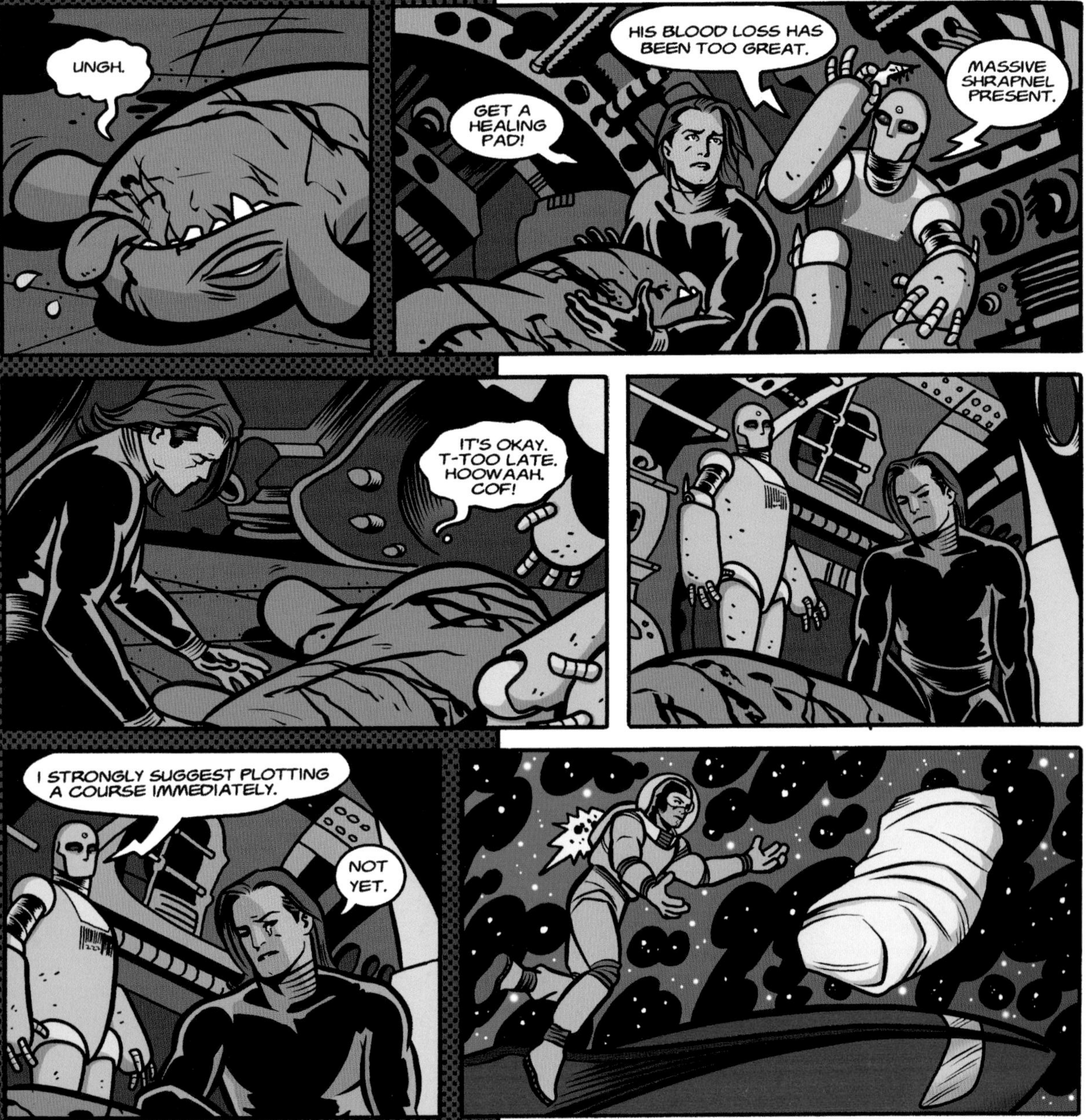
UNGH.
HIS BLOOD LOSS HAS BEEN TOO GREAT.
GET A HEALING PAD!
MASSIVE SHRAPNEL PRESENT.
IT'S OKAY. T-TOO LATE. HOOWAAH. COF!
I STRONGLY SUGGEST PLOTTING A COURSE IMMEDIATELY.
NOT YET.

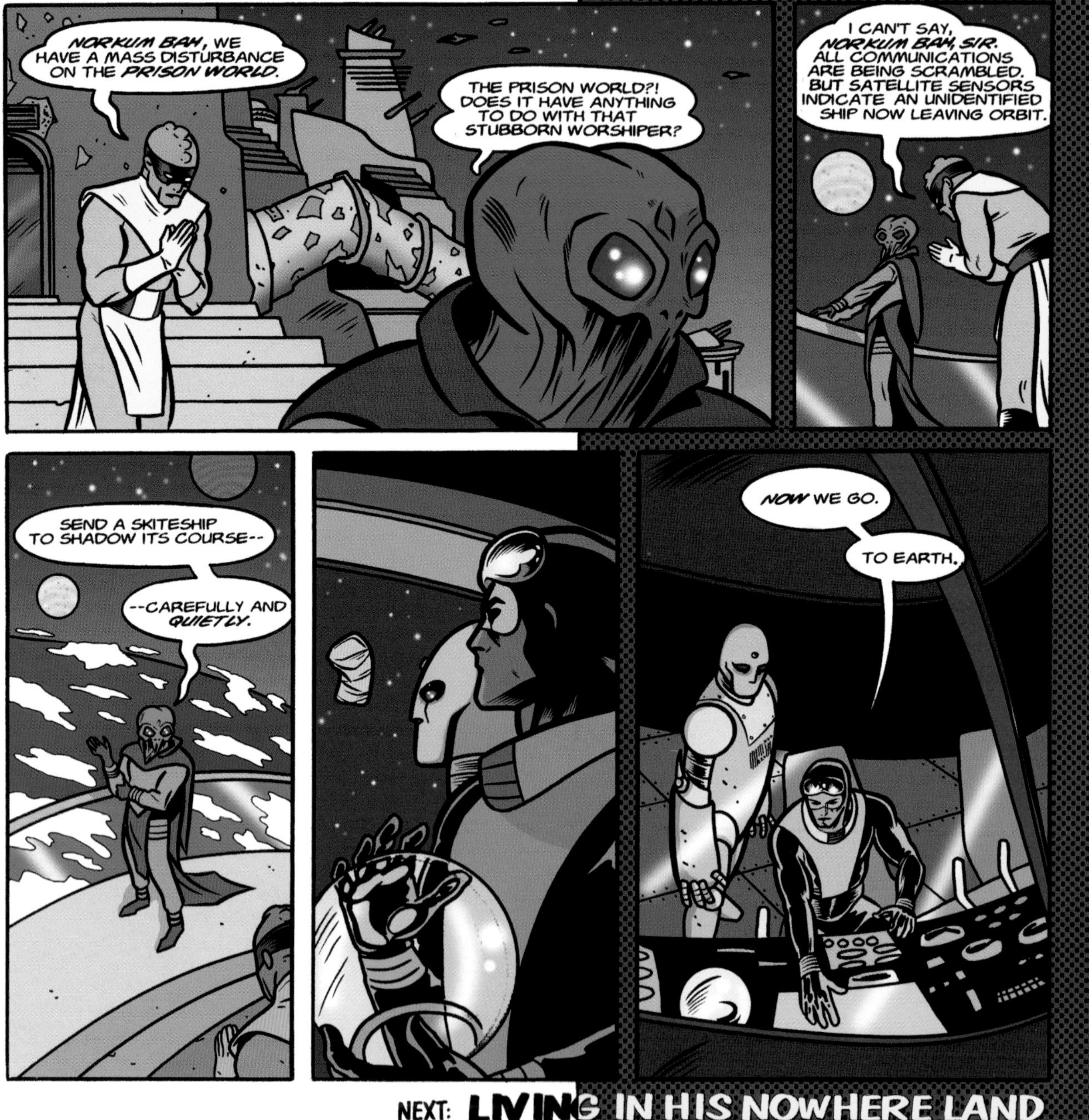
NORKUM BAH, WE HAVE A MASS DISTURBANCE ON THE PRISON WORLD.
THE PRISON WORLD?! DOES IT HAVE ANYTHING TO DO WITH THAT STUBBORN WORSHIPER?
I CAN'T SAY, NORKUM BAH, SIR. ALL COMMUNICATIONS ARE BEING SCRAMBLED. BUT SATELLITE SENSORS INDICATE AN UNIDENTIFIED SHIP NOW LEAVING ORBIT.
SEND A SKITESHIP TO SHADOW ITS COURSE--
--CAREFULLY AND QUIETLY.
NOW WE GO.
TO EARTH.

NEXT: LIVING IN HIS NOWHERE LAND

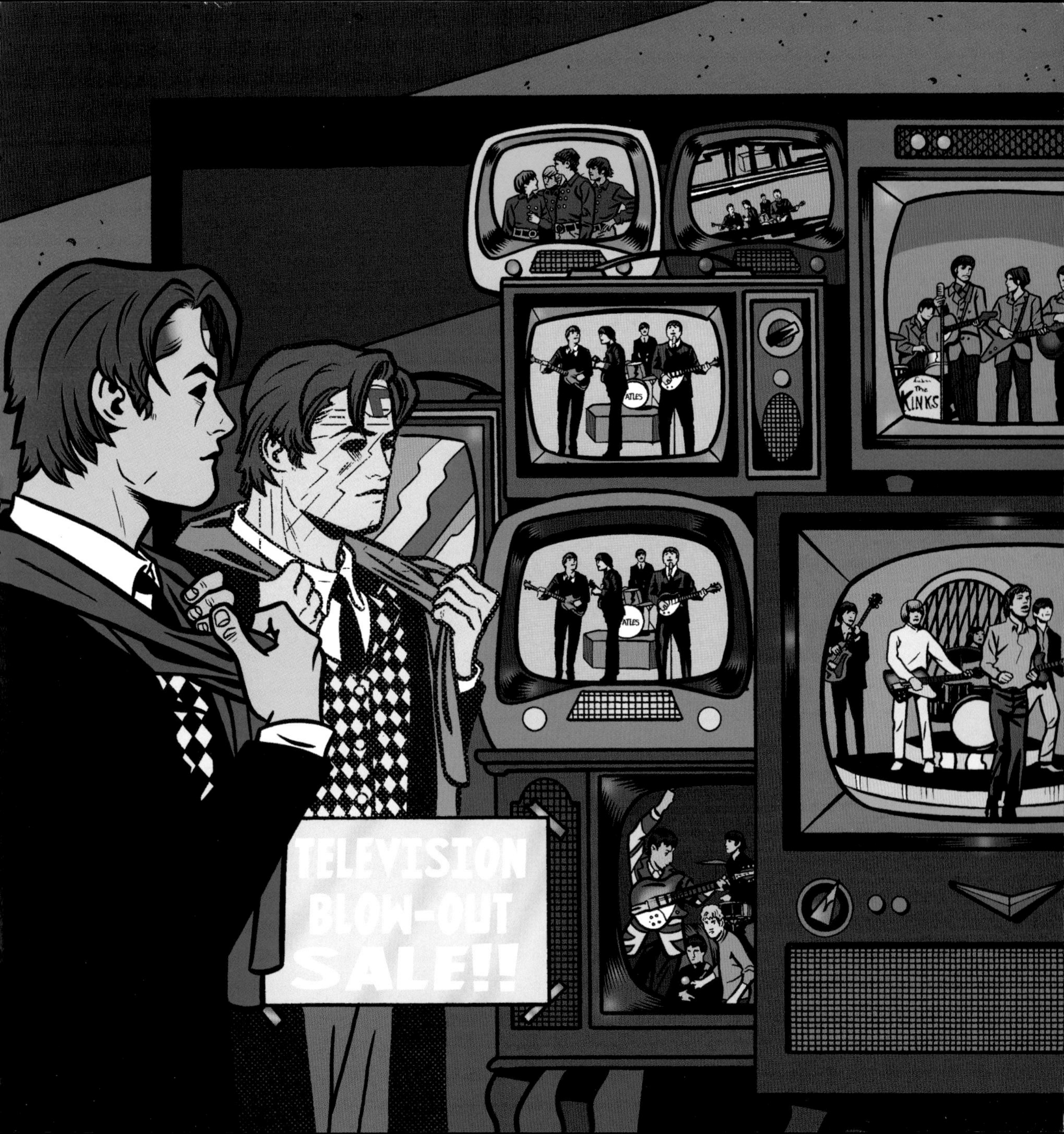
TELEVISION
BLOW-OUT
SALE!!

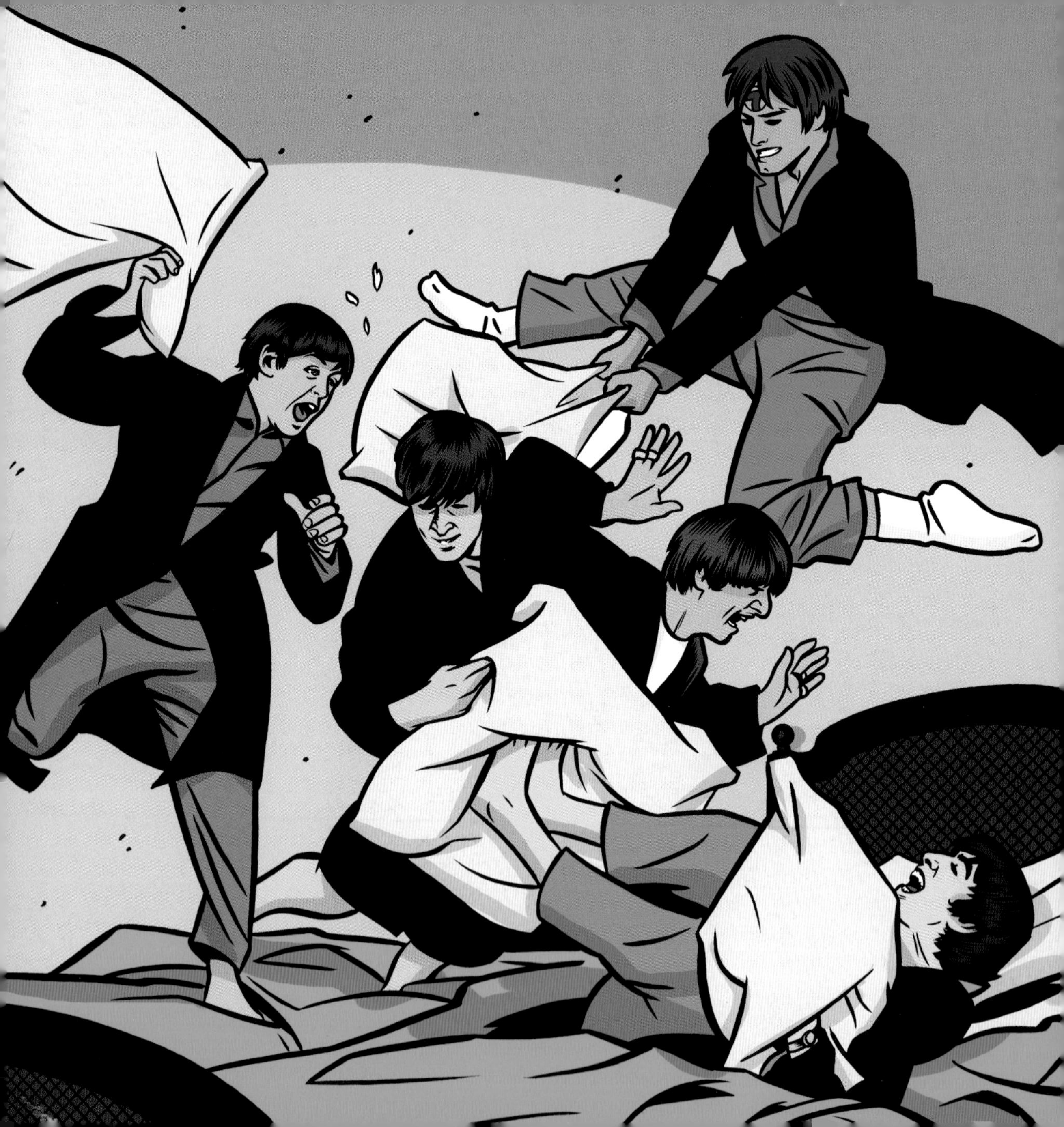

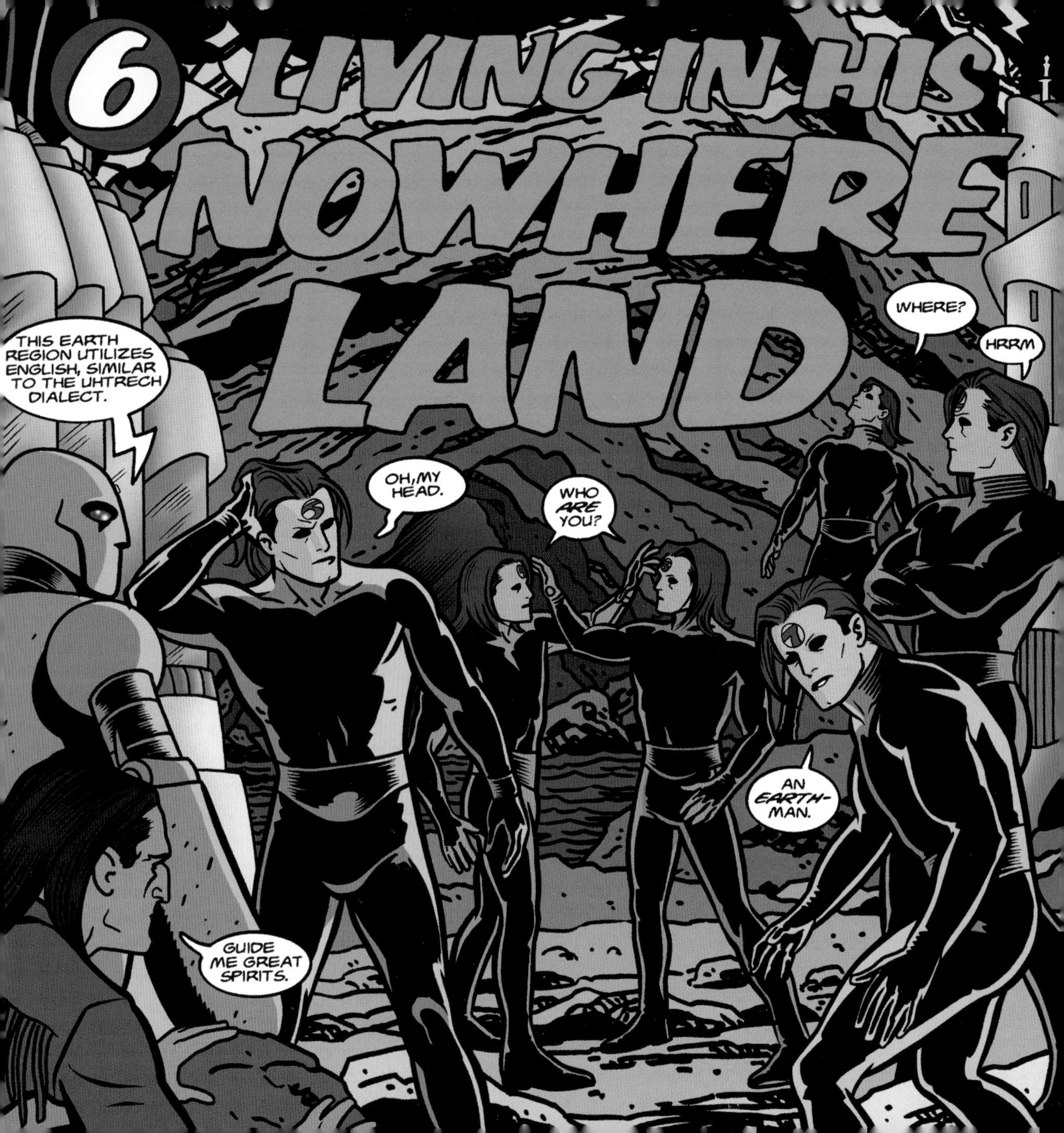
6 LIVING IN HIS NOWHERE LAND
THIS EARTH REGION UTILIZES ENGLISH, SIMILAR TO THE UHTRECH DIALECT.
WHERE?
HRRM
OH, MY HEAD.
WHO ARE YOU?
AN EARTH-MAN.
GUIDE ME GREAT SPIRITS.

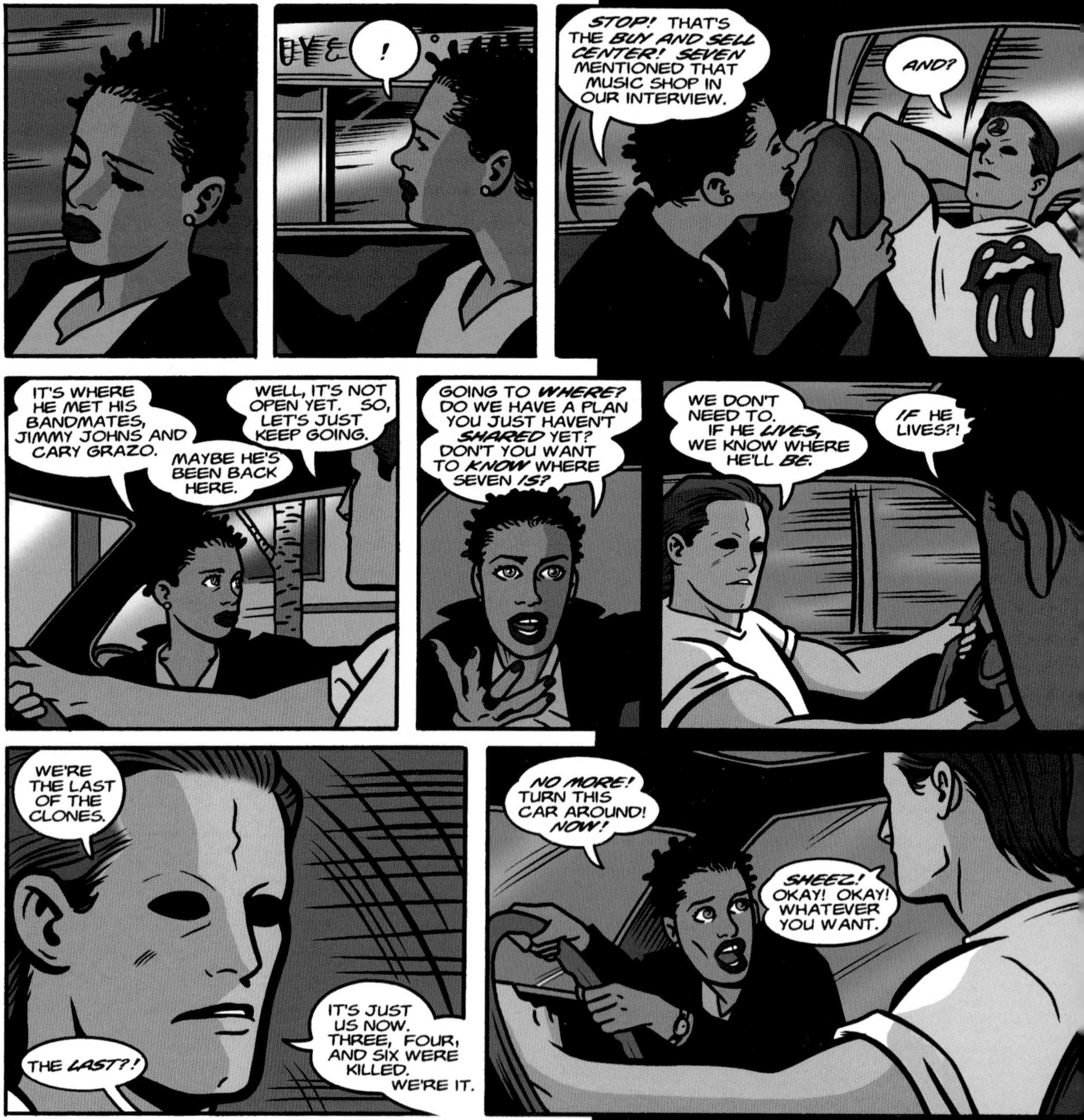
!
STOP! THAT'S THE BUY AND SELL CENTER! SEVEN MENTIONED THAT MUSIC SHOP IN OUR INTERVIEW.
AND?
IT'S WHERE HE MET HIS BANDMATES, JIMMY JOHNS AND CARY GRAZO.
MAYBE HE'S BEEN BACK HERE.
WELL, IT'S NOT OPEN YET. SO, LET'S JUST KEEP GOING.
GOING TO WHERE? DO WE HAVE A PLAN YOU JUST HAVEN'T SHARED YET? DON'T YOU WANT TO KNOW WHERE SEVEN IS?
WE DON'T NEED TO. IF HE LIVES, WE KNOW WHERE HE'LL BE.
IF HE LIVES?!
WE'RE THE LAST OF THE CLONES.
THE LAST?!
IT'S JUST US NOW. THREE, FOUR, AND SIX WERE KILLED. WE'RE IT.
NO MORE! TURN THIS CAR AROUND! NOW!
SHEEZ! OKAY! OKAY! WHATEVER YOU WANT.

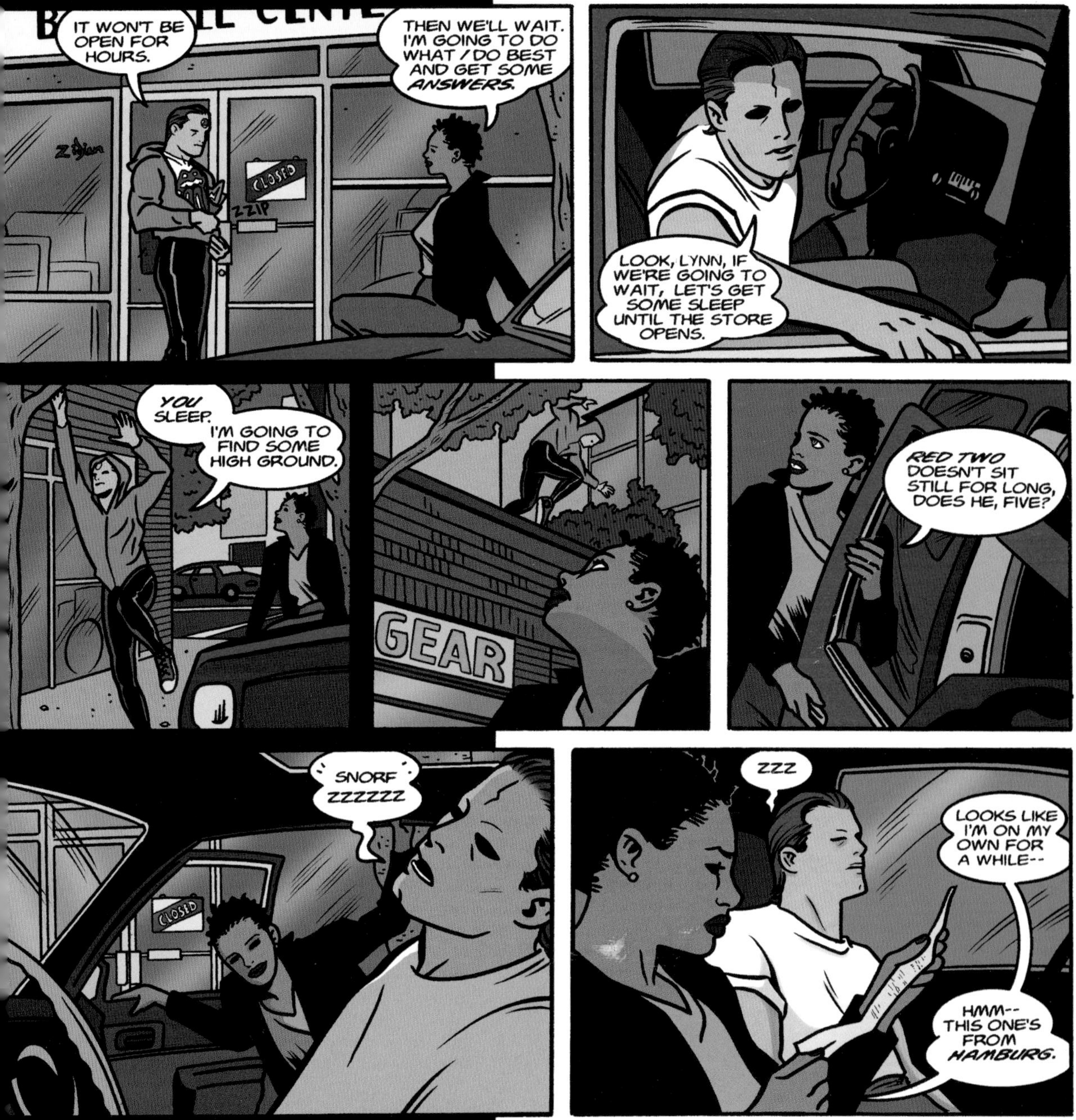
IT WON'T BE OPEN FOR HOURS.
THEN WE'LL WAIT. I'M GOING TO DO WHAT I DO BEST AND GET SOME ANSWERS.
CLOSED
ZZIP
LOOK, LYNN, IF WE'RE GOING TO WAIT, LET'S GET SOME SLEEP UNTIL THE STORE OPENS.
YOU SLEEP.
I'M GOING TO FIND SOME HIGH GROUND.
GEAR
RED TWO DOESN'T SIT STILL FOR LONG, DOES HE, FIVE?
SNORF ZZZZZZ
CLOSED
ZZZ
LOOKS LIKE I'M ON MY OWN FOR A WHILE--
HMM-- THIS ONE'S FROM HAMBURG.

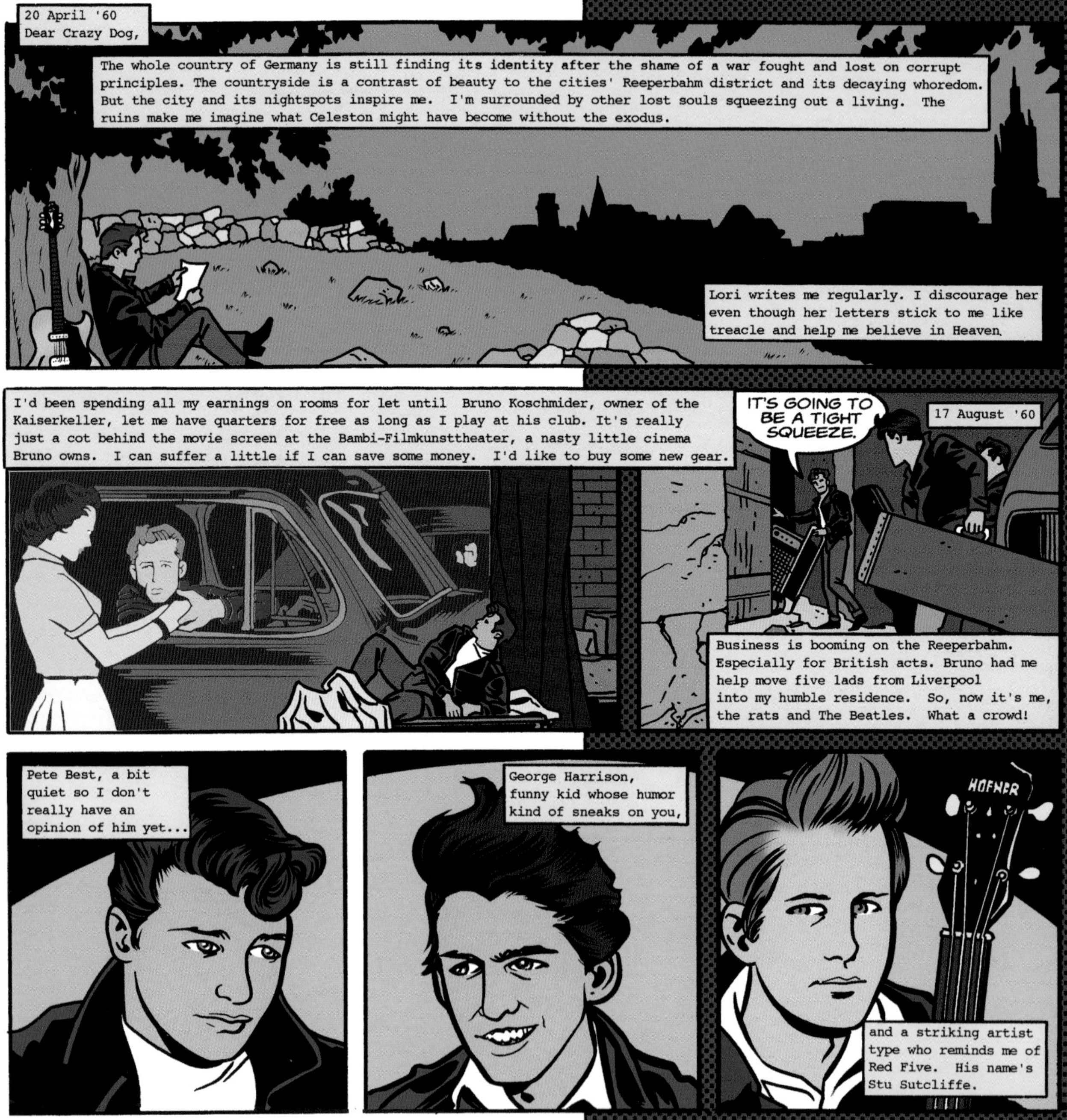
20 April '60
Dear Crazy Dog,
The whole country of Germany is still finding its identity after the shame of a war fought and lost on corrupt principles. The countryside is a contrast of beauty to the cities' Reeperbahm district and its decaying whoredom. But the city and its nightspots inspire me. I'm surrounded by other lost souls squeezing out a living. The ruins make me imagine what Celeston might have become without the exodus.
Lori writes me regularly. I discourage her even though her letters stick to me like treacle and help me believe in Heaven.
I'd been spending all my earnings on rooms for let until Bruno Koschmider, owner of the Kaiserkeller, let me have quarters for free as long as I play at his club. It's really just a cot behind the movie screen at the Bambi-Filmkunsttheater, a nasty little cinema Bruno owns. I can suffer a little if I can save some money. I'd like to buy some new gear.
17 August '60
IT'S GOING TO BE A TIGHT SQUEEZE.
Business is booming on the Reeperbahm. Especially for British acts. Bruno had me help move five lads from Liverpool into my humble residence. So, now it's me, the rats and The Beatles. What a crowd!
Pete Best, a bit quiet so I don't really have an opinion of him yet...
George Harrison, funny kid whose humor kind of sneaks on you,
HOFNER
and a striking artist type who reminds me of Red Five. His name's Stu Sutcliffe.

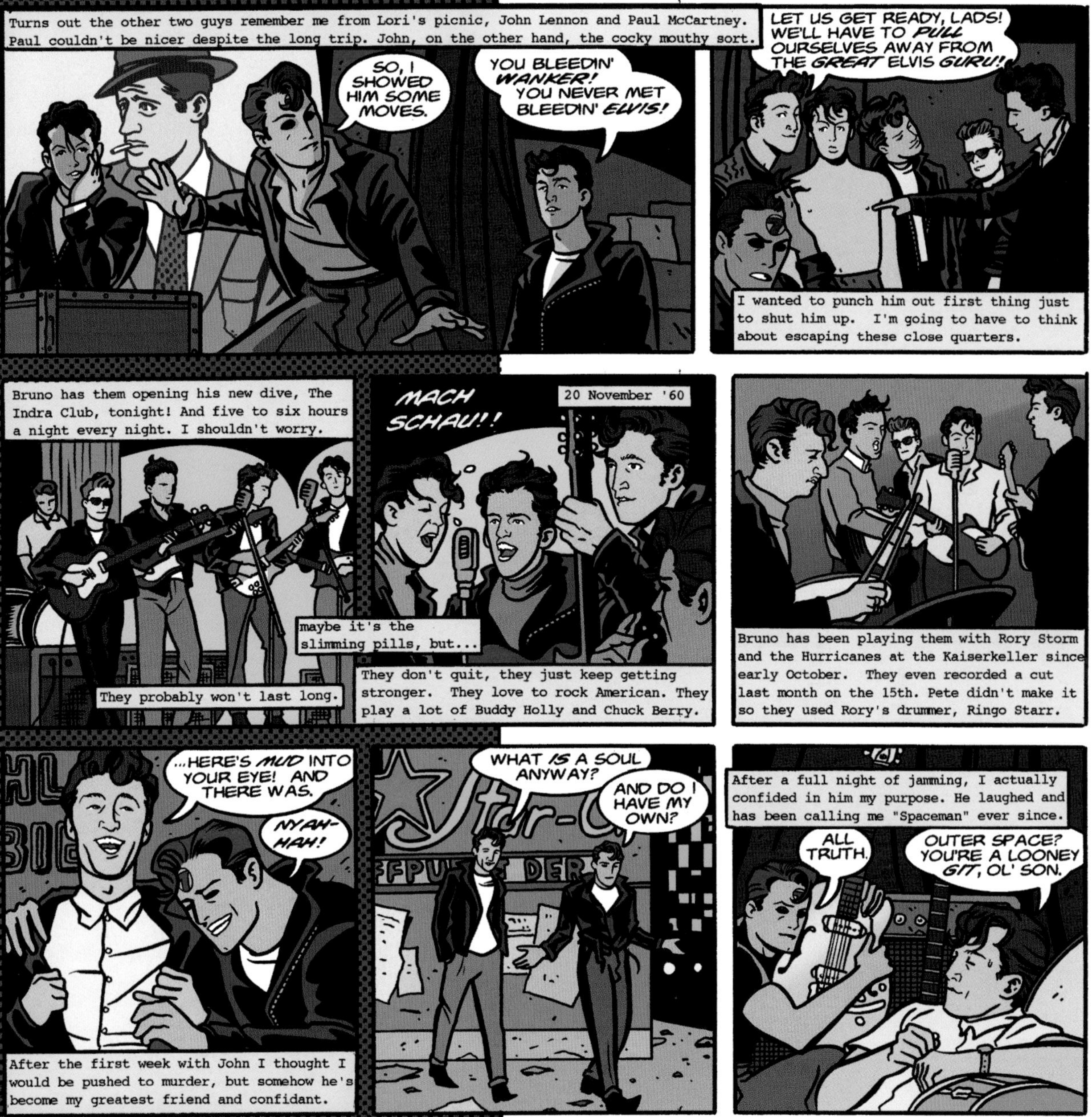
Turns out the other two guys remember me from Lori's picnic, John Lennon and Paul McCartney. Paul couldn't be nicer despite the long trip. John, on the other hand, the cocky mouthy sort.
SO, I SHOWED HIM SOME MOVES.
YOU BLEEDIN' WANKER! YOU NEVER MET BLEEDIN' ELVIS!
LET US GET READY, LADS! WE'LL HAVE TO PULL OURSELVES AWAY FROM THE GREAT ELVIS GURU!
I wanted to punch him out first thing just to shut him up. I'm going to have to think about escaping these close quarters.
Bruno has them opening his new dive, The Indra Club, tonight! And five to six hours a night every night. I shouldn't worry.
They probably won't last long.
MACH SCHAU!!
20 November '60
maybe it's the slimming pills, but...
They don't quit, they just keep getting stronger. They love to rock American. They play a lot of Buddy Holly and Chuck Berry.
Bruno has been playing them with Rory Storm and the Hurricanes at the Kaiserkeller since early October. They even recorded a cut last month on the 15th. Pete didn't make it so they used Rory's drummer, Ringo Starr.
...HERE'S MUD INTO YOUR EYE! AND THERE WAS.
NYAH-HAH!
After the first week with John I thought I would be pushed to murder, but somehow he's become my greatest friend and confidant.
WHAT IS A SOUL ANYWAY?
AND DO I HAVE MY OWN?
After a full night of jamming, I actually confided in him my purpose. He laughed and has been calling me "Spaceman" ever since.
ALL TRUTH.
OUTER SPACE? YOU'RE A LOONEY GIT, OL' SON.

15 April '61

DAS ROCKET?

I got a jolt last night when I thought I saw an Enfinite Assassin hiding on line at the club. I told the stage manager I was too sick to go on and begged off the bill.

Paul's picked up the bass since Stu lost interest in the band. Astrid and his paintings have taken their place in his heart.

1 May '61

Lori gave me the surprise of my short life on April 1st when she showed up with John, Paul, George and Pete when they returned to Hamburg to play the Top Ten Club.

They're not the same band I met last August. The immeasurable hours of constant playing have turned them into performing dynamos and hometown heroes in Liverpool.

Astrid has talked everyone but Pete into a new 'do that's all the rage in France.

19 Jan '62

YOU SHOULD *GO*, MATE! THE *MERSEY* SCENE IS REALLY *JUMPING* NOW.

NO. NOT YET.

I'm still not sure if I really saw an Enfinite but the thought has kept me off the stage. I'm looking for other ways to make money.

Hanging with Stu and Astrid, Lori and I have become a bit domesticated. With Lori here, no day is long enough.

I can't

shake the feeling that I'm not allowed a real life...that I don't deserve her.

20 March '62

I've gone back with Lori to Liverpool to meet her folks. At first they were thrilled just to have their daughter back safe and healthy.

I'LL KILL YOU! SHE'S JUST A *BABY*!

SHE'S A FULL-GROWN *WOMAN*, MAL!

But their resentment towards me didn't stay hidden long.

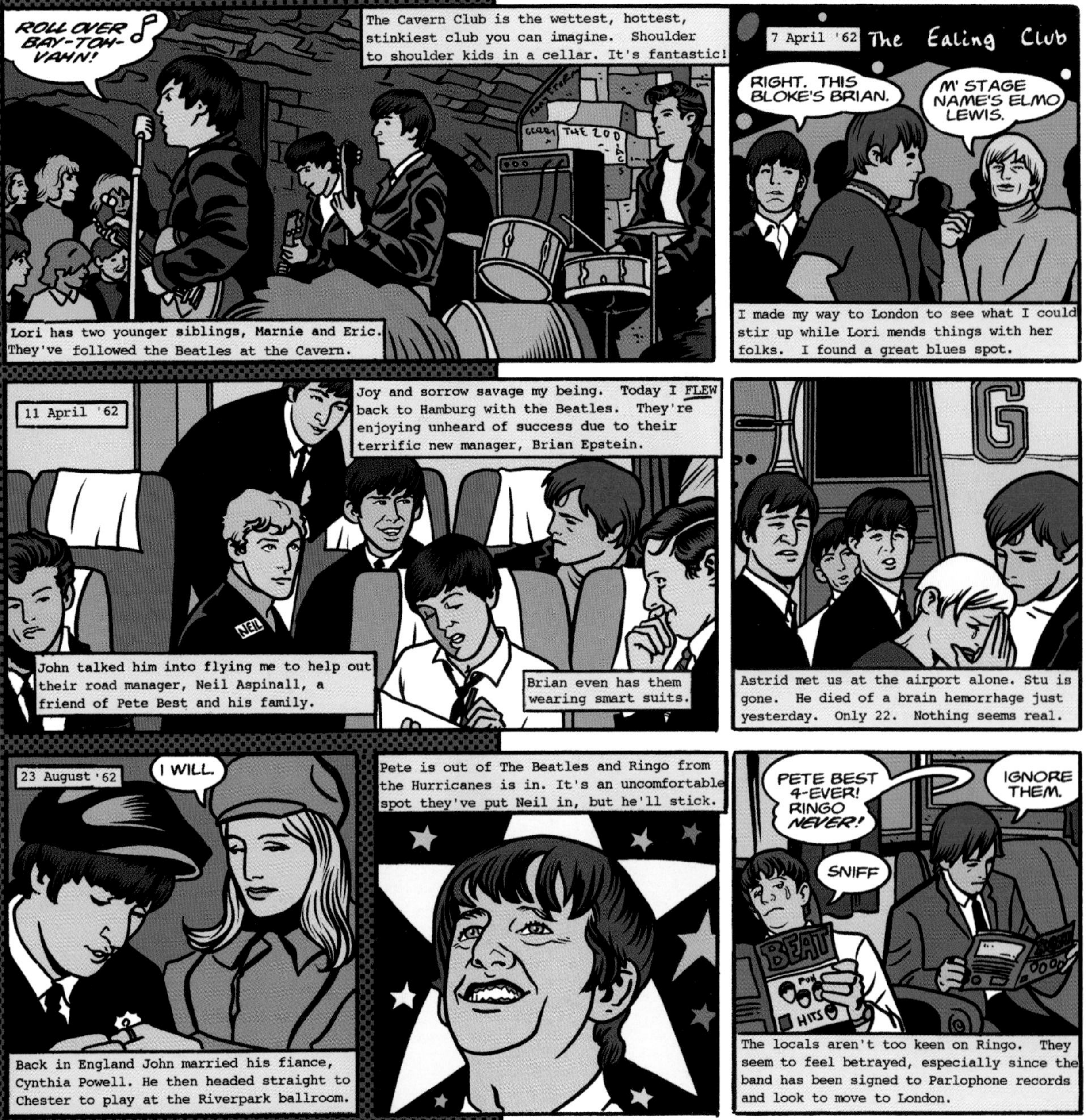
ROLL OVER BAY-TOH-VAHN!
The Cavern Club is the wettest, hottest, stinkiest club you can imagine. Shoulder to shoulder kids in a cellar. It's fantastic!
Lori has two younger siblings, Marnie and Eric. They've followed the Beatles at the Cavern.
7 April '62
The Ealing Club
RIGHT. THIS BLOKE'S BRIAN.
M' STAGE NAME'S ELMO LEWIS.
I made my way to London to see what I could stir up while Lori mends things with her folks. I found a great blues spot.
11 April '62
Joy and sorrow savage my being. Today I FLEW back to Hamburg with the Beatles. They're enjoying unheard of success due to their terrific new manager, Brian Epstein.
NEIL
John talked him into flying me to help out their road manager, Neil Aspinall, a friend of Pete Best and his family.
Brian even has them wearing smart suits.
G
Astrid met us at the airport alone. Stu is gone. He died of a brain hemorrhage just yesterday. Only 22. Nothing seems real.
23 August '62
I WILL.
Back in England John married his fiance, Cynthia Powell. He then headed straight to Chester to play at the Riverpark ballroom.
Pete is out of The Beatles and Ringo from the Hurricanes is in. It's an uncomfortable spot they've put Neil in, but he'll stick.
PETE BEST 4-EVER! RINGO NEVER!
IGNORE THEM.
SNIFF
BEAT
HITS
The locals aren't too keen on Ringo. They seem to feel betrayed, especially since the band has been signed to Parlophone records and look to move to London.

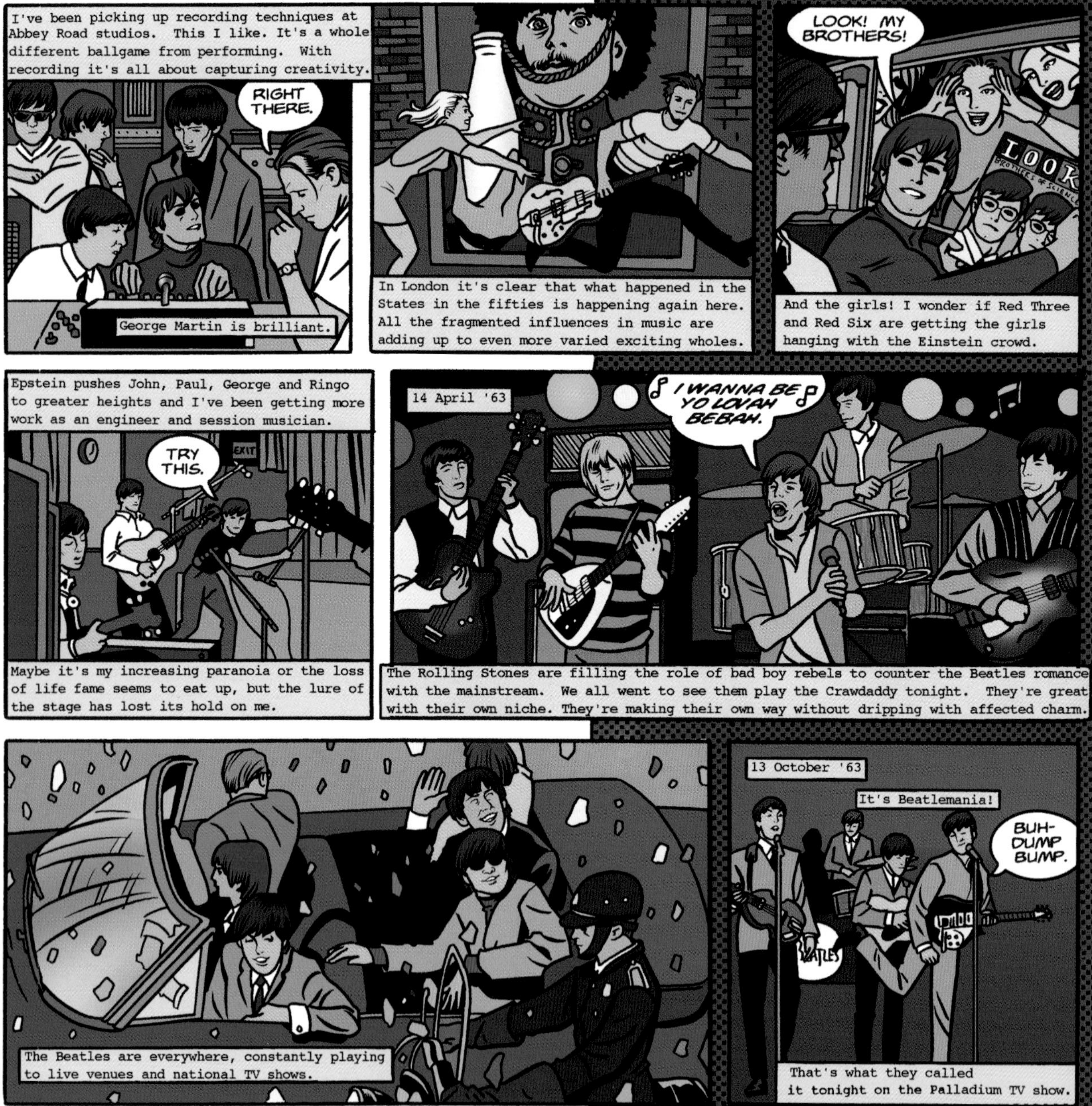

I've been picking up recording techniques at Abbey Road studios. This I like. It's a whole different ballgame from performing. With recording it's all about capturing creativity.
RIGHT THERE.
George Martin is brilliant.
In London it's clear that what happened in the States in the fifties is happening again here. All the fragmented influences in music are adding up to even more varied exciting wholes.
LOOK! MY BROTHERS!
LOOK
BROTHERS OF SCIENCE
And the girls! I wonder if Red Three and Red Six are getting the girls hanging with the Einstein crowd.
Epstein pushes John, Paul, George and Ringo to greater heights and I've been getting more work as an engineer and session musician.
TRY THIS.
EXIT
Maybe it's my increasing paranoia or the loss of life fame seems to eat up, but the lure of the stage has lost its hold on me.
14 April '63
I WANNA BE YO LOVAH BEBAH.
The Rolling Stones are filling the role of bad boy rebels to counter the Beatles romance with the mainstream. We all went to see them play the Crawdaddy tonight. They're great with their own niche. They're making their own way without dripping with affected charm.
The Beatles are everywhere, constantly playing to live venues and national TV shows.
13 October '63
It's Beatlemania!
BUH-DUMP BUMP.
BEATLES
That's what they called it tonight on the Palladium TV show.

The Beatles played the royal command performance tonight. It's official! National heroes! Still, it reminds me of Elvis singing to a hound dog. Could the same leather lads in Hamburg play for the Queen Mother? John managed to get off a good one.

4 November, '63

WOULD THOSE IN THE CHEAP SEATS *CLAP* THEIR HANDS. THE REST OF YOU CAN *RATTLE* YOUR JEWELRY.

I like being around it without being a part of it. I don't desire the adoration of faceless thousands. The love Lori gives me is more than I can accept or have a right to.

Fame is no temptation. Or is it fear?

23 November '63

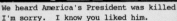

We heard America's President was killed. I'm sorry. I know you liked him.

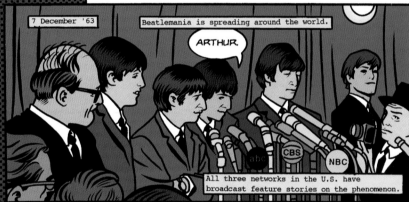

7 December '63

Beatlemania is spreading around the world.

ARTHUR

All three networks in the U.S. have broadcast feature stories on the phenomenon.

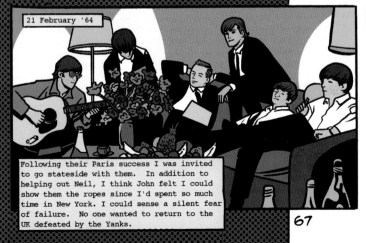

21 February '64

Following their Paris success I was invited to go stateside with them. In addition to helping out Neil, I think John felt I could show them the ropes since I'd spent so much time in New York. I could sense a silent fear of failure. No one wanted to return to the UK defeated by the Yanks.

Well, the opposite is happenning. Before the trip "I Want To Hold Your Hand" went from no.43 to no.1 in one week!

CHEERS!

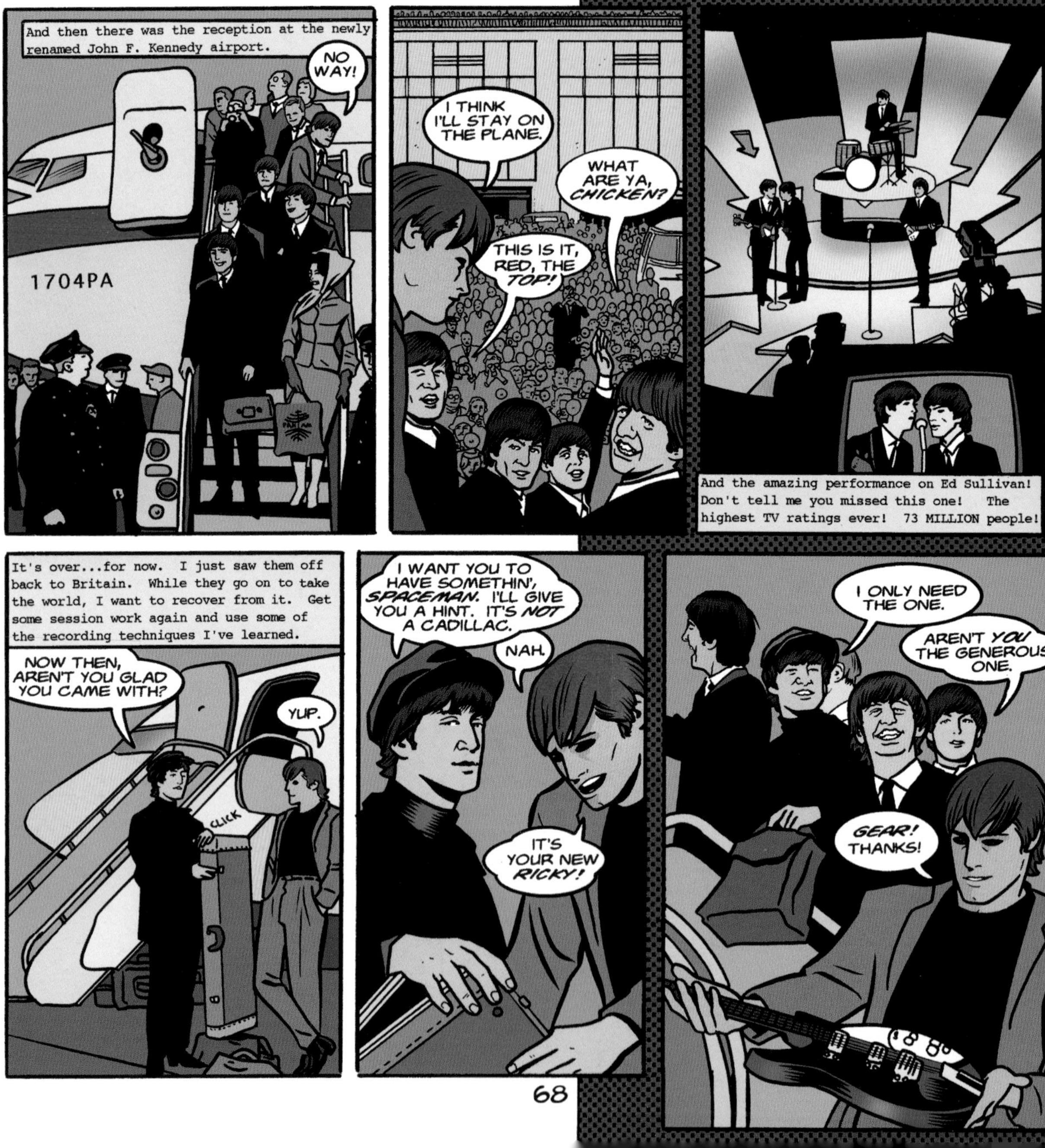

And then there was the reception at the newly renamed John F. Kennedy airport.
NO WAY!
1704PA
I THINK I'LL STAY ON THE PLANE.
WHAT ARE YA, *CHICKEN?*
THIS IS IT, RED, THE *TOP!*
And the amazing performance on Ed Sullivan! Don't tell me you missed this one! The highest TV ratings ever! 73 MILLION people!
It's over...for now. I just saw them off back to Britain. While they go on to take the world, I want to recover from it. Get some session work again and use some of the recording techniques I've learned.
NOW THEN, AREN'T YOU GLAD YOU CAME WITH?
YUP.
CLICK
I WANT YOU TO HAVE SOMETHIN', *SPACEMAN.* I'LL GIVE YOU A HINT. IT'S *NOT* A CADILLAC.
NAH.
IT'S YOUR NEW *RICKY!*
I ONLY NEED THE ONE.
AREN'T *YOU* THE GENEROUS ONE.
GEAR! THANKS!

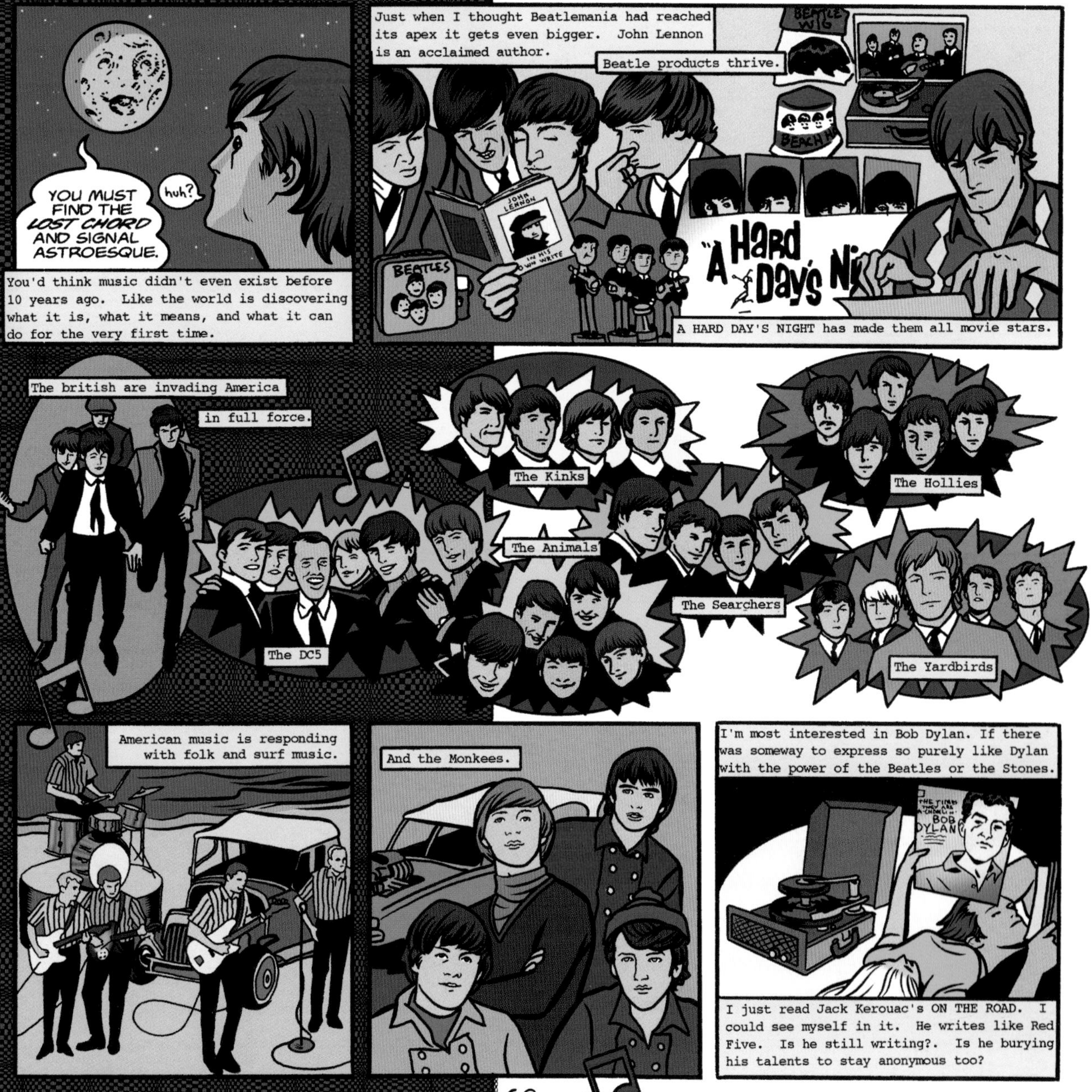
YOU MUST FIND THE LOST CHORD AND SIGNAL ASTROESQUE.
huh?
You'd think music didn't even exist before 10 years ago. Like the world is discovering what it is, what it means, and what it can do for the very first time.
Just when I thought Beatlemania had reached its apex it gets even bigger. John Lennon is an acclaimed author.
Beatle products thrive.
BEATLE WIG
JOHN LENNON
IN HIS OWN WRITE
BEATLES
"A Hard Day's
A HARD DAY'S NIGHT has made them all movie stars.
The british are invading America
in full force.
The Kinks
The Hollies
The Animals
The DC5
The Searchers
The Yardbirds
American music is responding with folk and surf music.
And the Monkees.
I'm most interested in Bob Dylan. If there was someway to express so purely like Dylan with the power of the Beatles or the Stones.
BOB DYLAN
I just read Jack Kerouac's ON THE ROAD. I could see myself in it. He writes like Red Five. Is he still writing?. Is he burying his talents to stay anonymous too?

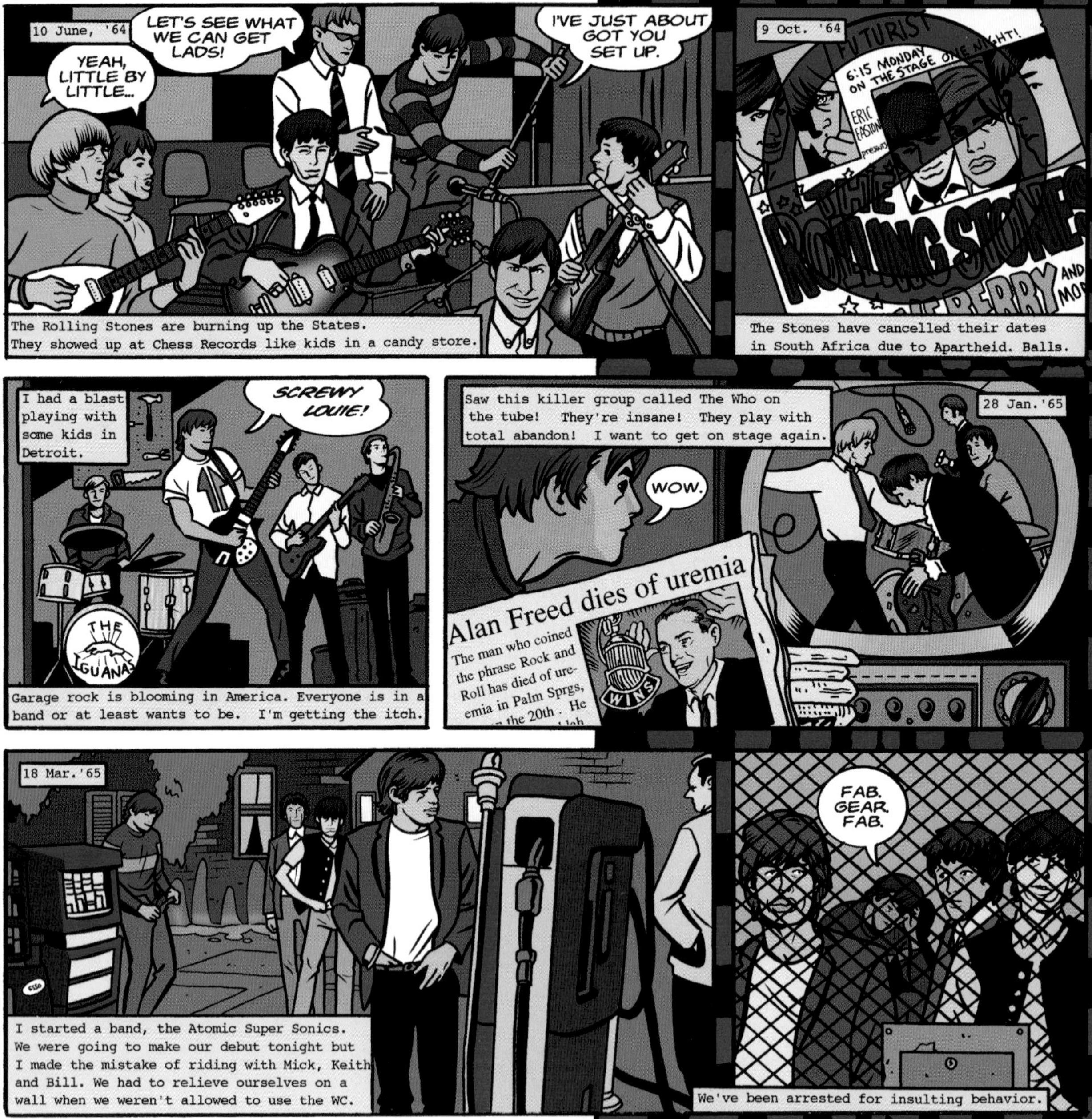
10 June, '64
YEAH, LITTLE BY LITTLE...
LET'S SEE WHAT WE CAN GET LADS!
I'VE JUST ABOUT GOT YOU SET UP.
The Rolling Stones are burning up the States.
They showed up at Chess Records like kids in a candy store.
9 Oct. '64
FUTURIST
6:15 MONDAY ON THE STAGE ONE NIGHT!
ERIC EASTON presents
THE ROLLING STONES
The Stones have cancelled their dates
in South Africa due to Apartheid. Balls.
I had a blast playing with some kids in Detroit.
SCREWY LOUIE!
THE IGUANAS
Garage rock is blooming in America. Everyone is in a
band or at least wants to be. I'm getting the itch.
Saw this killer group called The Who on
the tube! They're insane! They play with
total abandon! I want to get on stage again.
28 Jan.'65
WOW.
Alan Freed dies of uremia
The man who coined
the phrase Rock and
Roll has died of ure-
emia in Palm Sprgs,
the 20th . He
WINS
18 Mar.'65
I started a band, the Atomic Super Sonics.
We were going to make our debut tonight but
I made the mistake of riding with Mick, Keith
and Bill. We had to relieve ourselves on a
wall when we weren't allowed to use the WC.
FAB. GEAR. FAB.
We've been arrested for insulting behavior.

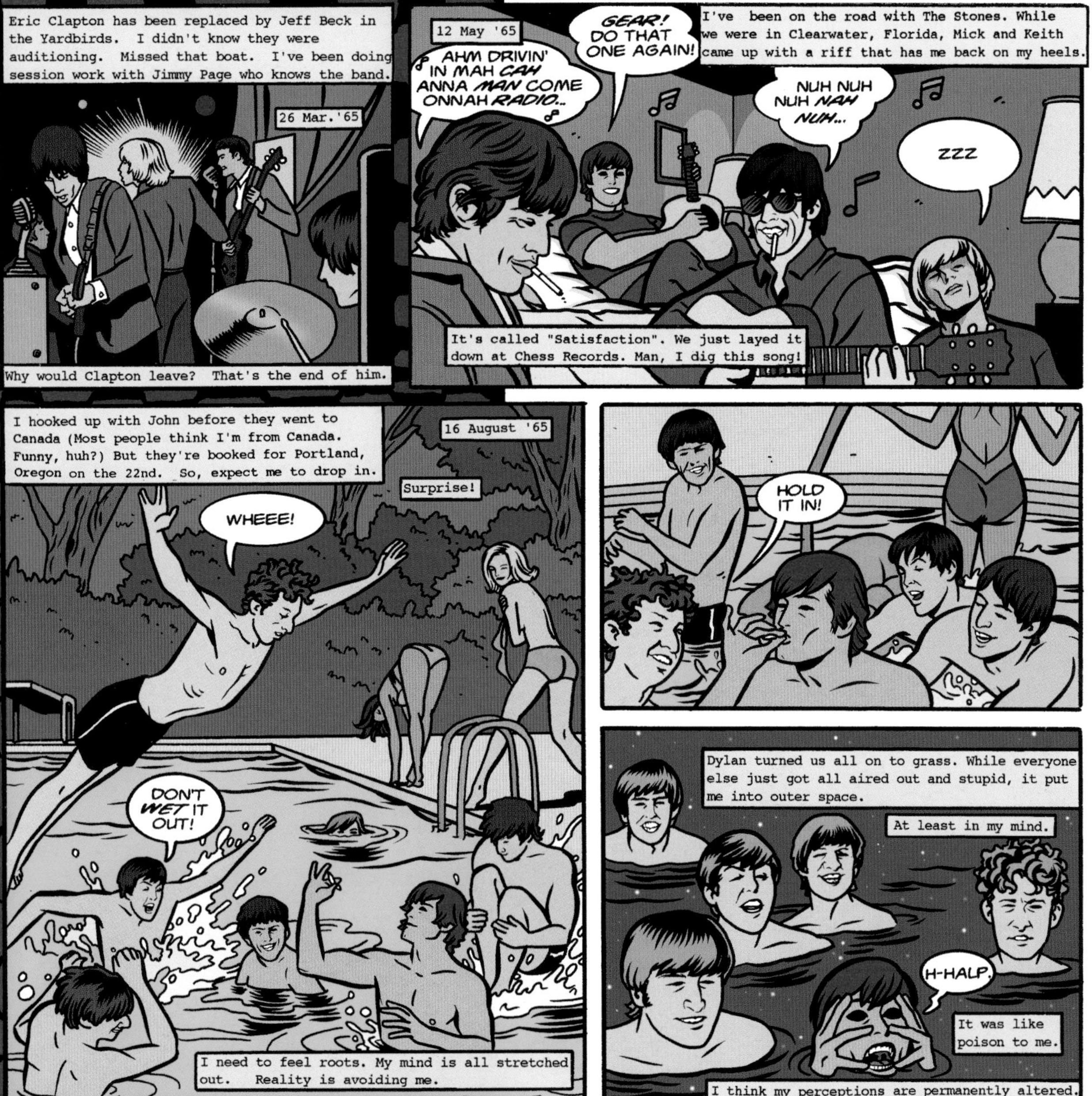

Eric Clapton has been replaced by Jeff Beck in the Yardbirds. I didn't know they were auditioning. Missed that boat. I've been doing session work with Jimmy Page who knows the band.
26 Mar.'65
Why would Clapton leave? That's the end of him.
12 May '65
AHM DRIVIN' IN MAH *CAH* ANNA *MAN* COME ONNAH *RADIO*...
GEAR! DO THAT ONE AGAIN!
I've been on the road with The Stones. While we were in Clearwater, Florida, Mick and Keith came up with a riff that has me back on my heels.
NUH NUH NUH *NAH NUH*...
ZZZ
It's called "Satisfaction". We just layed it down at Chess Records. Man, I dig this song!
I hooked up with John before they went to Canada (Most people think I'm from Canada. Funny, huh?) But they're booked for Portland, Oregon on the 22nd. So, expect me to drop in.
16 August '65
Surprise!
WHEEE!
DON'T *WET* IT OUT!
I need to feel roots. My mind is all stretched out. Reality is avoiding me.
HOLD IT IN!
Dylan turned us all on to grass. While everyone else just got all aired out and stupid, it put me into outer space.
At least in my mind.
H-HALP.
It was like poison to me.
I think my perceptions are permanently altered.

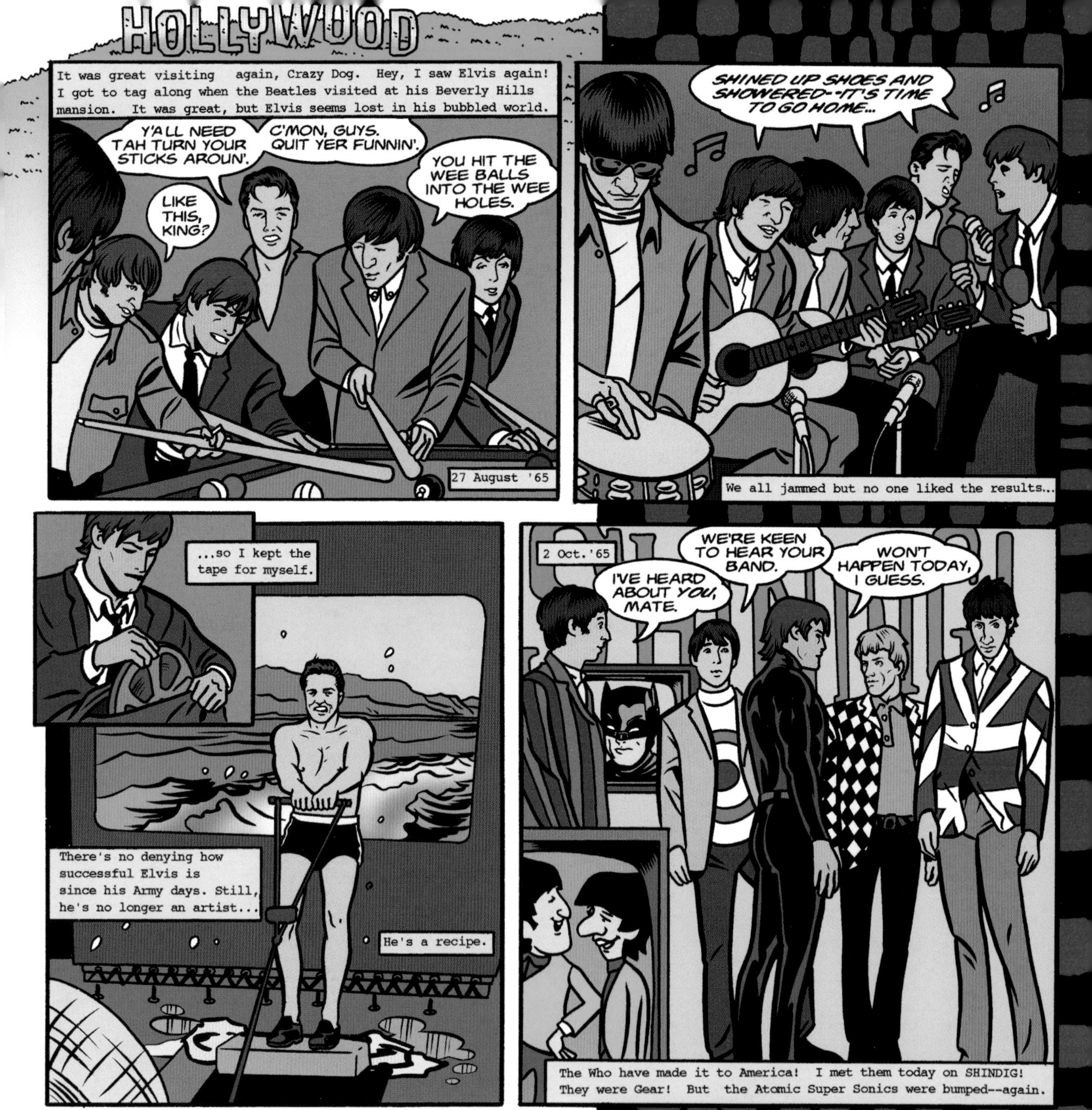
HOLLYWOOD
It was great visiting again, Crazy Dog. Hey, I saw Elvis again! I got to tag along when the Beatles visited at his Beverly Hills mansion. It was great, but Elvis seems lost in his bubbled world.
Y'ALL NEED TAH TURN YOUR STICKS AROUN'.
C'MON, GUYS. QUIT YER FUNNIN'.
LIKE THIS, KING?
YOU HIT THE WEE BALLS INTO THE WEE HOLES.
27 August '65
SHINED UP SHOES AND SHOWERED--IT'S TIME TO GO HOME...
We all jammed but no one liked the results...
...so I kept the tape for myself.
There's no denying how successful Elvis is since his Army days. Still, he's no longer an artist...
He's a recipe.
2 Oct.'65
I'VE HEARD ABOUT YOU, MATE.
WE'RE KEEN TO HEAR YOUR BAND.
WON'T HAPPEN TODAY, I GUESS.
The Who have made it to America! I met them today on SHINDIG! They were Gear! But the Atomic Super Sonics were bumped--again.

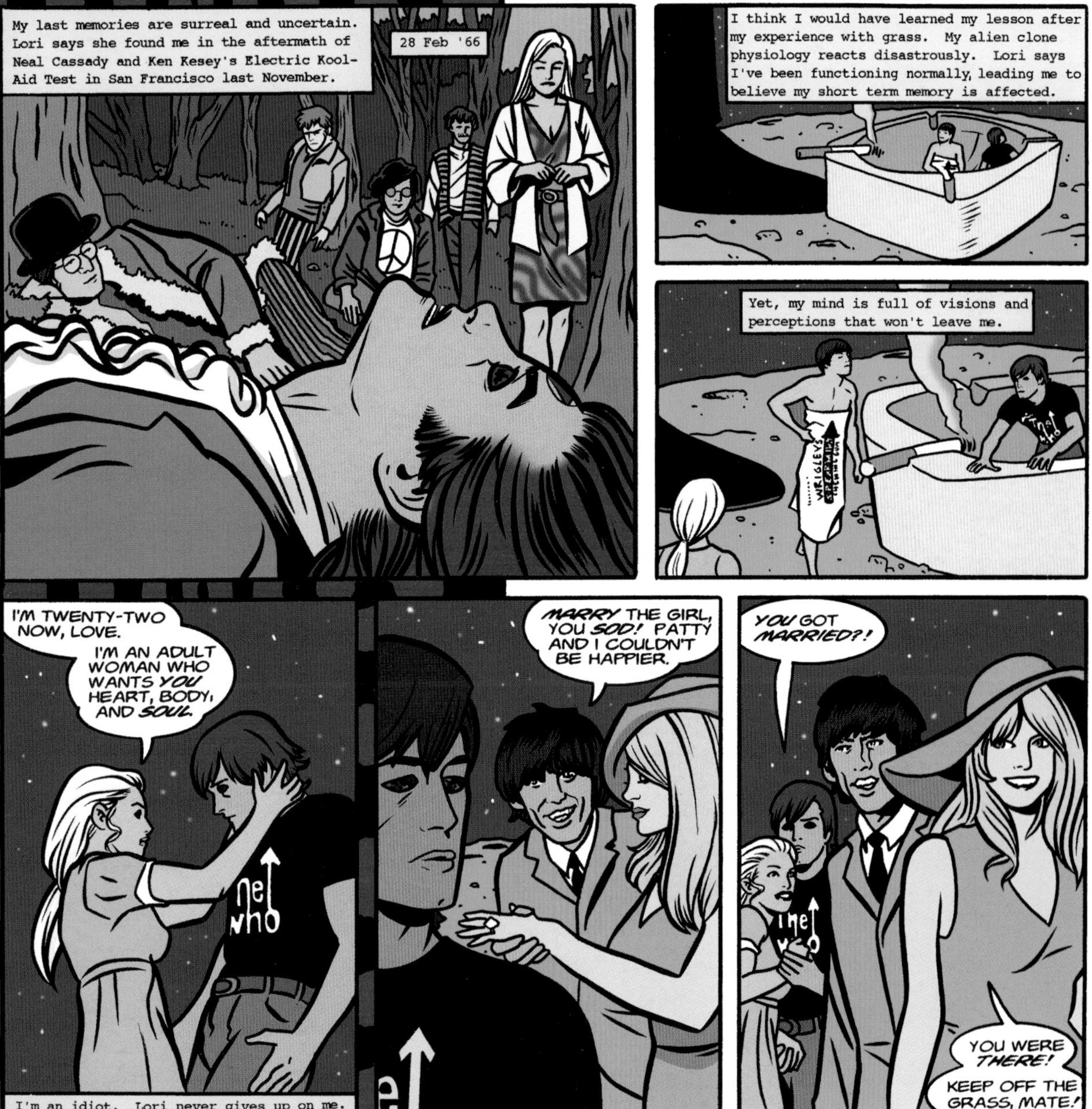
My last memories are surreal and uncertain. Lori says she found me in the aftermath of Neal Cassady and Ken Kesey's Electric Kool-Aid Test in San Francisco last November.
28 Feb '66
I think I would have learned my lesson after my experience with grass. My alien clone physiology reacts disastrously. Lori says I've been functioning normally, leading me to believe my short term memory is affected.
Yet, my mind is full of visions and perceptions that won't leave me.
WRIGLEY'S SPEARMINT
I'M TWENTY-TWO NOW, LOVE.
I'M AN ADULT WOMAN WHO WANTS YOU HEART, BODY, AND SOUL.
I'm an idiot. Lori never gives up on me.
MARRY THE GIRL, YOU SOD! PATTY AND I COULDN'T BE HAPPIER.
YOU GOT MARRIED?!
YOU WERE THERE!
KEEP OFF THE GRASS, MATE!

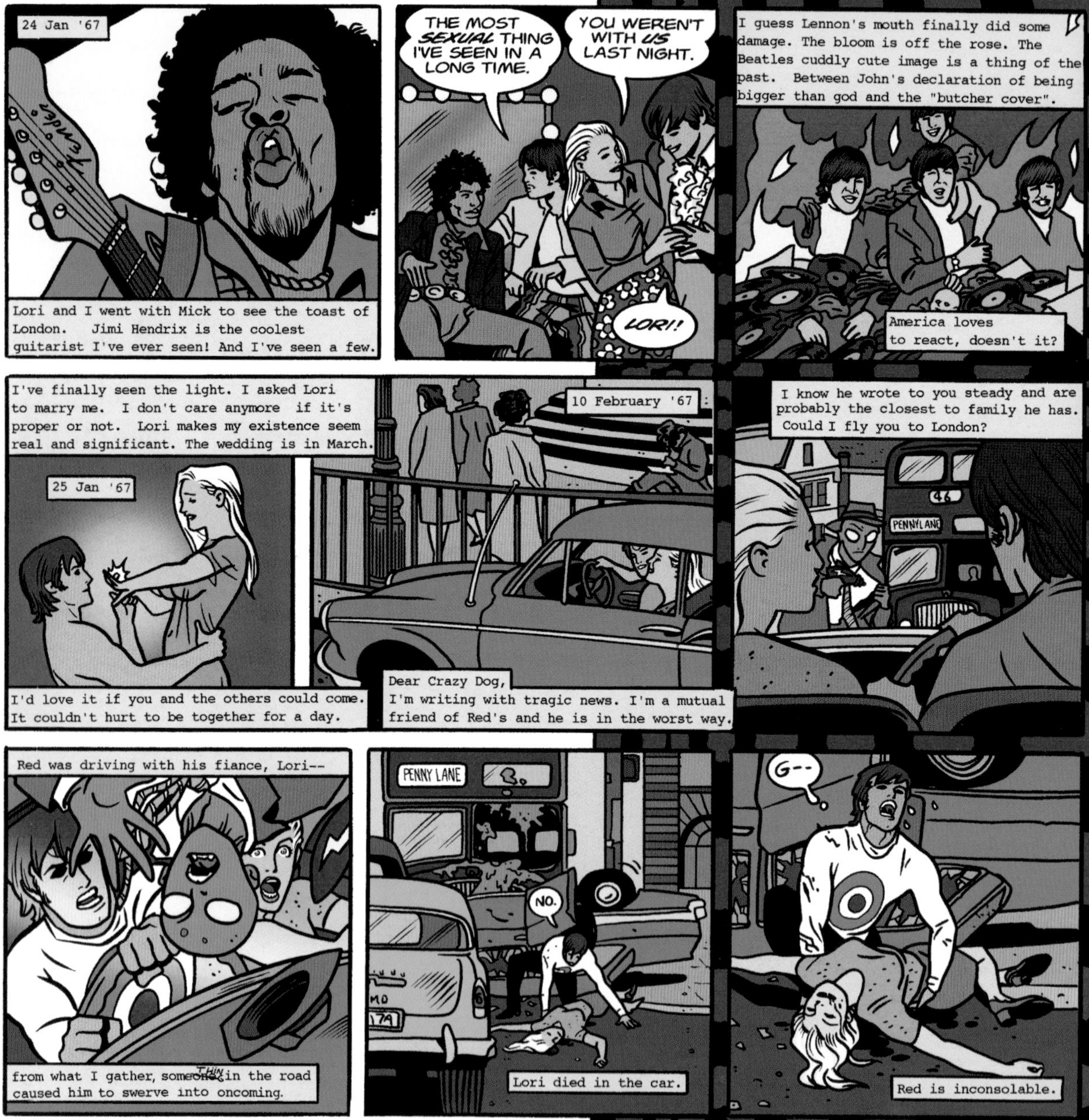

24 Jan '67
Lori and I went with Mick to see the toast of London. Jimi Hendrix is the coolest guitarist I've ever seen! And I've seen a few.
THE MOST SEXUAL THING I'VE SEEN IN A LONG TIME.
YOU WEREN'T WITH US LAST NIGHT.
LORI!!
I guess Lennon's mouth finally did some damage. The bloom is off the rose. The Beatles cuddly cute image is a thing of the past. Between John's declaration of being bigger than god and the "butcher cover".
America loves to react, doesn't it?
I've finally seen the light. I asked Lori to marry me. I don't care anymore if it's proper or not. Lori makes my existence seem real and significant. The wedding is in March.
25 Jan '67
I'd love it if you and the others could come. It couldn't hurt to be together for a day.
10 February '67
Dear Crazy Dog,
I'm writing with tragic news. I'm a mutual friend of Red's and he is in the worst way.
I know he wrote to you steady and are probably the closest to family he has. Could I fly you to London?
46
PENNYLANE
Red was driving with his fiance, Lori--
from what I gather, some~~one~~ THIN in the road caused him to swerve into oncoming.
PENNY LANE
NO.
Lori died in the car.
G--
Red is inconsolable.

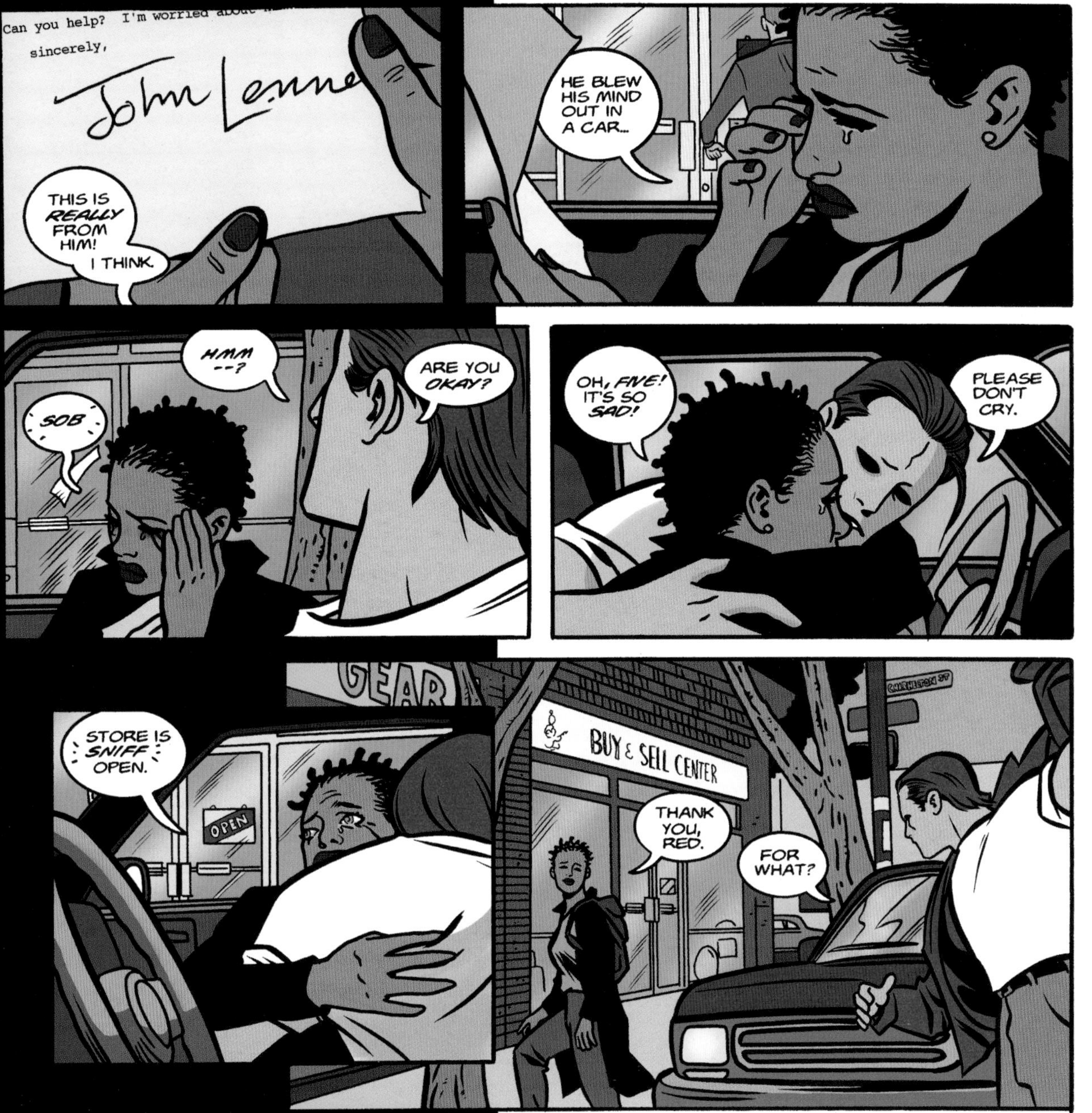

Can you help? I'm worried about
sincerely,
John Lenne
THIS IS REALLY FROM HIM! I THINK.
HE BLEW HIS MIND OUT IN A CAR...
SOB
HMM --?
ARE YOU OKAY?
OH, FIVE! IT'S SO SAD!
PLEASE DON'T CRY.
GEAR
STORE IS SNIFF OPEN.
OPEN
BUY & SELL CENTER
THANK YOU, RED.
FOR WHAT?

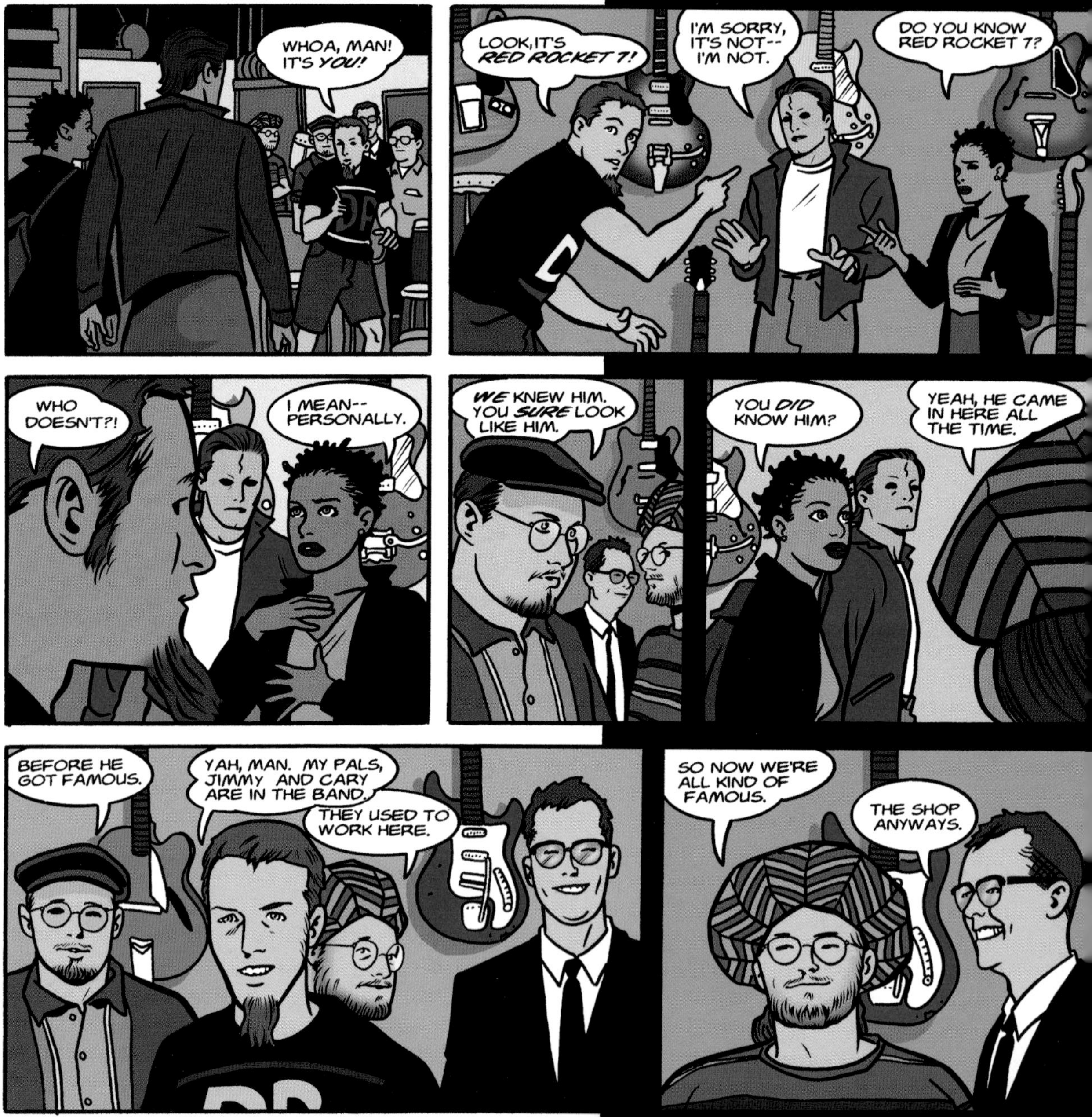
WHOA, MAN! IT'S YOU!
LOOK, IT'S RED ROCKET 7!
I'M SORRY, IT'S NOT-- I'M NOT.
DO YOU KNOW RED ROCKET 7?
WHO DOESN'T?!
I MEAN-- PERSONALLY.
WE KNEW HIM. YOU SURE LOOK LIKE HIM.
YOU DID KNOW HIM?
YEAH, HE CAME IN HERE ALL THE TIME.
BEFORE HE GOT FAMOUS.
YAH, MAN. MY PALS, JIMMY AND CARY ARE IN THE BAND.
THEY USED TO WORK HERE.
SO NOW WE'RE ALL KIND OF FAMOUS.
THE SHOP ANYWAYS.

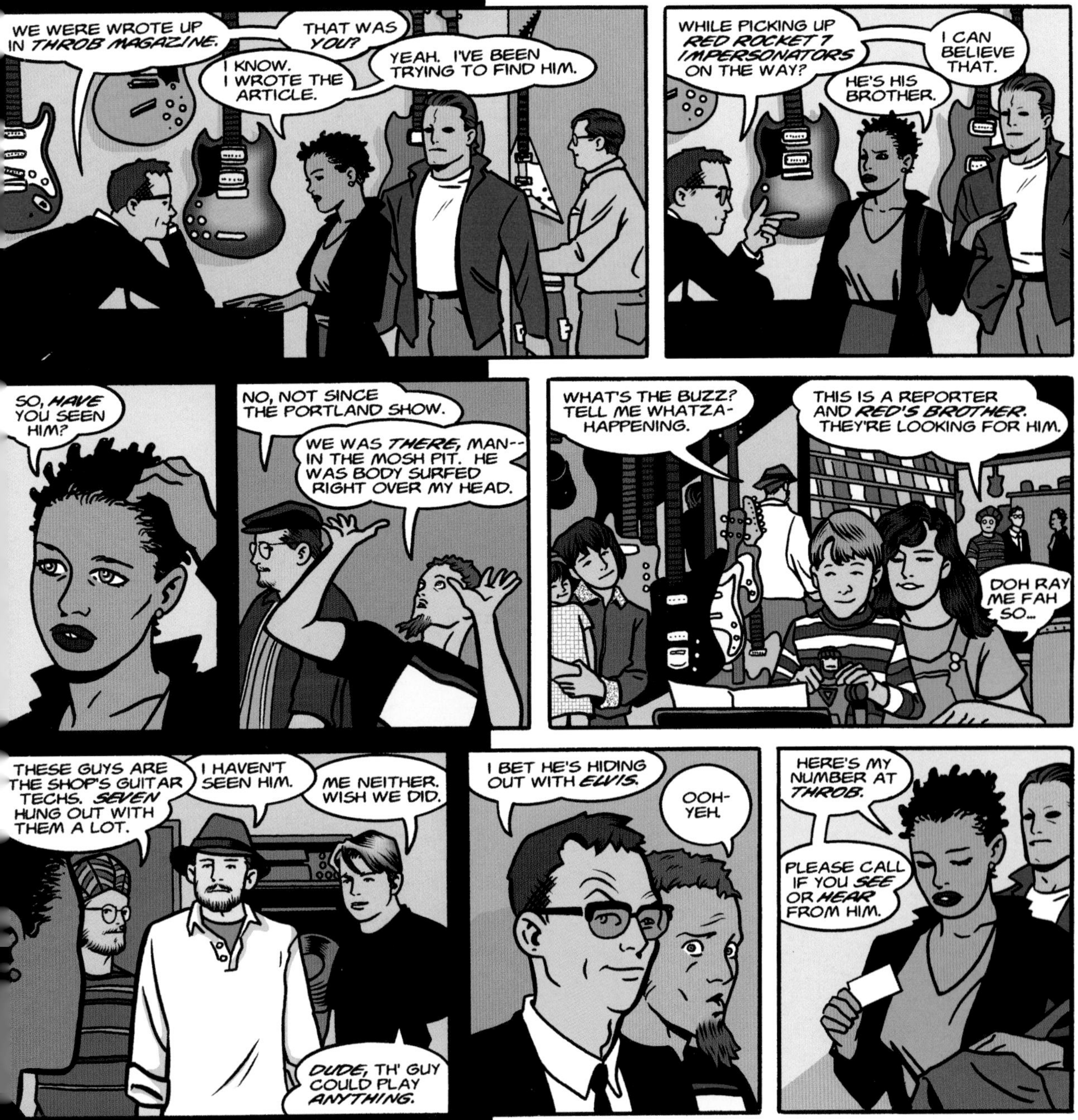
WE WERE WROTE UP IN THROB MAGAZINE.
THAT WAS YOU?
I KNOW. I WROTE THE ARTICLE.
YEAH. I'VE BEEN TRYING TO FIND HIM.
WHILE PICKING UP RED ROCKET 7 IMPERSONATORS ON THE WAY?
I CAN BELIEVE THAT.
HE'S HIS BROTHER.
SO, HAVE YOU SEEN HIM?
NO, NOT SINCE THE PORTLAND SHOW.
WE WAS THERE, MAN-- IN THE MOSH PIT. HE WAS BODY SURFED RIGHT OVER MY HEAD.
WHAT'S THE BUZZ? TELL ME WHATZA-HAPPENING.
THIS IS A REPORTER AND RED'S BROTHER. THEY'RE LOOKING FOR HIM.
DOH RAY ME FAH SO...
THESE GUYS ARE THE SHOP'S GUITAR TECHS. SEVEN HUNG OUT WITH THEM A LOT.
I HAVEN'T SEEN HIM.
ME NEITHER. WISH WE DID.
DUDE, TH' GUY COULD PLAY ANYTHING.
I BET HE'S HIDING OUT WITH ELVIS.
OOH-YEH.
HERE'S MY NUMBER AT THROB.
PLEASE CALL IF YOU SEE OR HEAR FROM HIM.

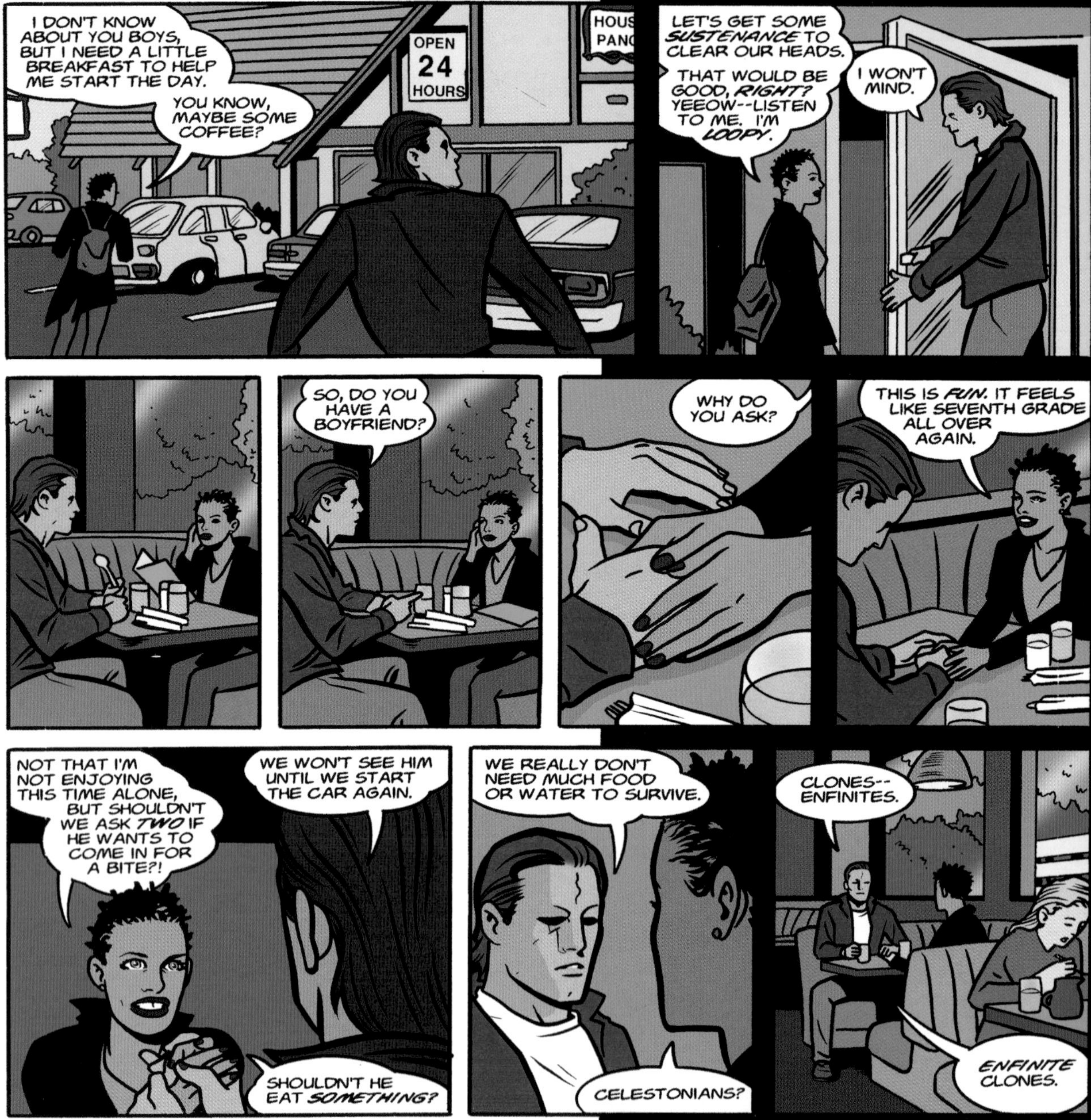

I DON'T KNOW ABOUT YOU BOYS, BUT I NEED A LITTLE BREAKFAST TO HELP ME START THE DAY.
YOU KNOW, MAYBE SOME COFFEE?
OPEN 24 HOURS
LET'S GET SOME SUSTENANCE TO CLEAR OUR HEADS.
THAT WOULD BE GOOD, RIGHT? YEEOW--LISTEN TO ME. I'M LOOPY.
I WON'T MIND.
SO, DO YOU HAVE A BOYFRIEND?
WHY DO YOU ASK?
THIS IS FUN. IT FEELS LIKE SEVENTH GRADE ALL OVER AGAIN.
NOT THAT I'M NOT ENJOYING THIS TIME ALONE, BUT SHOULDN'T WE ASK TWO IF HE WANTS TO COME IN FOR A BITE?!
WE WON'T SEE HIM UNTIL WE START THE CAR AGAIN.
SHOULDN'T HE EAT SOMETHING?
WE REALLY DON'T NEED MUCH FOOD OR WATER TO SURVIVE.
CELESTONIANS?
CLONES--ENFINITES.
ENFINITE CLONES.

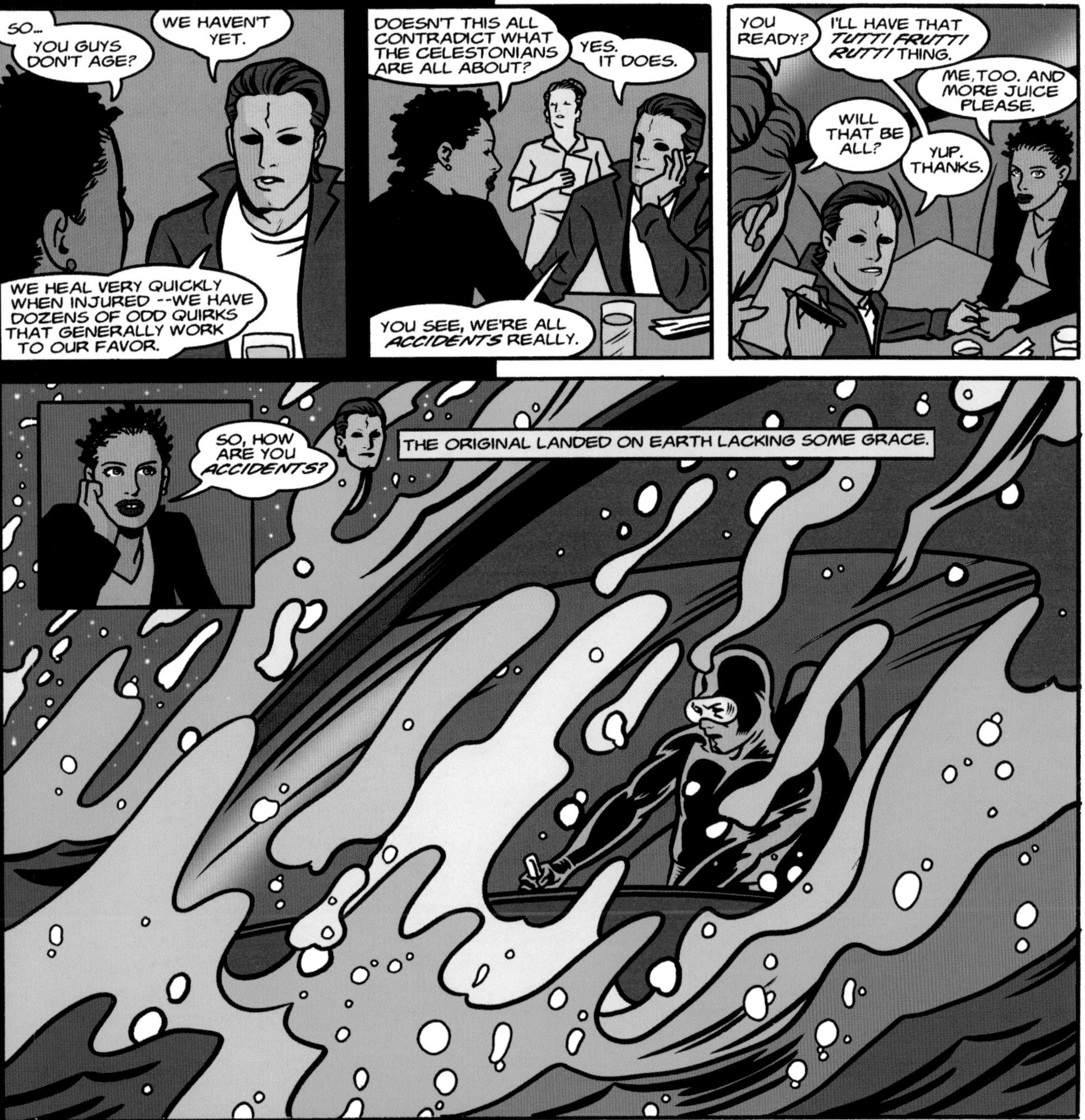
SO... YOU GUYS DON'T AGE?
WE HAVEN'T YET.
WE HEAL VERY QUICKLY WHEN INJURED --WE HAVE DOZENS OF ODD QUIRKS THAT GENERALLY WORK TO OUR FAVOR.
DOESN'T THIS ALL CONTRADICT WHAT THE CELESTONIANS ARE ALL ABOUT?
YES. IT DOES.
YOU SEE, WE'RE ALL ACCIDENTS REALLY.
YOU READY?
I'LL HAVE THAT TUTTI FRUTTI RUTTI THING.
ME, TOO. AND MORE JUICE PLEASE.
WILL THAT BE ALL?
YUP. THANKS.
SO, HOW ARE YOU ACCIDENTS?
THE ORIGINAL LANDED ON EARTH LACKING SOME GRACE.

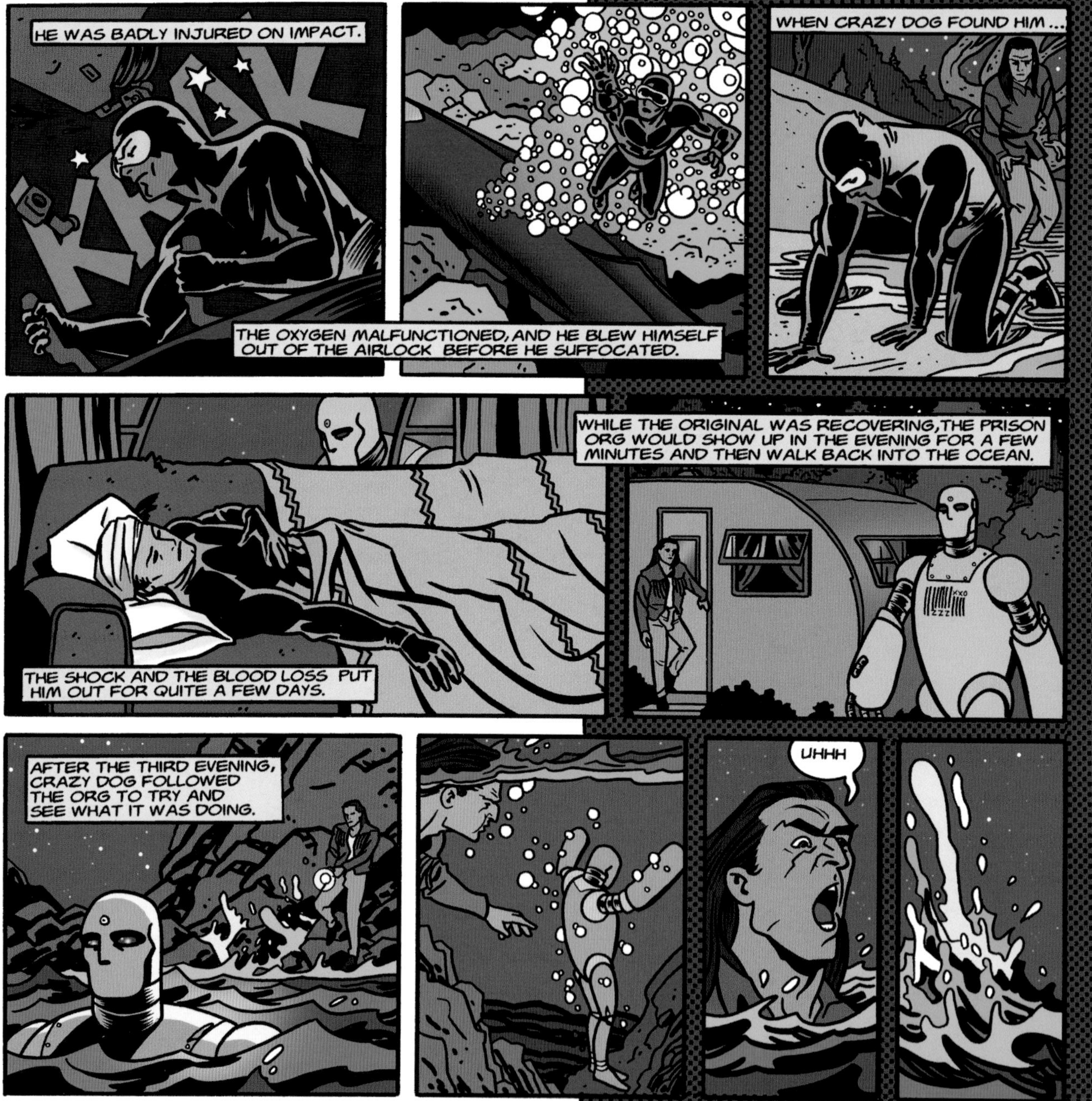
HE WAS BADLY INJURED ON IMPACT.
KRAK
THE OXYGEN MALFUNCTIONED, AND HE BLEW HIMSELF OUT OF THE AIRLOCK BEFORE HE SUFFOCATED.
WHEN CRAZY DOG FOUND HIM ...
THE SHOCK AND THE BLOOD LOSS PUT HIM OUT FOR QUITE A FEW DAYS.
WHILE THE ORIGINAL WAS RECOVERING, THE PRISON ORG WOULD SHOW UP IN THE EVENING FOR A FEW MINUTES AND THEN WALK BACK INTO THE OCEAN.
AFTER THE THIRD EVENING, CRAZY DOG FOLLOWED THE ORG TO TRY AND SEE WHAT IT WAS DOING.
UHHH

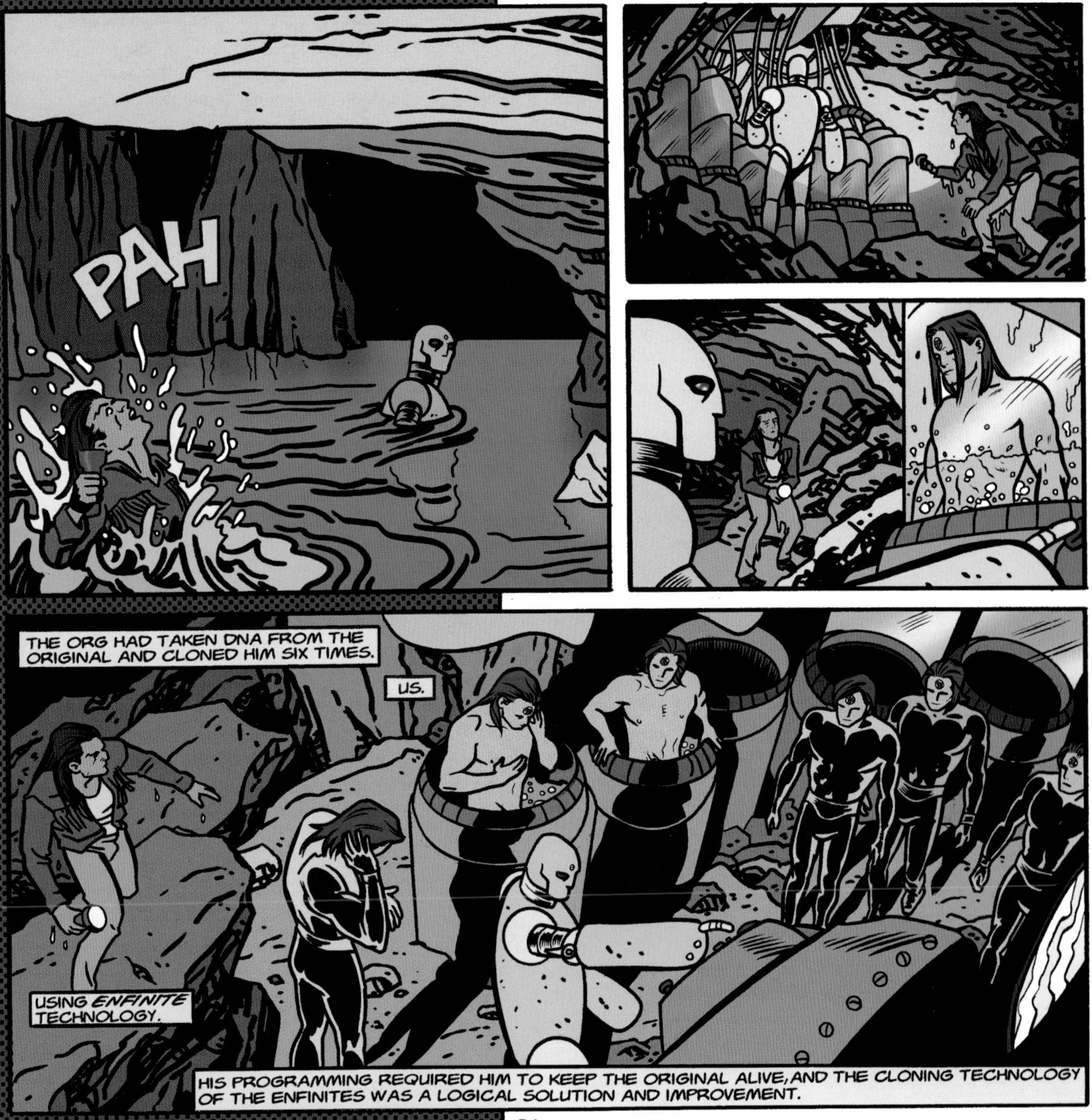
PAH
THE ORG HAD TAKEN DNA FROM THE ORIGINAL AND CLONED HIM SIX TIMES.
US.
USING *ENFINITE* TECHNOLOGY.
HIS PROGRAMMING REQUIRED HIM TO KEEP THE ORIGINAL ALIVE, AND THE CLONING TECHNOLOGY OF THE ENFINITES WAS A LOGICAL SOLUTION AND IMPROVEMENT.

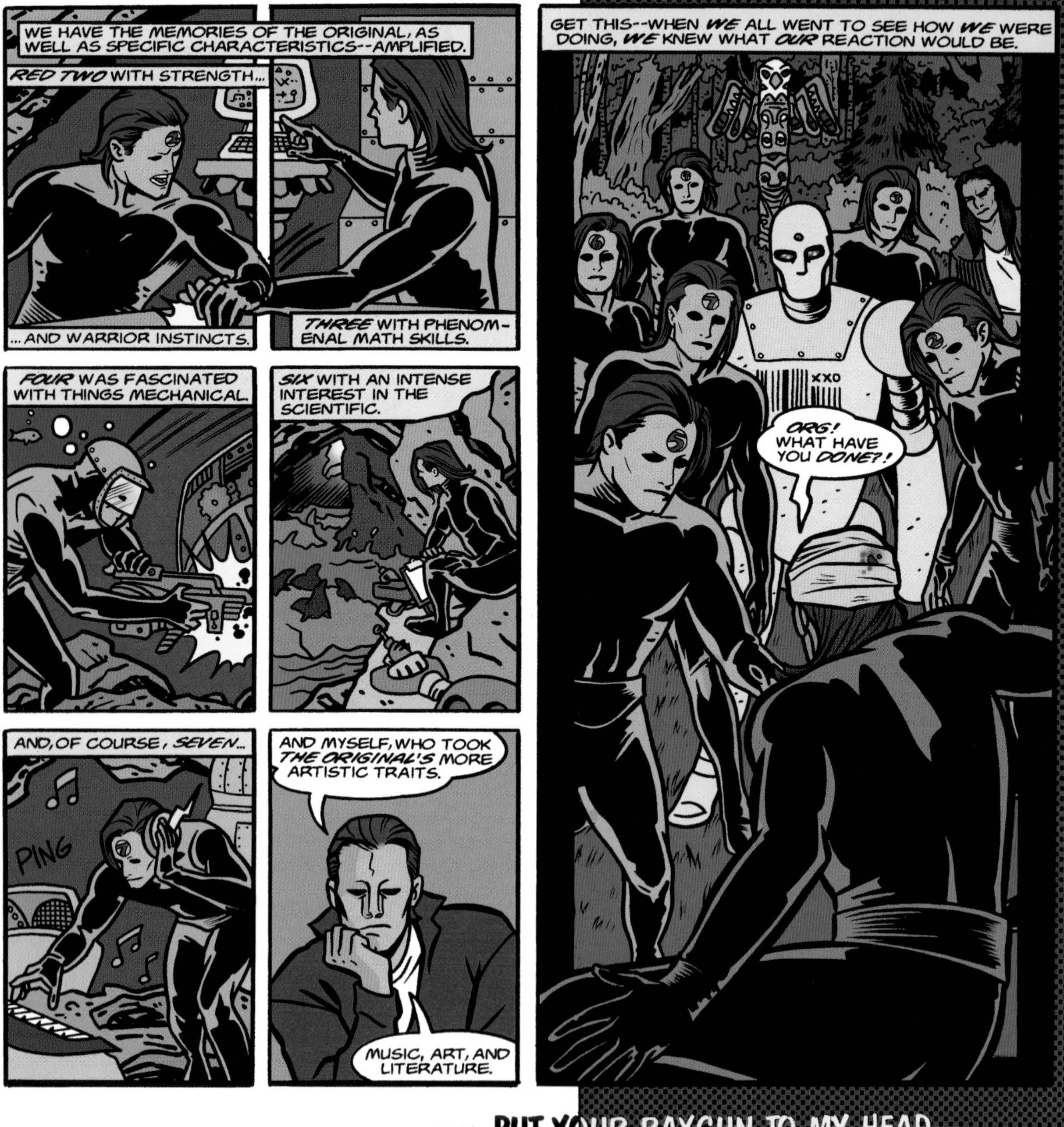
WE HAVE THE MEMORIES OF THE ORIGINAL, AS WELL AS SPECIFIC CHARACTERISTICS--AMPLIFIED.
RED TWO WITH STRENGTH...
...AND WARRIOR INSTINCTS.
THREE WITH PHENOMENAL MATH SKILLS.
FOUR WAS FASCINATED WITH THINGS MECHANICAL.
SIX WITH AN INTENSE INTEREST IN THE SCIENTIFIC.
AND, OF COURSE, SEVEN...
PING
AND MYSELF, WHO TOOK THE ORIGINAL'S MORE ARTISTIC TRAITS.
MUSIC, ART, AND LITERATURE.
GET THIS--WHEN WE ALL WENT TO SEE HOW WE WERE DOING, WE KNEW WHAT OUR REACTION WOULD BE.
XXO
ORG! WHAT HAVE YOU DONE?!

NEXT: **PUT YOUR RAYGUN TO MY HEAD**

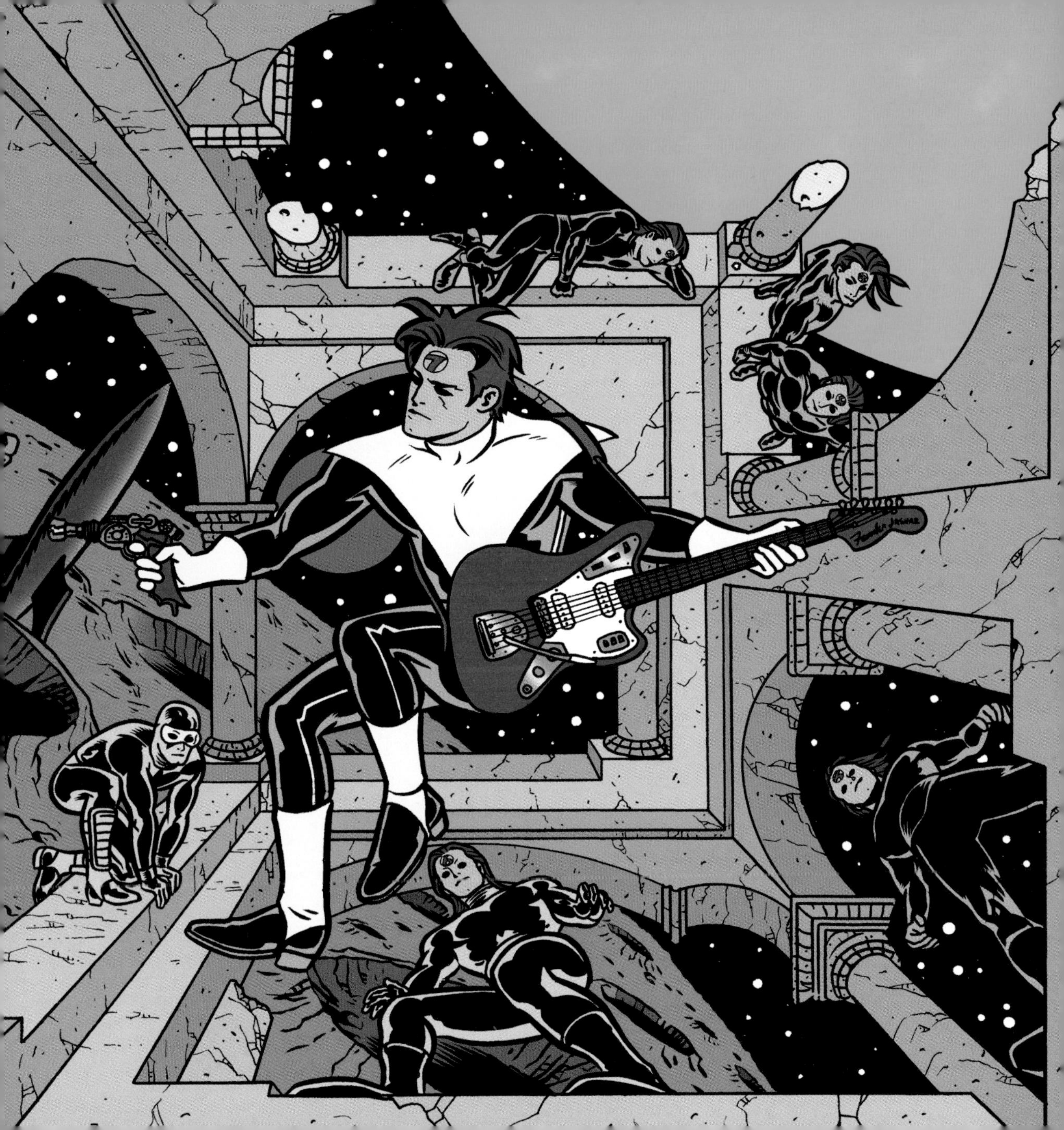
Fender Jaguar

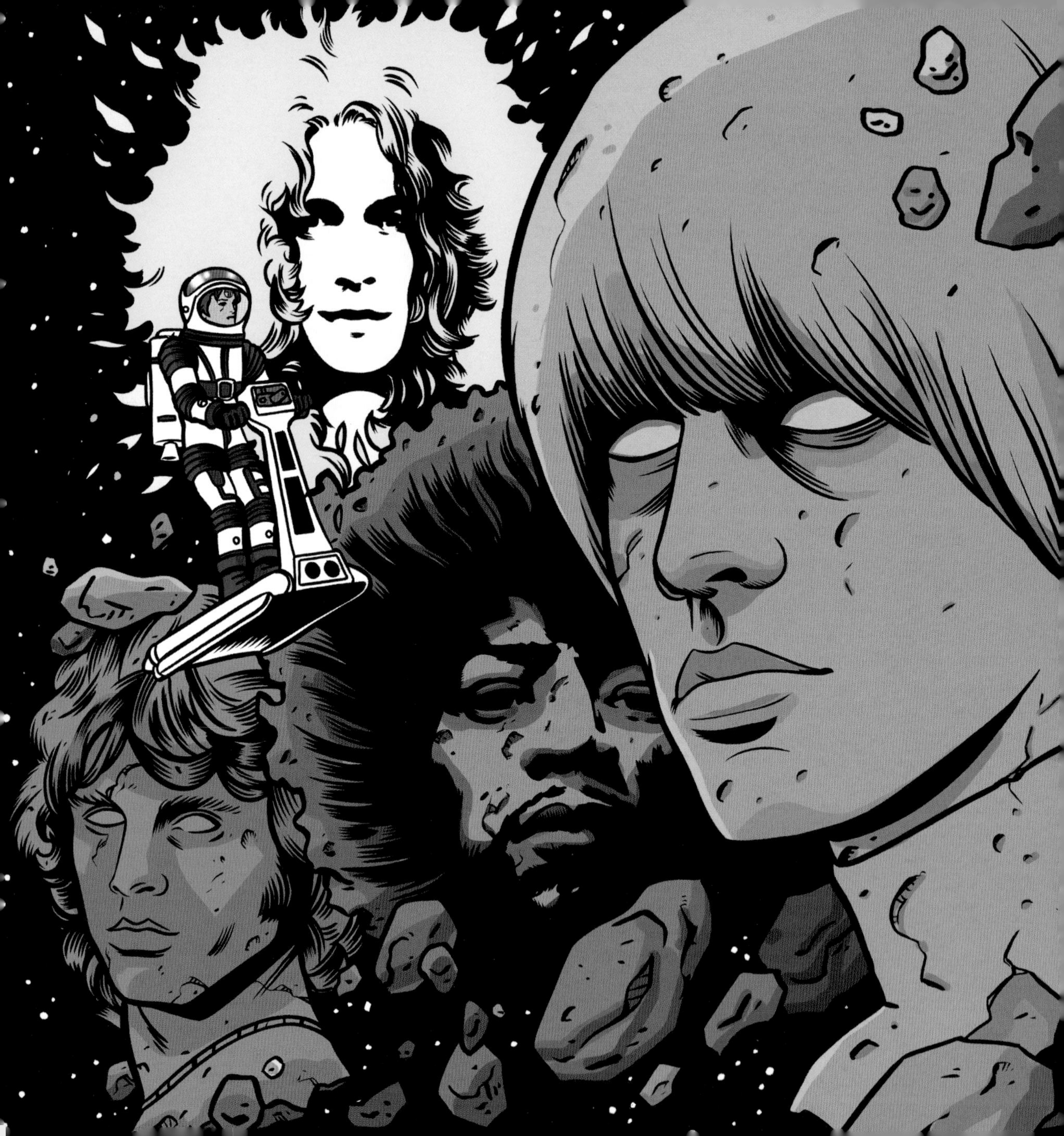

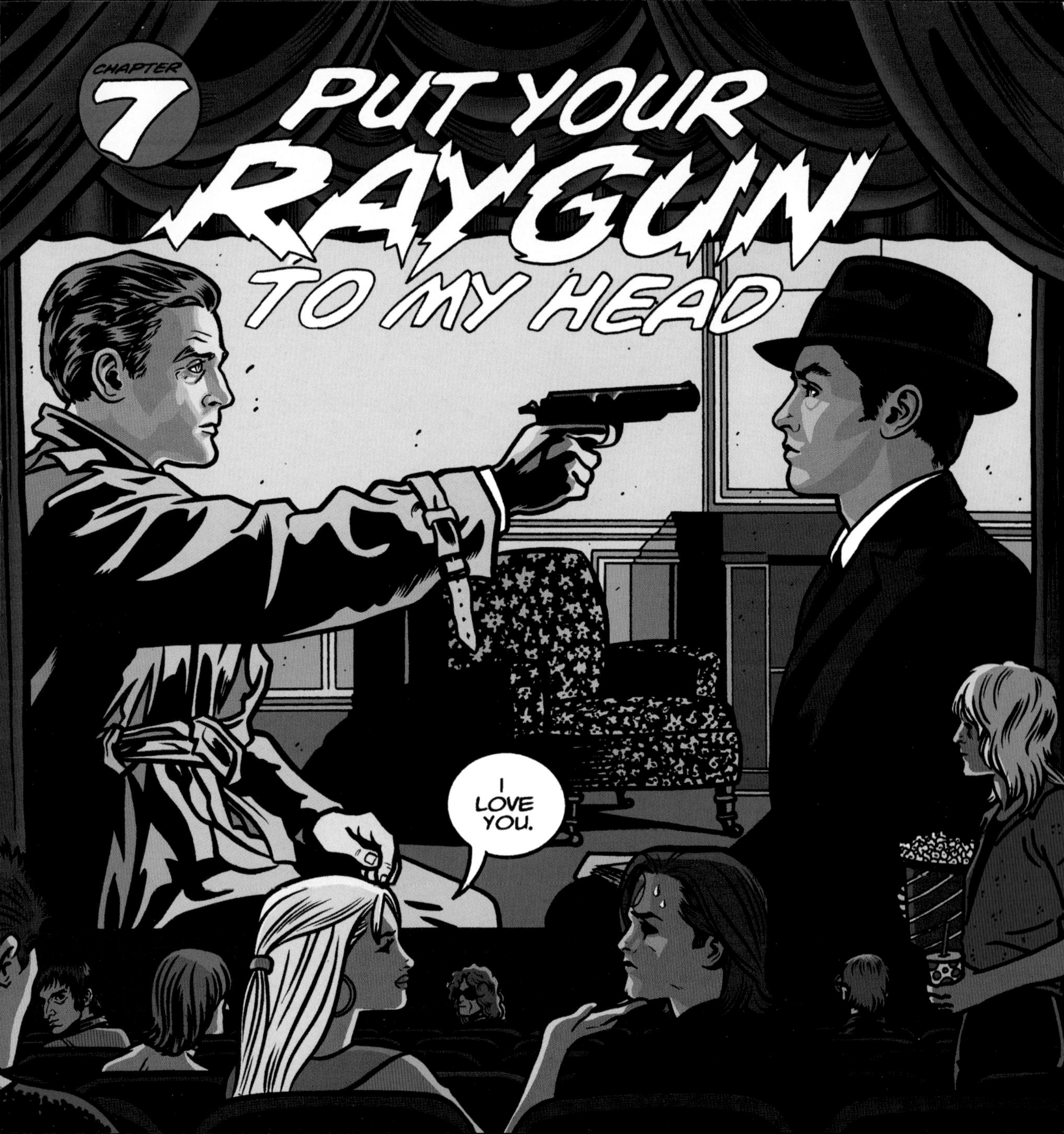
CHAPTER 7
PUT YOUR RAYGUN TO MY HEAD
I LOVE YOU.

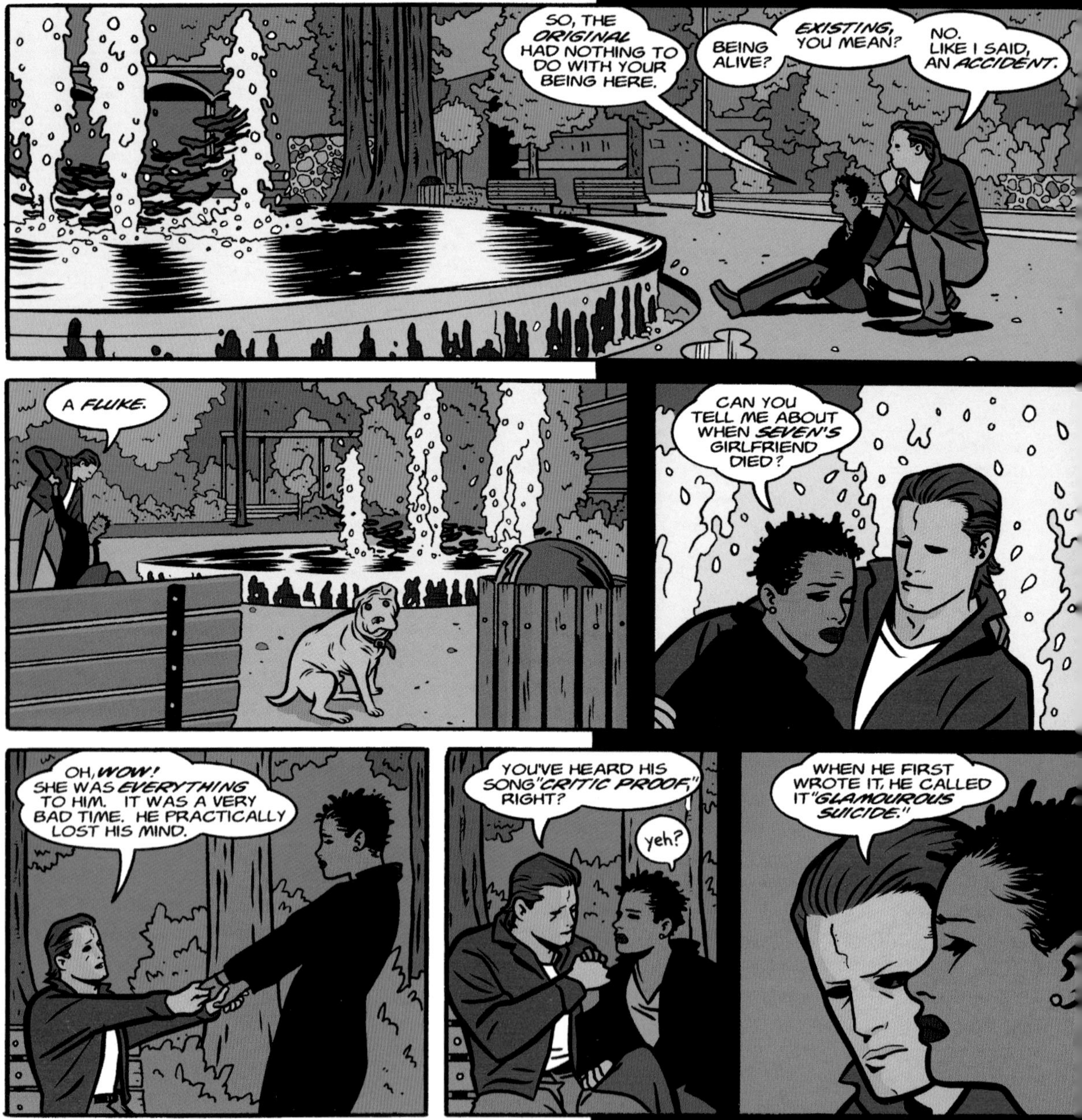
SO, THE *ORIGINAL* HAD NOTHING TO DO WITH YOUR BEING HERE.
BEING ALIVE?
EXISTING, YOU MEAN?
NO. LIKE I SAID, AN *ACCIDENT*.
A *FLUKE*.
CAN YOU TELL ME ABOUT WHEN *SEVEN'S* GIRLFRIEND DIED?
OH, *WOW!* SHE WAS *EVERYTHING* TO HIM. IT WAS A VERY BAD TIME. HE PRACTICALLY LOST HIS MIND.
YOU'VE HEARD HIS SONG "*CRITIC PROOF*," RIGHT?
yeh?
WHEN HE FIRST WROTE IT, HE CALLED IT "*GLAMOUROUS SUICIDE*."

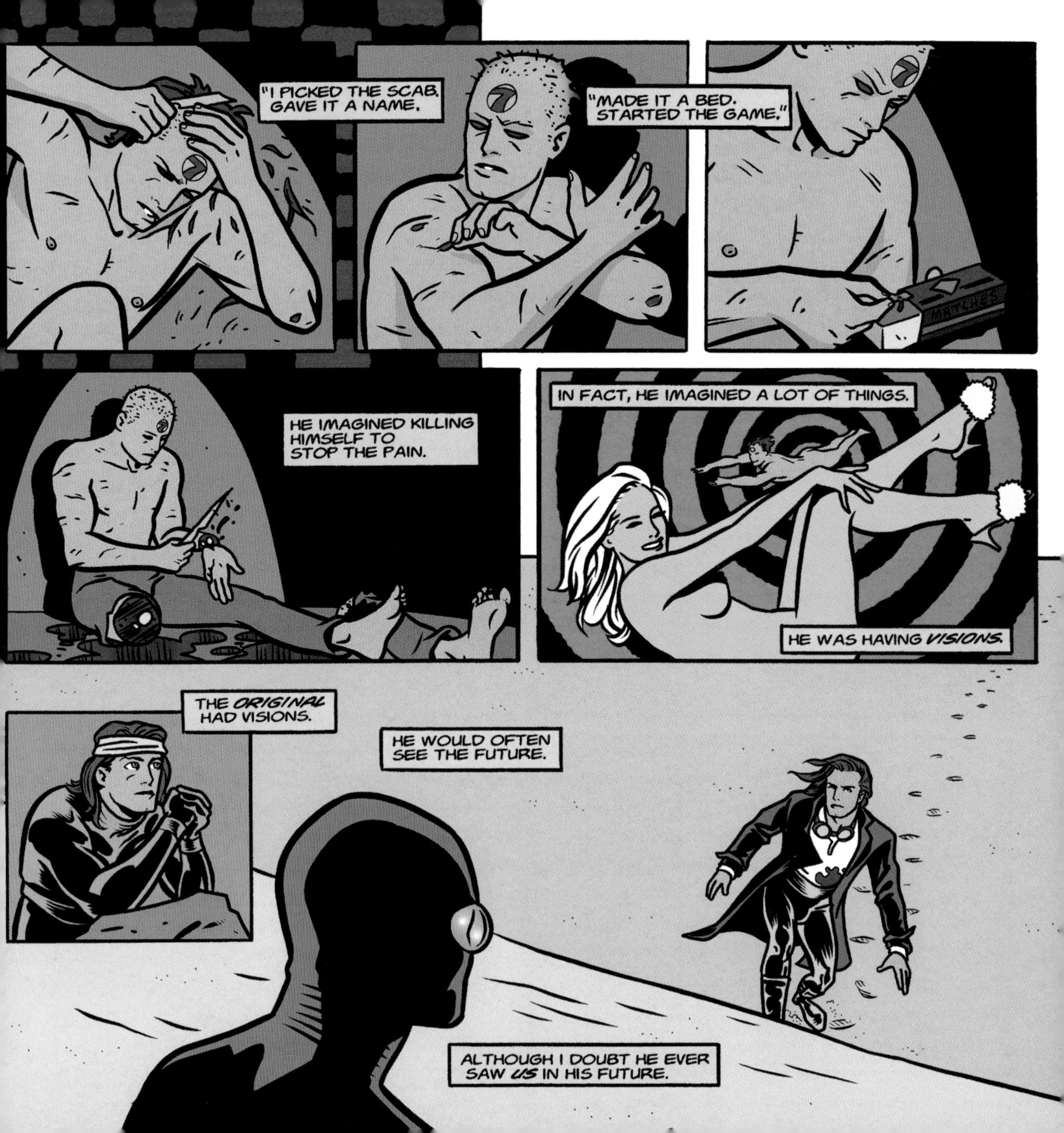
"I PICKED THE SCAB. GAVE IT A NAME.
"MADE IT A BED. STARTED THE GAME."
HE IMAGINED KILLING HIMSELF TO STOP THE PAIN.
IN FACT, HE IMAGINED A LOT OF THINGS.
HE WAS HAVING *VISIONS*.
THE *ORIGINAL* HAD VISIONS.
HE WOULD OFTEN SEE THE FUTURE.
ALTHOUGH I DOUBT HE EVER SAW *US* IN HIS FUTURE.

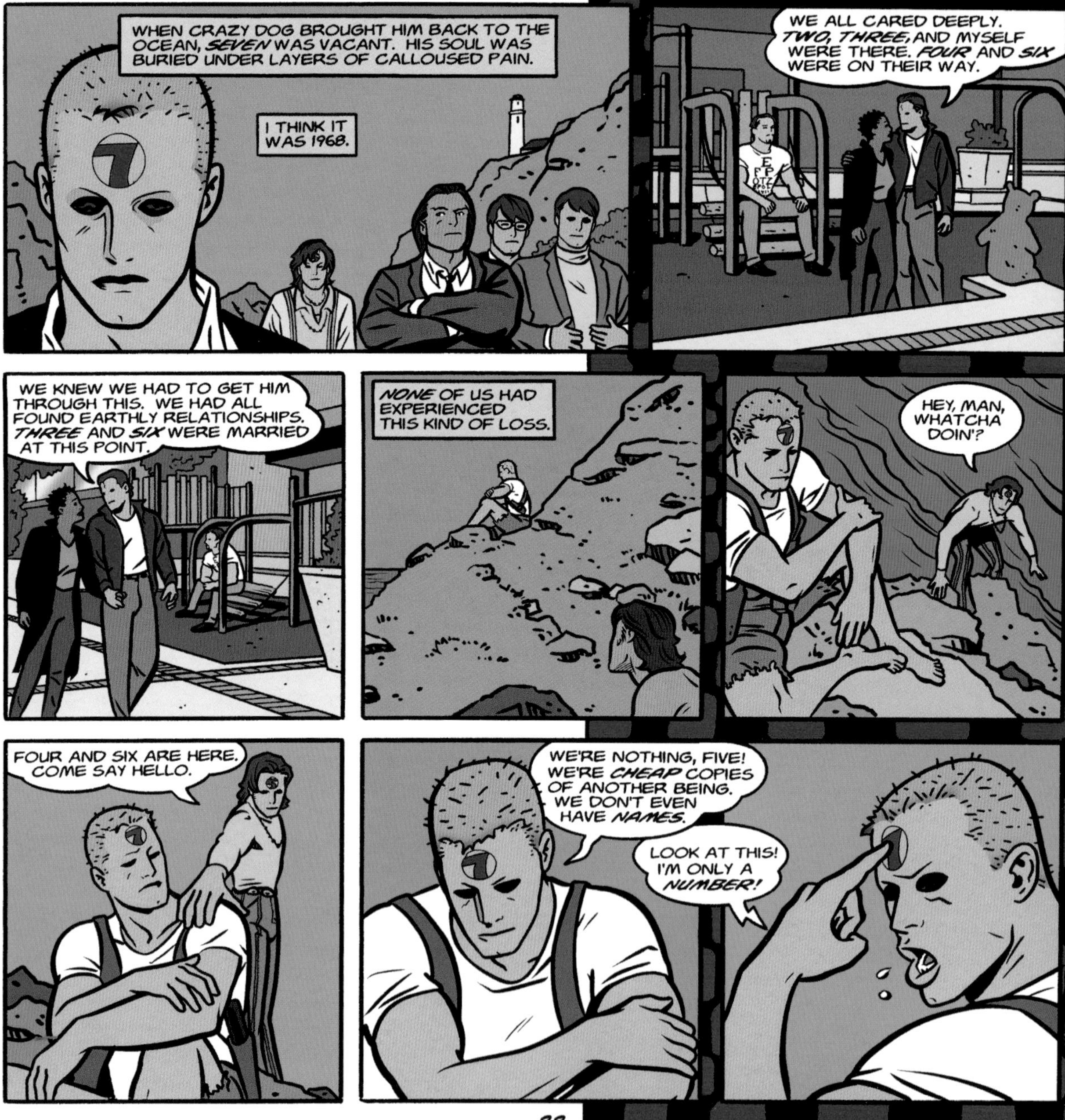
WHEN CRAZY DOG BROUGHT HIM BACK TO THE OCEAN, SEVEN WAS VACANT. HIS SOUL WAS BURIED UNDER LAYERS OF CALLOUSED PAIN.
I THINK IT WAS 1968.
WE ALL CARED DEEPLY. TWO, THREE, AND MYSELF WERE THERE. FOUR AND SIX WERE ON THEIR WAY.
WE KNEW WE HAD TO GET HIM THROUGH THIS. WE HAD ALL FOUND EARTHLY RELATIONSHIPS. THREE AND SIX WERE MARRIED AT THIS POINT.
NONE OF US HAD EXPERIENCED THIS KIND OF LOSS.
HEY, MAN, WHATCHA DOIN'?
FOUR AND SIX ARE HERE. COME SAY HELLO.
WE'RE NOTHING, FIVE! WE'RE CHEAP COPIES OF ANOTHER BEING. WE DON'T EVEN HAVE NAMES.
LOOK AT THIS! I'M ONLY A NUMBER!

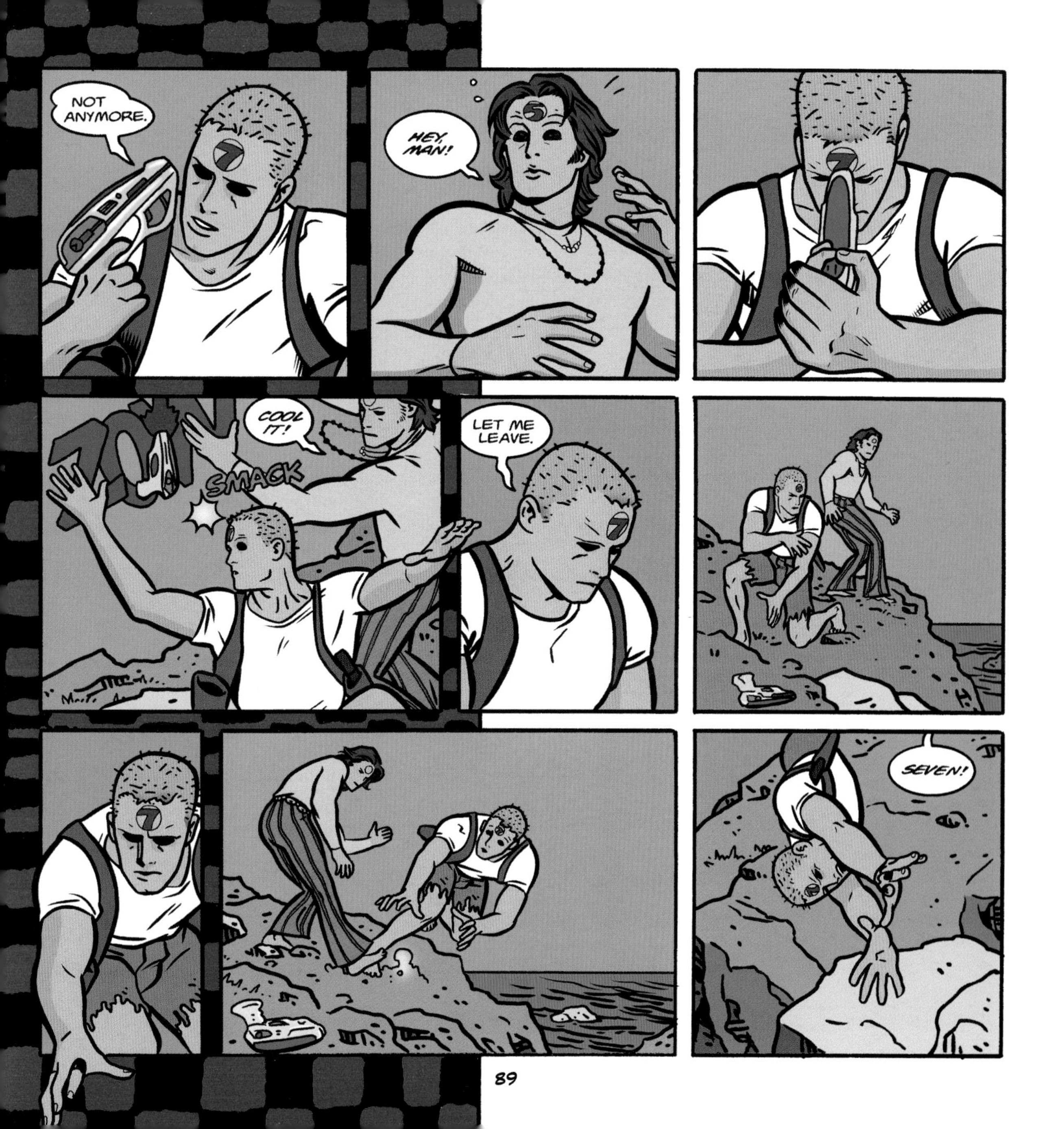
NOT ANYMORE.
HEY, MAN!
COOL IT!
SMACK
LET ME LEAVE.
SEVEN!

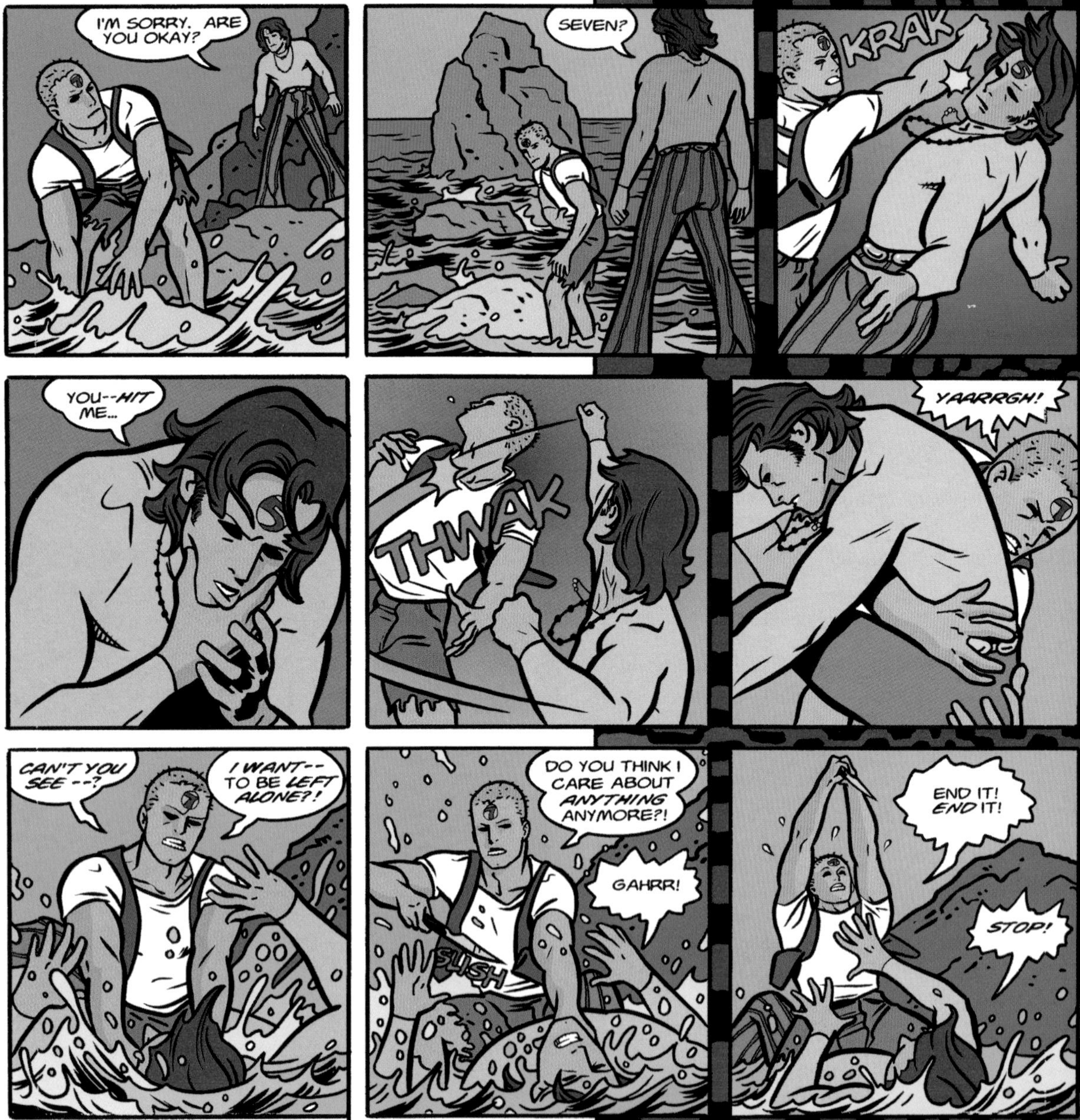

I'M SORRY. ARE YOU OKAY?
SEVEN?
KRAK
YOU--HIT ME...
THWAK
YAARRGH!
CAN'T YOU SEE --?
I WANT-- TO BE LEFT ALONE?!
DO YOU THINK I CARE ABOUT ANYTHING ANYMORE?!
GAHRR!
SLISH
END IT! END IT!
STOP!

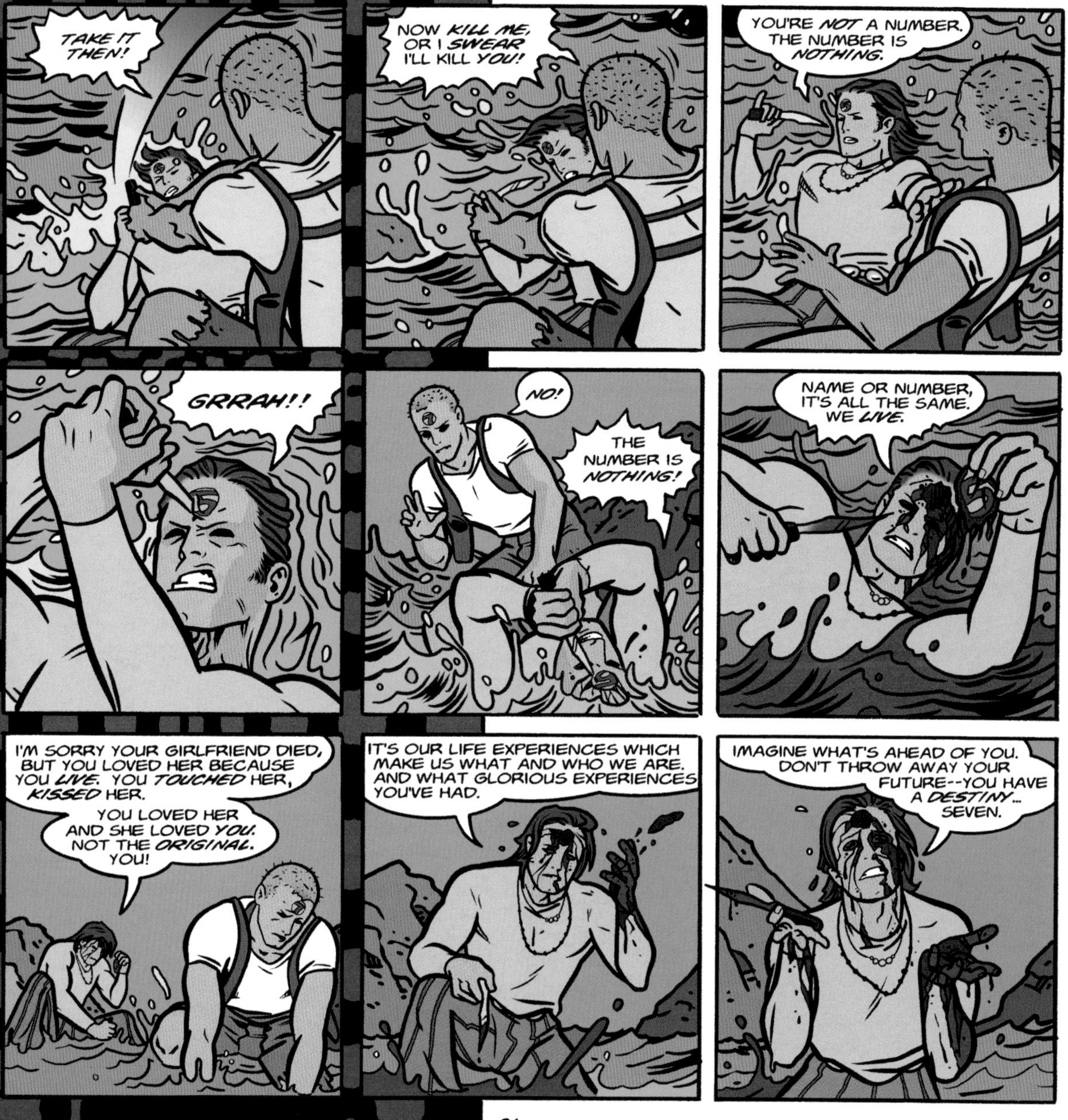
TAKE IT THEN!
NOW KILL ME, OR I SWEAR I'LL KILL YOU!
YOU'RE NOT A NUMBER. THE NUMBER IS NOTHING.
GRRAH!!
NO!
THE NUMBER IS NOTHING!
NAME OR NUMBER, IT'S ALL THE SAME. WE LIVE.
I'M SORRY YOUR GIRLFRIEND DIED, BUT YOU LOVED HER BECAUSE YOU LIVE. YOU TOUCHED HER, KISSED HER.
YOU LOVED HER AND SHE LOVED YOU. NOT THE ORIGINAL. YOU!
IT'S OUR LIFE EXPERIENCES WHICH MAKE US WHAT AND WHO WE ARE. AND WHAT GLORIOUS EXPERIENCES YOU'VE HAD.
IMAGINE WHAT'S AHEAD OF YOU. DON'T THROW AWAY YOUR FUTURE--YOU HAVE A DESTINY... SEVEN.

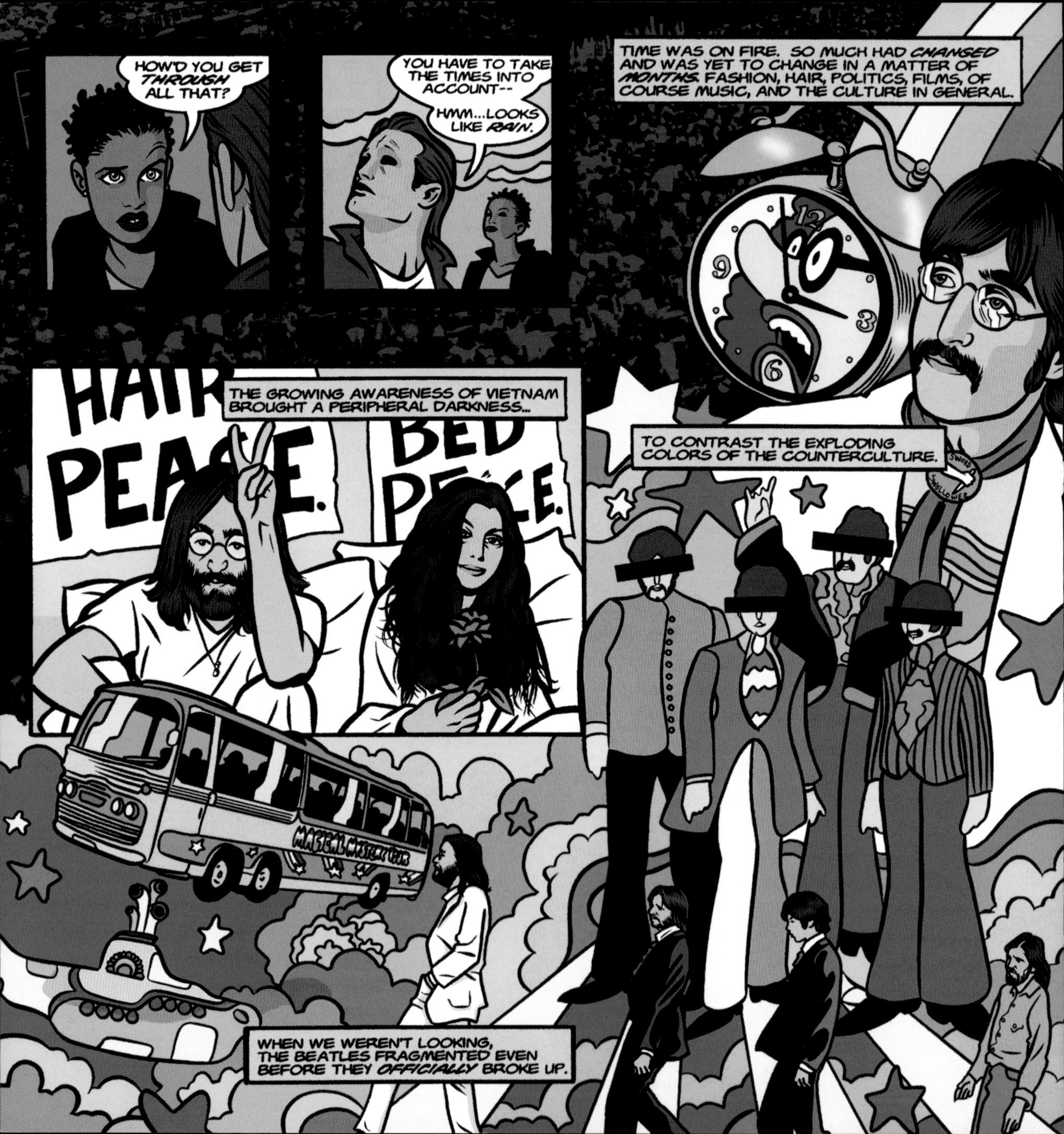

HOW'D YOU GET *THROUGH* ALL THAT?
YOU HAVE TO TAKE THE TIMES INTO ACCOUNT--
HMM...LOOKS LIKE *RAIN*.
TIME WAS ON FIRE. SO MUCH HAD *CHANGED* AND WAS YET TO CHANGE IN A MATTER OF *MONTHS*. FASHION, HAIR, POLITICS, FILMS, OF COURSE MUSIC, AND THE CULTURE IN GENERAL.
HAIR
BED
THE GROWING AWARENESS OF VIETNAM BROUGHT A PERIPHERAL DARKNESS...
TO CONTRAST THE EXPLODING COLORS OF THE COUNTERCULTURE.
SWORD SWALLOWER
WHEN WE WEREN'T LOOKING, THE BEATLES FRAGMENTED EVEN BEFORE THEY *OFFICIALLY* BROKE UP.

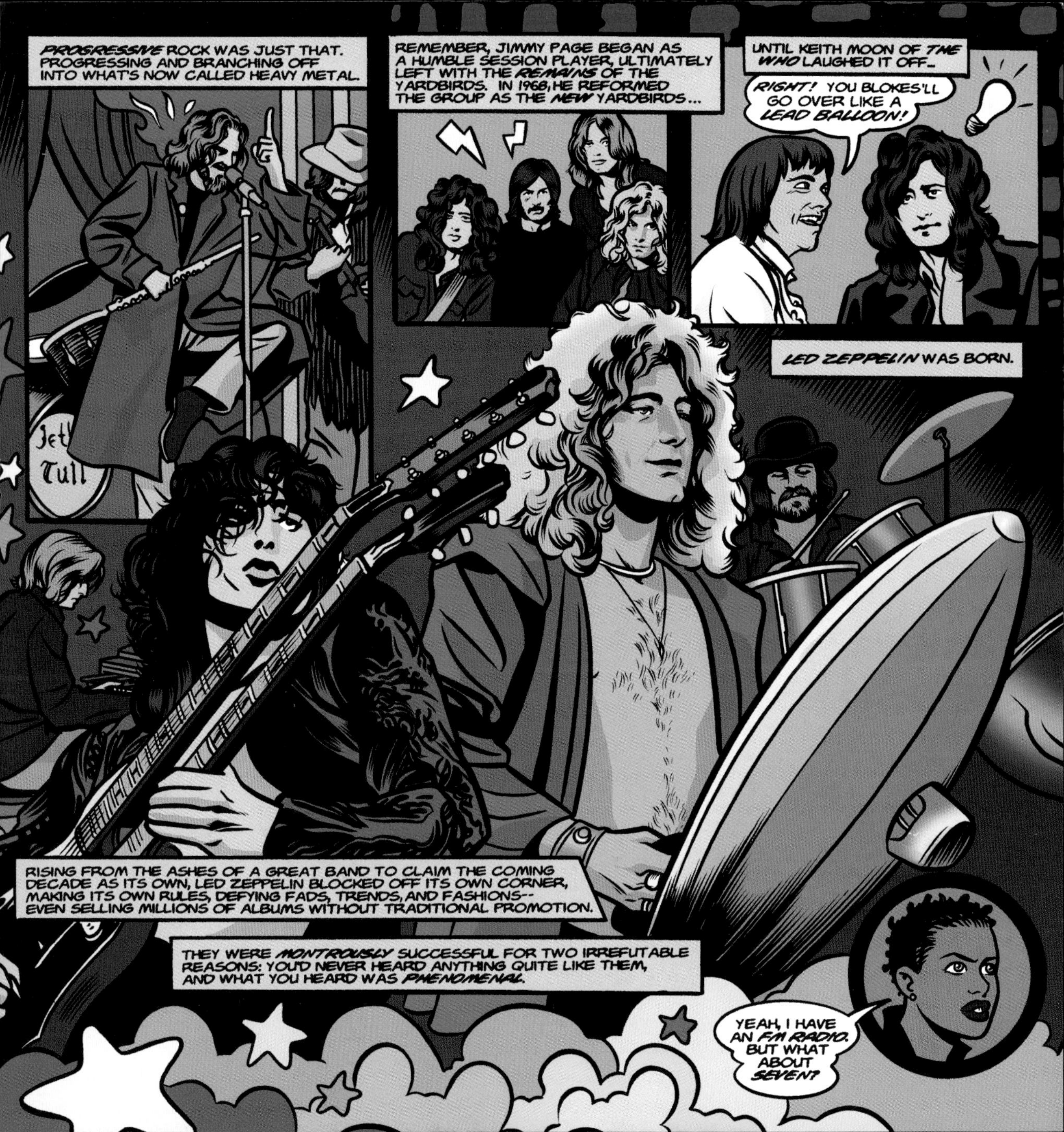
PROGRESSIVE ROCK WAS JUST THAT. PROGRESSING AND BRANCHING OFF INTO WHAT'S NOW CALLED HEAVY METAL.
Jeth Tull
REMEMBER, JIMMY PAGE BEGAN AS A HUMBLE SESSION PLAYER, ULTIMATELY LEFT WITH THE REMAINS OF THE YARDBIRDS. IN 1968, HE REFORMED THE GROUP AS THE NEW YARDBIRDS...
UNTIL KEITH MOON OF THE WHO LAUGHED IT OFF...
RIGHT! YOU BLOKES'LL GO OVER LIKE A LEAD BALLOON!
LED ZEPPELIN WAS BORN.
RISING FROM THE ASHES OF A GREAT BAND TO CLAIM THE COMING DECADE AS ITS OWN, LED ZEPPELIN BLOCKED OFF ITS OWN CORNER, MAKING ITS OWN RULES, DEFYING FADS, TRENDS, AND FASHIONS-- EVEN SELLING MILLIONS OF ALBUMS WITHOUT TRADITIONAL PROMOTION.
THEY WERE MONTROUSLY SUCCESSFUL FOR TWO IRREFUTABLE REASONS: YOU'D NEVER HEARD ANYTHING QUITE LIKE THEM, AND WHAT YOU HEARD WAS PHENOMENAL.
YEAH, I HAVE AN FM RADIO. BUT WHAT ABOUT SEVEN?

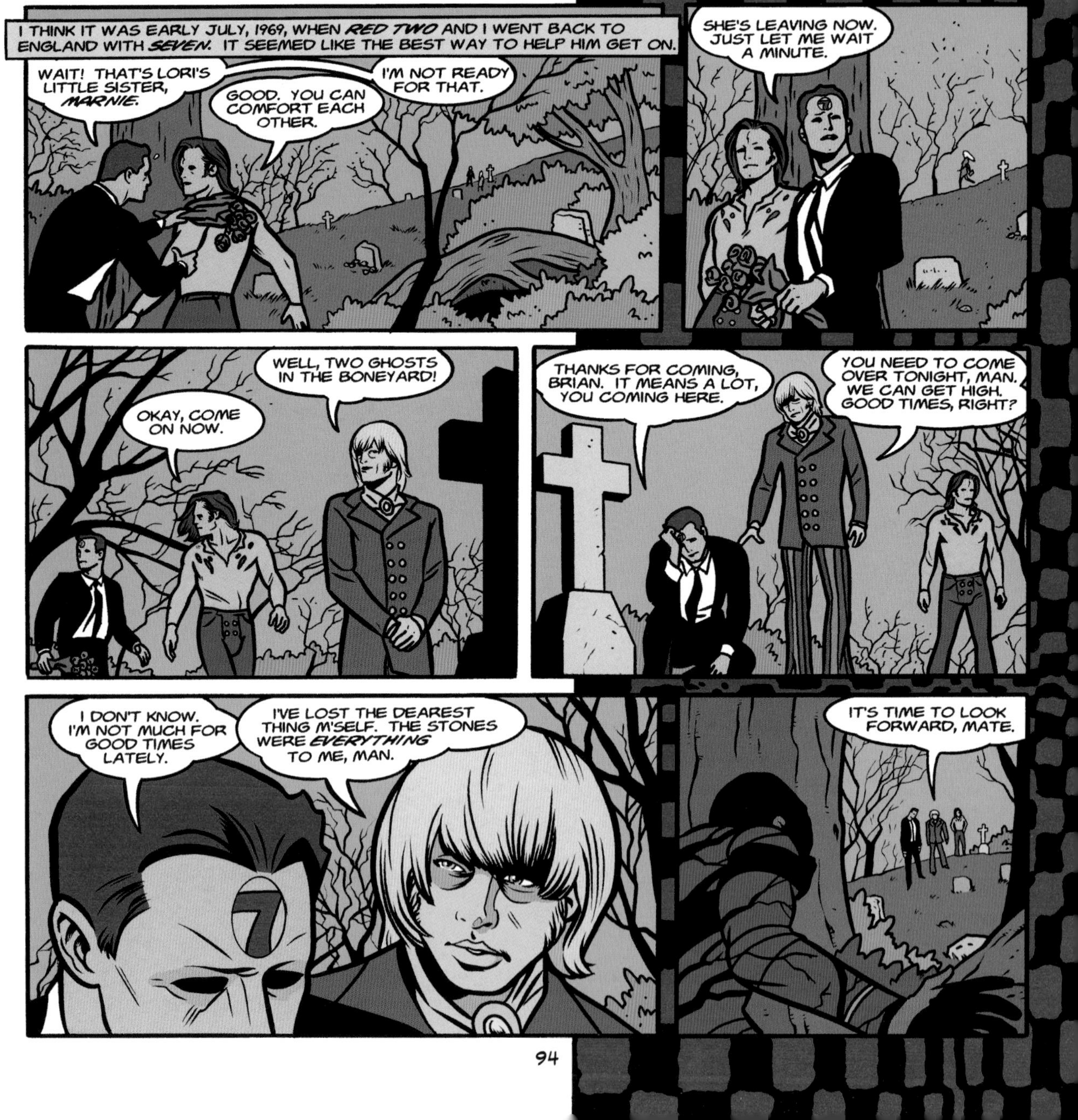

I THINK IT WAS EARLY JULY, 1969, WHEN RED TWO AND I WENT BACK TO ENGLAND WITH SEVEN. IT SEEMED LIKE THE BEST WAY TO HELP HIM GET ON.
WAIT! THAT'S LORI'S LITTLE SISTER, MARNIE.
GOOD. YOU CAN COMFORT EACH OTHER.
I'M NOT READY FOR THAT.
SHE'S LEAVING NOW. JUST LET ME WAIT A MINUTE.
WELL, TWO GHOSTS IN THE BONEYARD!
OKAY, COME ON NOW.
THANKS FOR COMING, BRIAN. IT MEANS A LOT, YOU COMING HERE.
YOU NEED TO COME OVER TONIGHT, MAN. WE CAN GET HIGH. GOOD TIMES, RIGHT?
I DON'T KNOW. I'M NOT MUCH FOR GOOD TIMES LATELY.
I'VE LOST THE DEAREST THING M'SELF. THE STONES WERE EVERYTHING TO ME, MAN.
IT'S TIME TO LOOK FORWARD, MATE.

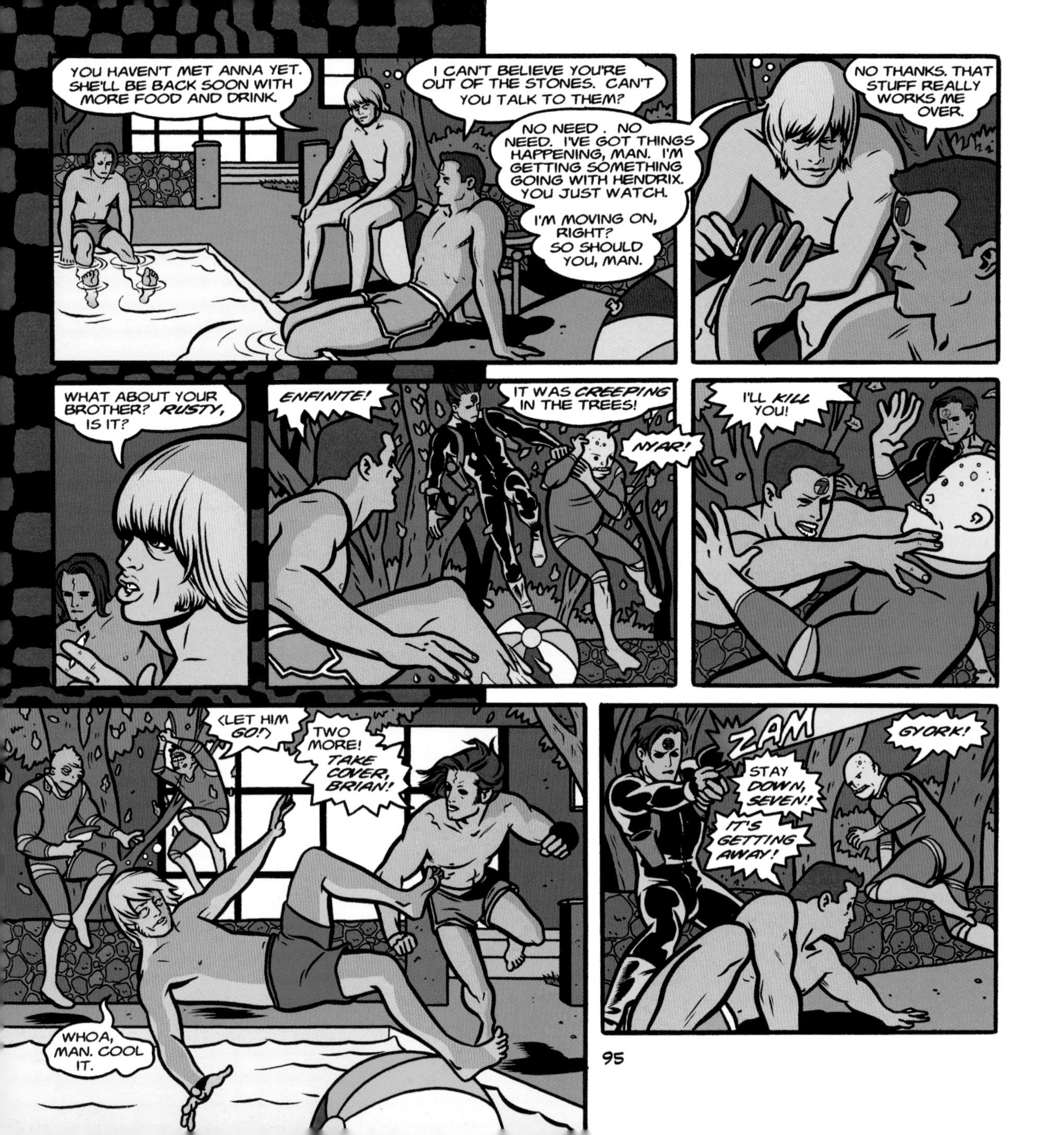
YOU HAVEN'T MET ANNA YET. SHE'LL BE BACK SOON WITH MORE FOOD AND DRINK.
I CAN'T BELIEVE YOU'RE OUT OF THE STONES. CAN'T YOU TALK TO THEM?
NO NEED. NO NEED. I'VE GOT THINGS HAPPENING, MAN. I'M GETTING SOMETHING GOING WITH HENDRIX. YOU JUST WATCH.
I'M MOVING ON, RIGHT? SO SHOULD YOU, MAN.
NO THANKS. THAT STUFF REALLY WORKS ME OVER.
WHAT ABOUT YOUR BROTHER? RUSTY, IS IT?
ENFINITE!
IT WAS CREEPING IN THE TREES!
NYAR!
I'LL KILL YOU!
<LET HIM GO!>
TWO MORE! TAKE COVER, BRIAN!
WHOA, MAN. COOL IT.
ZAM
GYORK!
STAY DOWN, SEVEN!
IT'S GETTING AWAY!

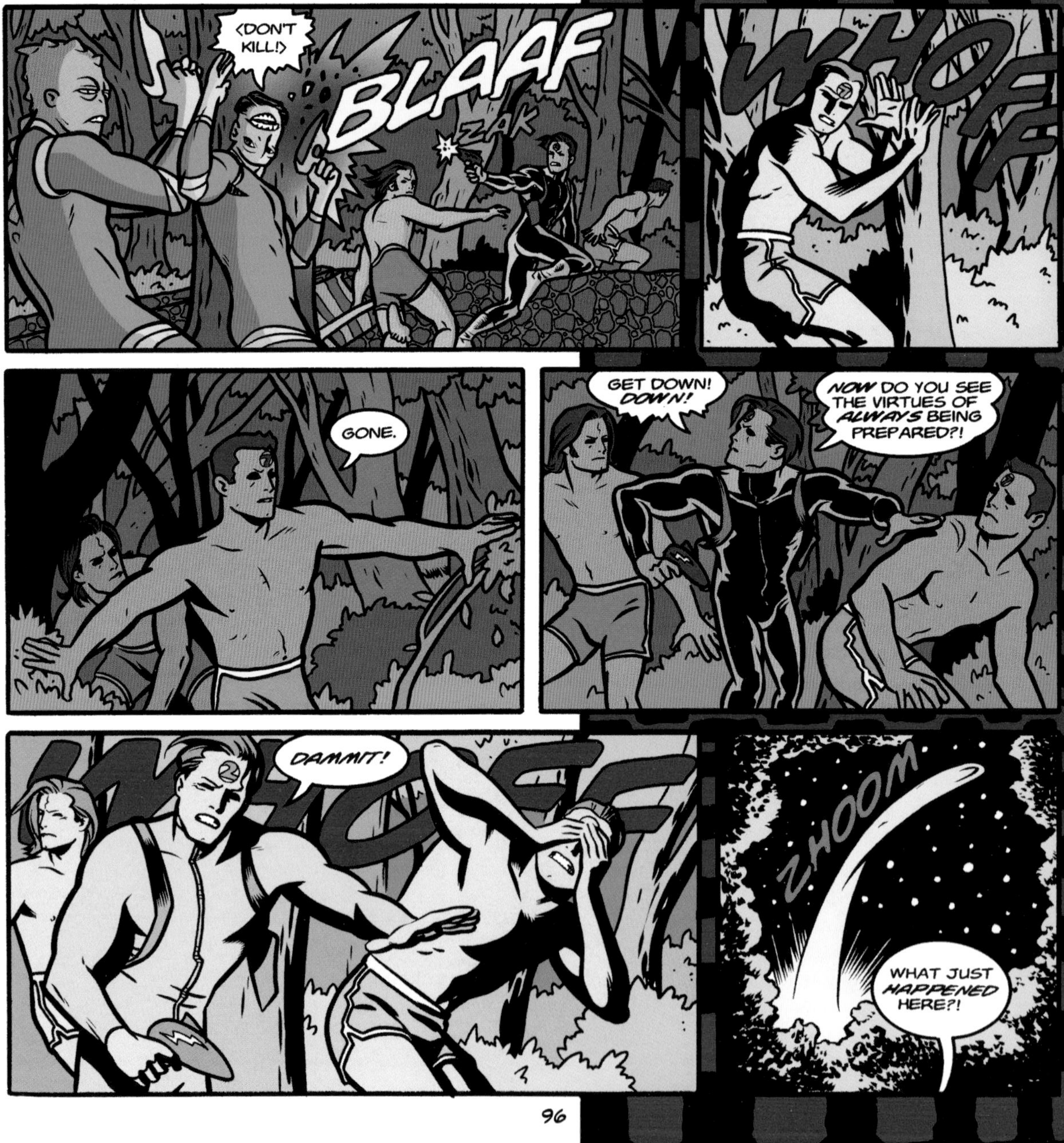
<DON'T KILL!>
BLAAF
ZAK
WHOFF
GONE.
GET DOWN! DOWN!
NOW DO YOU SEE THE VIRTUES OF ALWAYS BEING PREPARED?!
DAMMIT!
ZHOOM
WHAT JUST HAPPENED HERE?!

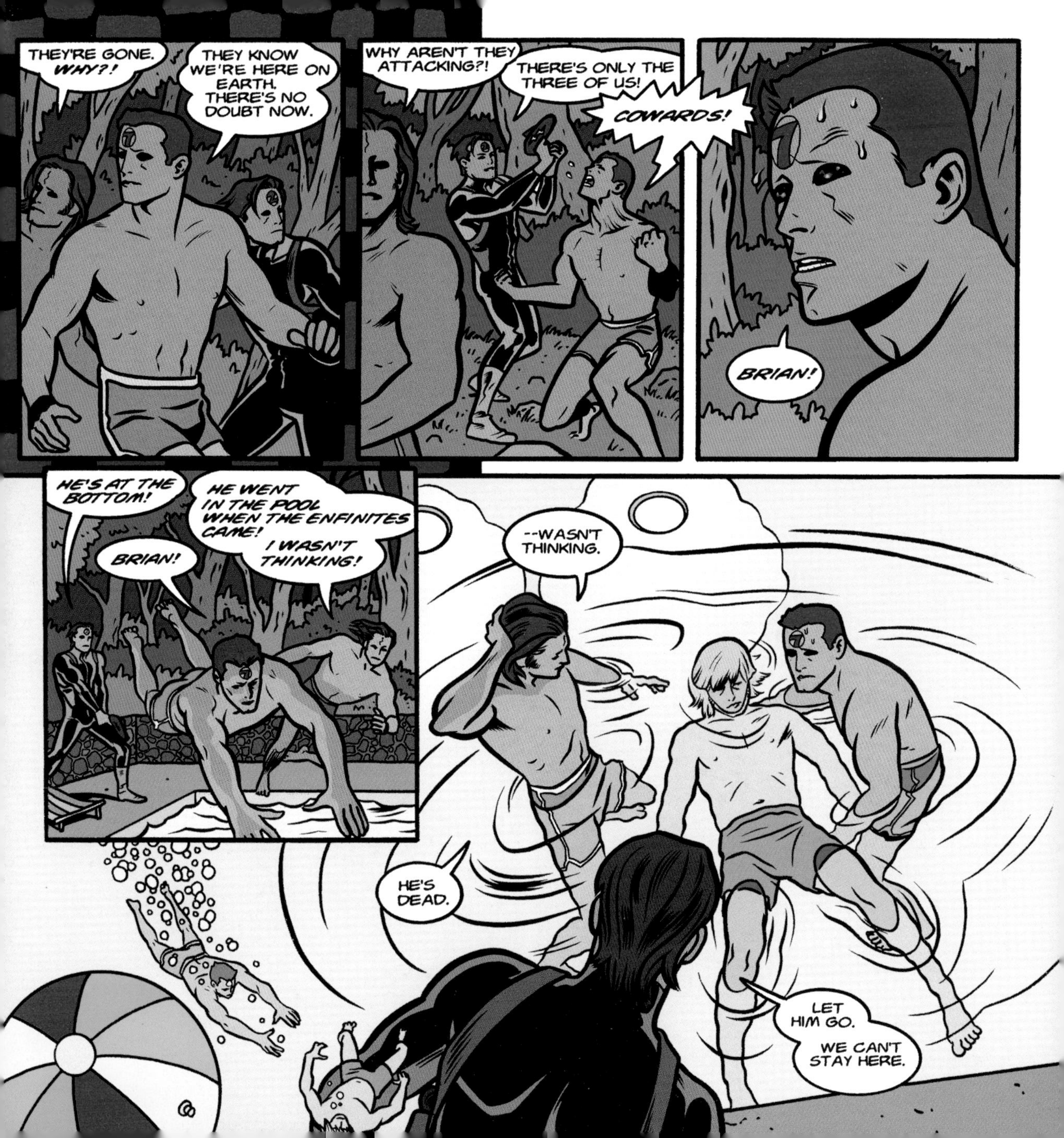

THEY'RE GONE. WHY?!
THEY KNOW WE'RE HERE ON EARTH. THERE'S NO DOUBT NOW.
WHY AREN'T THEY ATTACKING?!
THERE'S ONLY THE THREE OF US!
COWARDS!
BRIAN!
HE'S AT THE BOTTOM!
BRIAN!
HE WENT IN THE POOL WHEN THE ENFINITES CAME!
I WASN'T THINKING!
--WASN'T THINKING.
HE'S DEAD.
LET HIM GO.
WE CAN'T STAY HERE.

'EAVEN'S LIGHT F'EVEH SHINES, EHTH'S SHADOHS FLOY.

THE STONES WERE TO INTRODUCE THEIR NEW GUITARIST, MICK TAYLOR, A COUPLE OF DAYS LATER AT THEIR FREE HYDE PARK SHOW--IT BECAME A MEMORIAL TO BRIAN INSTEAD.

RED?

LOR--

M-*MARNIE!* WH-WHAT ARE--

HI.

DO YOUR FOLKS KNOW YOU'RE HERE?

COME ON. I'LL GET YOU HOME.

I'M QUITE ALL RIGHT BEING HERE.

I'M FINE GETTING AROUND ON MY OWN.

YEAH. I REMEMBER YOU, *TEN* YEARS OLD, SNEAKING INTO *THE CAVERN* TO WATCH THE BEATLES. I'LL HAVE TO KEEP AN *EYE* ON YOU.

I'D LIKE THAT.

HEY, *SEVEN!* WE'LL CATCH UP WITH YOU AT THE HOTEL.

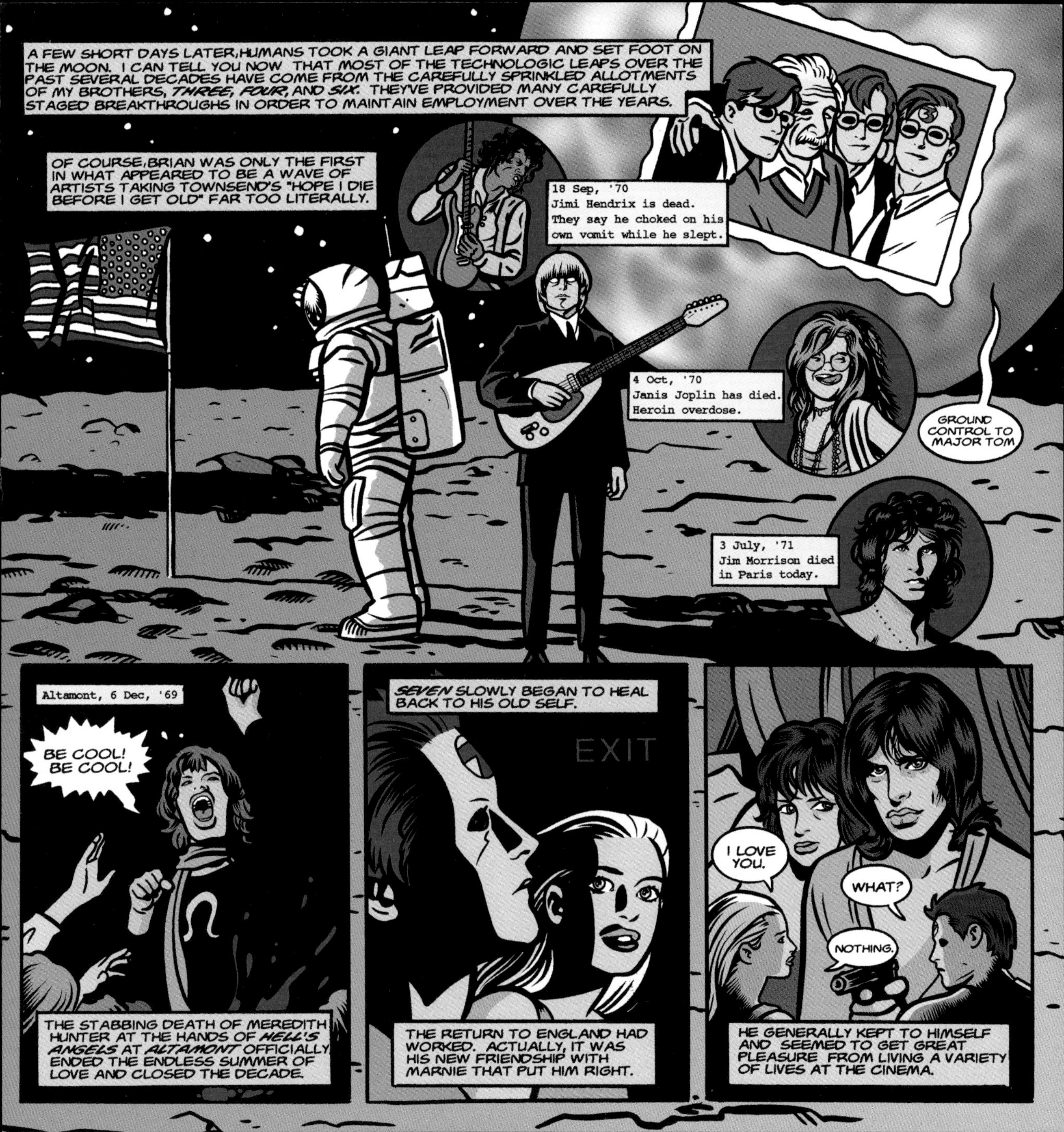
A FEW SHORT DAYS LATER, HUMANS TOOK A GIANT LEAP FORWARD AND SET FOOT ON THE MOON. I CAN TELL YOU NOW THAT MOST OF THE TECHNOLOGIC LEAPS OVER THE PAST SEVERAL DECADES HAVE COME FROM THE CAREFULLY SPRINKLED ALLOTMENTS OF MY BROTHERS, THREE, FOUR, AND SIX. THEY'VE PROVIDED MANY CAREFULLY STAGED BREAKTHROUGHS IN ORDER TO MAINTAIN EMPLOYMENT OVER THE YEARS.
OF COURSE, BRIAN WAS ONLY THE FIRST IN WHAT APPEARED TO BE A WAVE OF ARTISTS TAKING TOWNSEND'S "HOPE I DIE BEFORE I GET OLD" FAR TOO LITERALLY.
18 Sep, '70 Jimi Hendrix is dead. They say he choked on his own vomit while he slept.
4 Oct, '70 Janis Joplin has died. Heroin overdose.
GROUND CONTROL TO MAJOR TOM
3 July, '71 Jim Morrison died in Paris today.
Altamont, 6 Dec, '69
BE COOL! BE COOL!
THE STABBING DEATH OF MEREDITH HUNTER AT THE HANDS OF HELL'S ANGELS AT ALTAMONT OFFICIALLY ENDED THE ENDLESS SUMMER OF LOVE AND CLOSED THE DECADE.
SEVEN SLOWLY BEGAN TO HEAL BACK TO HIS OLD SELF.
EXIT
THE RETURN TO ENGLAND HAD WORKED. ACTUALLY, IT WAS HIS NEW FRIENDSHIP WITH MARNIE THAT PUT HIM RIGHT.
I LOVE YOU.
WHAT?
NOTHING.
HE GENERALLY KEPT TO HIMSELF AND SEEMED TO GET GREAT PLEASURE FROM LIVING A VARIETY OF LIVES AT THE CINEMA.

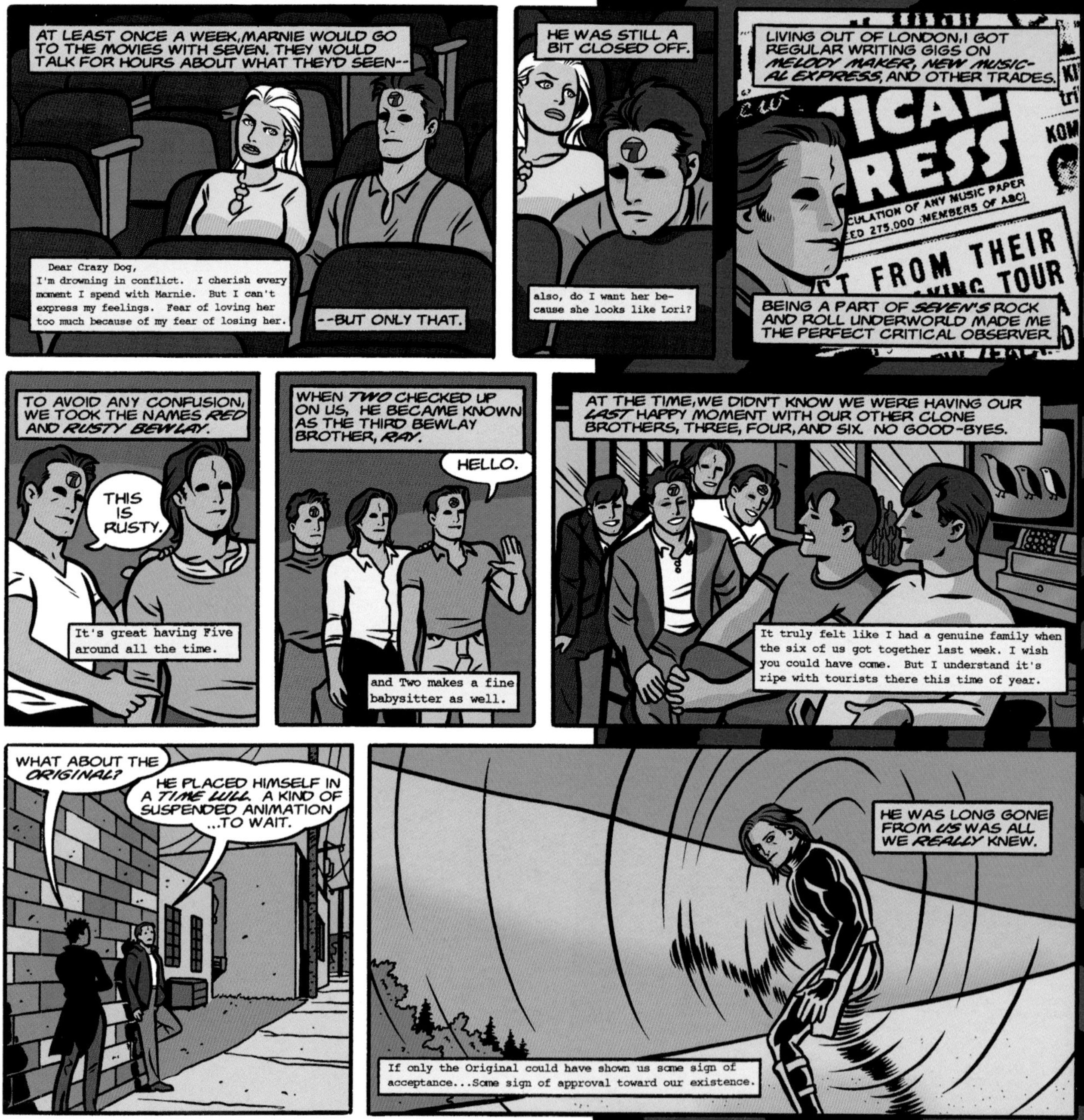

AT LEAST ONCE A WEEK, MARNIE WOULD GO TO THE MOVIES WITH SEVEN. THEY WOULD TALK FOR HOURS ABOUT WHAT THEY'D SEEN--
Dear Crazy Dog,
I'm drowning in conflict. I cherish every moment I spend with Marnie. But I can't express my feelings. Fear of loving her too much because of my fear of losing her.
--BUT ONLY THAT.
HE WAS STILL A BIT CLOSED OFF.
also, do I want her because she looks like Lori?
LIVING OUT OF LONDON, I GOT REGULAR WRITING GIGS ON MELODY MAKER, NEW MUSICAL EXPRESS, AND OTHER TRADES.
BEING A PART OF SEVEN'S ROCK AND ROLL UNDERWORLD MADE ME THE PERFECT CRITICAL OBSERVER.
TO AVOID ANY CONFUSION, WE TOOK THE NAMES RED AND RUSTY BEWLAY.
THIS IS RUSTY.
It's great having Five around all the time.
WHEN TWO CHECKED UP ON US, HE BECAME KNOWN AS THE THIRD BEWLAY BROTHER, RAY.
HELLO.
and Two makes a fine babysitter as well.
AT THE TIME, WE DIDN'T KNOW WE WERE HAVING OUR LAST HAPPY MOMENT WITH OUR OTHER CLONE BROTHERS, THREE, FOUR, AND SIX. NO GOOD-BYES.
It truly felt like I had a genuine family when the six of us got together last week. I wish you could have come. But I understand it's ripe with tourists there this time of year.
WHAT ABOUT THE ORIGINAL?
HE PLACED HIMSELF IN A TIME LULL. A KIND OF SUSPENDED ANIMATION ...TO WAIT.
HE WAS LONG GONE FROM US WAS ALL WE REALLY KNEW.
If only the Original could have shown us some sign of acceptance...Some sign of approval toward our existence.

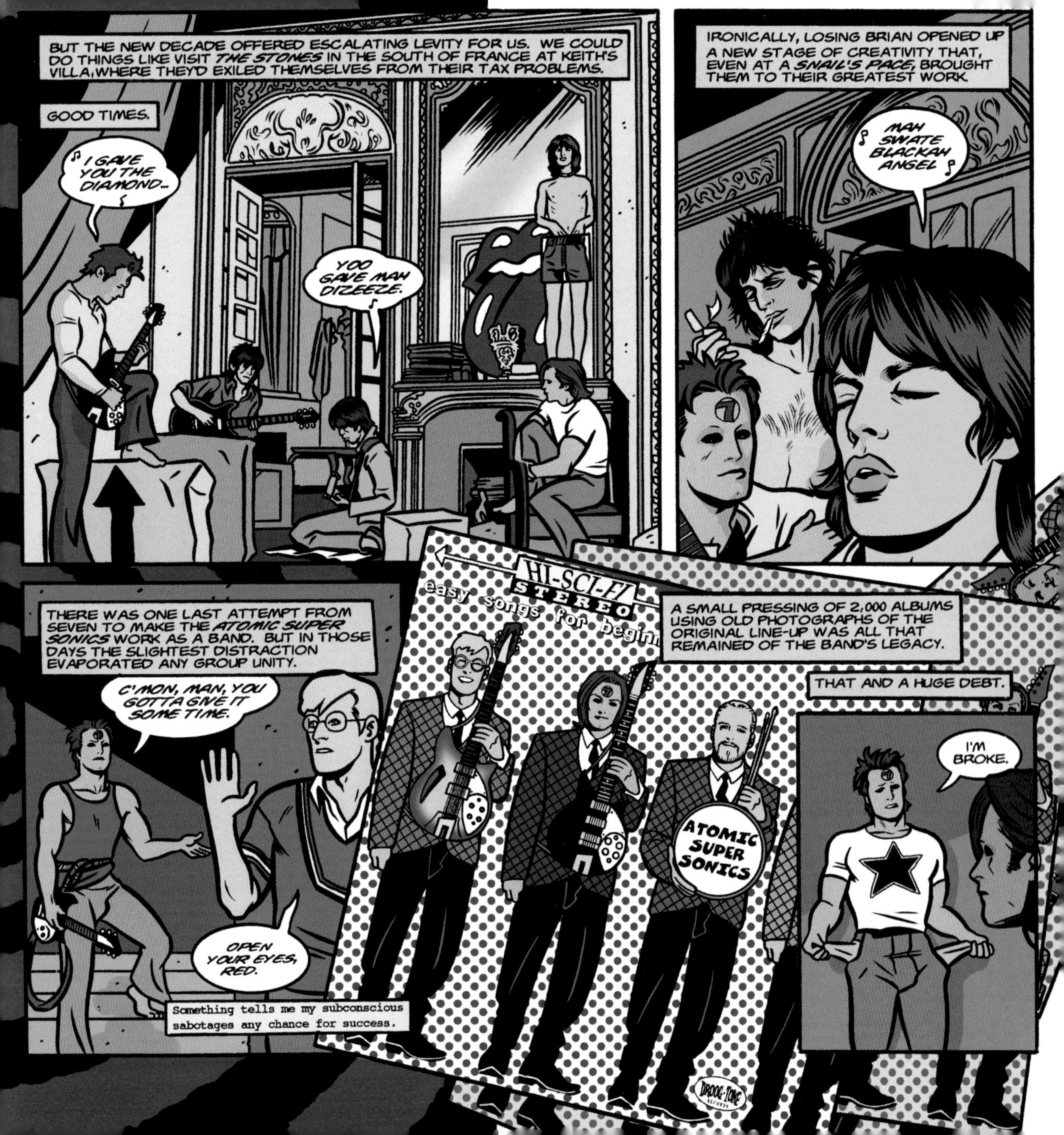

BUT THE NEW DECADE OFFERED ESCALATING LEVITY FOR US. WE COULD DO THINGS LIKE VISIT THE STONES IN THE SOUTH OF FRANCE AT KEITH'S VILLA, WHERE THEY'D EXILED THEMSELVES FROM THEIR TAX PROBLEMS.
GOOD TIMES.
I GAVE YOU THE DIAMOND...
YOO GAVE MAH DIZEEZE.
IRONICALLY, LOSING BRIAN OPENED UP A NEW STAGE OF CREATIVITY THAT, EVEN AT A SNAIL'S PACE, BROUGHT THEM TO THEIR GREATEST WORK.
MAH SWATE BLACKAH ANGEL
THERE WAS ONE LAST ATTEMPT FROM SEVEN TO MAKE THE ATOMIC SUPER SONICS WORK AS A BAND. BUT IN THOSE DAYS THE SLIGHTEST DISTRACTION EVAPORATED ANY GROUP UNITY.
C'MON, MAN, YOU GOTTA GIVE IT SOME TIME.
OPEN YOUR EYES, RED.
Something tells me my subconscious sabotages any chance for success.
HI-SCI-FI
STEREO
easy songs for beginn
ATOMIC SUPER SONICS
DROOG-TONE RECORDS
A SMALL PRESSING OF 2,000 ALBUMS USING OLD PHOTOGRAPHS OF THE ORIGINAL LINE-UP WAS ALL THAT REMAINED OF THE BAND'S LEGACY.
THAT AND A HUGE DEBT.
I'M BROKE.

AFTER SETTLING INTO REGULAR RECORDING ENGINEER WORK, SEVEN MET *MICK RONSON*, AN AMAZING GUITARIST FROM HULL, WHO WAS THRILLED WHEN HE FOUND OUT SEVEN WAS LEADER OF *THE A.S.S.*

THAT WAS *YOUR* BAND? NICE *CRUNCH!*

THANKS!

SEVEN'S EFFORTS HADN'T GONE COMPLETELY UNNOTICED.

THEY STRUCK UP A HARD-CORE FRIENDSHIP IMMEDIATELY-- LIKED ALL THE SAME THINGS. YOU KNOW HOW IT IS.

I *DIG* THAT ALBUM!

GROOVY!

Mick"Ronno"Ronson is so cool! One of the nicest & unselfish people I've met on this world.

Rolling Stones Beggar's Banquet

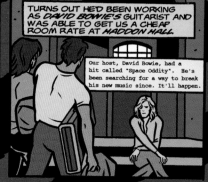

TURNS OUT HE'D BEEN WORKING AS *DAVID BOWIE'S* GUITARIST AND WAS ABLE TO GET US A CHEAP ROOM RATE AT *MADDON HALL.*

Our host, David Bowie, had a hit called "Space Oddity". He's been searching for a way to break his new music since. It'll happen.

THIS WAS AN EXOTIC TIME WHEN THE HIPPIE LIFESTYLE WAS STILL CLINGING LIKE IVY AND INCENSE.

I HEAR A CHORD IN MY HEAD, BUT *I'VE NEVER BEEN* ABLE TO *PLAY IT.*

MUSICALLY, YOU NEEDED A MAP.

I HAVE MEMORIES OF FLYING *PAST* THE MOON, ALTHOUGH I'VE NEVER *PHYSICALLY* BEEN THERE.

He seems interested in all my experiences.

IT WAS ANYBODY'S PLAY TO BE THE NEXT BIG THING.

ESTABLISHED ACTS AND ONE-HIT-WONDERS RULED THE CHARTS AS USUAL, BUT THE ROCK WORLD WAS SALIVATING FOR SOMETHING NEW.

SNIP

IT SUITS YOU.

WE DIDN'T KNOW IT AT THE TIME, BUT WE WERE AT THE *EPICENTER* OF THE NEXT INFLUENTIAL, REVOLUTIONARY, *TRENDIEST* MOVEMENT.

THIS IS THE LOOK, RONNO.

I'LL GET USED TO IT.

THE EXPLOSION OF *GLAM ROCK.*

David's music is so visual and with Ronno's guitar, it's raw with power.

He just needs to find a way to break from the pack.

NO ONE COULD DENY ITS POWER.

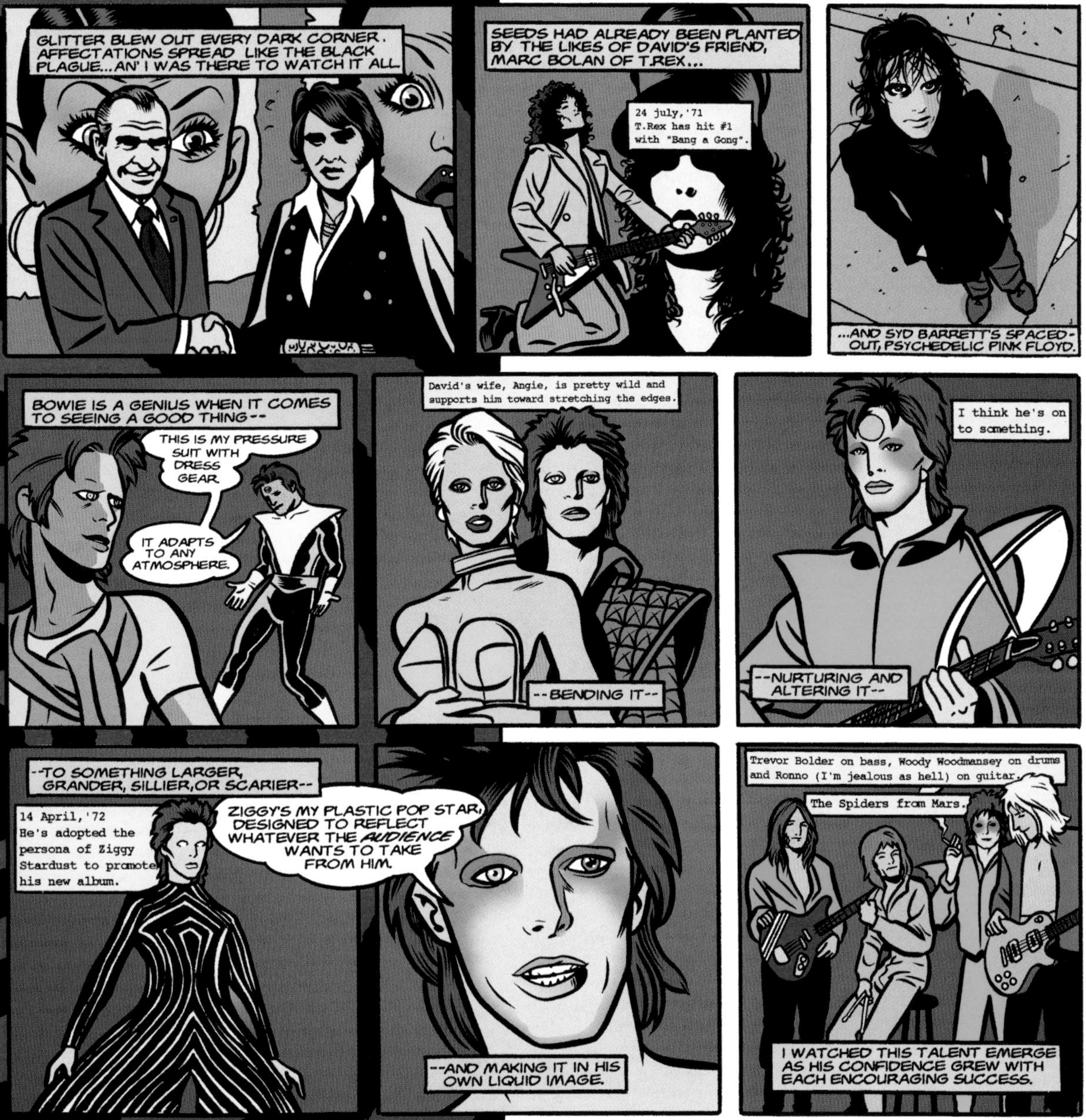
GLITTER BLEW OUT EVERY DARK CORNER. AFFECTATIONS SPREAD LIKE THE BLACK PLAGUE...AN' I WAS THERE TO WATCH IT ALL.
SEEDS HAD ALREADY BEEN PLANTED BY THE LIKES OF DAVID'S FRIEND, MARC BOLAN OF T.REX...
24 july,'71 T.Rex has hit #1 with "Bang a Gong".
...AND SYD BARRETT'S SPACED-OUT, PSYCHEDELIC PINK FLOYD.
BOWIE IS A GENIUS WHEN IT COMES TO SEEING A GOOD THING--
THIS IS MY PRESSURE SUIT WITH DRESS GEAR.
IT ADAPTS TO ANY ATMOSPHERE.
David's wife, Angie, is pretty wild and supports him toward stretching the edges.
--BENDING IT--
I think he's on to something.
--NURTURING AND ALTERING IT--
--TO SOMETHING LARGER, GRANDER, SILLIER, OR SCARIER--
14 April,'72 He's adopted the persona of Ziggy Stardust to promote his new album.
ZIGGY'S MY PLASTIC POP STAR, DESIGNED TO REFLECT WHATEVER THE *AUDIENCE* WANTS TO TAKE FROM HIM.
--AND MAKING IT IN HIS OWN LIQUID IMAGE.
Trevor Bolder on bass, Woody Woodmansey on drums and Ronno (I'm jealous as hell) on guitar.
The Spiders from Mars.
I WATCHED THIS TALENT EMERGE AS HIS CONFIDENCE GREW WITH EACH ENCOURAGING SUCCESS.

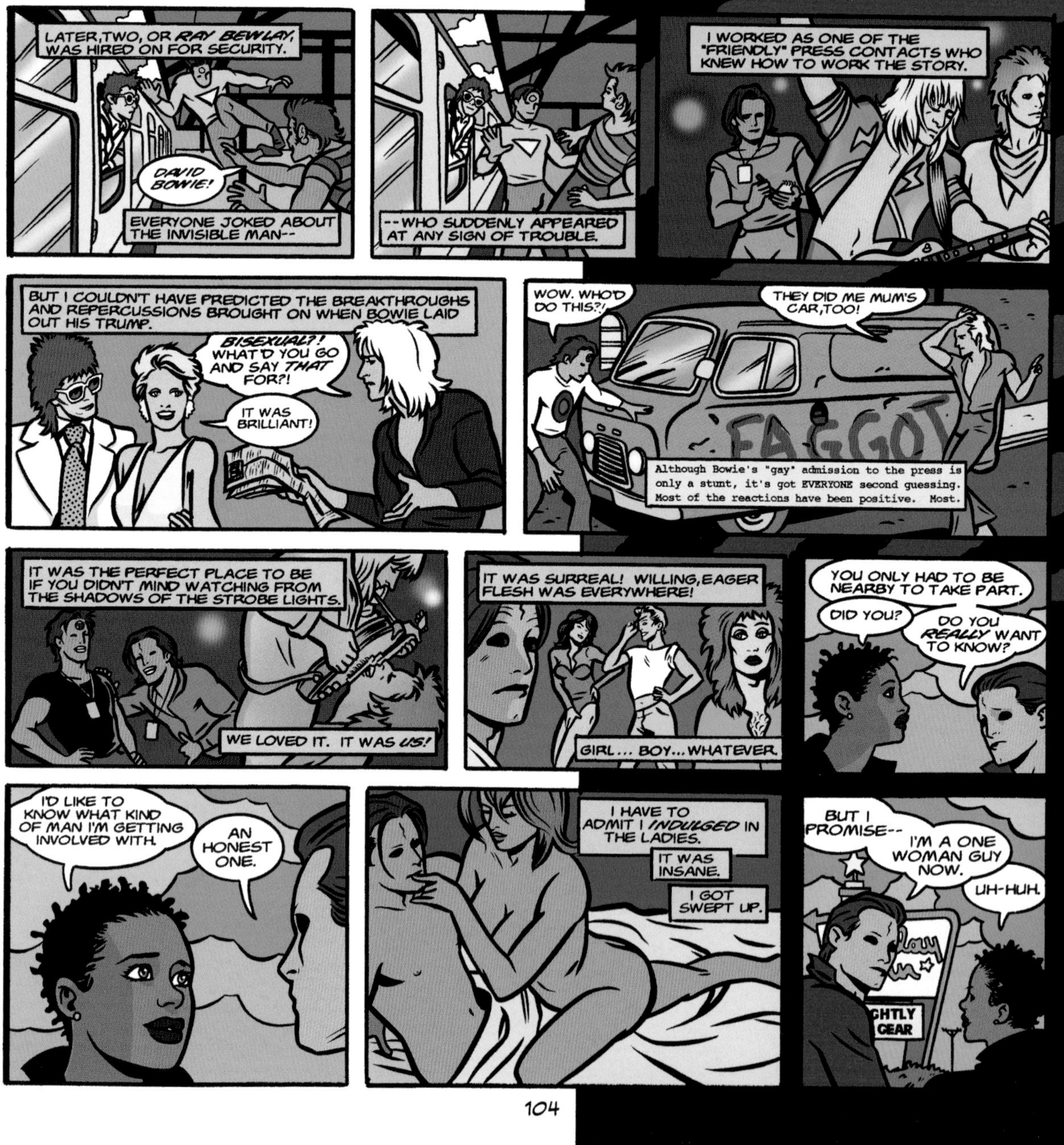
LATER, TWO, OR *RAY BEWLAY*, WAS HIRED ON FOR SECURITY.
DAVID BOWIE!
EVERYONE JOKED ABOUT THE INVISIBLE MAN--
--WHO SUDDENLY APPEARED AT ANY SIGN OF TROUBLE.
I WORKED AS ONE OF THE "FRIENDLY" PRESS CONTACTS WHO KNEW HOW TO WORK THE STORY.
BUT I COULDN'T HAVE PREDICTED THE BREAKTHROUGHS AND REPERCUSSIONS BROUGHT ON WHEN BOWIE LAID OUT HIS TRUMP.
BISEXUAL?! WHAT'D YOU GO AND SAY *THAT* FOR?!
IT WAS BRILLIANT!
WOW. WHO'D DO THIS?!
THEY DID ME MUM'S CAR, TOO!
FAGGOT
Although Bowie's "gay" admission to the press is only a stunt, it's got EVERYONE second guessing. Most of the reactions have been positive. Most.
IT WAS THE PERFECT PLACE TO BE IF YOU DIDN'T MIND WATCHING FROM THE SHADOWS OF THE STROBE LIGHTS.
WE LOVED IT. IT WAS *US!*
IT WAS SURREAL! WILLING, EAGER FLESH WAS EVERYWHERE!
GIRL... BOY... WHATEVER.
YOU ONLY HAD TO BE NEARBY TO TAKE PART.
DID YOU?
DO YOU *REALLY* WANT TO KNOW?
I'D LIKE TO KNOW WHAT KIND OF MAN I'M GETTING INVOLVED WITH.
AN HONEST ONE.
I HAVE TO ADMIT I *INDULGED* IN THE LADIES.
IT WAS INSANE.
I GOT SWEPT UP.
BUT I PROMISE--
I'M A ONE WOMAN GUY NOW.
UH-HUH.

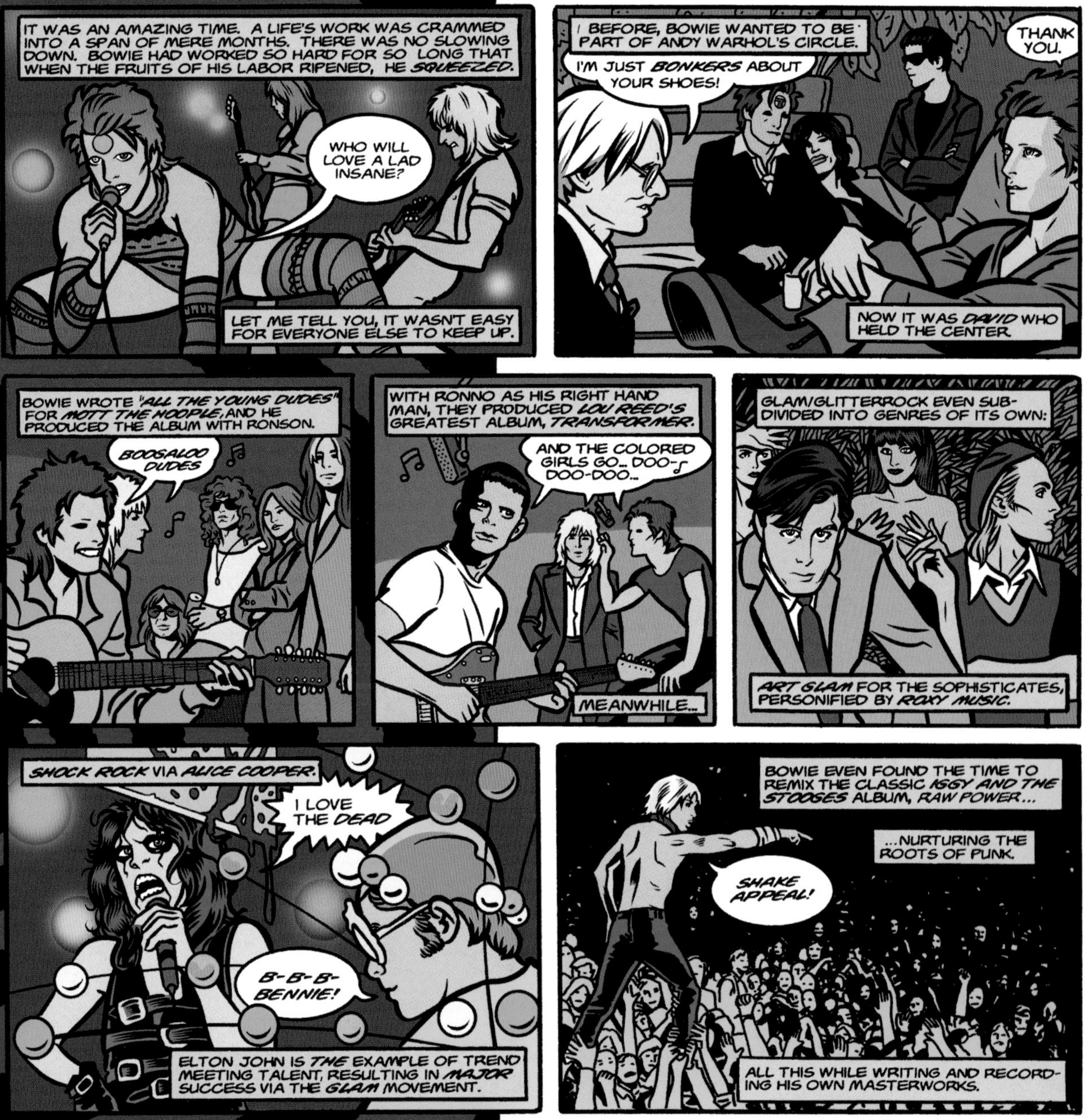
IT WAS AN AMAZING TIME. A LIFE'S WORK WAS CRAMMED INTO A SPAN OF MERE MONTHS. THERE WAS NO SLOWING DOWN. BOWIE HAD WORKED SO HARD FOR SO LONG THAT WHEN THE FRUITS OF HIS LABOR RIPENED, HE SQUEEZED.
WHO WILL LOVE A LAD INSANE?
LET ME TELL YOU, IT WASN'T EASY FOR EVERYONE ELSE TO KEEP UP.
BEFORE, BOWIE WANTED TO BE PART OF ANDY WARHOL'S CIRCLE.
I'M JUST BONKERS ABOUT YOUR SHOES!
THANK YOU.
NOW IT WAS DAVID WHO HELD THE CENTER.
BOWIE WROTE "ALL THE YOUNG DUDES" FOR MOTT THE HOOPLE, AND HE PRODUCED THE ALBUM WITH RONSON.
BOOGALOO DUDES
WITH RONNO AS HIS RIGHT HAND MAN, THEY PRODUCED LOU REED'S GREATEST ALBUM, TRANSFORMER.
AND THE COLORED GIRLS GO... DOO-DOO-DOO-DOO...
MEANWHILE...
GLAM/GLITTERROCK EVEN SUB-DIVIDED INTO GENRES OF ITS OWN:
ART GLAM FOR THE SOPHISTICATES, PERSONIFIED BY ROXY MUSIC.
SHOCK ROCK VIA ALICE COOPER.
I LOVE THE DEAD
B-B-B-BENNIE!
ELTON JOHN IS THE EXAMPLE OF TREND MEETING TALENT, RESULTING IN MAJOR SUCCESS VIA THE GLAM MOVEMENT.
BOWIE EVEN FOUND THE TIME TO REMIX THE CLASSIC IGGY AND THE STOOGES ALBUM, RAW POWER...
...NURTURING THE ROOTS OF PUNK.
SHAKE APPEAL!
ALL THIS WHILE WRITING AND RECORDING HIS OWN MASTERWORKS.

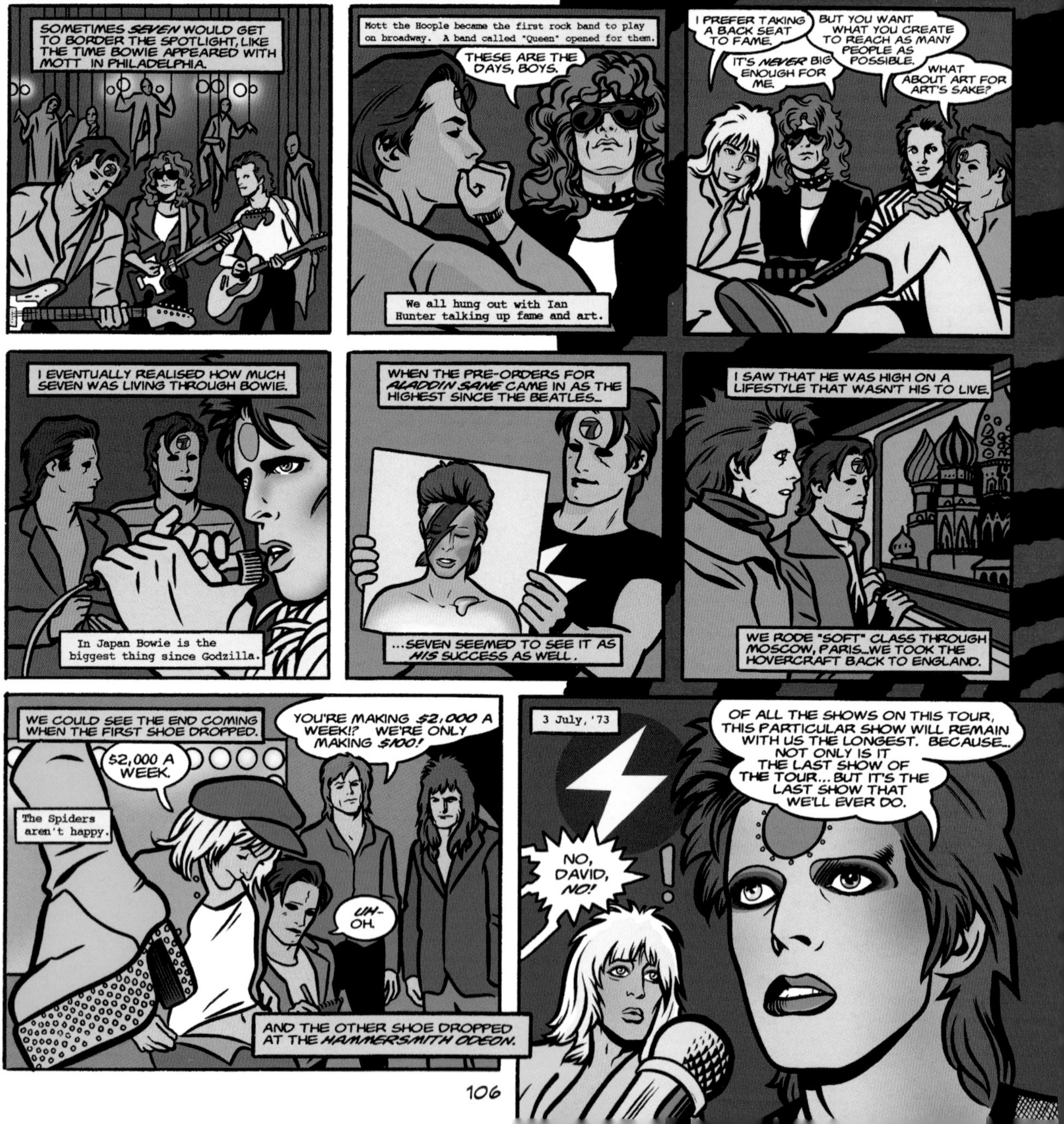
SOMETIMES SEVEN WOULD GET TO BORDER THE SPOTLIGHT, LIKE THE TIME BOWIE APPEARED WITH MOTT IN PHILADELPHIA.
Mott the Hoople became the first rock band to play on broadway. A band called "Queen" opened for them.
THESE ARE THE DAYS, BOYS.
We all hung out with Ian Hunter talking up fame and art.
I PREFER TAKING A BACK SEAT TO FAME.
IT'S NEVER BIG ENOUGH FOR ME.
BUT YOU WANT WHAT YOU CREATE TO REACH AS MANY PEOPLE AS POSSIBLE.
WHAT ABOUT ART FOR ART'S SAKE?
I EVENTUALLY REALISED HOW MUCH SEVEN WAS LIVING THROUGH BOWIE.
In Japan Bowie is the biggest thing since Godzilla.
WHEN THE PRE-ORDERS FOR ALADDIN SANE CAME IN AS THE HIGHEST SINCE THE BEATLES...
...SEVEN SEEMED TO SEE IT AS HIS SUCCESS AS WELL.
I SAW THAT HE WAS HIGH ON A LIFESTYLE THAT WASN'T HIS TO LIVE.
WE RODE "SOFT" CLASS THROUGH MOSCOW, PARIS...WE TOOK THE HOVERCRAFT BACK TO ENGLAND.
WE COULD SEE THE END COMING WHEN THE FIRST SHOE DROPPED.
$2,000 A WEEK.
YOU'RE MAKING $2,000 A WEEK!? WE'RE ONLY MAKING $100!
The Spiders aren't happy.
UH-OH.
AND THE OTHER SHOE DROPPED AT THE HAMMERSMITH ODEON.
3 July, '73
OF ALL THE SHOWS ON THIS TOUR, THIS PARTICULAR SHOW WILL REMAIN WITH US THE LONGEST. BECAUSE... NOT ONLY IS IT THE LAST SHOW OF THE TOUR... BUT IT'S THE LAST SHOW THAT WE'LL EVER DO.
NO, DAVID, NO!
!

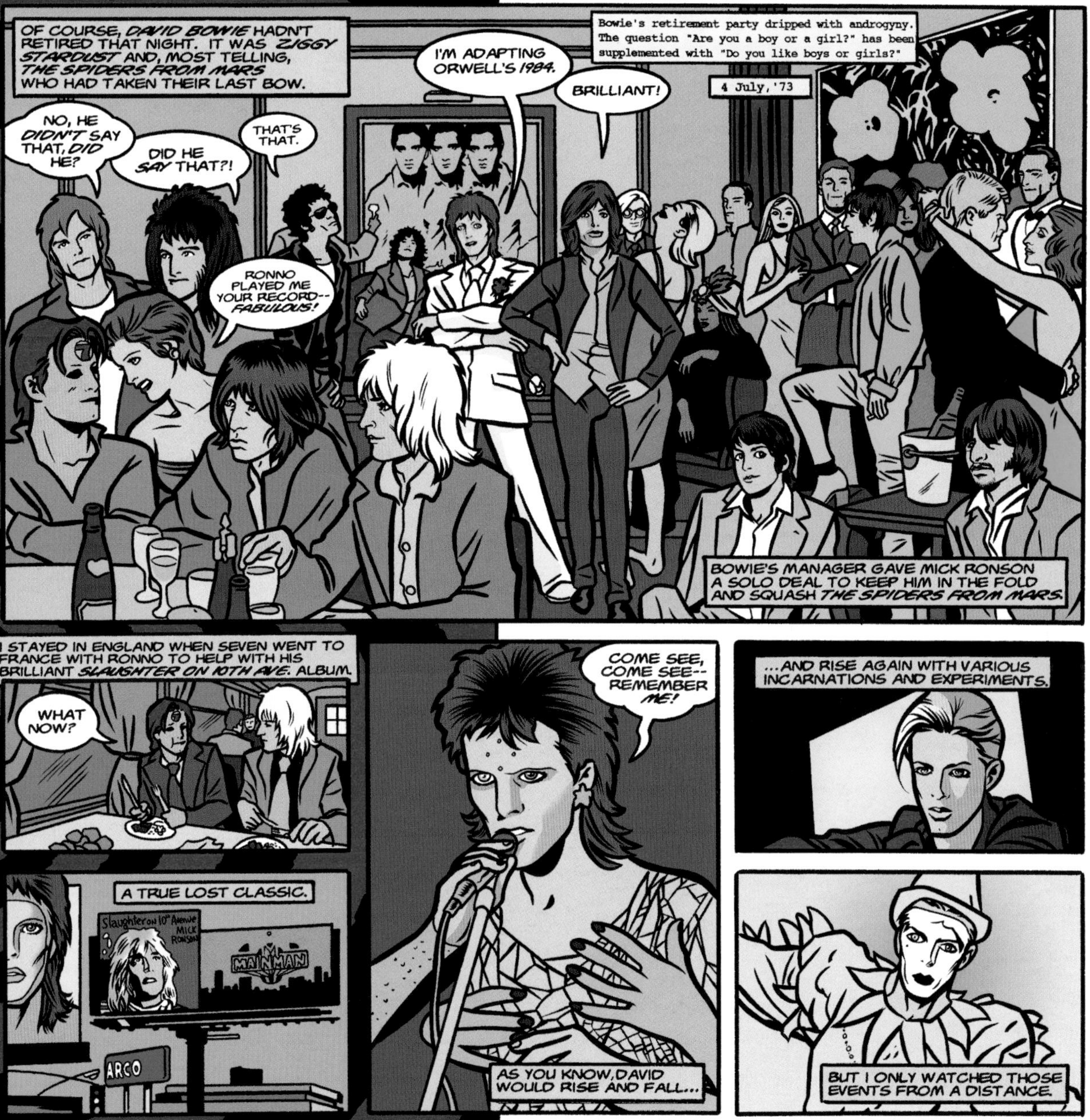
OF COURSE, *DAVID BOWIE* HADN'T RETIRED THAT NIGHT. IT WAS *ZIGGY STARDUST* AND, MOST TELLING, *THE SPIDERS FROM MARS* WHO HAD TAKEN THEIR LAST BOW.
I'M ADAPTING ORWELL'S *1984*.
Bowie's retirement party dripped with androgyny. The question "Are you a boy or a girl?" has been supplemented with "Do you like boys or girls?"
BRILLIANT!
4 July, '73
NO, HE *DIDN'T* SAY THAT, *DID* HE?
DID HE *SAY* THAT?!
THAT'S THAT.
RONNO PLAYED ME YOUR RECORD-- *FABULOUS!*
BOWIE'S MANAGER GAVE MICK RONSON A SOLO DEAL TO KEEP HIM IN THE FOLD AND SQUASH *THE SPIDERS FROM MARS*.
I STAYED IN ENGLAND WHEN SEVEN WENT TO FRANCE WITH RONNO TO HELP WITH HIS BRILLIANT *SLAUGHTER ON 10TH AVE.* ALBUM.
WHAT NOW?
A TRUE LOST CLASSIC.
Slaughter on 10th Avenue
MICK RONSON
MAINMAN
ARCO
COME SEE, COME SEE-- REMEMBER *ME!*
AS YOU KNOW, DAVID WOULD RISE AND FALL...
...AND RISE AGAIN WITH VARIOUS INCARNATIONS AND EXPERIMENTS.
BUT I ONLY WATCHED THOSE EVENTS FROM A DISTANCE.

WE WERE FINALLY REUNITED WHEN WE WERE HIRED AS TECHNICAL ADVISORS ON BOWIE'S FIRST FEATURE.

24 July, '75

MAN WHO FELL TO EARTH
roll 7 scene 3 take 1 MOS
director N. ROEG
cinematographer ANTHONY RICHMOND sound B. GREGORY
24

We're on location in New Mexico. I got Marnie a job helping with make-up and costumes. We still go see movies together.

SO, HOW LONG HAVE YOU KNOWN RED? ARE YOU AN ITEM?

I WISH. I'VE HAD A THING FOR HIM FOREVER

SOMEDAY.

I'LL SAY IT AGAIN... I *LOVE* YOU. DO *YOU* LOVE ME?

M-M-M-MARNIE, I...

I GOTTA GET SOME POPCORN! DO YOU WANT SOME?

NO!

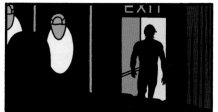

EXIT

ZAP

ORANGE R

RED?!

⟨THIS IS THE LAST OF THEM.⟩

⟨ARE YOU SURE?⟩

⟨I'VE BEEN GATHERING DATA FOR OVER TWENTY EARTH YEARS. I'M SURE.⟩

NEXT: **BETTER TO BURN OUT**

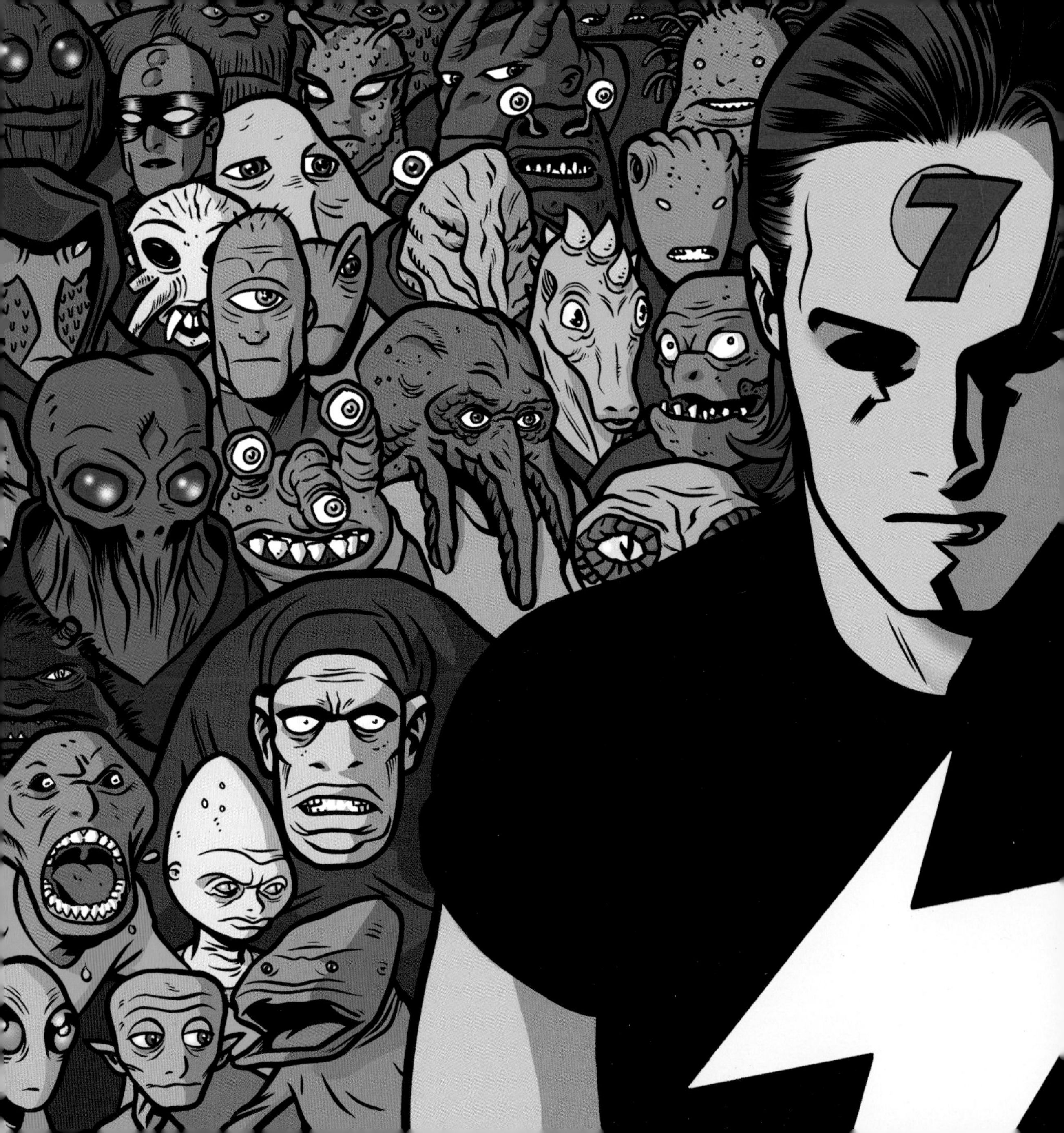

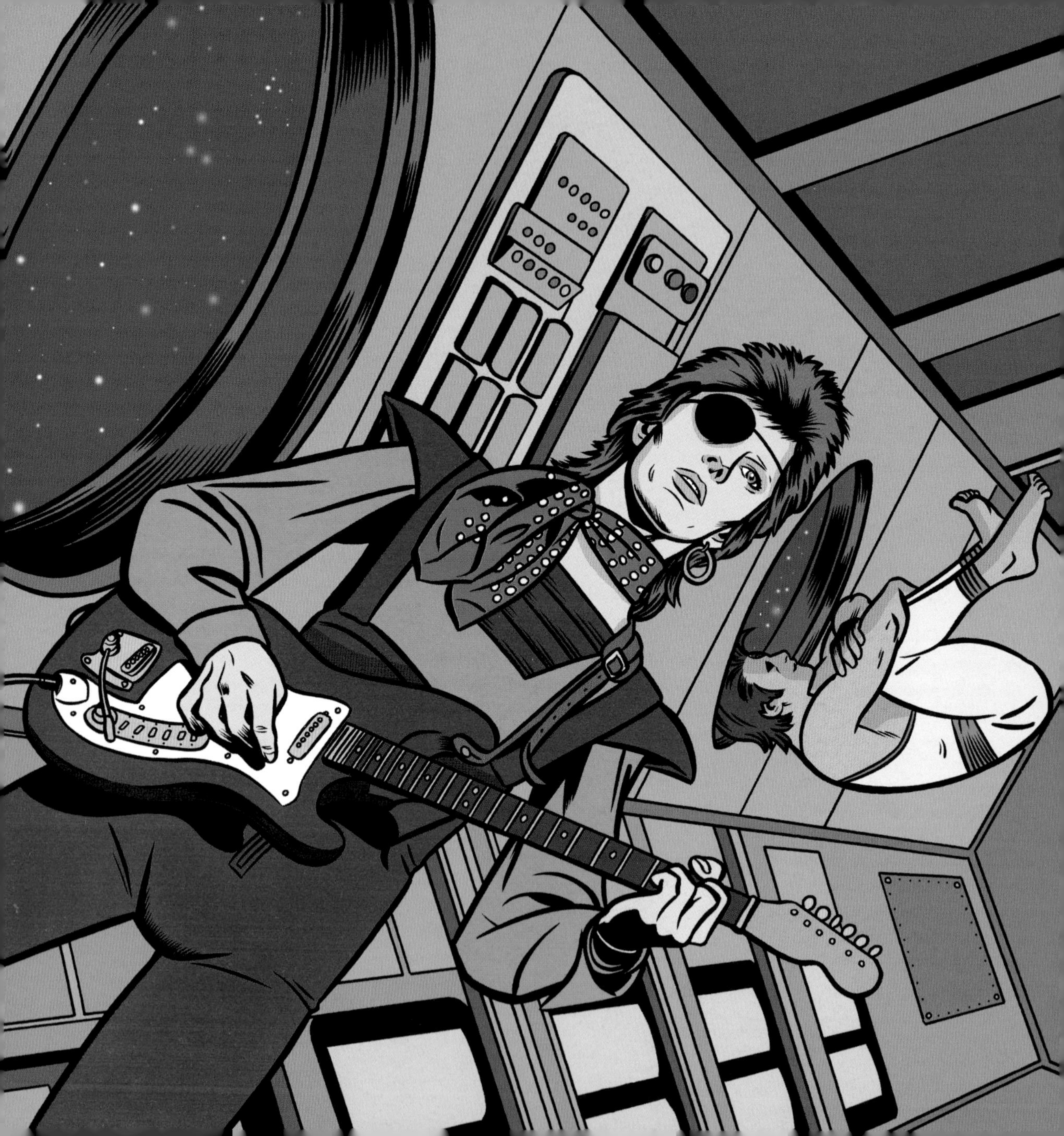

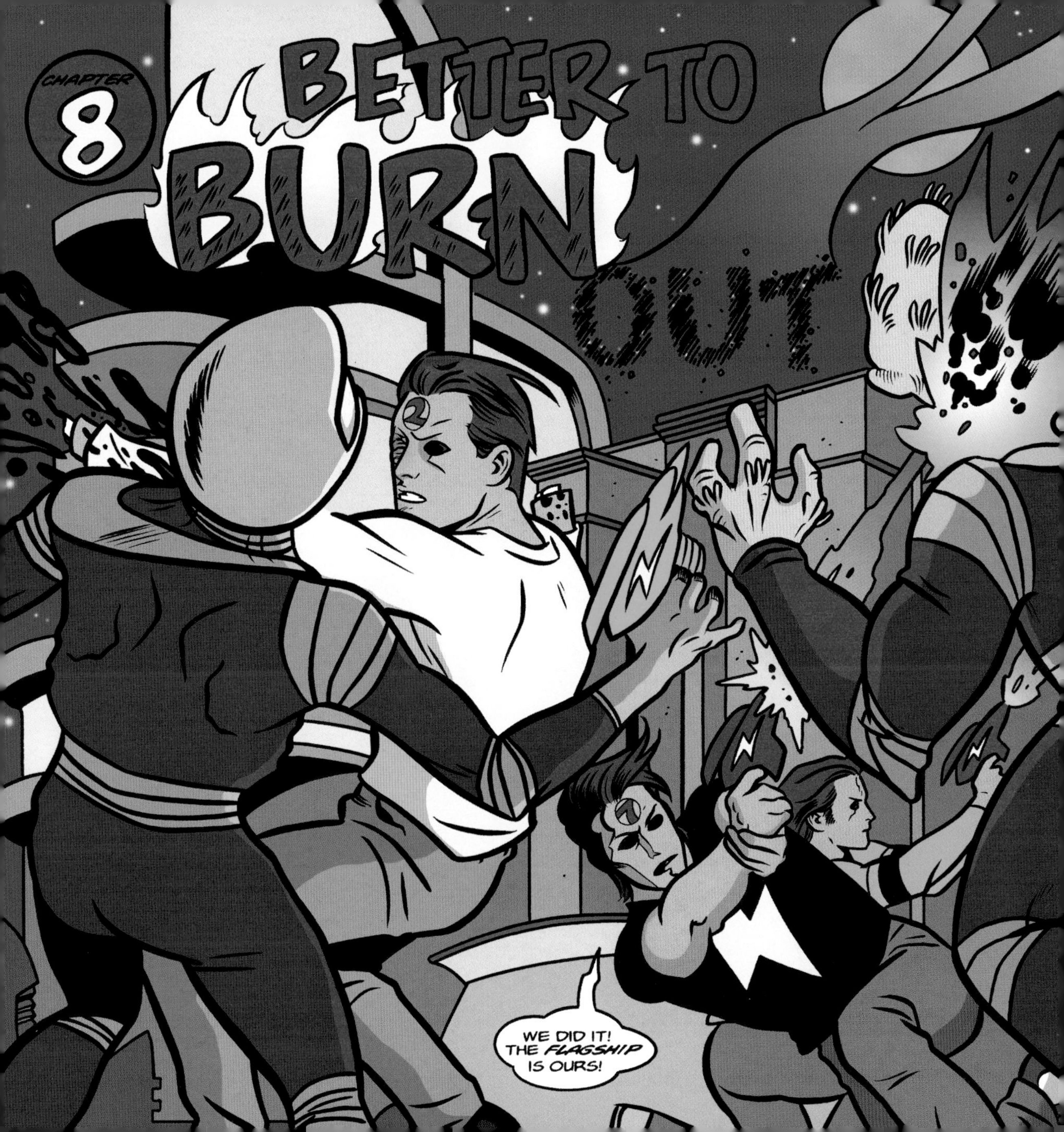
CHAPTER
8
BETTER TO
BURN
OUT
WE DID IT! THE FLAGSHIP IS OURS!

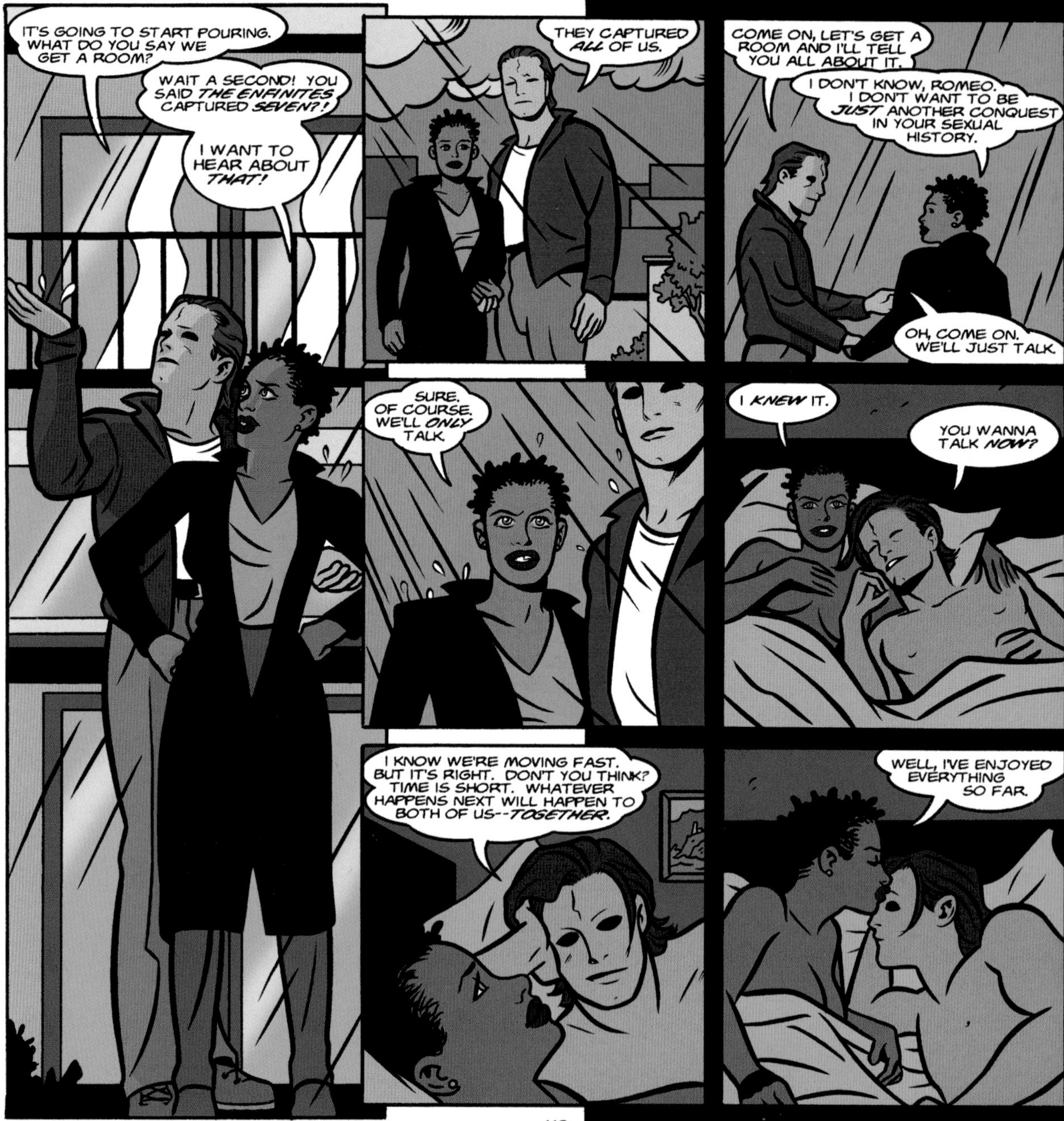
IT'S GOING TO START POURING. WHAT DO YOU SAY WE GET A ROOM?
WAIT A SECOND! YOU SAID *THE ENFINITES* CAPTURED *SEVEN?!*
I WANT TO HEAR ABOUT *THAT!*
THEY CAPTURED *ALL* OF US.
COME ON, LET'S GET A ROOM AND I'LL TELL YOU ALL ABOUT IT.
I DON'T KNOW, ROMEO. I DON'T WANT TO BE *JUST* ANOTHER CONQUEST IN YOUR SEXUAL HISTORY.
OH, COME ON. WE'LL JUST TALK.
SURE. OF COURSE. WE'LL *ONLY* TALK.
I *KNEW* IT.
YOU WANNA TALK *NOW?*
I KNOW WE'RE MOVING FAST. BUT IT'S RIGHT. DON'T YOU THINK? TIME IS SHORT. WHATEVER HAPPENS NEXT WILL HAPPEN TO BOTH OF US--*TOGETHER.*
WELL, I'VE ENJOYED EVERYTHING SO FAR.

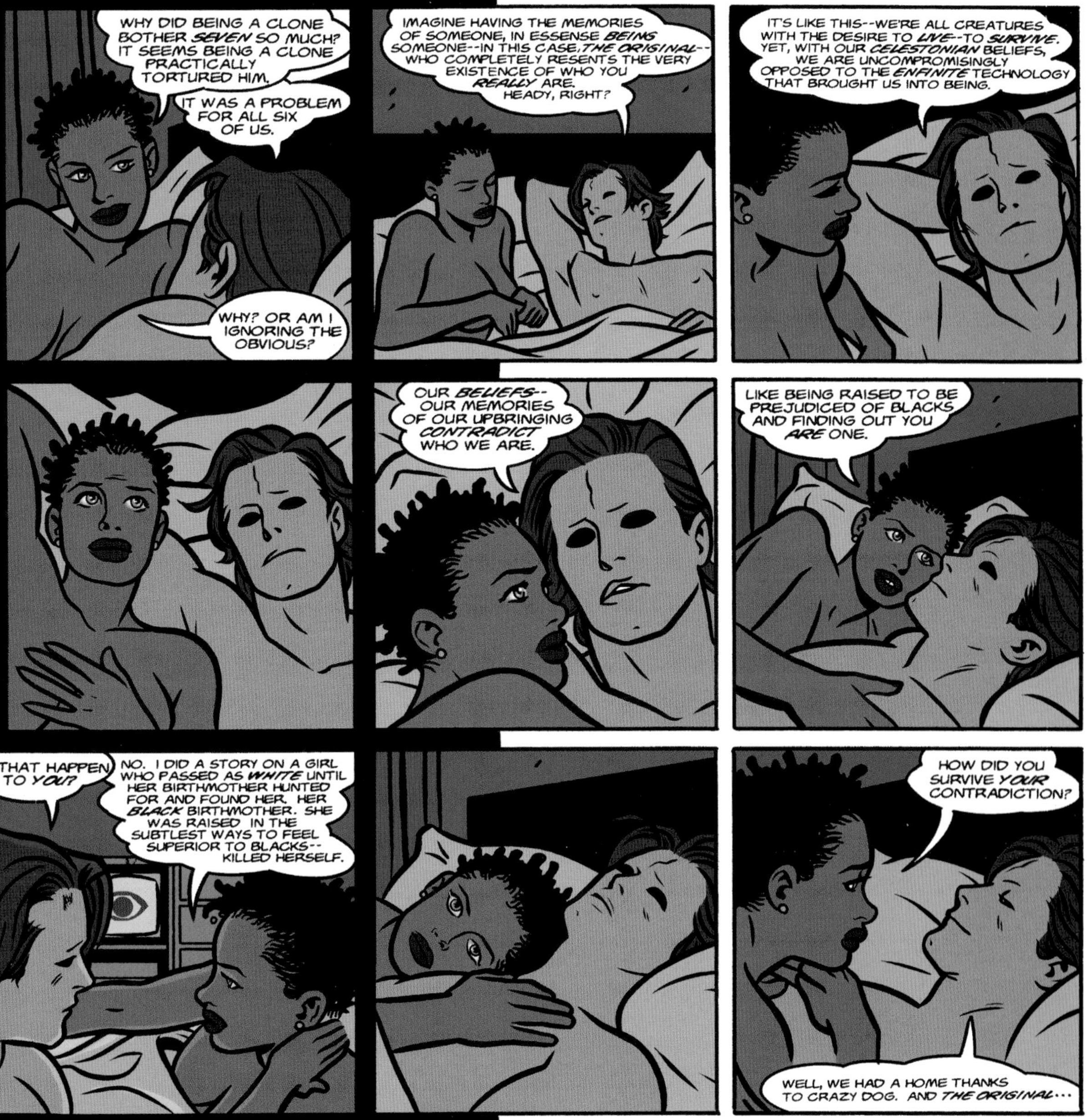
WHY DID BEING A CLONE BOTHER SEVEN SO MUCH? IT SEEMS BEING A CLONE PRACTICALLY TORTURED HIM.
IT WAS A PROBLEM FOR ALL SIX OF US.
WHY? OR AM I IGNORING THE OBVIOUS?
IMAGINE HAVING THE MEMORIES OF SOMEONE, IN ESSENSE BEING SOMEONE--IN THIS CASE, THE ORIGINAL--WHO COMPLETELY RESENTS THE VERY EXISTENCE OF WHO YOU REALLY ARE. HEADY, RIGHT?
IT'S LIKE THIS--WE'RE ALL CREATURES WITH THE DESIRE TO LIVE--TO SURVIVE. YET, WITH OUR CELESTONIAN BELIEFS, WE ARE UNCOMPROMISINGLY OPPOSED TO THE ENFINITE TECHNOLOGY THAT BROUGHT US INTO BEING.
OUR BELIEFS--OUR MEMORIES OF OUR UPBRINGING CONTRADICT WHO WE ARE.
LIKE BEING RAISED TO BE PREJUDICED OF BLACKS AND FINDING OUT YOU ARE ONE.
THAT HAPPEN TO YOU?
NO. I DID A STORY ON A GIRL WHO PASSED AS WHITE UNTIL HER BIRTHMOTHER HUNTED FOR AND FOUND HER. HER BLACK BIRTHMOTHER. SHE WAS RAISED IN THE SUBTLEST WAYS TO FEEL SUPERIOR TO BLACKS--KILLED HERSELF.
HOW DID YOU SURVIVE YOUR CONTRADICTION?
WELL, WE HAD A HOME THANKS TO CRAZY DOG. AND THE ORIGINAL...

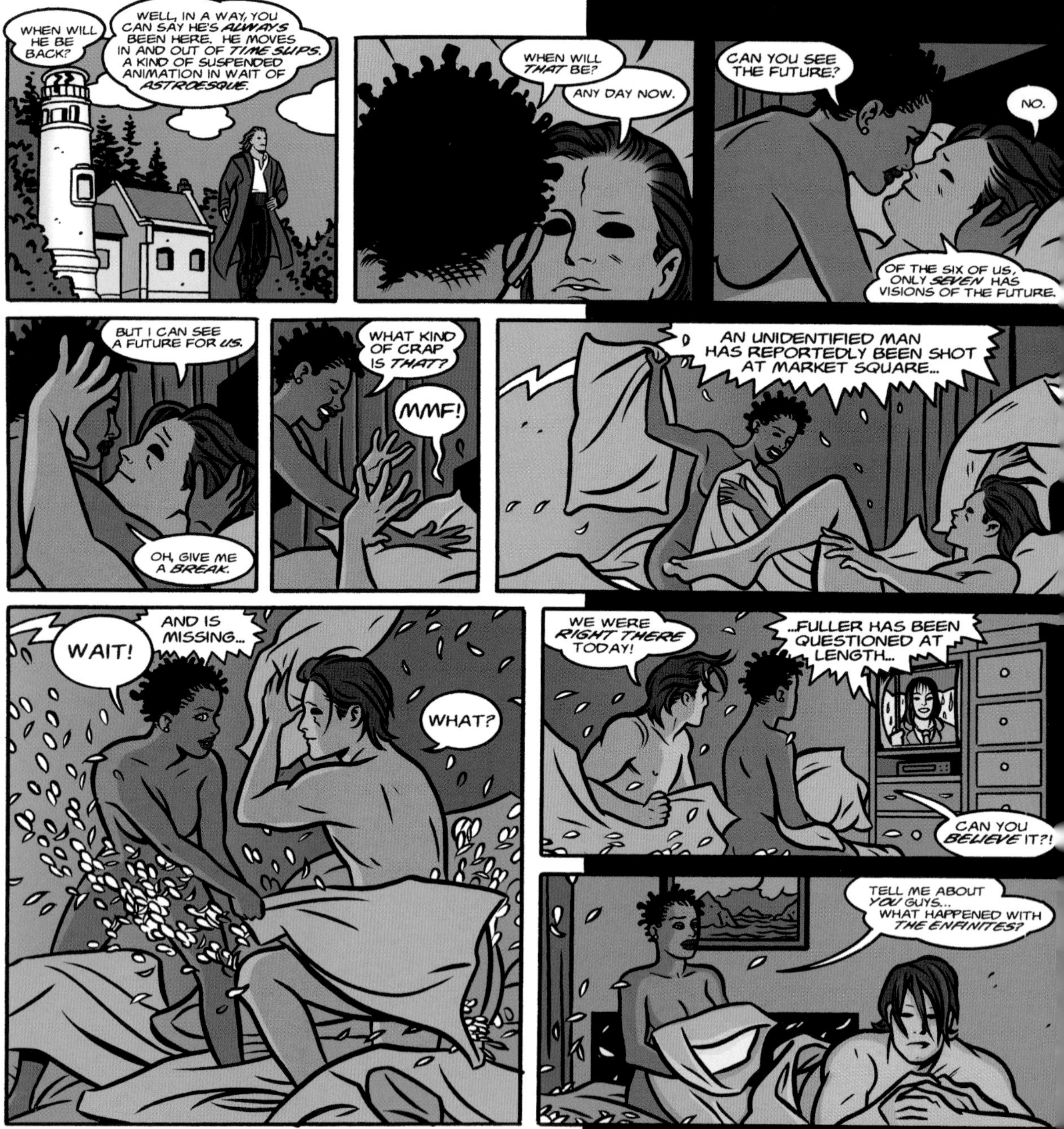
WHEN WILL HE BE BACK?
WELL, IN A WAY, YOU CAN SAY HE'S ALWAYS BEEN HERE. HE MOVES IN AND OUT OF TIME SLIPS. A KIND OF SUSPENDED ANIMATION IN WAIT OF ASTROESQUE.
WHEN WILL THAT BE?
ANY DAY NOW.
CAN YOU SEE THE FUTURE?
NO.
OF THE SIX OF US, ONLY SEVEN HAS VISIONS OF THE FUTURE.
BUT I CAN SEE A FUTURE FOR US.
OH, GIVE ME A BREAK.
WHAT KIND OF CRAP IS THAT?
MMF!
AN UNIDENTIFIED MAN HAS REPORTEDLY BEEN SHOT AT MARKET SQUARE...
AND IS MISSING...
WAIT!
WHAT?
WE WERE RIGHT THERE TODAY!
...FULLER HAS BEEN QUESTIONED AT LENGTH...
CAN YOU BELIEVE IT?!
TELL ME ABOUT YOU GUYS... WHAT HAPPENED WITH THE ENFINITES?

THEY'D FOLLOWED *THE ORIGINAL'S* COURSE TO EARTH. THEY'D RECOGNIZED THE *EXPLOSION* OF TECHNOLOGY BROUGHT ABOUT BY THREE, FOUR, AND SIX AND DISCOVERED THEIR EXISTENCE.

KNOWING THEY WERE *CLONES* OF THE *ORIGINAL*, THEY PATIENTLY WAITED FOR SOME DISCLOSURE OF HIS WHEREABOUTS.

BUT SEVEN'S LETTERS SUGGESTED *THE ENFINITES* HAD BEEN ON EARTH SINCE *THE FIFTIES*. WHY'D IT TAKE THEM 'TIL *1975* TO CAPTURE YOU?

THEIR ONLY DIRECTIVE WAS TO *RECAPTURE* THE *ORIGINAL*. UNTIL THEY COULD LOCATE HIM, THEIR ONLY LINK TO HIM WAS US.

DL RECORDS

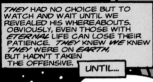

THEY HAD NO CHOICE BUT TO WATCH AND WAIT UNTIL WE REVEALED HIS WHEREABOUTS. OBVIOUSLY, EVEN THOSE WITH *ETERNAL* LIFE CAN LOSE THEIR PATIENCE. *THEY* KNEW *WE* KNEW *THEY* WERE ON *EARTH*, BUT HADN'T TAKEN THE OFFENSIVE.

UNTIL...

WE'LL DETAIN THE CLONES FOR INTERROGATION AS ORDERED.

TAKE THEM TO THE *LUXURY FACILITY* ON *BERUM 12.* WE WILL SEE IF *FRIENDLY COAXING* CAN RESULT IN OBTAINING THE INFORMATION WE DESIRE.

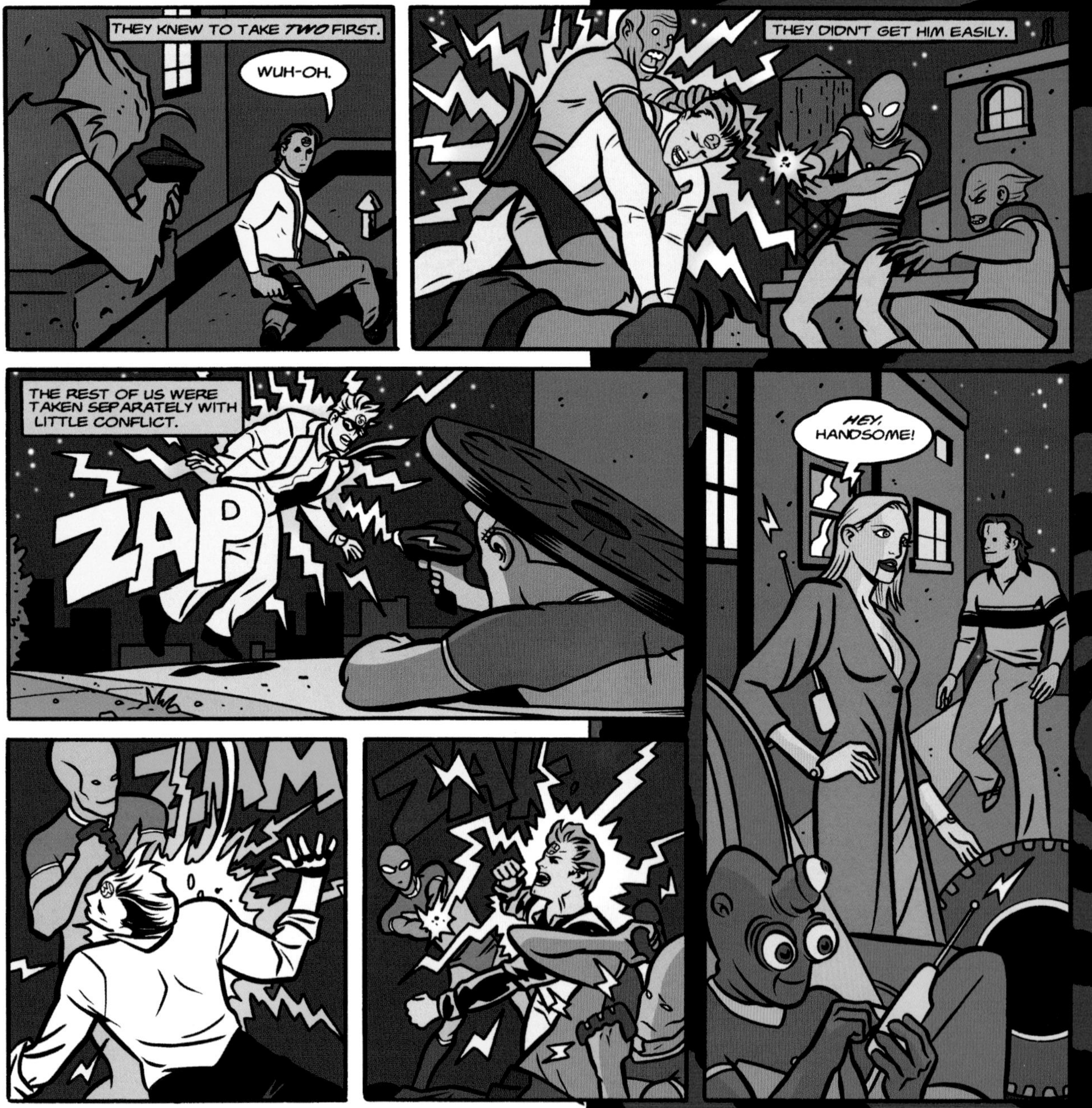
THEY KNEW TO TAKE TWO FIRST.
WUH-OH.
THEY DIDN'T GET HIM EASILY.
THE REST OF US WERE TAKEN SEPARATELY WITH LITTLE CONFLICT.
ZAP
HEY, HANDSOME!

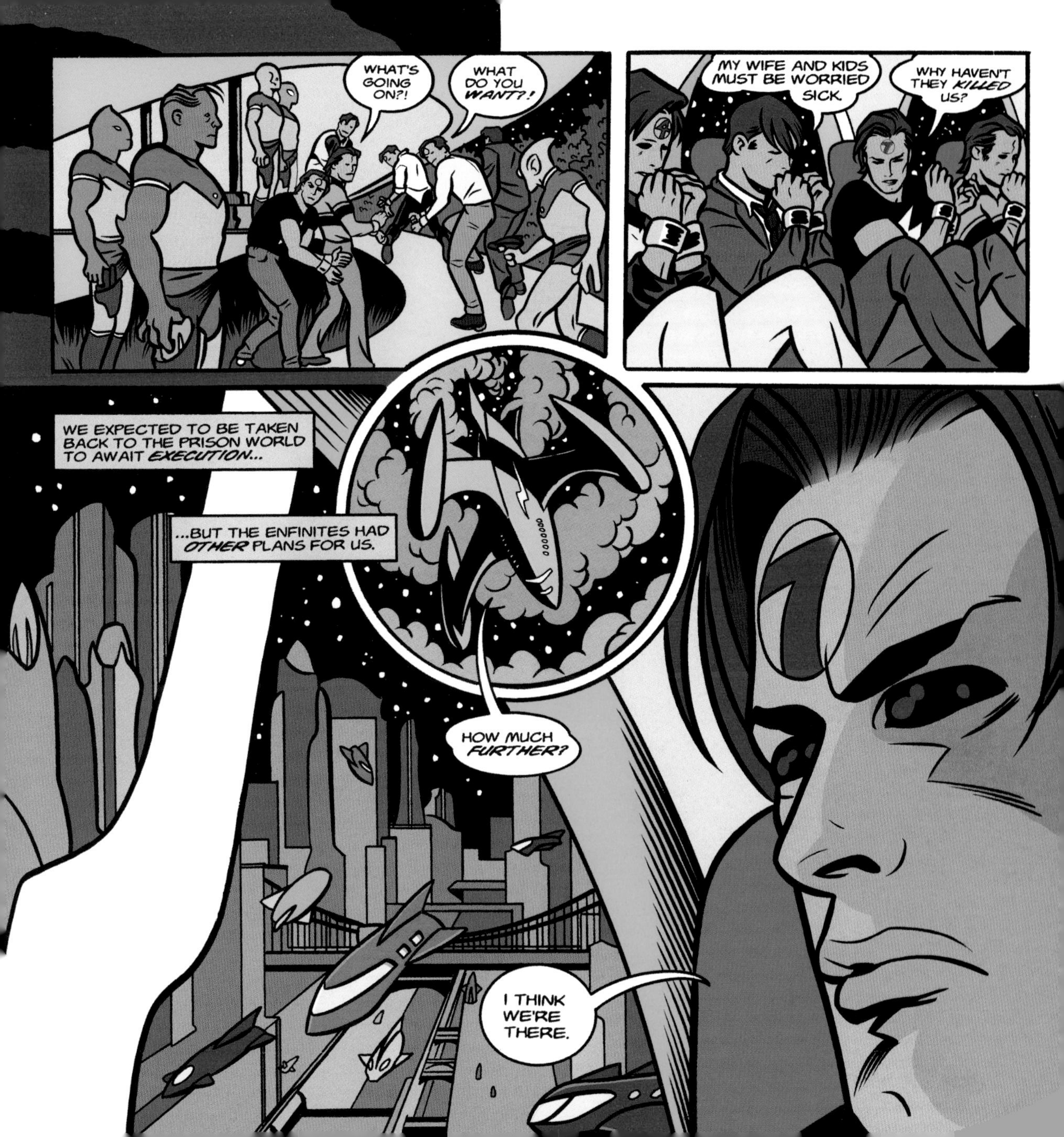
WHAT'S GOING ON?!
WHAT DO YOU WANT?!
MY WIFE AND KIDS MUST BE WORRIED SICK.
WHY HAVEN'T THEY KILLED US?
WE EXPECTED TO BE TAKEN BACK TO THE PRISON WORLD TO AWAIT EXECUTION...
...BUT THE ENFINITES HAD OTHER PLANS FOR US.
HOW MUCH FURTHER?
I THINK WE'RE THERE.

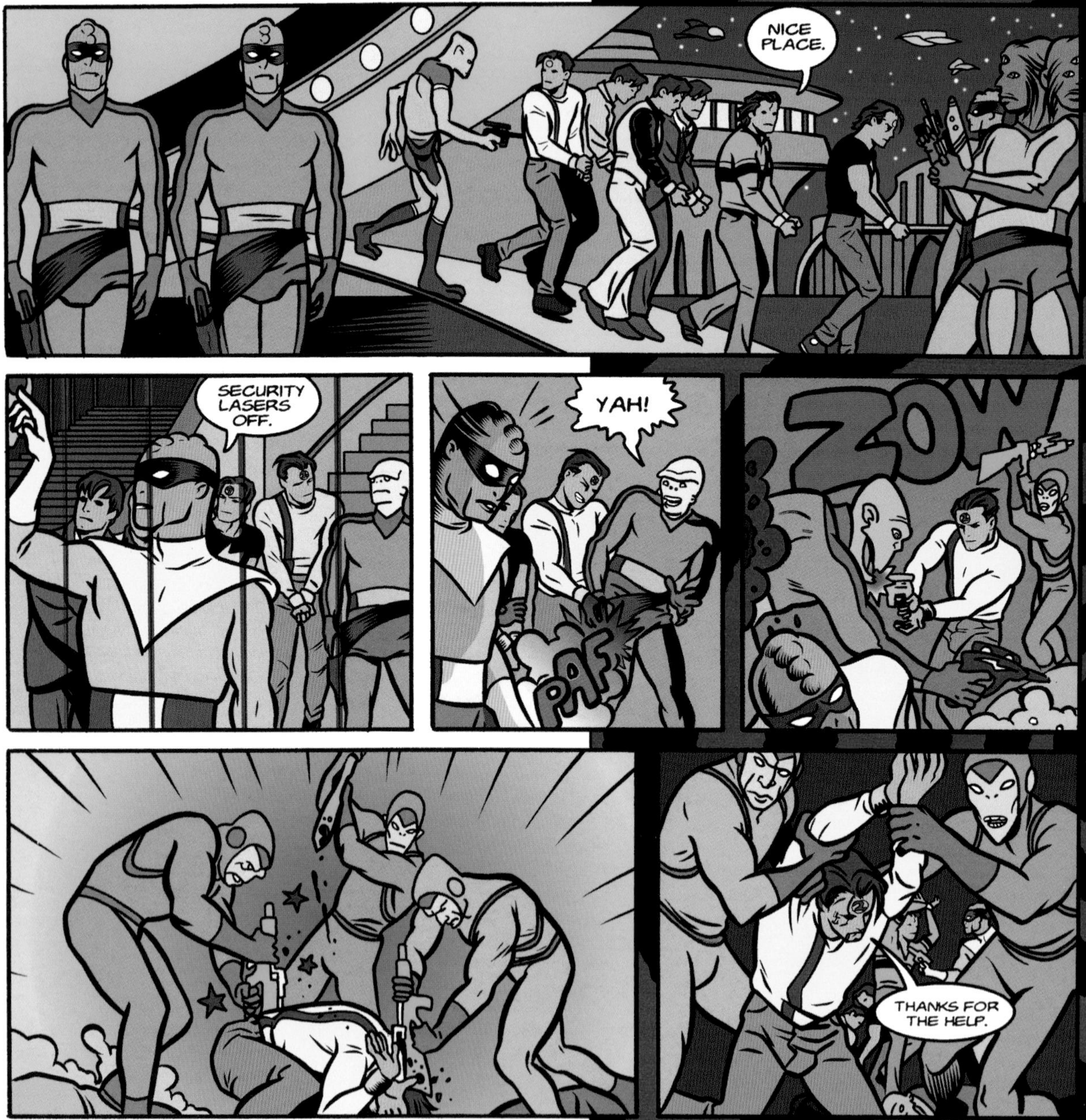
NICE PLACE.
SECURITY LASERS OFF.
YAH!
PAF
ZOW
THANKS FOR THE HELP.

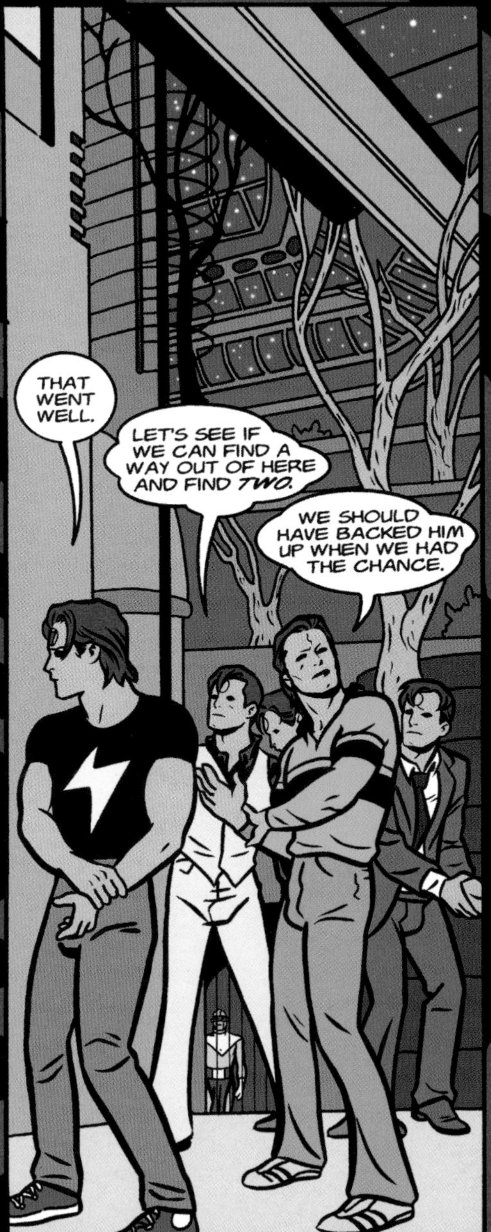
THAT WENT WELL.
LET'S SEE IF WE CAN FIND A WAY OUT OF HERE AND FIND *TWO.*
WE SHOULD HAVE BACKED HIM UP WHEN WE HAD THE CHANCE.

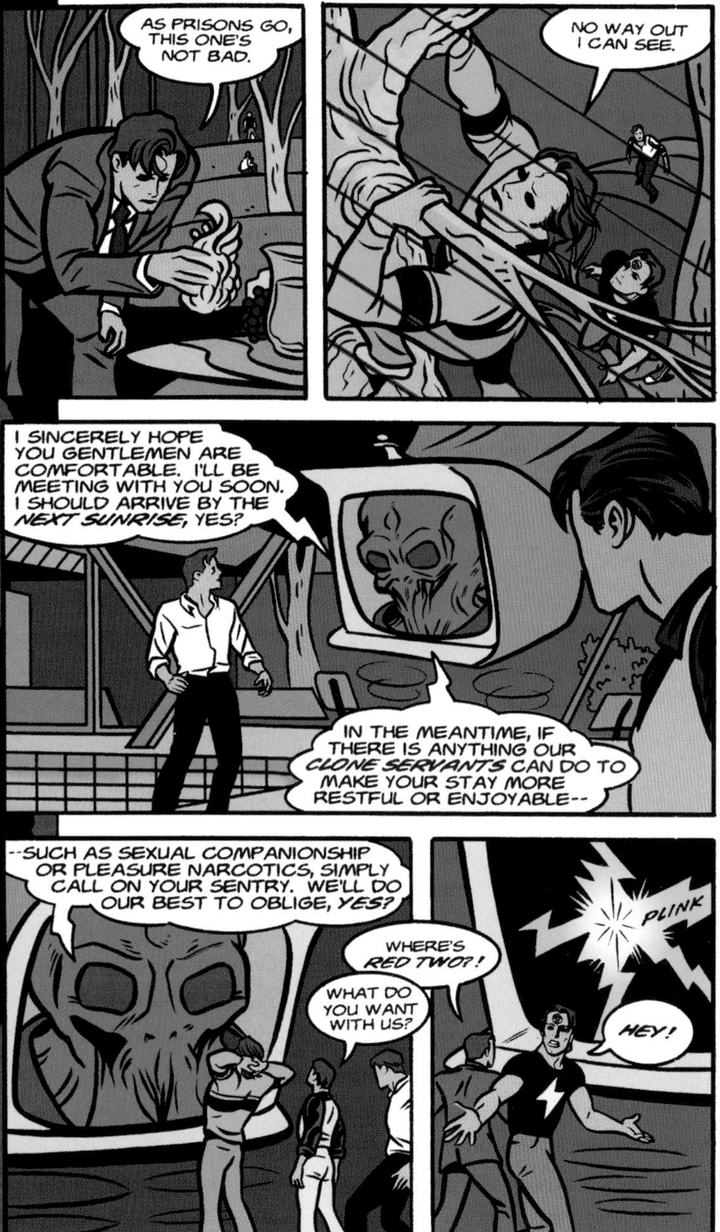
AS PRISONS GO, THIS ONE'S NOT BAD.
NO WAY OUT I CAN SEE.
I SINCERELY HOPE YOU GENTLEMEN ARE COMFORTABLE. I'LL BE MEETING WITH YOU SOON. I SHOULD ARRIVE BY THE *NEXT SUNRISE,* YES?
IN THE MEANTIME, IF THERE IS ANYTHING OUR *CLONE SERVANTS* CAN DO TO MAKE YOUR STAY MORE RESTFUL OR ENJOYABLE--
--SUCH AS SEXUAL COMPANIONSHIP OR PLEASURE NARCOTICS, SIMPLY CALL ON YOUR SENTRY. WE'LL DO OUR BEST TO OBLIGE, *YES?*
WHERE'S *RED TWO?!*
WHAT DO YOU WANT WITH US?
PLINK
HEY!

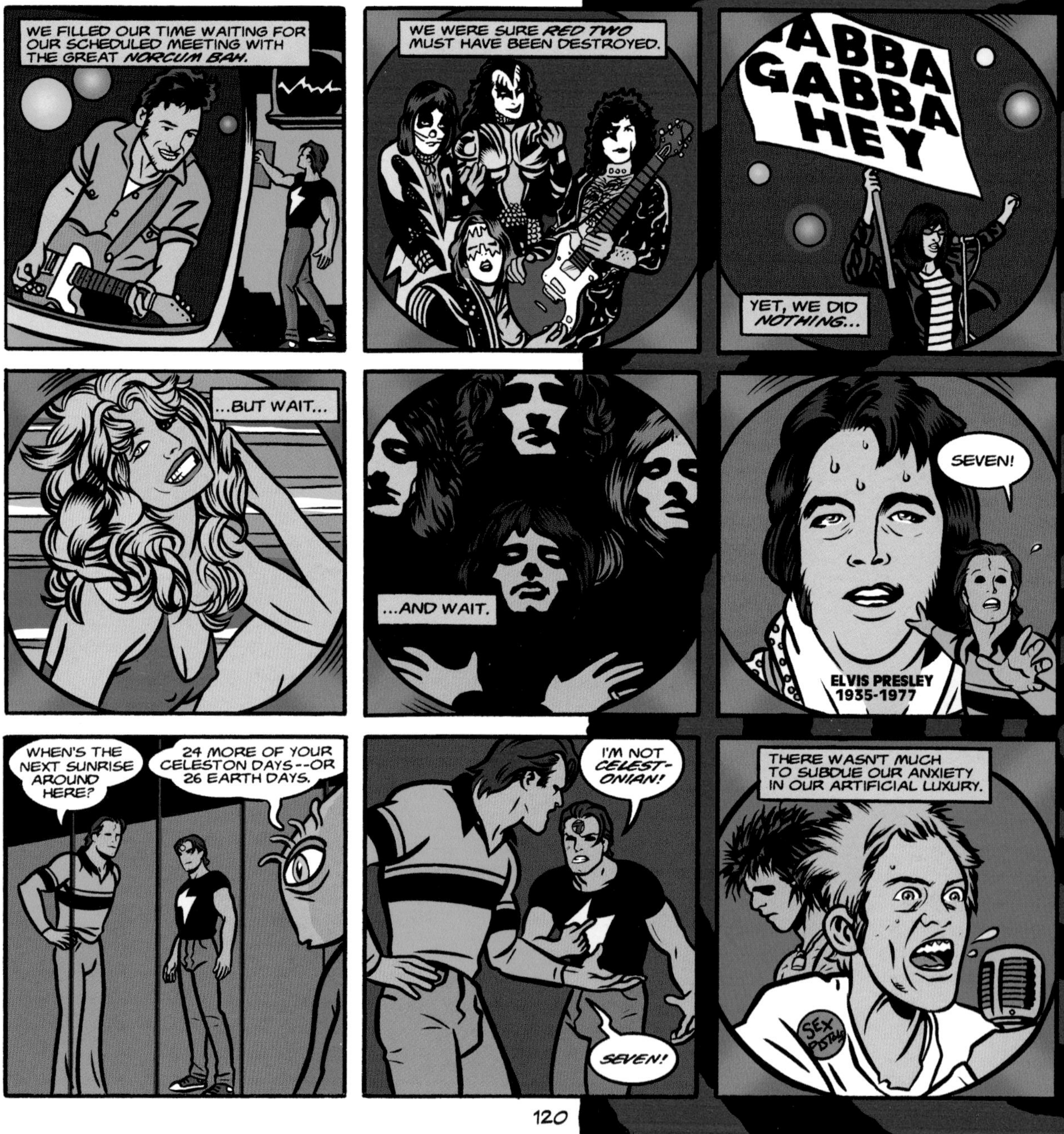
WE FILLED OUR TIME WAITING FOR OUR SCHEDULED MEETING WITH THE GREAT NORCUM BAH.
WE WERE SURE RED TWO MUST HAVE BEEN DESTROYED.
GABBA GABBA HEY
YET, WE DID NOTHING...
...BUT WAIT...
...AND WAIT.
SEVEN!
ELVIS PRESLEY 1935-1977
WHEN'S THE NEXT SUNRISE AROUND HERE?
24 MORE OF YOUR CELESTON DAYS--OR 26 EARTH DAYS.
I'M NOT CELESTONIAN!
SEVEN!
THERE WASN'T MUCH TO SUBDUE OUR ANXIETY IN OUR ARTIFICIAL LUXURY.
SEX PISTOLS

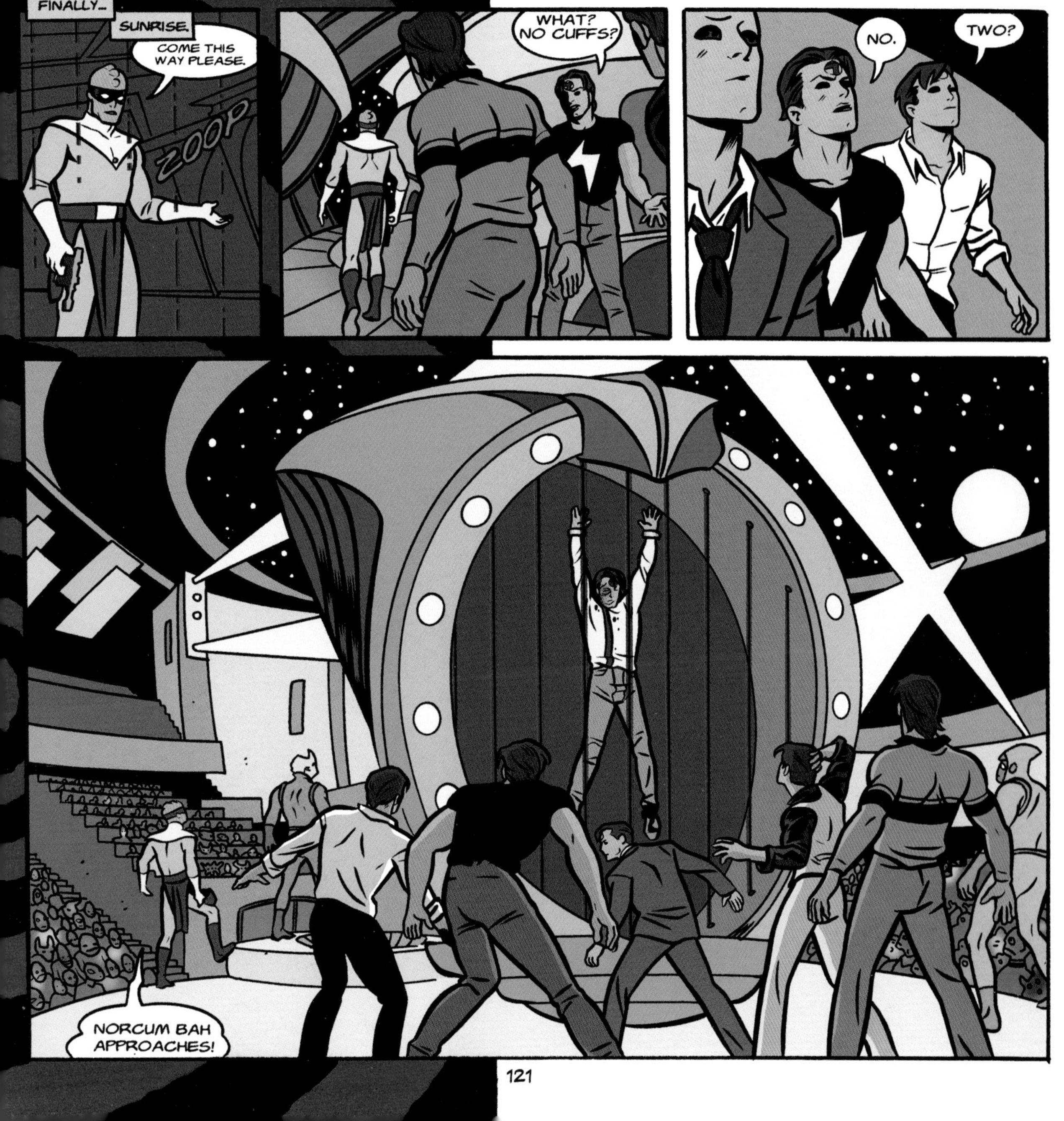
FINALLY...
SUNRISE.
COME THIS WAY PLEASE.
ZOOP
WHAT? NO CUFFS?
NO.
TWO?
NORCUM BAH APPROACHES!

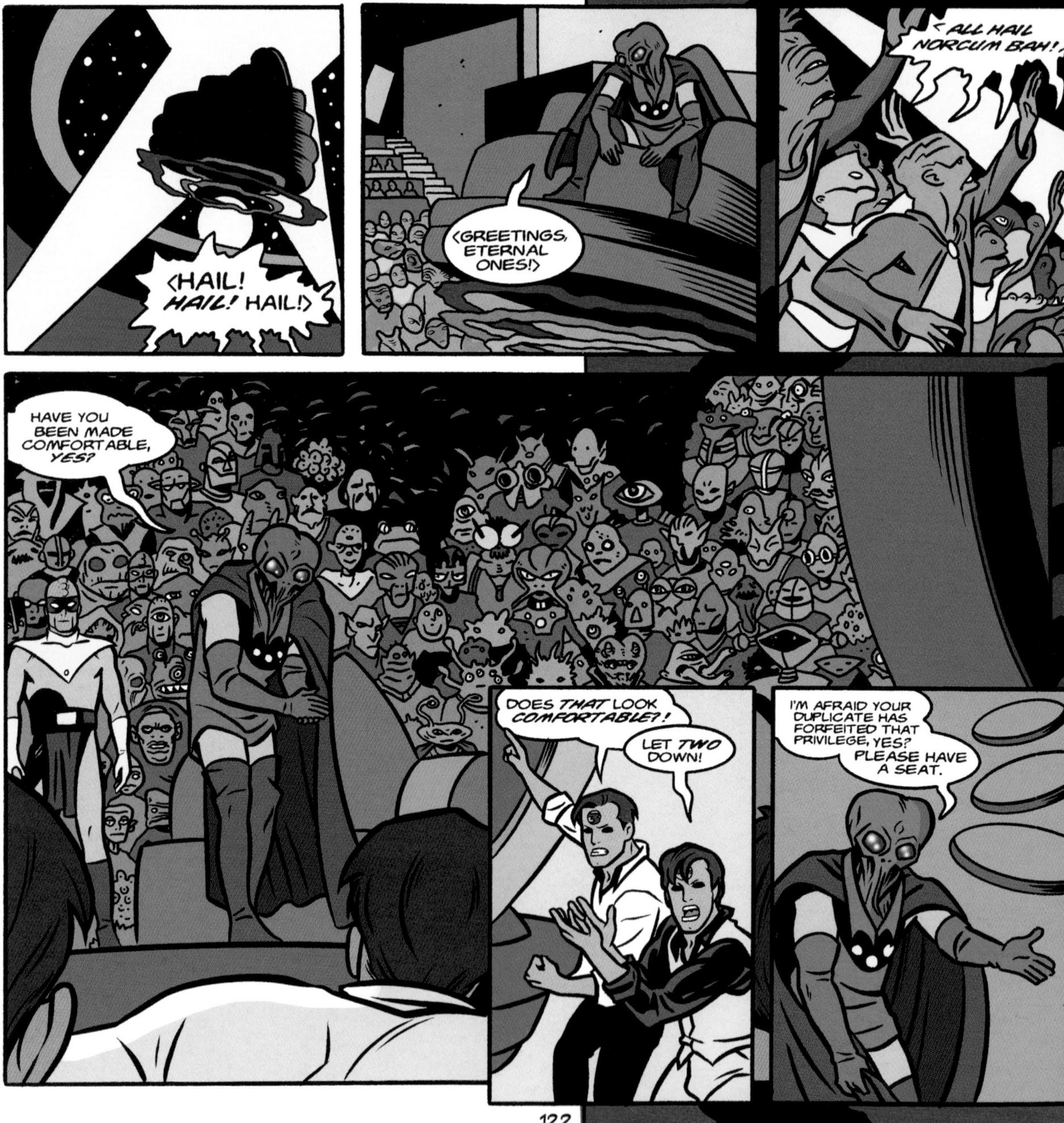
<HAIL! HAIL! HAIL!>
<GREETINGS, ETERNAL ONES!>
<ALL HAIL NORCUM BAH!>
HAVE YOU BEEN MADE COMFORTABLE, YES?
DOES THAT LOOK COMFORTABLE?!
LET TWO DOWN!
I'M AFRAID YOUR DUPLICATE HAS FORFEITED THAT PRIVILEGE, YES?
PLEASE HAVE A SEAT.

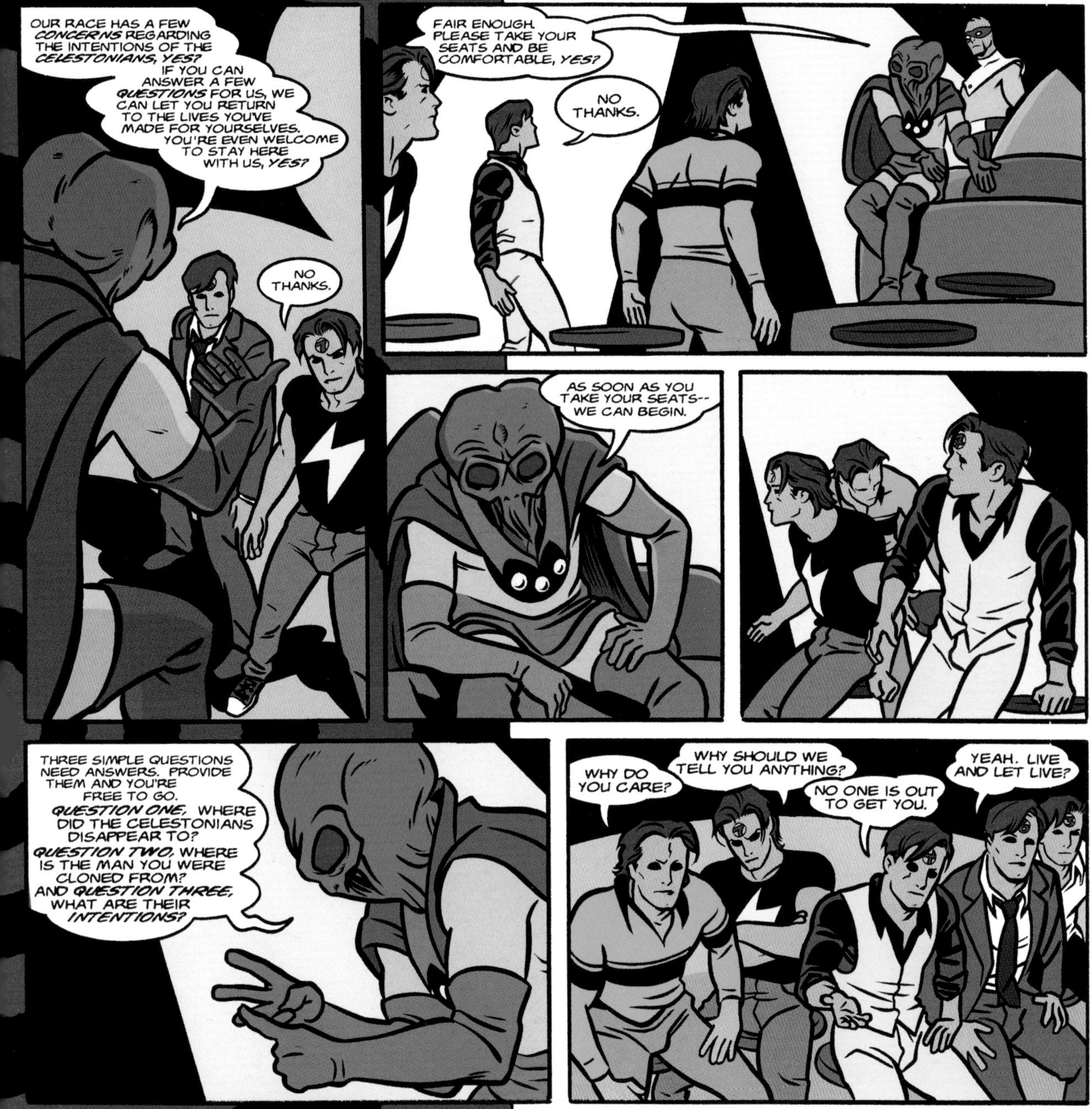
OUR RACE HAS A FEW *CONCERNS* REGARDING THE INTENTIONS OF THE *CELESTONIANS, YES?*
IF YOU CAN ANSWER A FEW *QUESTIONS* FOR US, WE CAN LET YOU RETURN TO THE LIVES YOU'VE MADE FOR YOURSELVES.
YOU'RE EVEN WELCOME TO STAY HERE WITH US, *YES?*
NO THANKS.
FAIR ENOUGH. PLEASE TAKE YOUR SEATS AND BE COMFORTABLE, *YES?*
NO THANKS.
AS SOON AS YOU TAKE YOUR SEATS-- WE CAN BEGIN.
THREE SIMPLE QUESTIONS NEED ANSWERS. PROVIDE THEM AND YOU'RE FREE TO GO.
QUESTION ONE, WHERE DID THE CELESTONIANS DISAPPEAR TO?
QUESTION TWO, WHERE IS THE MAN YOU WERE CLONED FROM?
AND *QUESTION THREE,* WHAT ARE THEIR *INTENTIONS?*
WHY DO YOU CARE?
WHY SHOULD WE TELL YOU ANYTHING?
NO ONE IS OUT TO GET YOU.
YEAH. LIVE AND LET LIVE?

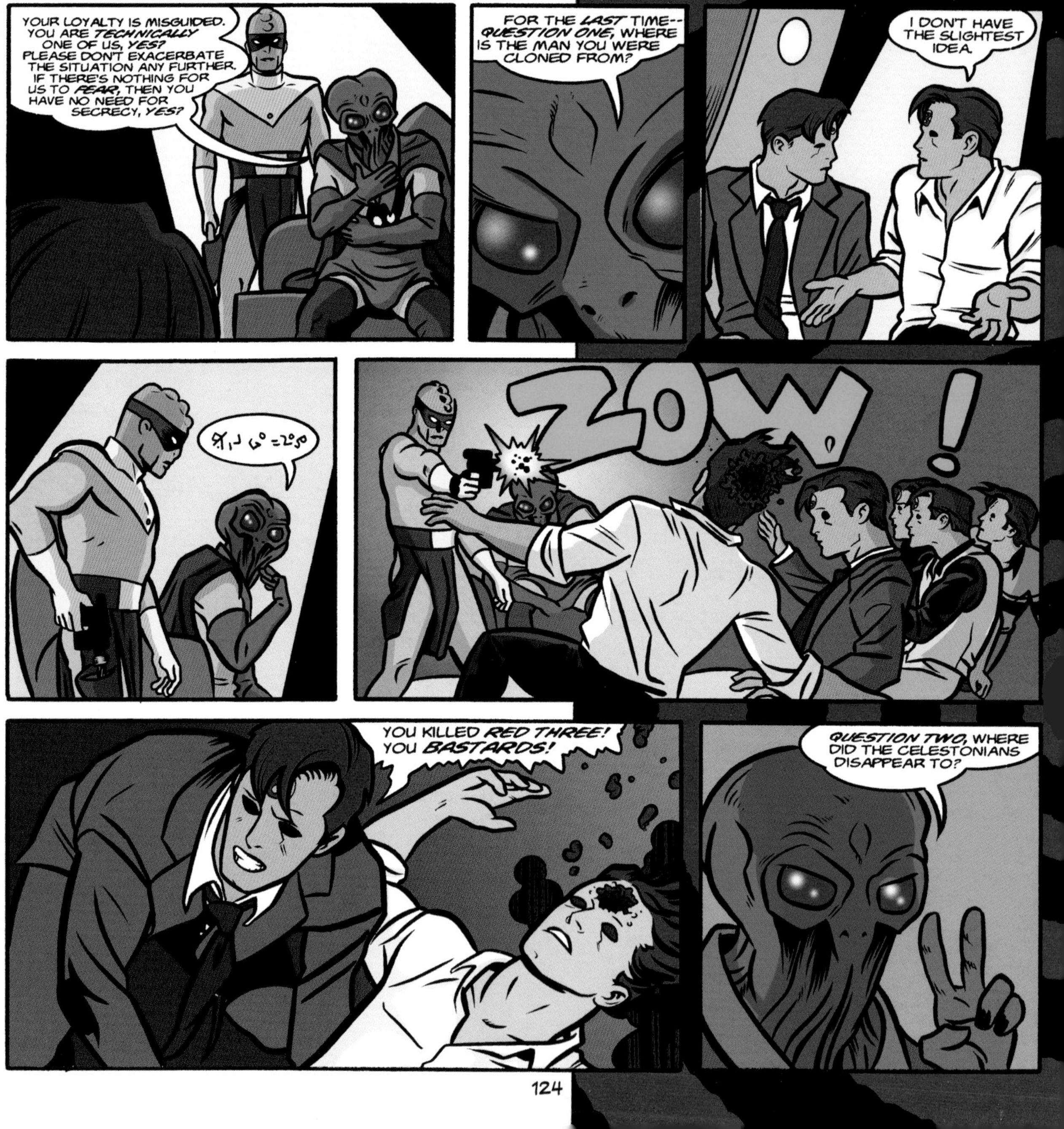
YOUR LOYALTY IS MISGUIDED. YOU ARE TECHNICALLY ONE OF US, YES? PLEASE DON'T EXACERBATE THE SITUATION ANY FURTHER. IF THERE'S NOTHING FOR US TO FEAR, THEN YOU HAVE NO NEED FOR SECRECY, YES?
FOR THE LAST TIME-- QUESTION ONE, WHERE IS THE MAN YOU WERE CLONED FROM?
I DON'T HAVE THE SLIGHTEST IDEA.
ZOW!
YOU KILLED RED THREE! YOU BASTARDS!
QUESTION TWO, WHERE DID THE CELESTONIANS DISAPPEAR TO?

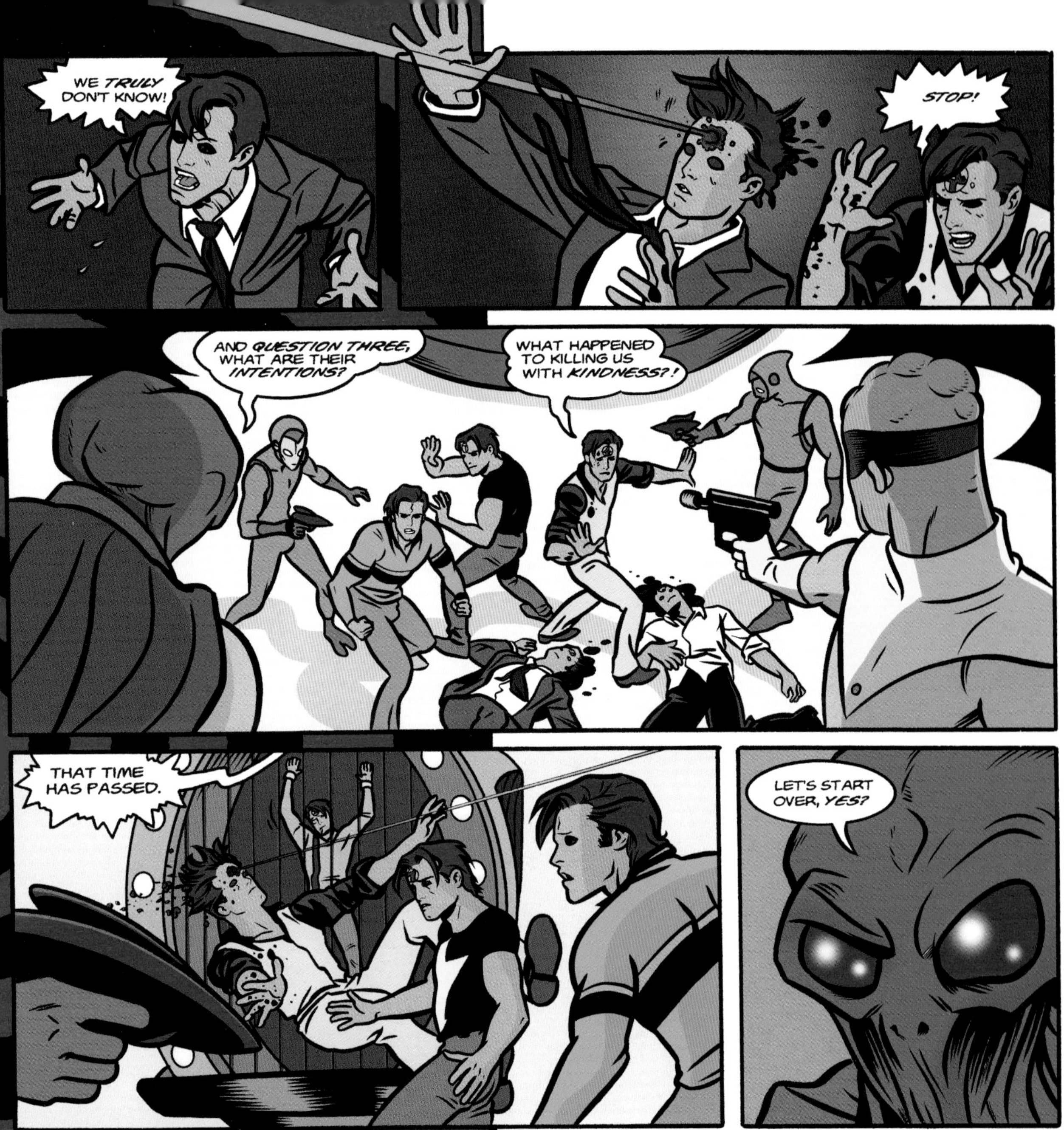
WE TRULY DON'T KNOW!
STOP!
AND QUESTION THREE, WHAT ARE THEIR INTENTIONS?
WHAT HAPPENED TO KILLING US WITH KINDNESS?!
THAT TIME HAS PASSED.
LET'S START OVER, YES?

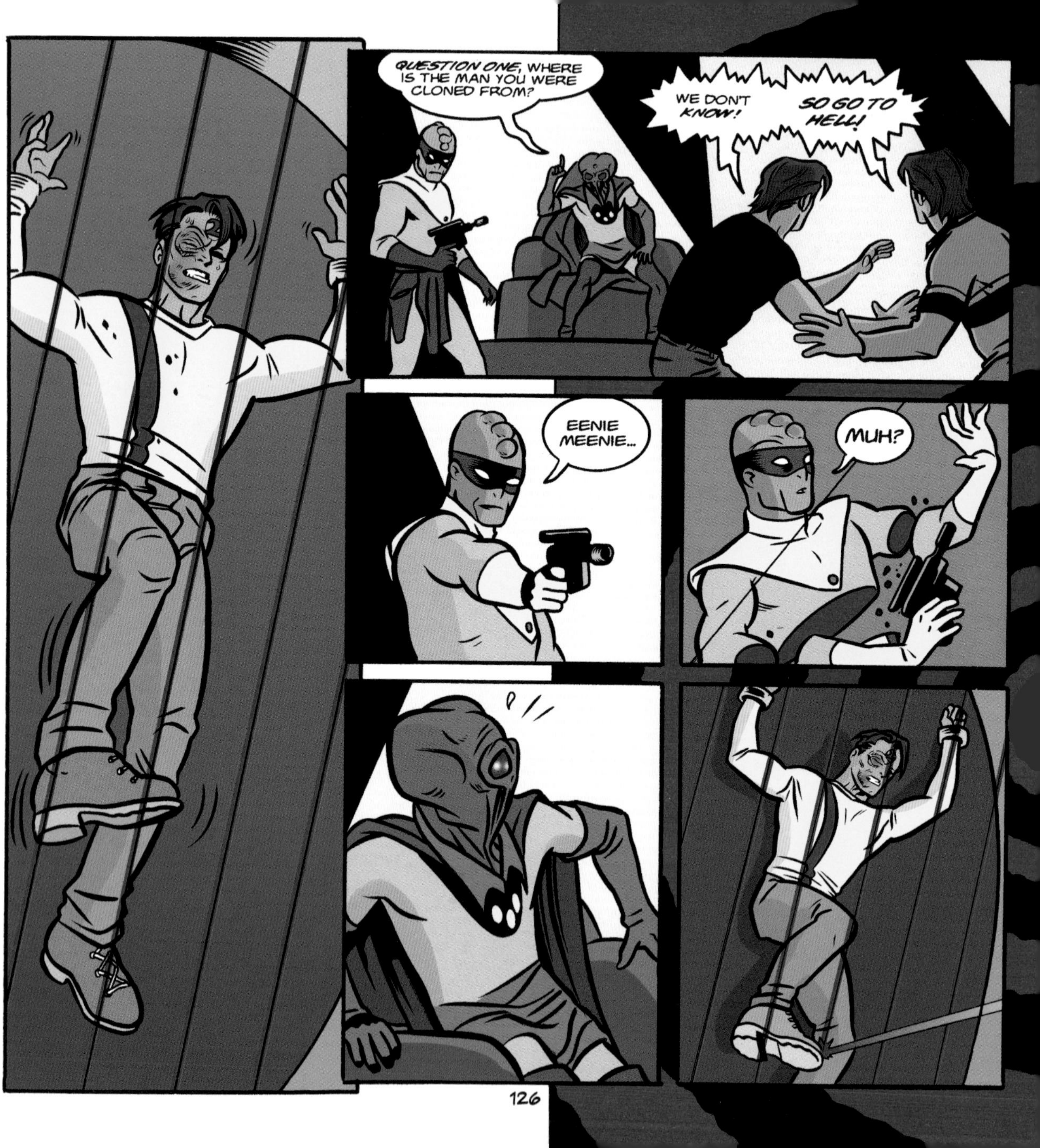
QUESTION ONE, WHERE IS THE MAN YOU WERE CLONED FROM?
WE DON'T KNOW!
SO GO TO HELL!
EENIE MEENIE...
MUH?

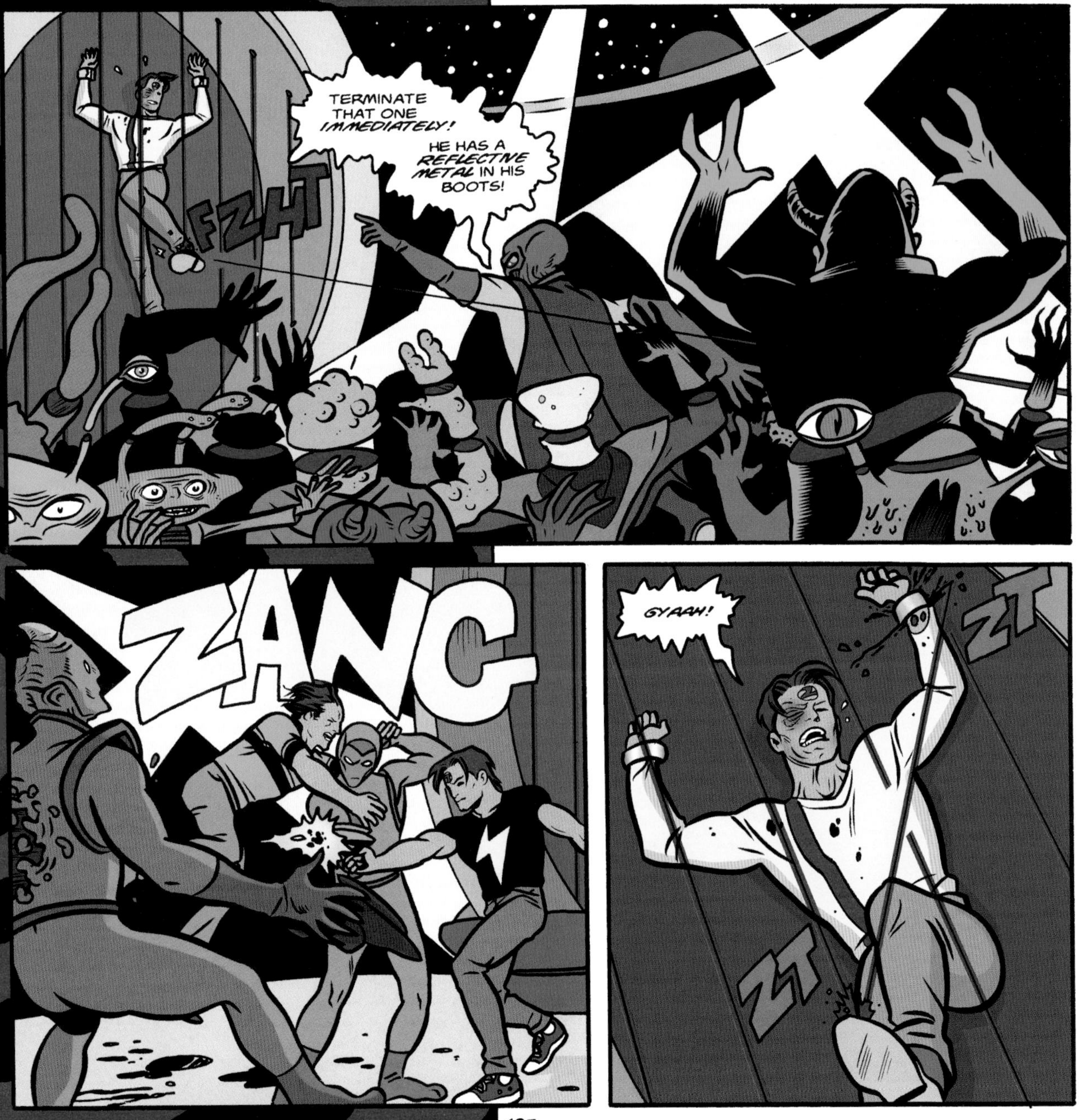
TERMINATE THAT ONE IMMEDIATELY!
HE HAS A REFLECTIVE METAL IN HIS BOOTS!
FZHT
ZANC
GYAAH!
ZT
ZT

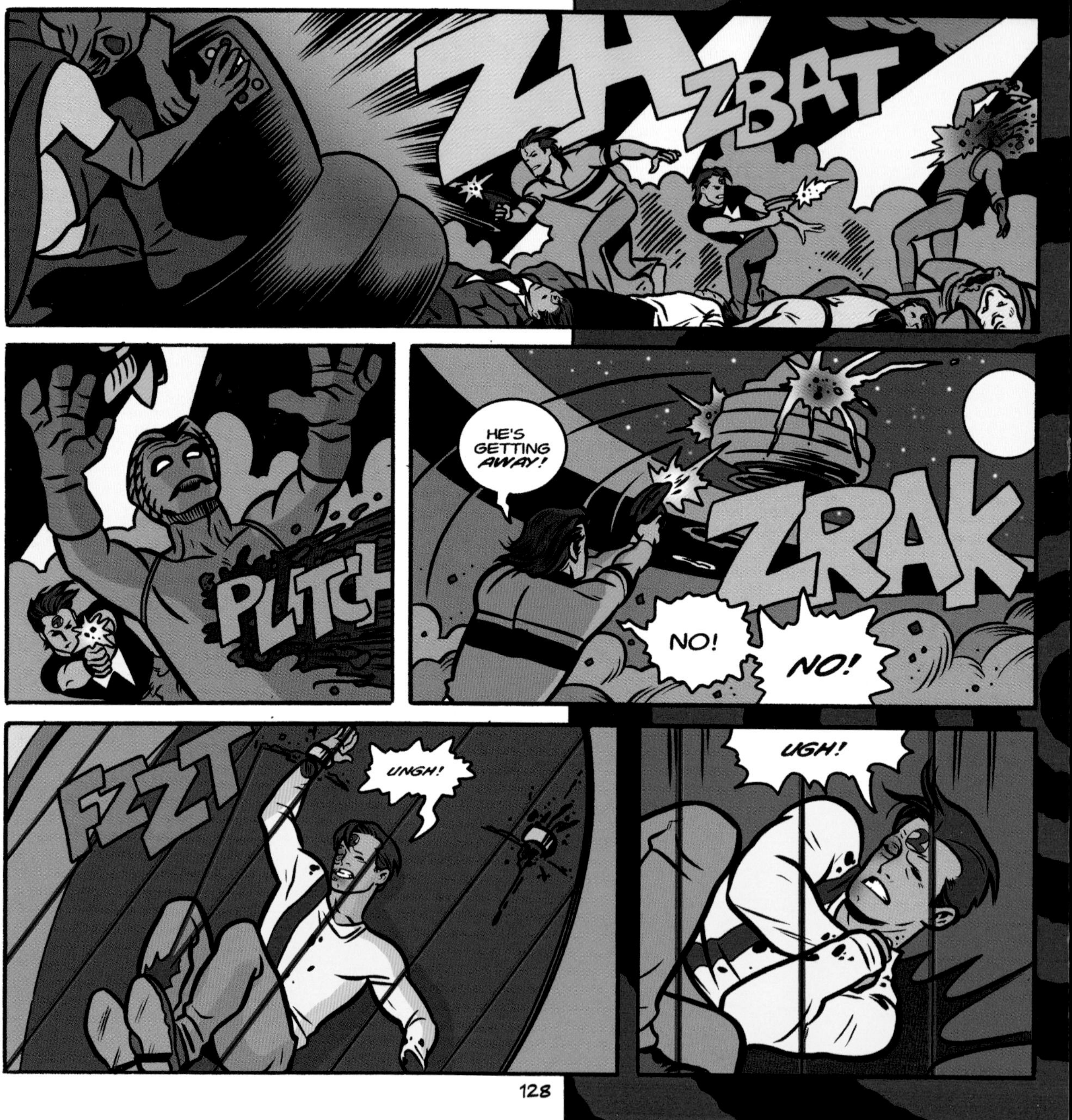
ZAP
ZBAT
PLITCH
HE'S GETTING AWAY!
ZRAK
NO!
NO!
FZZT
UNGH!
UGH!

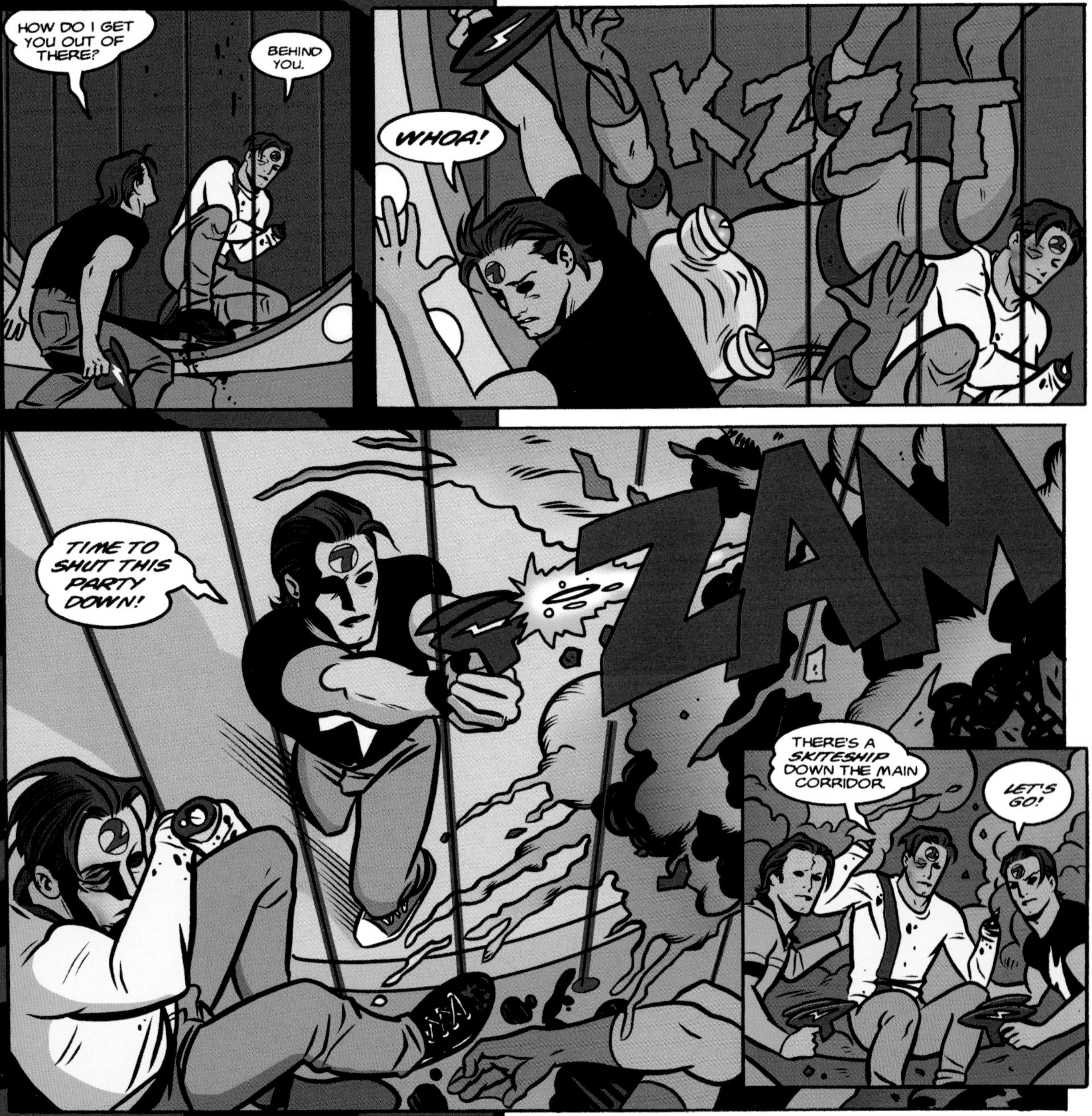
HOW DO I GET YOU OUT OF THERE?
BEHIND YOU.
WHOA!
KZZZT
TIME TO SHUT THIS PARTY DOWN!
ZAM
THERE'S A SKITESHIP DOWN THE MAIN CORRIDOR.
LET'S GO!

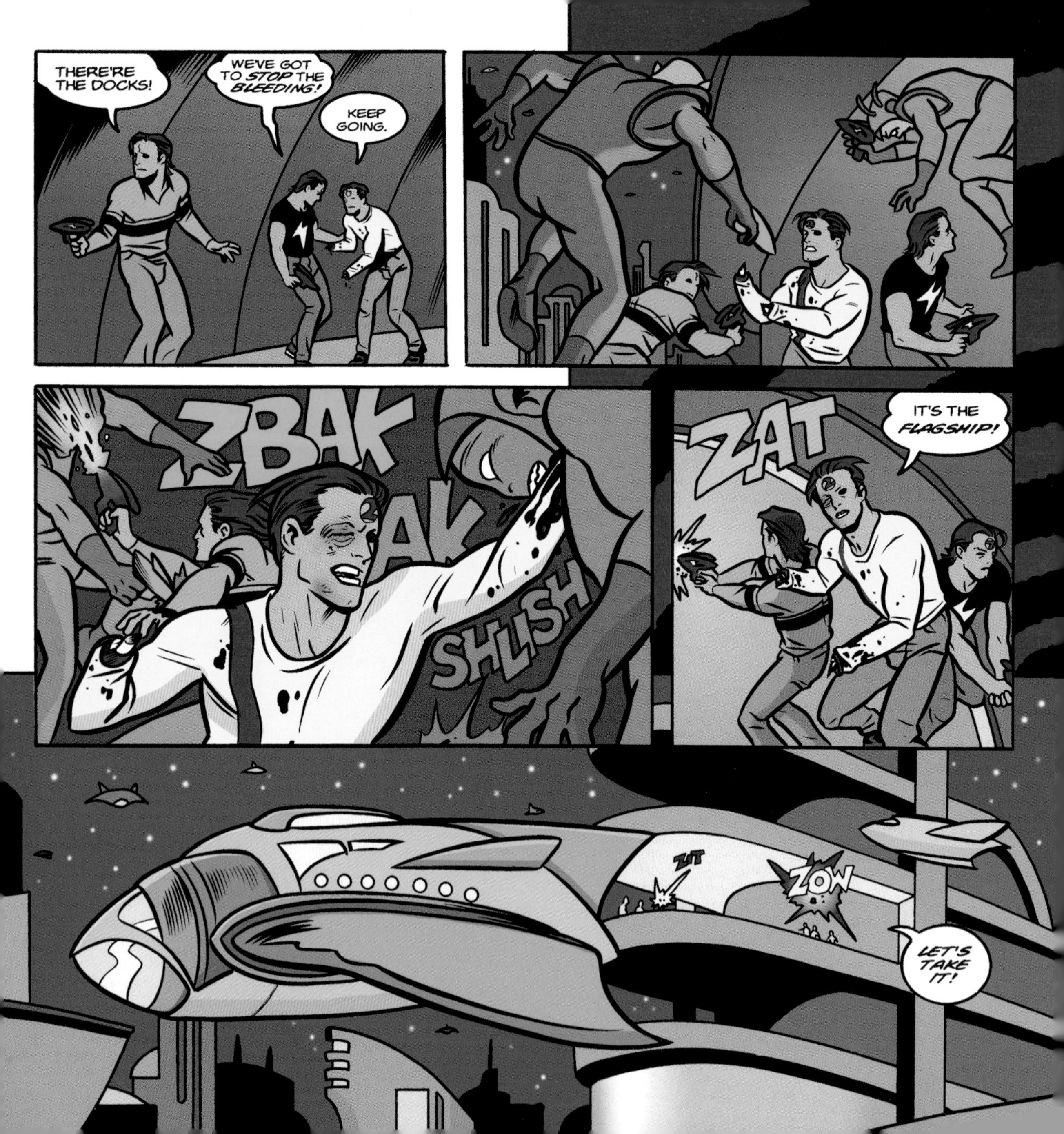
THERE'RE THE DOCKS!
WE'VE GOT TO STOP THE BLEEDING!
KEEP GOING.
ZBAK
AK
SHLISH
ZAT
IT'S THE FLAGSHIP!
ZIT
ZOW
LET'S TAKE IT!

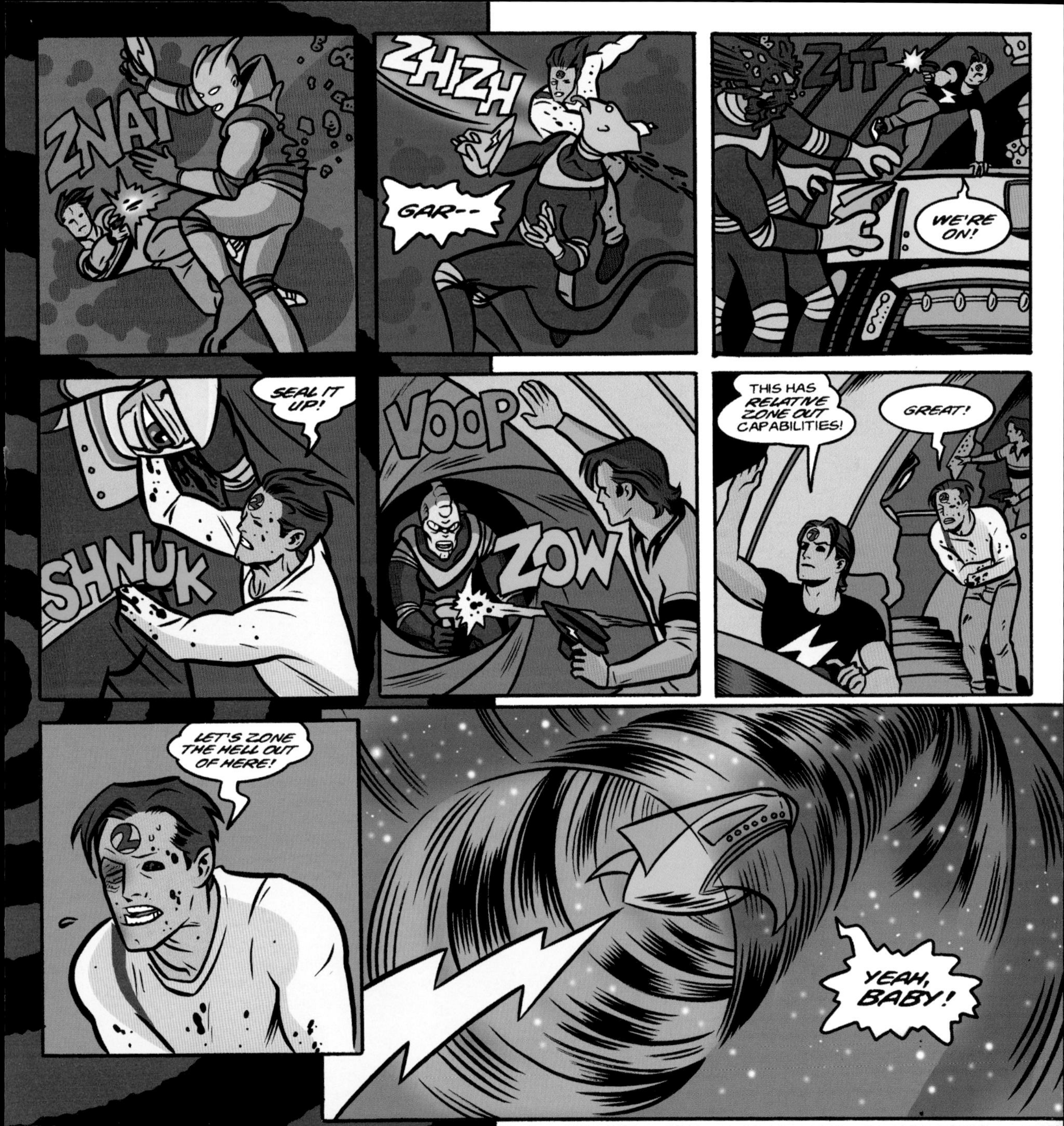
ZNAT
ZHIZH
GAR--
ZIT
WE'RE ON!
SEAL IT UP!
SHNUK
VOOP
ZOW
THIS HAS RELATIVE ZONE OUT CAPABILITIES!
GREAT!
LET'S ZONE THE HELL OUT OF HERE!
YEAH, BABY!

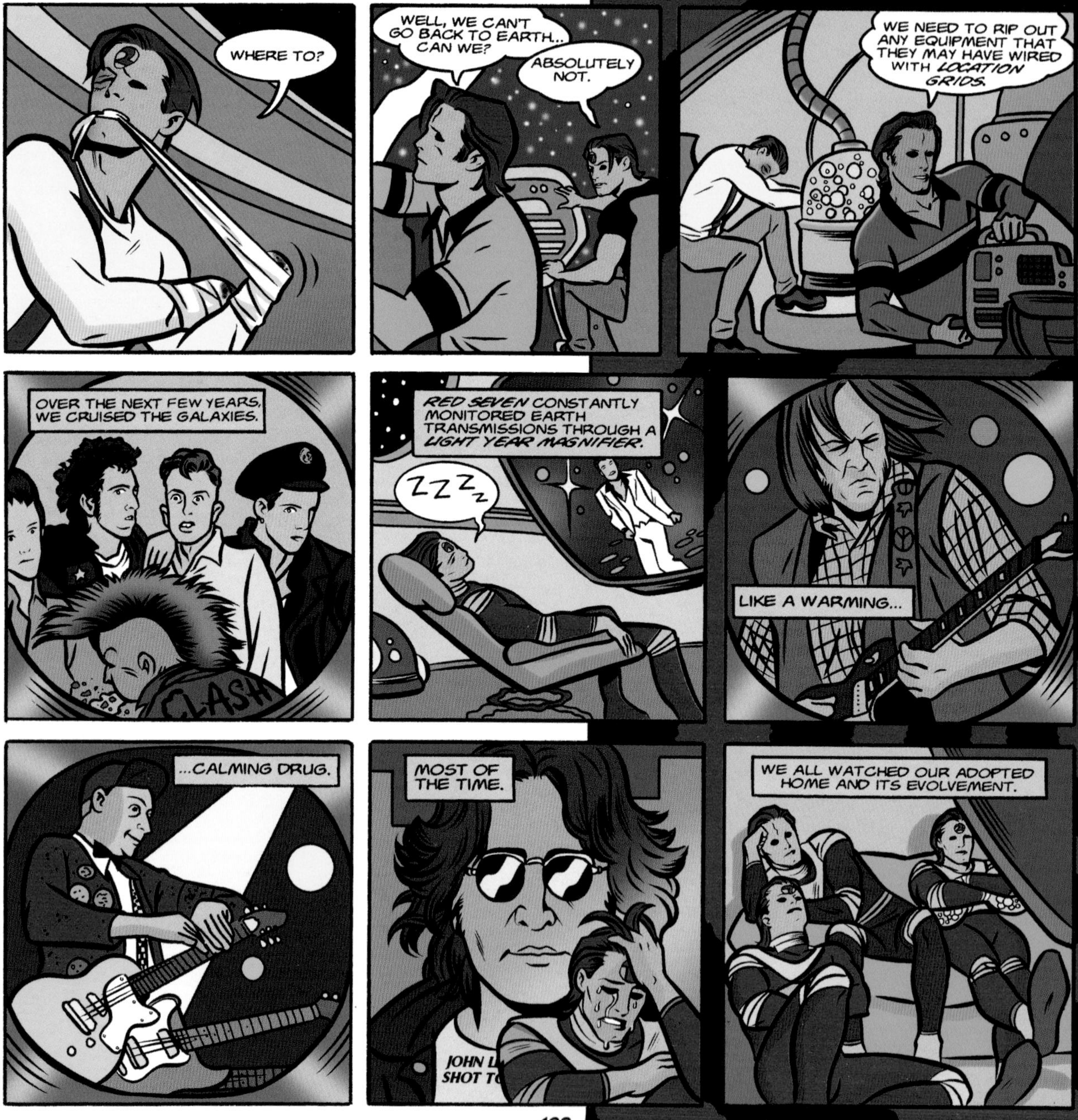
WHERE TO?
WELL, WE CAN'T GO BACK TO EARTH... CAN WE?
ABSOLUTELY NOT.
WE NEED TO RIP OUT ANY EQUIPMENT THAT THEY MAY HAVE WIRED WITH LOCATION GRIDS.
OVER THE NEXT FEW YEARS, WE CRUISED THE GALAXIES.
CLASH
RED SEVEN CONSTANTLY MONITORED EARTH TRANSMISSIONS THROUGH A LIGHT YEAR MAGNIFIER.
ZZZZ
LIKE A WARMING...
...CALMING DRUG.
MOST OF THE TIME.
JOHN L
SHOT T
WE ALL WATCHED OUR ADOPTED HOME AND ITS EVOLVEMENT.

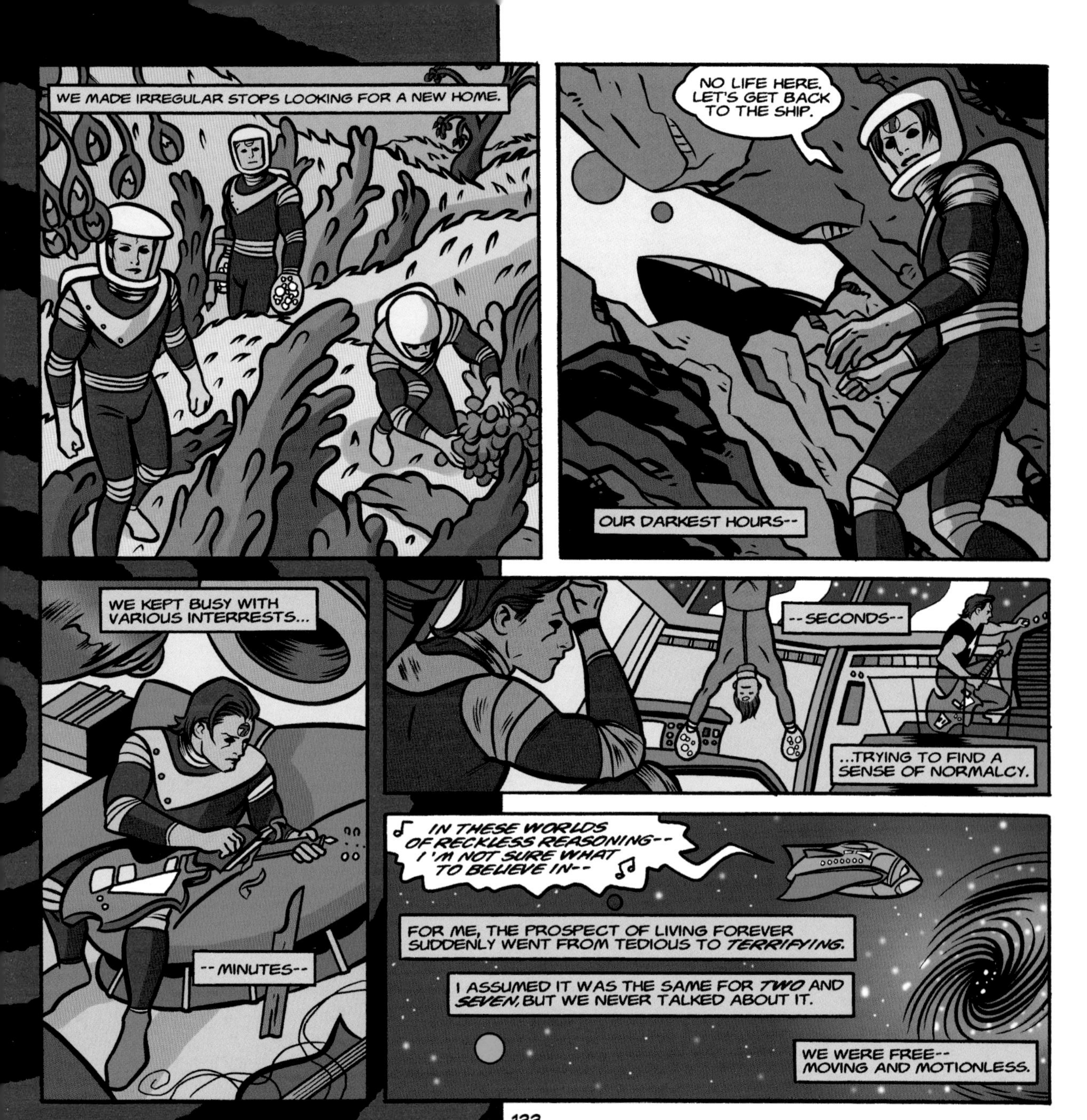
WE MADE IRREGULAR STOPS LOOKING FOR A NEW HOME.
NO LIFE HERE. LET'S GET BACK TO THE SHIP.
OUR DARKEST HOURS--
WE KEPT BUSY WITH VARIOUS INTERRESTS...
--SECONDS--
...TRYING TO FIND A SENSE OF NORMALCY.
--MINUTES--
IN THESE WORLDS OF RECKLESS REASONING-- I'M NOT SURE WHAT TO BELIEVE IN--
FOR ME, THE PROSPECT OF LIVING FOREVER SUDDENLY WENT FROM TEDIOUS TO TERRIFYING.
I ASSUMED IT WAS THE SAME FOR TWO AND SEVEN, BUT WE NEVER TALKED ABOUT IT.
WE WERE FREE-- MOVING AND MOTIONLESS.

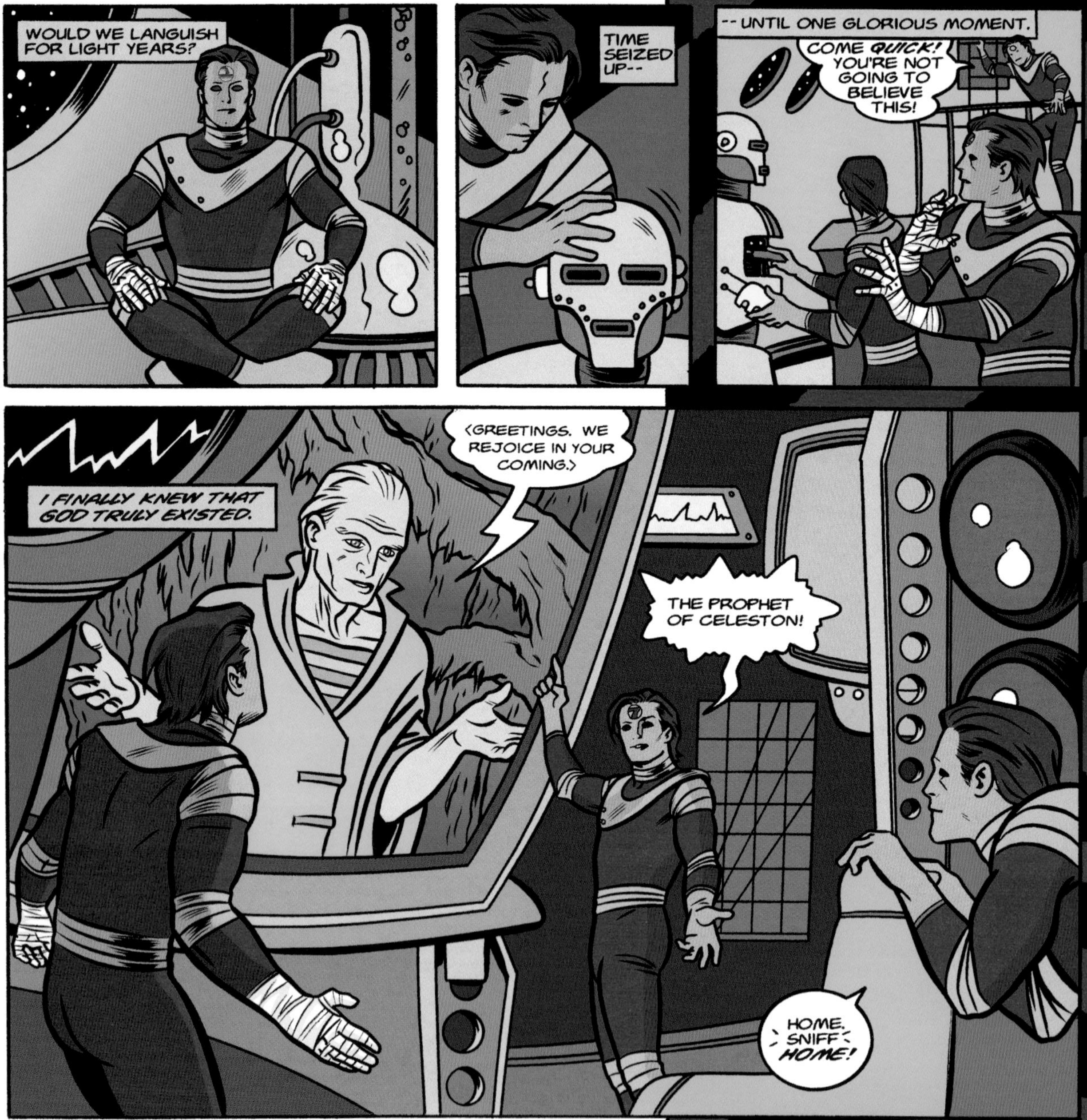
WOULD WE LANGUISH FOR LIGHT YEARS?
TIME SEIZED UP--
--UNTIL ONE GLORIOUS MOMENT.
COME QUICK! YOU'RE NOT GOING TO BELIEVE THIS!
I FINALLY KNEW THAT GOD TRULY EXISTED.
<GREETINGS. WE REJOICE IN YOUR COMING.>
THE PROPHET OF CELESTON!
HOME. SNIFF HOME!

NEXT: ALL APOLOGIES

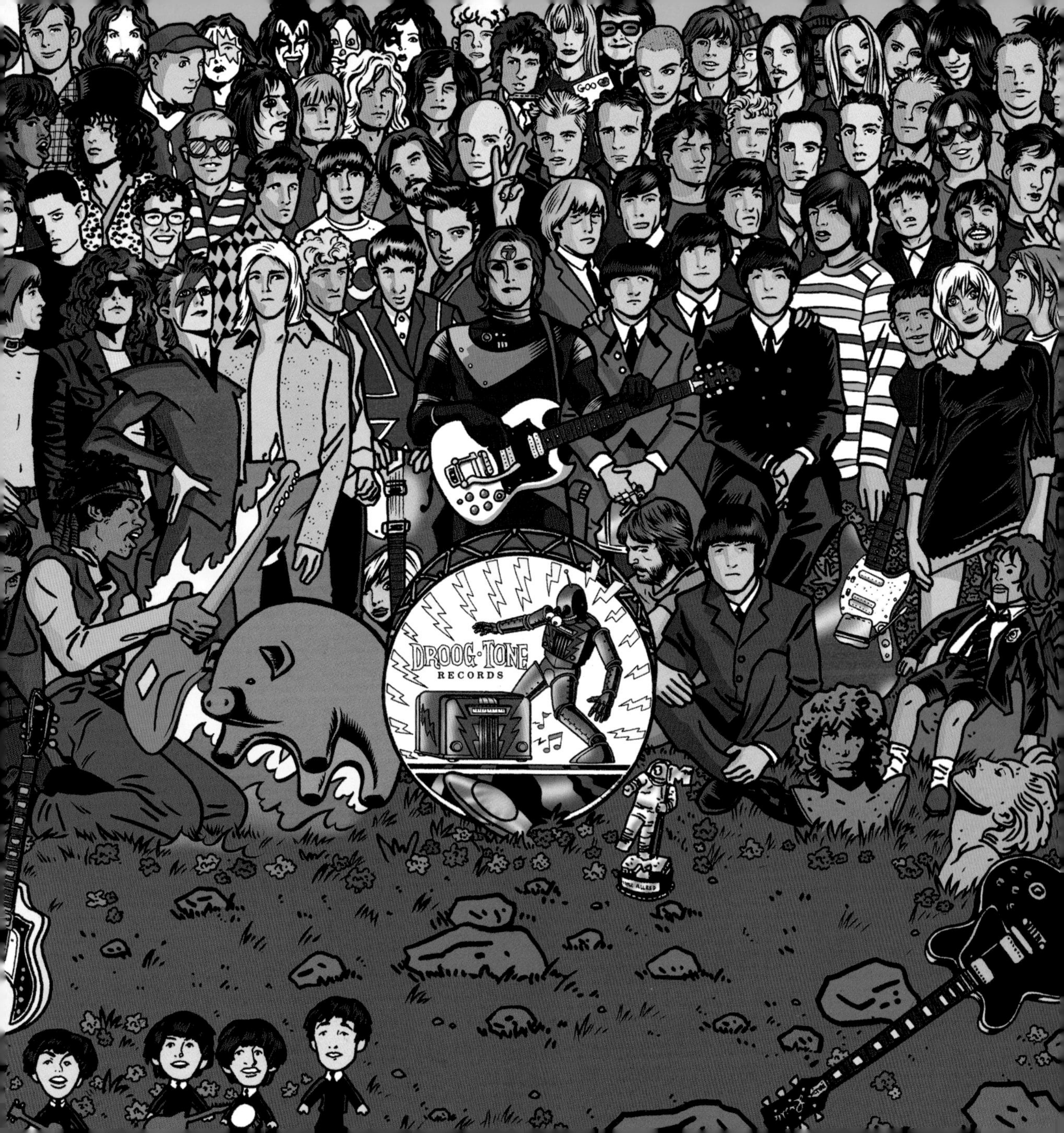
DROOG·TONE
RECORDS

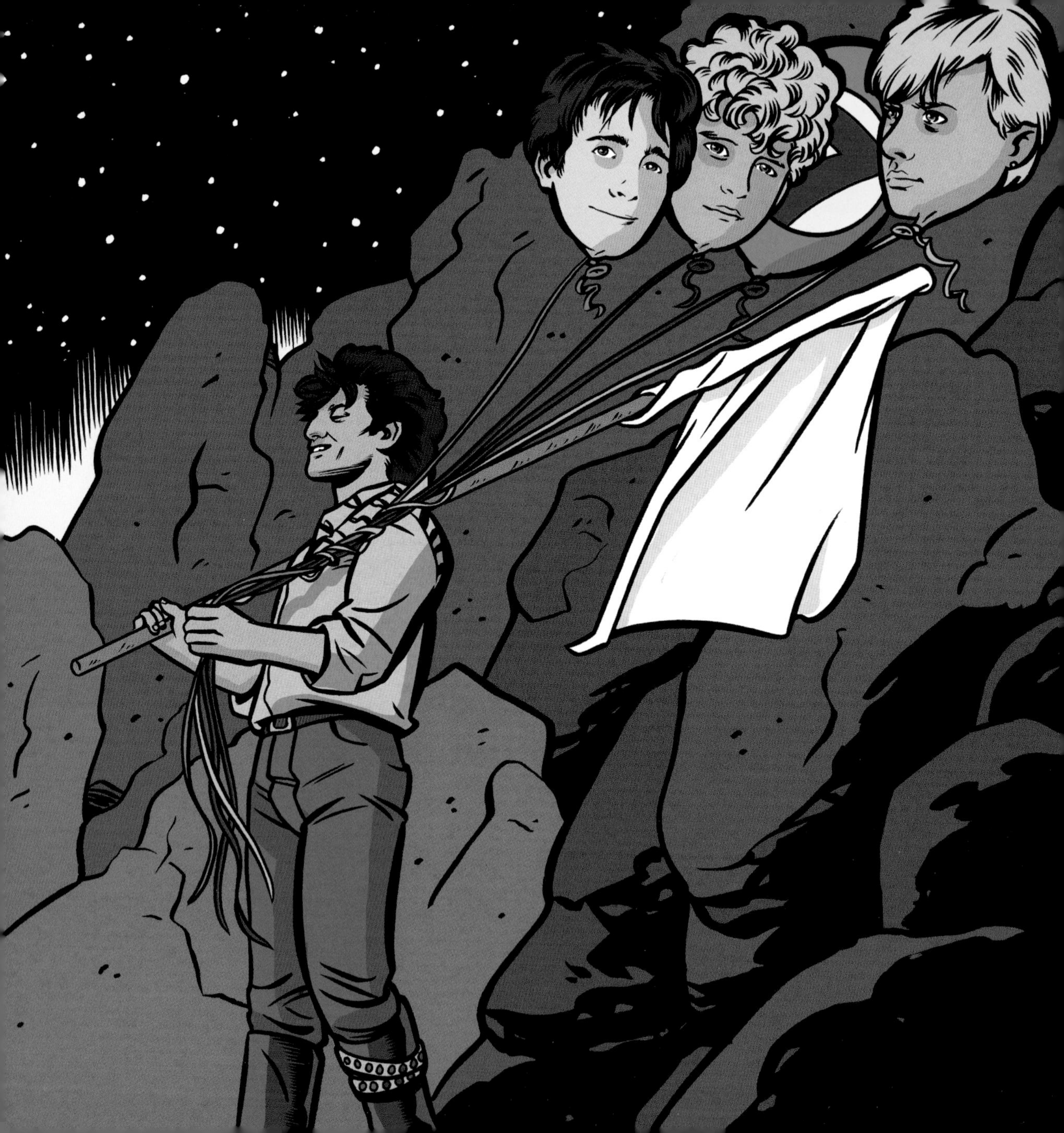

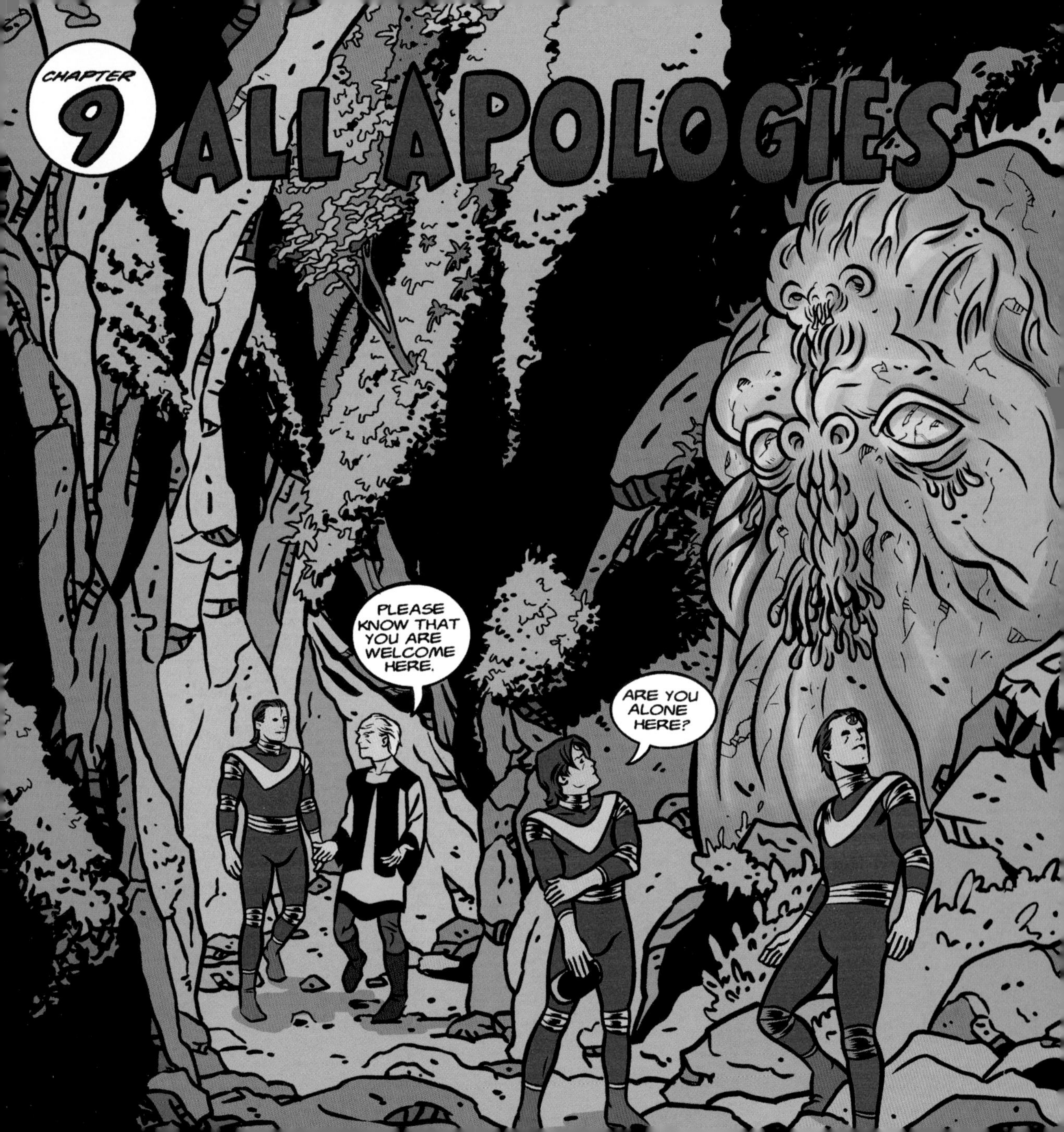
CHAPTER 9
ALL APOLOGIES
PLEASE KNOW THAT YOU ARE WELCOME HERE.
ARE YOU ALONE HERE?

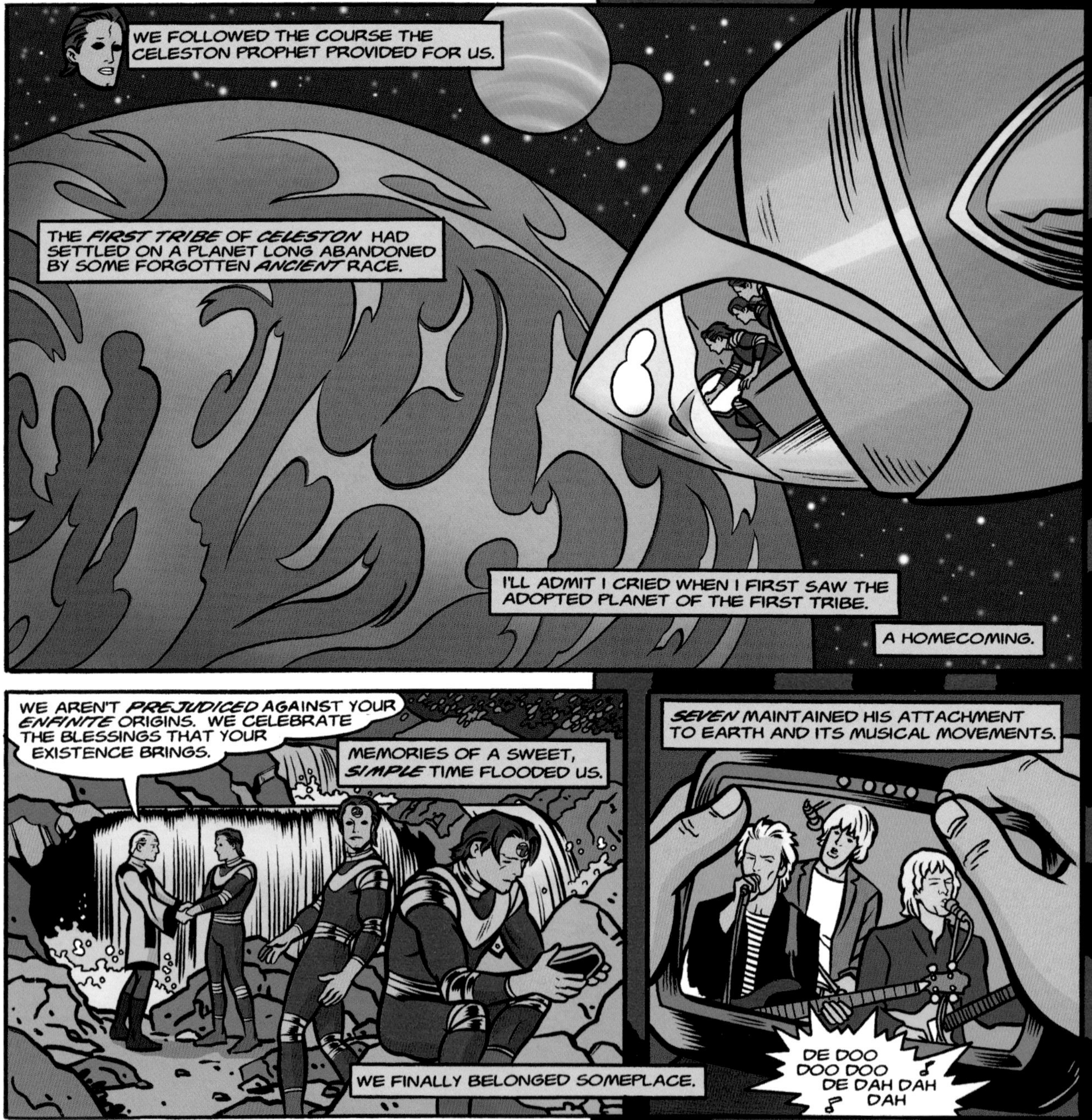
WE FOLLOWED THE COURSE THE CELESTON PROPHET PROVIDED FOR US.
THE *FIRST TRIBE* OF *CELESTON* HAD SETTLED ON A PLANET LONG ABANDONED BY SOME FORGOTTEN *ANCIENT* RACE.
I'LL ADMIT I CRIED WHEN I FIRST SAW THE ADOPTED PLANET OF THE FIRST TRIBE.
A HOMECOMING.
WE AREN'T *PREJUDICED* AGAINST YOUR *ENFINITE* ORIGINS. WE CELEBRATE THE BLESSINGS THAT YOUR EXISTENCE BRINGS.
MEMORIES OF A SWEET, *SIMPLE* TIME FLOODED US.
WE FINALLY BELONGED SOMEPLACE.
SEVEN MAINTAINED HIS ATTACHMENT TO EARTH AND ITS MUSICAL MOVEMENTS.
DE DOO DOO DOO DE DAH DAH DAH

THE ENFINITES DOMINATE THE *UNIVERSE*. WHY DO THEY WANT THE *CELESTONIANS* DESTROYED SO BADLY?

THEY SIMPLY FEAR WHAT THEY DON'T UNDERSTAND. THE THOUGHT OF OUR RACE BREEDING AND DYING CONTINUOUSLY IS PROBABLY DISGUSTING TO THEM.

I CAN'T CLAIM TO UNDERSTAND THE MIND OF ONE WHO WOULD JOIN THE ENFINITE MOVEMENT.

BUT YOU DON'T FEAR THEM.

NO. AND I DO NOT *FEAR DEATH*. I HAVE MY FAITH. THE SCRIPTURE CODES TELL OF OUR *ETERNAL* REWARDS IF WE LIVE IN RIGHTEOUSNESS.

DEATH IS SIMPLY A SPIRITUAL DOORWAY TO THE NEXT LEVEL IN GOD'S PLAN. OUR *HISTORIES*, AS WELL AS OUR *FUTURES*, ARE WRITTEN IN THE SCRIPTURES.

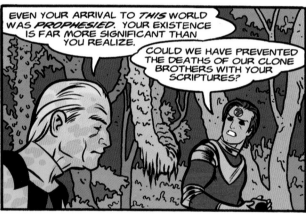

EVEN YOUR ARRIVAL TO *THIS* WORLD WAS *PROPHESIED*. YOUR EXISTENCE IS FAR MORE SIGNIFICANT THAN YOU REALIZE.

COULD WE HAVE PREVENTED THE DEATHS OF OUR CLONE BROTHERS WITH YOUR SCRIPTURES?

WALK WITH ME, AND OPEN YOUR HEART AND MIND.

I KNOW YOU'VE SUFFERED GREAT PAIN.

YOU EACH HAVE YOUR OWN SWEET SPIRIT. LIFE IS LIFE. YOUR BROTHERS HAVE PASSED ON. BE *SAD*, BUT DON'T BE *UNHAPPY*. YOU CAN HEAL THE SCARS ON YOUR HEART AND SOFTEN THE CALLUSES ON YOUR MIND.

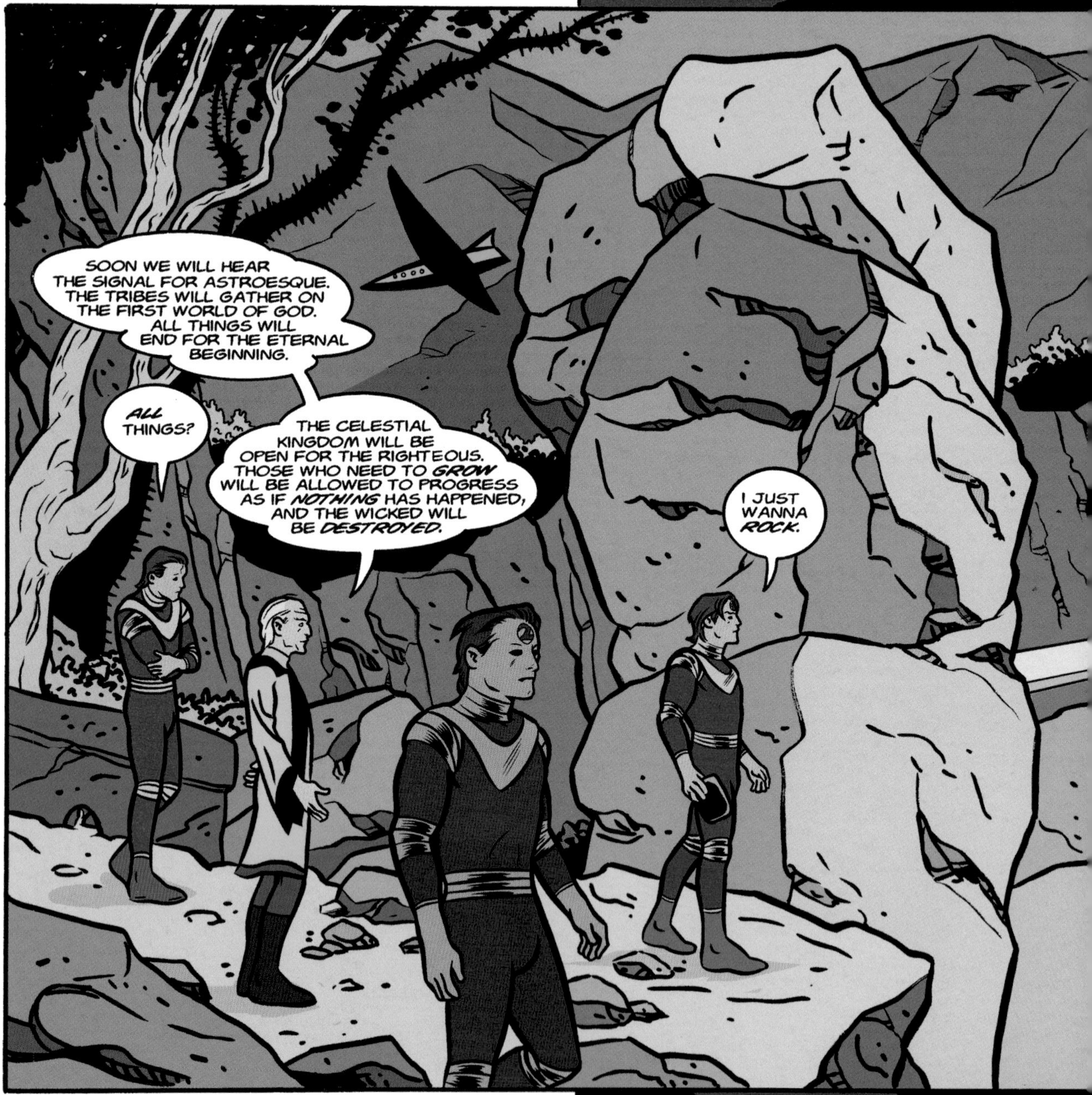
SOON WE WILL HEAR THE SIGNAL FOR ASTROESQUE. THE TRIBES WILL GATHER ON THE FIRST WORLD OF GOD. ALL THINGS WILL END FOR THE ETERNAL BEGINNING.
ALL THINGS?
THE CELESTIAL KINGDOM WILL BE OPEN FOR THE RIGHTEOUS. THOSE WHO NEED TO GROW WILL BE ALLOWED TO PROGRESS AS IF NOTHING HAS HAPPENED, AND THE WICKED WILL BE DESTROYED.
I JUST WANNA ROCK.

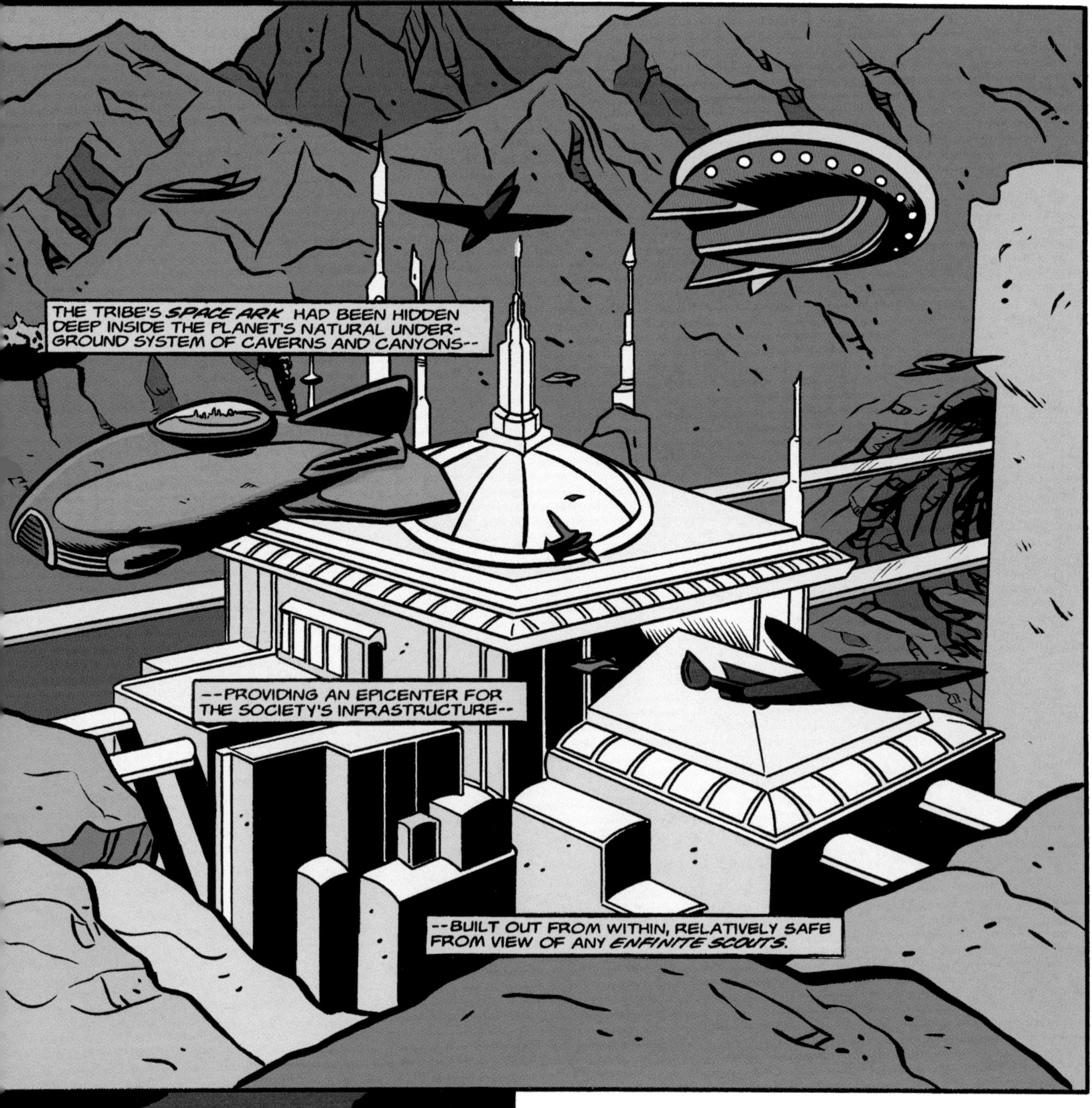
THE TRIBE'S SPACE ARK HAD BEEN HIDDEN DEEP INSIDE THE PLANET'S NATURAL UNDER-GROUND SYSTEM OF CAVERNS AND CANYONS--
--PROVIDING AN EPICENTER FOR THE SOCIETY'S INFRASTRUCTURE--
--BUILT OUT FROM WITHIN, RELATIVELY SAFE FROM VIEW OF ANY ENFINITE SCOUTS.

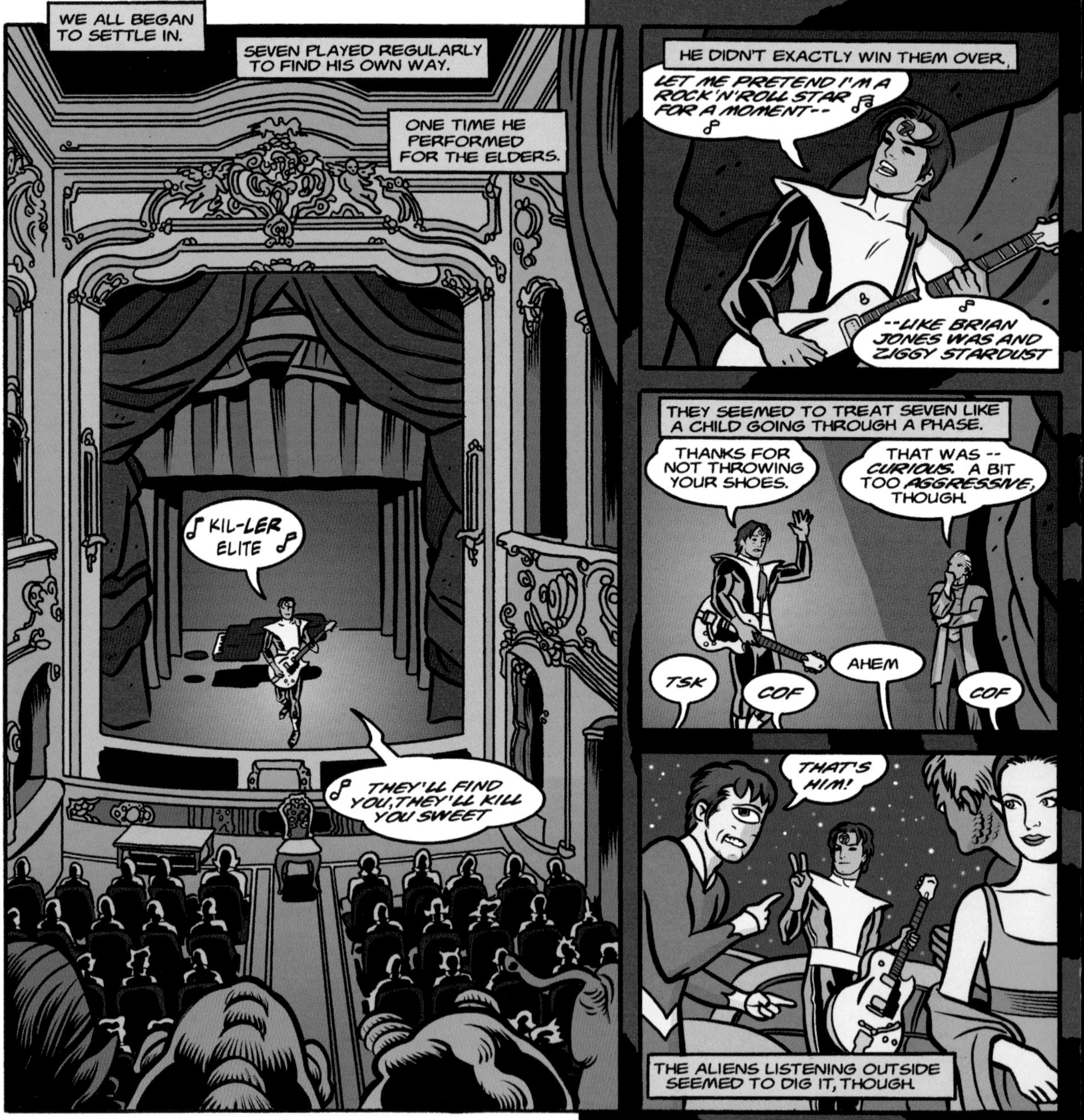
WE ALL BEGAN TO SETTLE IN.
SEVEN PLAYED REGULARLY TO FIND HIS OWN WAY.
ONE TIME HE PERFORMED FOR THE ELDERS.
KIL-LER ELITE
THEY'LL FIND YOU, THEY'LL KILL YOU SWEET
HE DIDN'T EXACTLY WIN THEM OVER.
LET ME PRETEND I'M A ROCK'N'ROLL STAR FOR A MOMENT--
--LIKE BRIAN JONES WAS AND ZIGGY STARDUST
THEY SEEMED TO TREAT SEVEN LIKE A CHILD GOING THROUGH A PHASE.
THANKS FOR NOT THROWING YOUR SHOES.
THAT WAS -- CURIOUS. A BIT TOO AGGRESSIVE, THOUGH.
TSK
COF
AHEM
COF
THAT'S HIM!
THE ALIENS LISTENING OUTSIDE SEEMED TO DIG IT, THOUGH.

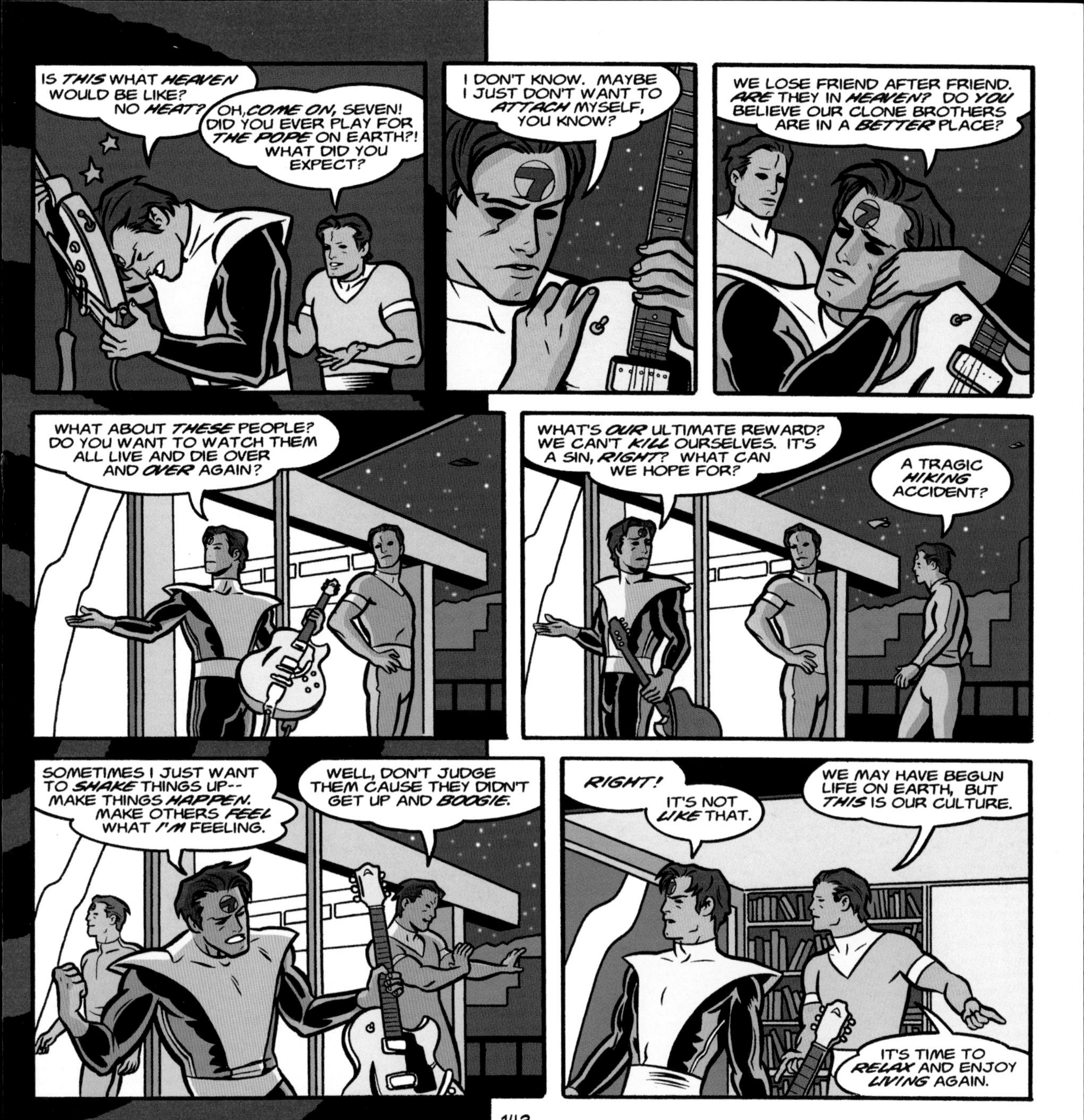
IS THIS WHAT HEAVEN WOULD BE LIKE? NO HEAT?
OH, COME ON, SEVEN! DID YOU EVER PLAY FOR THE POPE ON EARTH?! WHAT DID YOU EXPECT?
I DON'T KNOW. MAYBE I JUST DON'T WANT TO ATTACH MYSELF, YOU KNOW?
WE LOSE FRIEND AFTER FRIEND. ARE THEY IN HEAVEN? DO YOU BELIEVE OUR CLONE BROTHERS ARE IN A BETTER PLACE?
WHAT ABOUT THESE PEOPLE? DO YOU WANT TO WATCH THEM ALL LIVE AND DIE OVER AND OVER AGAIN?
WHAT'S OUR ULTIMATE REWARD? WE CAN'T KILL OURSELVES. IT'S A SIN, RIGHT? WHAT CAN WE HOPE FOR?
A TRAGIC HIKING ACCIDENT?
SOMETIMES I JUST WANT TO SHAKE THINGS UP-- MAKE THINGS HAPPEN. MAKE OTHERS FEEL WHAT I'M FEELING.
WELL, DON'T JUDGE THEM CAUSE THEY DIDN'T GET UP AND BOOGIE.
RIGHT!
IT'S NOT LIKE THAT.
WE MAY HAVE BEGUN LIFE ON EARTH, BUT THIS IS OUR CULTURE.
IT'S TIME TO RELAX AND ENJOY LIVING AGAIN.

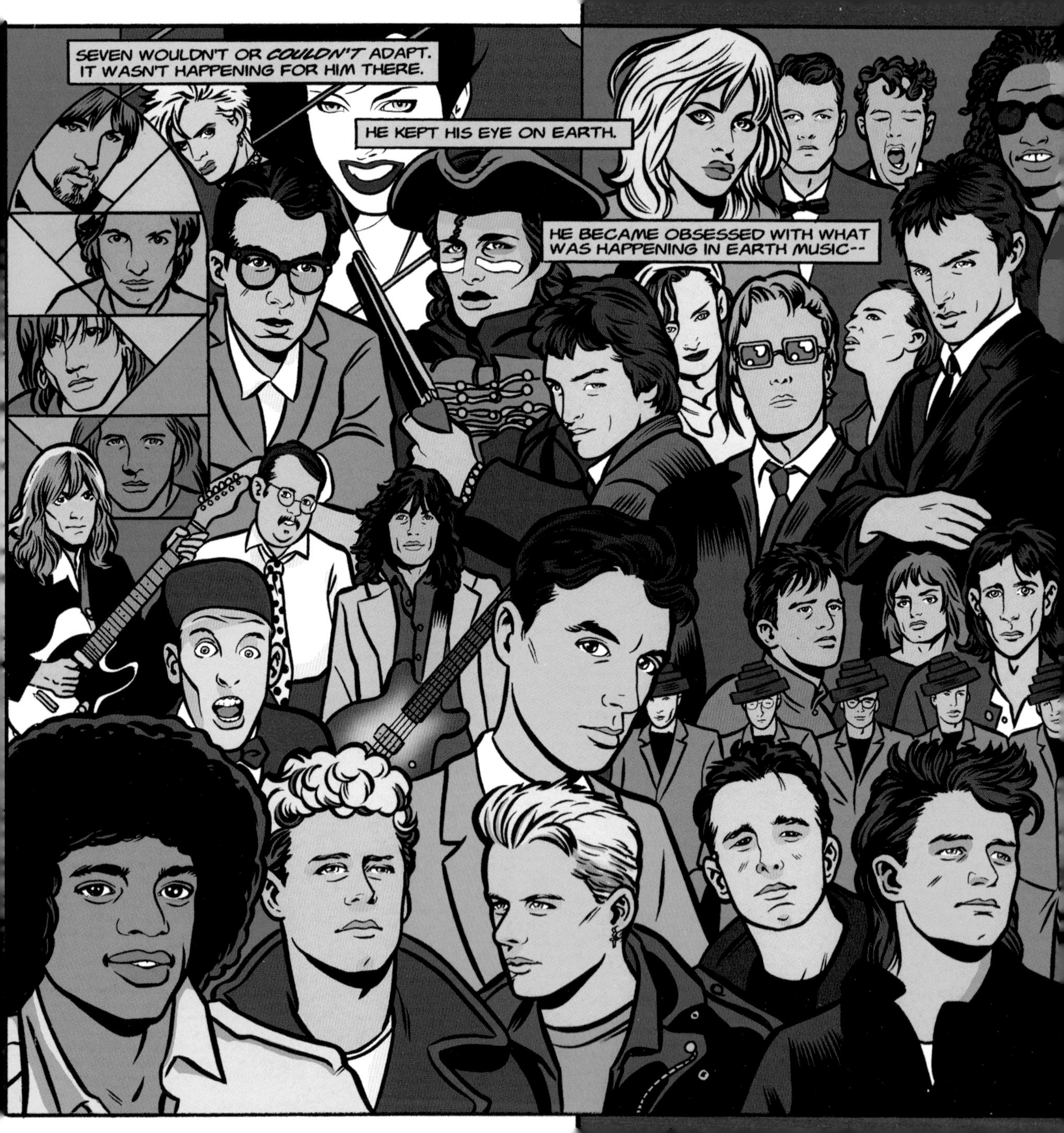
SEVEN WOULDN'T OR *COULDN'T* ADAPT. IT WASN'T HAPPENING FOR HIM THERE.
HE KEPT HIS EYE ON EARTH.
HE BECAME OBSESSED WITH WHAT WAS HAPPENING IN EARTH MUSIC--

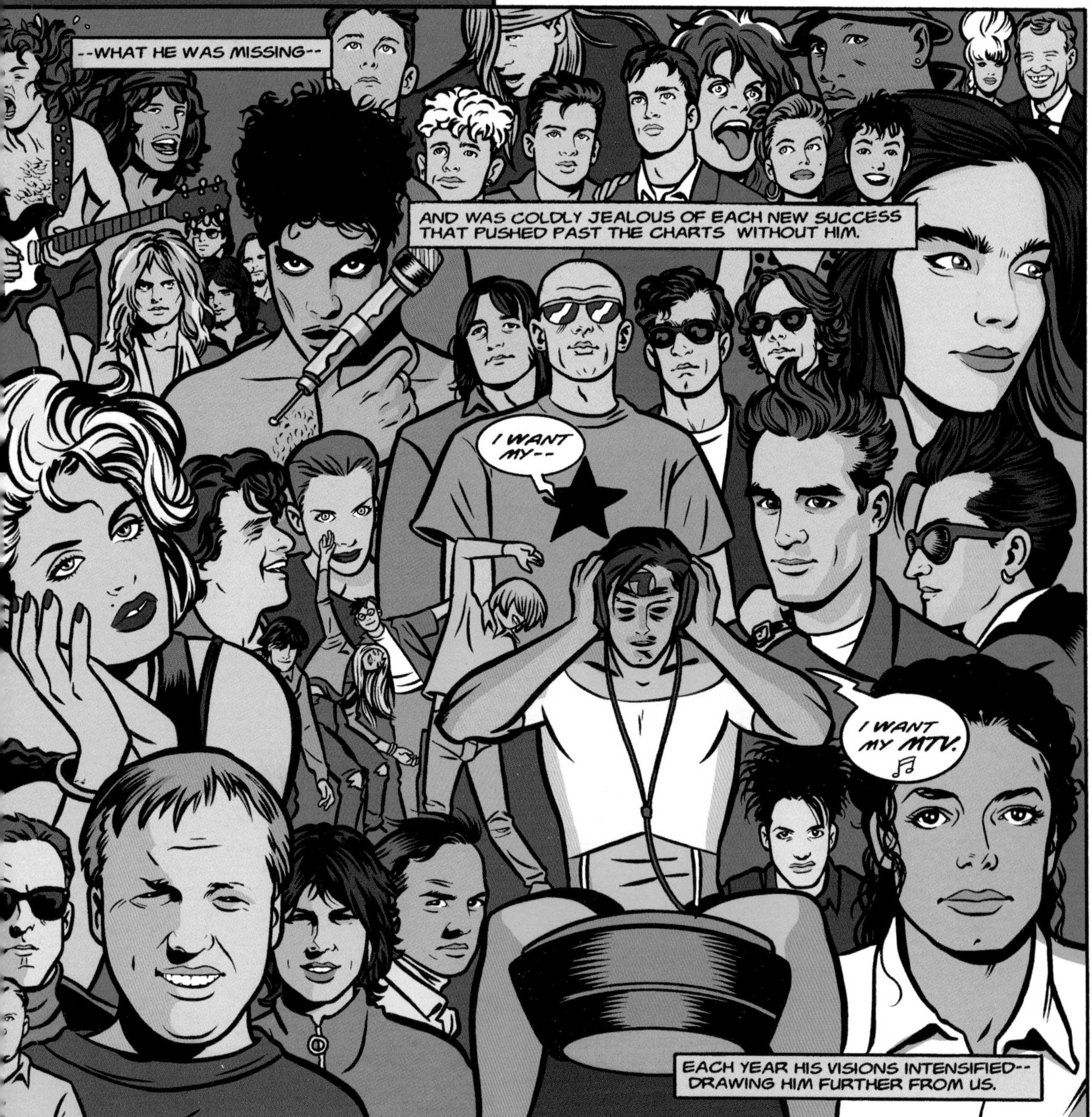
--WHAT HE WAS MISSING--
AND WAS COLDLY JEALOUS OF EACH NEW SUCCESS THAT PUSHED PAST THE CHARTS WITHOUT HIM.
I WANT MY--
I WANT MY MTV.
EACH YEAR HIS VISIONS INTENSIFIED-- DRAWING HIM FURTHER FROM US.

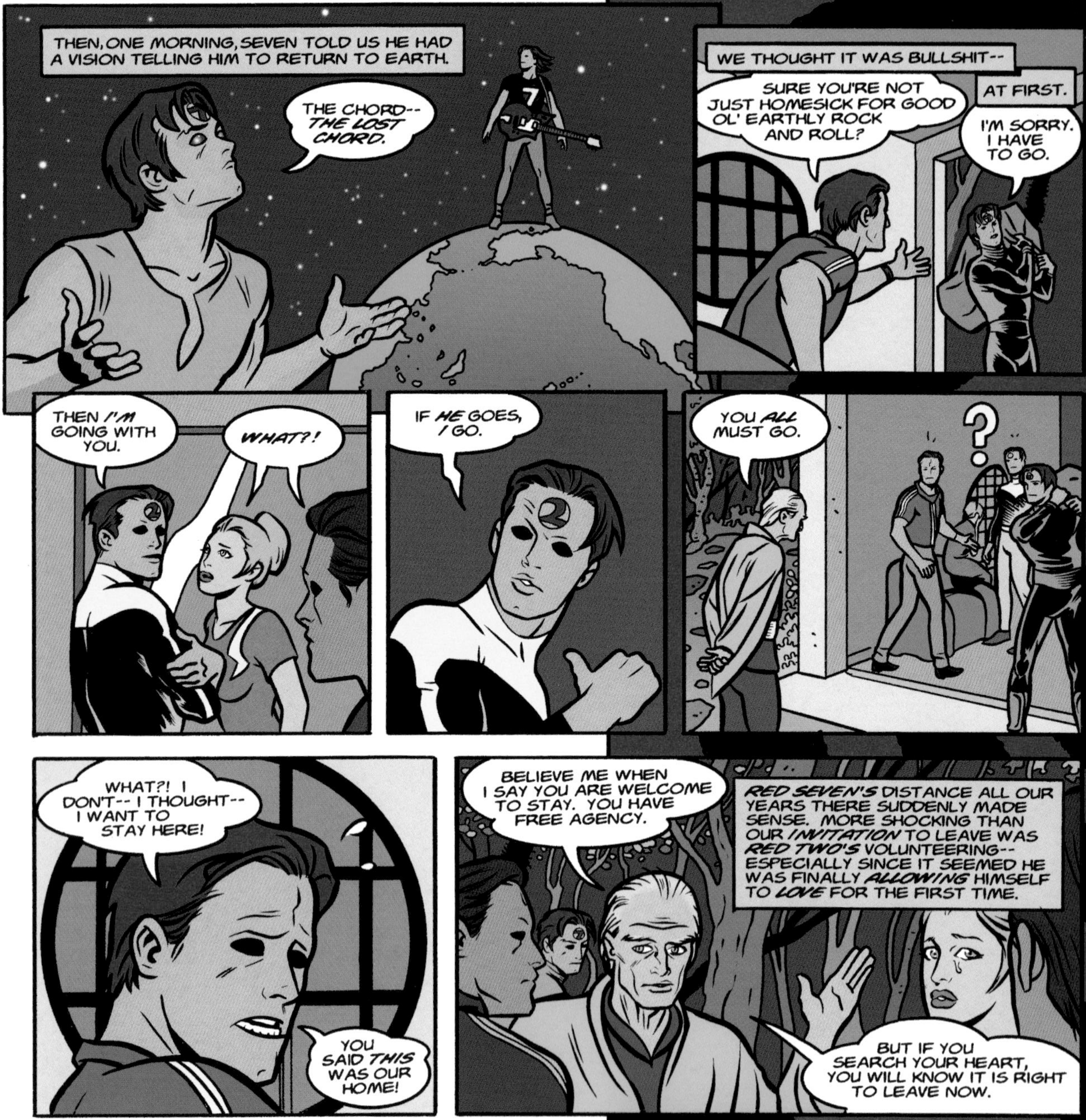
THEN, ONE MORNING, SEVEN TOLD US HE HAD A VISION TELLING HIM TO RETURN TO EARTH.
THE CHORD-- THE LOST CHORD.
WE THOUGHT IT WAS BULLSHIT--
SURE YOU'RE NOT JUST HOMESICK FOR GOOD OL' EARTHLY ROCK AND ROLL?
AT FIRST.
I'M SORRY. I HAVE TO GO.
THEN I'M GOING WITH YOU.
WHAT?!
IF HE GOES, I GO.
YOU ALL MUST GO.
?
WHAT?! I DON'T-- I THOUGHT-- I WANT TO STAY HERE!
YOU SAID THIS WAS OUR HOME!
BELIEVE ME WHEN I SAY YOU ARE WELCOME TO STAY. YOU HAVE FREE AGENCY.
RED SEVEN'S DISTANCE ALL OUR YEARS THERE SUDDENLY MADE SENSE. MORE SHOCKING THAN OUR INVITATION TO LEAVE WAS RED TWO'S VOLUNTEERING-- ESPECIALLY SINCE IT SEEMED HE WAS FINALLY ALLOWING HIMSELF TO LOVE FOR THE FIRST TIME.
BUT IF YOU SEARCH YOUR HEART, YOU WILL KNOW IT IS RIGHT TO LEAVE NOW.

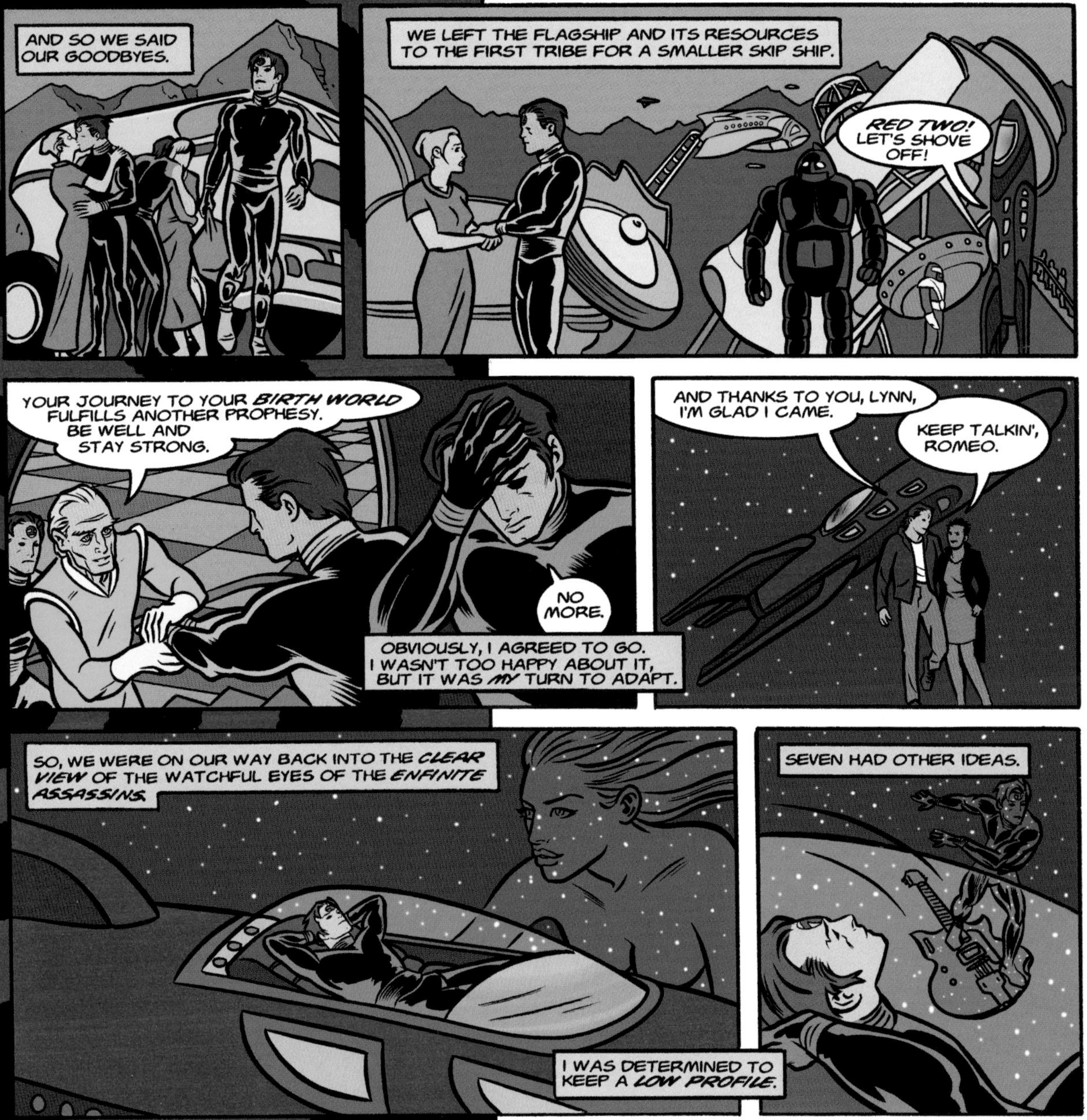
AND SO WE SAID OUR GOODBYES.
WE LEFT THE FLAGSHIP AND ITS RESOURCES TO THE FIRST TRIBE FOR A SMALLER SKIP SHIP.
RED TWO! LET'S SHOVE OFF!
YOUR JOURNEY TO YOUR BIRTH WORLD FULFILLS ANOTHER PROPHESY. BE WELL AND STAY STRONG.
NO MORE.
OBVIOUSLY, I AGREED TO GO. I WASN'T TOO HAPPY ABOUT IT, BUT IT WAS MY TURN TO ADAPT.
AND THANKS TO YOU, LYNN, I'M GLAD I CAME.
KEEP TALKIN', ROMEO.
SO, WE WERE ON OUR WAY BACK INTO THE CLEAR VIEW OF THE WATCHFUL EYES OF THE ENFINITE ASSASSINS.
I WAS DETERMINED TO KEEP A LOW PROFILE.
SEVEN HAD OTHER IDEAS.

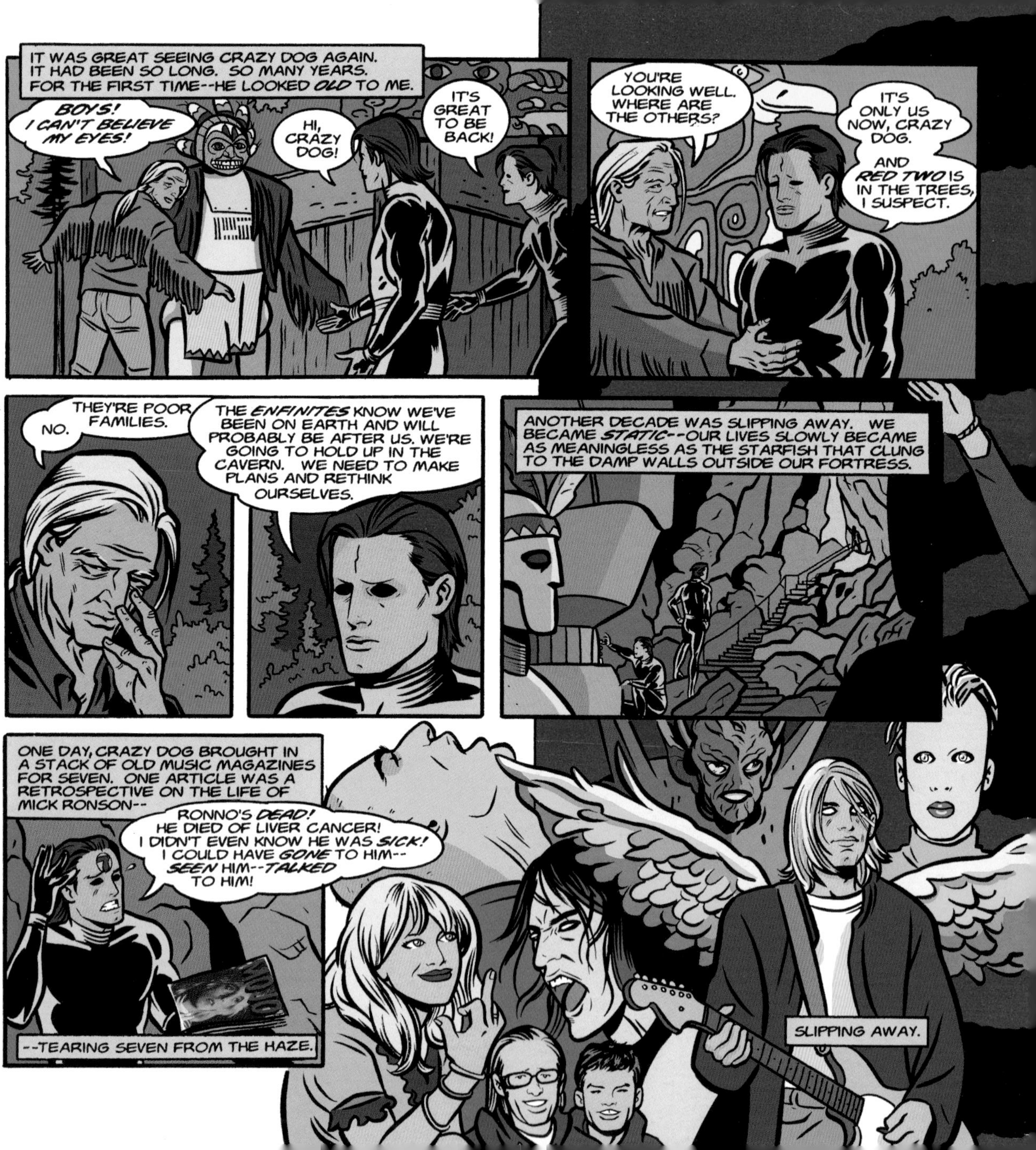
IT WAS GREAT SEEING CRAZY DOG AGAIN. IT HAD BEEN SO LONG. SO MANY YEARS. FOR THE FIRST TIME--HE LOOKED *OLD* TO ME.
BOYS! I CAN'T BELIEVE MY EYES!
HI, CRAZY DOG!
IT'S GREAT TO BE BACK!
YOU'RE LOOKING WELL. WHERE ARE THE OTHERS?
IT'S ONLY US NOW, CRAZY DOG.
AND *RED TWO* IS IN THE TREES, I SUSPECT.
NO.
THEY'RE POOR FAMILIES.
THE *ENFINITES* KNOW WE'VE BEEN ON EARTH AND WILL PROBABLY BE AFTER US. WE'RE GOING TO HOLD UP IN THE CAVERN. WE NEED TO MAKE PLANS AND RETHINK OURSELVES.
ANOTHER DECADE WAS SLIPPING AWAY. WE BECAME *STATIC*--OUR LIVES SLOWLY BECAME AS MEANINGLESS AS THE STARFISH THAT CLUNG TO THE DAMP WALLS OUTSIDE OUR FORTRESS.
ONE DAY, CRAZY DOG BROUGHT IN A STACK OF OLD MUSIC MAGAZINES FOR SEVEN. ONE ARTICLE WAS A RETROSPECTIVE ON THE LIFE OF MICK RONSON--
RONNO'S *DEAD!* HE DIED OF LIVER CANCER! I DIDN'T EVEN KNOW HE WAS *SICK!* I COULD HAVE *GONE* TO HIM-- *SEEN* HIM--*TALKED* TO HIM!
--TEARING SEVEN FROM THE HAZE.
SLIPPING AWAY.

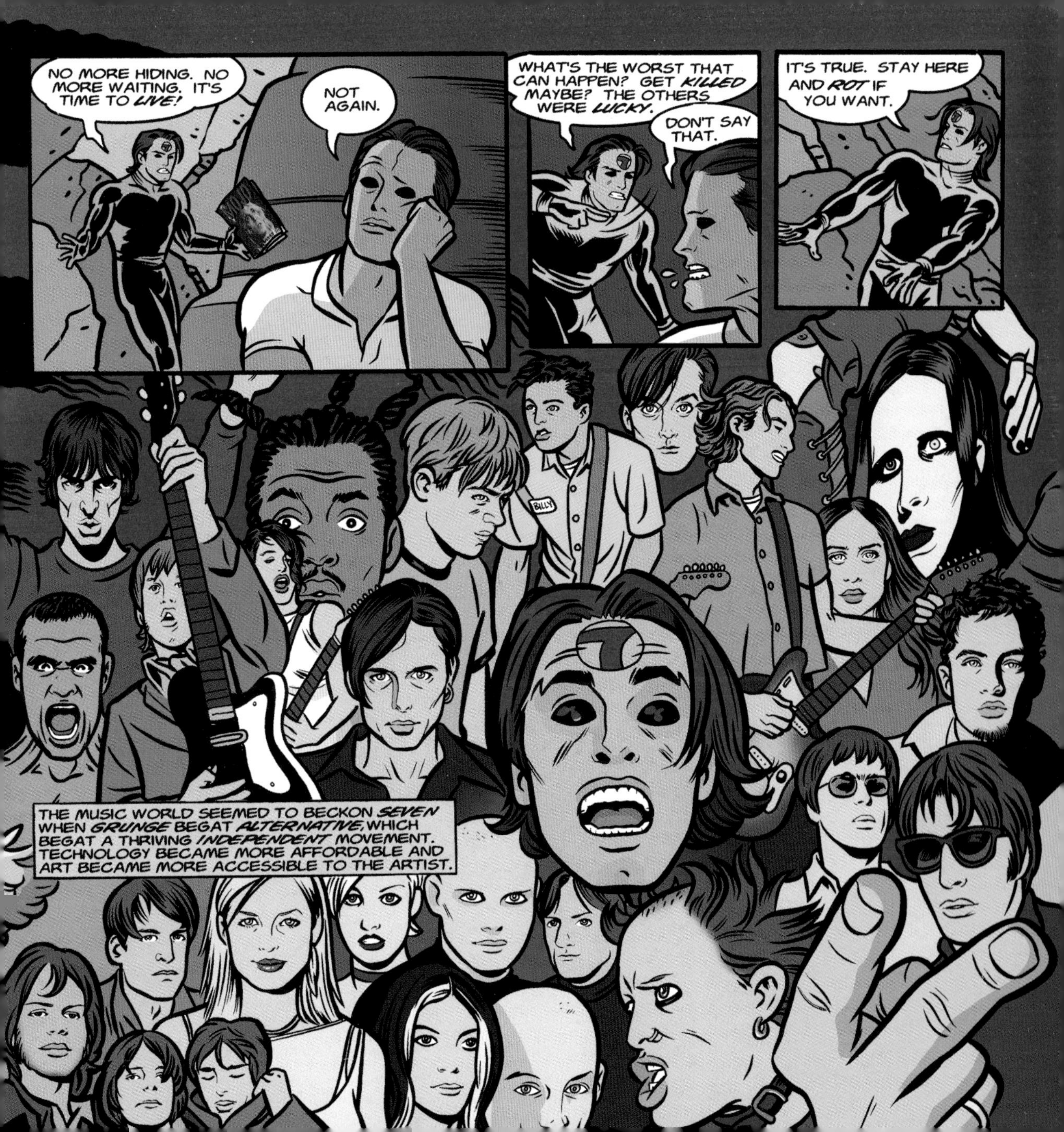
NO MORE HIDING. NO MORE WAITING. IT'S TIME TO *LIVE!*
NOT AGAIN.
WHAT'S THE WORST THAT CAN HAPPEN? GET *KILLED* MAYBE? THE OTHERS WERE *LUCKY.*
DON'T SAY THAT.
IT'S TRUE. STAY HERE AND *ROT* IF YOU WANT.
BILLY
THE MUSIC WORLD SEEMED TO BECKON *SEVEN* WHEN *GRUNGE* BEGAT *ALTERNATIVE,* WHICH BEGAT A THRIVING *INDEPENDENT* MOVEMENT. TECHNOLOGY BECAME MORE AFFORDABLE AND ART BECAME MORE ACCESSIBLE TO THE ARTIST.

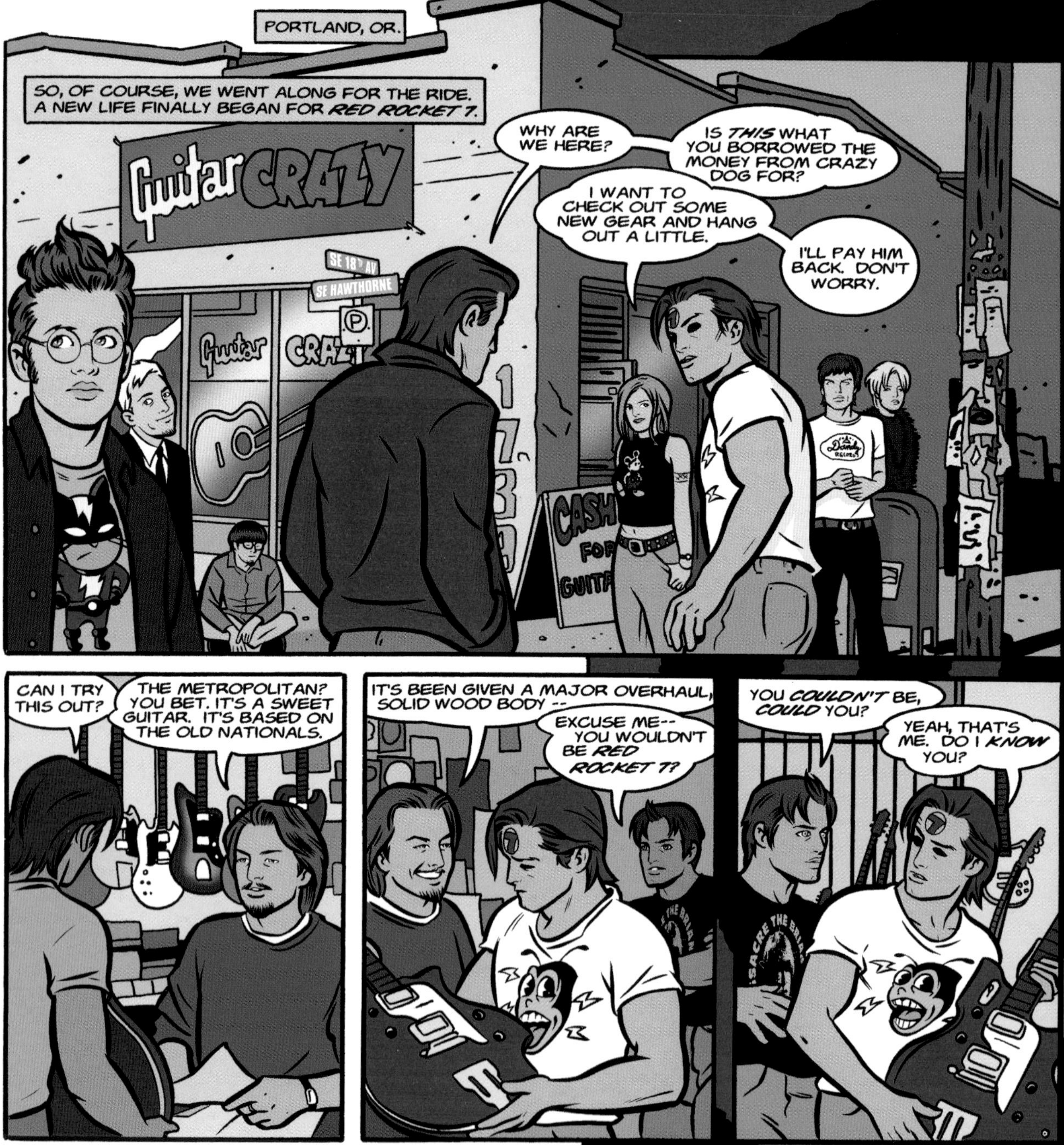

PORTLAND, OR.
SO, OF COURSE, WE WENT ALONG FOR THE RIDE. A NEW LIFE FINALLY BEGAN FOR *RED ROCKET 7.*
Guitar CRAZY
WHY ARE WE HERE?
IS *THIS* WHAT YOU BORROWED THE MONEY FROM CRAZY DOG FOR?
I WANT TO CHECK OUT SOME NEW GEAR AND HANG OUT A LITTLE.
I'LL PAY HIM BACK. DON'T WORRY.
SE 18TH AV
SE HAWTHORNE
CAN I TRY THIS OUT?
THE METROPOLITAN? YOU BET. IT'S A SWEET GUITAR. IT'S BASED ON THE OLD NATIONALS.
IT'S BEEN GIVEN A MAJOR OVERHAUL, SOLID WOOD BODY --
EXCUSE ME-- YOU WOULDN'T BE *RED ROCKET 7?*
YOU *COULDN'T* BE, *COULD* YOU?
YEAH, THAT'S ME. DO I *KNOW* YOU?

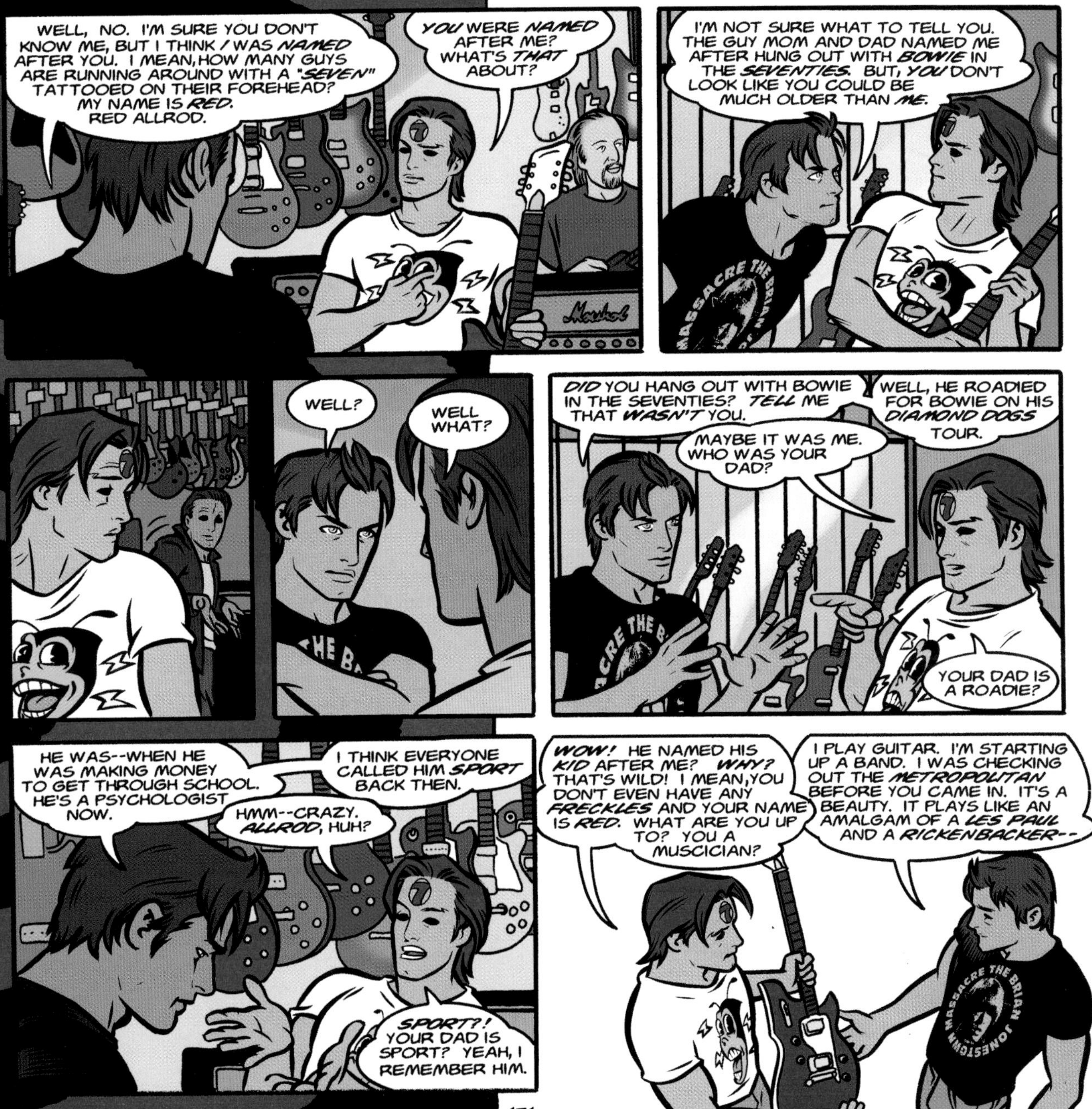
WELL, NO. I'M SURE YOU DON'T KNOW ME, BUT I THINK I WAS NAMED AFTER YOU. I MEAN, HOW MANY GUYS ARE RUNNING AROUND WITH A "SEVEN" TATTOOED ON THEIR FOREHEAD? MY NAME IS RED. RED ALLROD.
YOU WERE NAMED AFTER ME? WHAT'S THAT ABOUT?
I'M NOT SURE WHAT TO TELL YOU. THE GUY MOM AND DAD NAMED ME AFTER HUNG OUT WITH BOWIE IN THE SEVENTIES. BUT, YOU DON'T LOOK LIKE YOU COULD BE MUCH OLDER THAN ME.
MASSACRE THE BRIAN
WELL?
WELL WHAT?
DID YOU HANG OUT WITH BOWIE IN THE SEVENTIES? TELL ME THAT WASN'T YOU.
MAYBE IT WAS ME. WHO WAS YOUR DAD?
WELL, HE ROADIED FOR BOWIE ON HIS DIAMOND DOGS TOUR.
YOUR DAD IS A ROADIE?
HE WAS--WHEN HE WAS MAKING MONEY TO GET THROUGH SCHOOL. HE'S A PSYCHOLOGIST NOW.
I THINK EVERYONE CALLED HIM SPORT BACK THEN.
HMM--CRAZY. ALLROD, HUH?
SPORT?! YOUR DAD IS SPORT? YEAH, I REMEMBER HIM.
WOW! HE NAMED HIS KID AFTER ME? WHY? THAT'S WILD! I MEAN, YOU DON'T EVEN HAVE ANY FRECKLES AND YOUR NAME IS RED. WHAT ARE YOU UP TO? YOU A MUSCICIAN?
I PLAY GUITAR. I'M STARTING UP A BAND. I WAS CHECKING OUT THE METROPOLITAN BEFORE YOU CAME IN. IT'S A BEAUTY. IT PLAYS LIKE AN AMALGAM OF A LES PAUL AND A RICKENBACKER--
MASSACRE THE BRIAN JONESTOWN

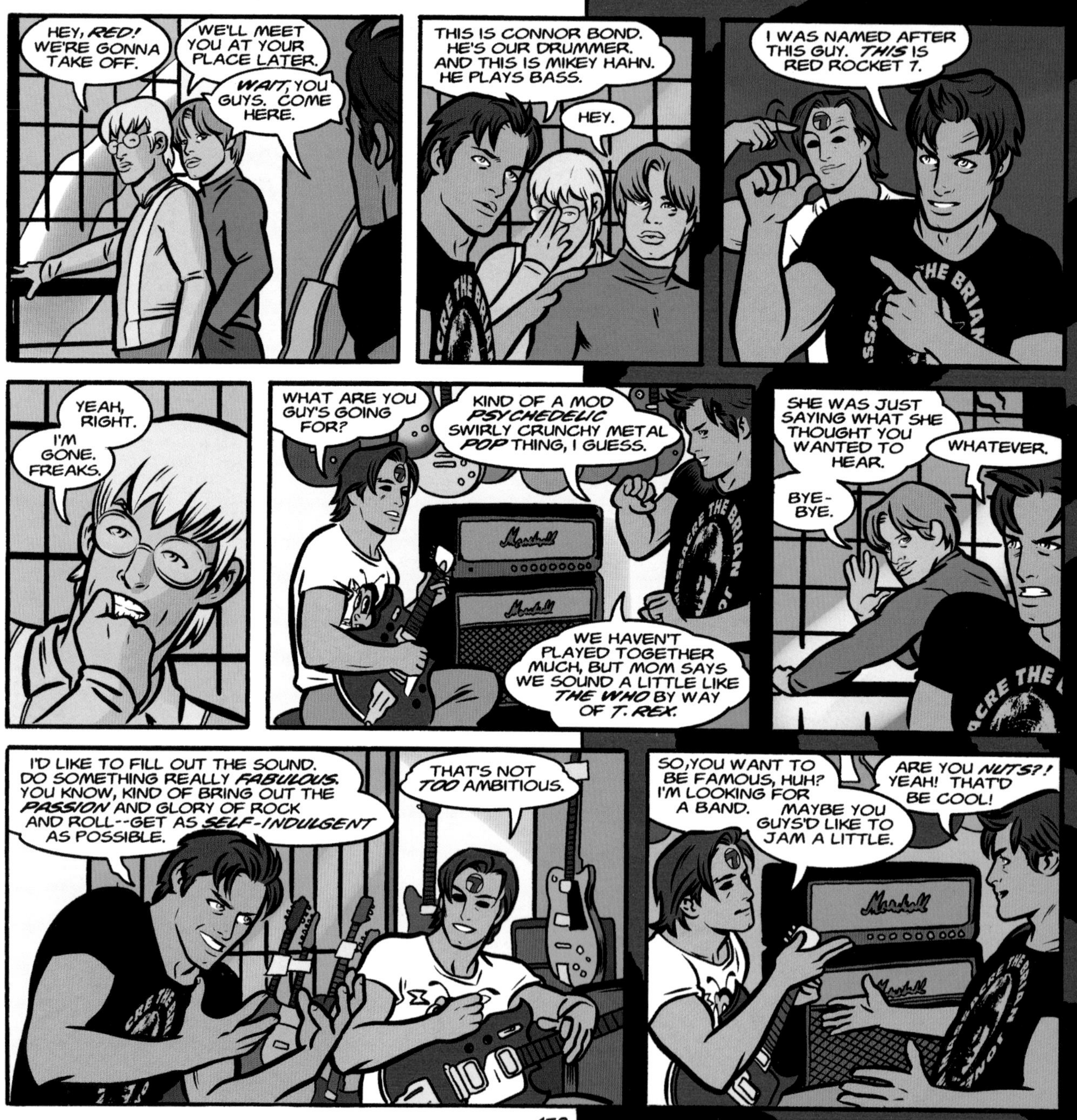
HEY, RED! WE'RE GONNA TAKE OFF.
WE'LL MEET YOU AT YOUR PLACE LATER.
WAIT, YOU GUYS. COME HERE.
THIS IS CONNOR BOND. HE'S OUR DRUMMER. AND THIS IS MIKEY HAHN. HE PLAYS BASS.
HEY.
I WAS NAMED AFTER THIS GUY. THIS IS RED ROCKET 7.
YEAH, RIGHT.
I'M GONE. FREAKS.
WHAT ARE YOU GUY'S GOING FOR?
KIND OF A MOD PSYCHEDELIC SWIRLY CRUNCHY METAL POP THING, I GUESS.
WE HAVEN'T PLAYED TOGETHER MUCH, BUT MOM SAYS WE SOUND A LITTLE LIKE THE WHO BY WAY OF T. REX.
SHE WAS JUST SAYING WHAT SHE THOUGHT YOU WANTED TO HEAR.
WHATEVER.
BYE-BYE.
I'D LIKE TO FILL OUT THE SOUND. DO SOMETHING REALLY FABULOUS. YOU KNOW, KIND OF BRING OUT THE PASSION AND GLORY OF ROCK AND ROLL--GET AS SELF-INDULGENT AS POSSIBLE.
THAT'S NOT TOO AMBITIOUS.
SO, YOU WANT TO BE FAMOUS, HUH? I'M LOOKING FOR A BAND.
MAYBE YOU GUYS'D LIKE TO JAM A LITTLE.
ARE YOU NUTS?! YEAH! THAT'D BE COOL!

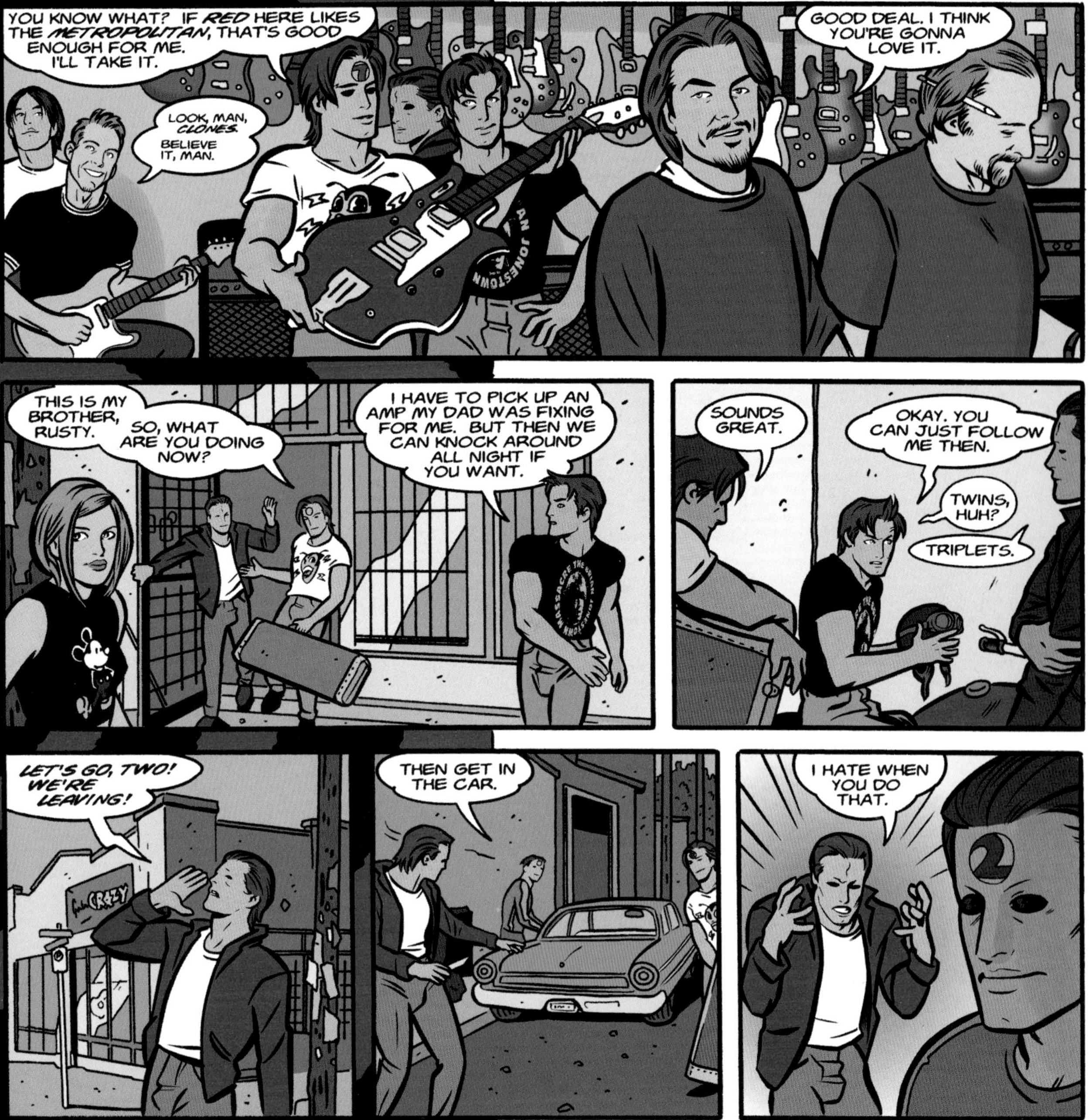

YOU KNOW WHAT? IF RED HERE LIKES THE METROPOLITAN, THAT'S GOOD ENOUGH FOR ME. I'LL TAKE IT.
LOOK, MAN, CLONES.
BELIEVE IT, MAN.
GOOD DEAL. I THINK YOU'RE GONNA LOVE IT.
THIS IS MY BROTHER, RUSTY.
SO, WHAT ARE YOU DOING NOW?
I HAVE TO PICK UP AN AMP MY DAD WAS FIXING FOR ME. BUT THEN WE CAN KNOCK AROUND ALL NIGHT IF YOU WANT.
SOUNDS GREAT.
OKAY. YOU CAN JUST FOLLOW ME THEN.
TWINS, HUH?
TRIPLETS.
LET'S GO, TWO! WE'RE LEAVING!
THEN GET IN THE CAR.
I HATE WHEN YOU DO THAT.

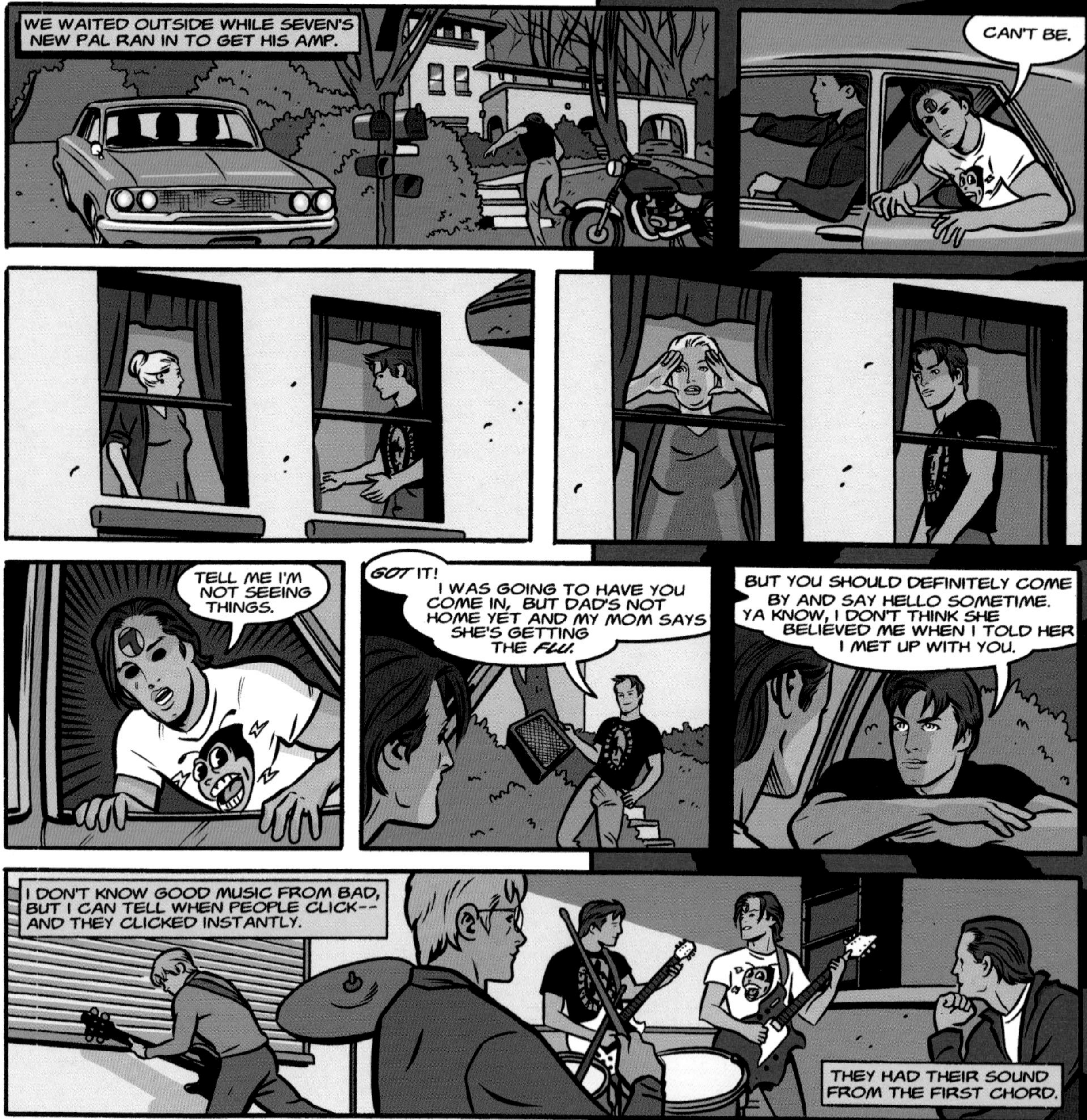
WE WAITED OUTSIDE WHILE SEVEN'S NEW PAL RAN IN TO GET HIS AMP.
CAN'T BE.
TELL ME I'M NOT SEEING THINGS.
GOT IT!
I WAS GOING TO HAVE YOU COME IN, BUT DAD'S NOT HOME YET AND MY MOM SAYS SHE'S GETTING THE FLU.
BUT YOU SHOULD DEFINITELY COME BY AND SAY HELLO SOMETIME. YA KNOW, I DON'T THINK SHE BELIEVED ME WHEN I TOLD HER I MET UP WITH YOU.
I DON'T KNOW GOOD MUSIC FROM BAD, BUT I CAN TELL WHEN PEOPLE CLICK-- AND THEY CLICKED INSTANTLY.
THEY HAD THEIR SOUND FROM THE FIRST CHORD.

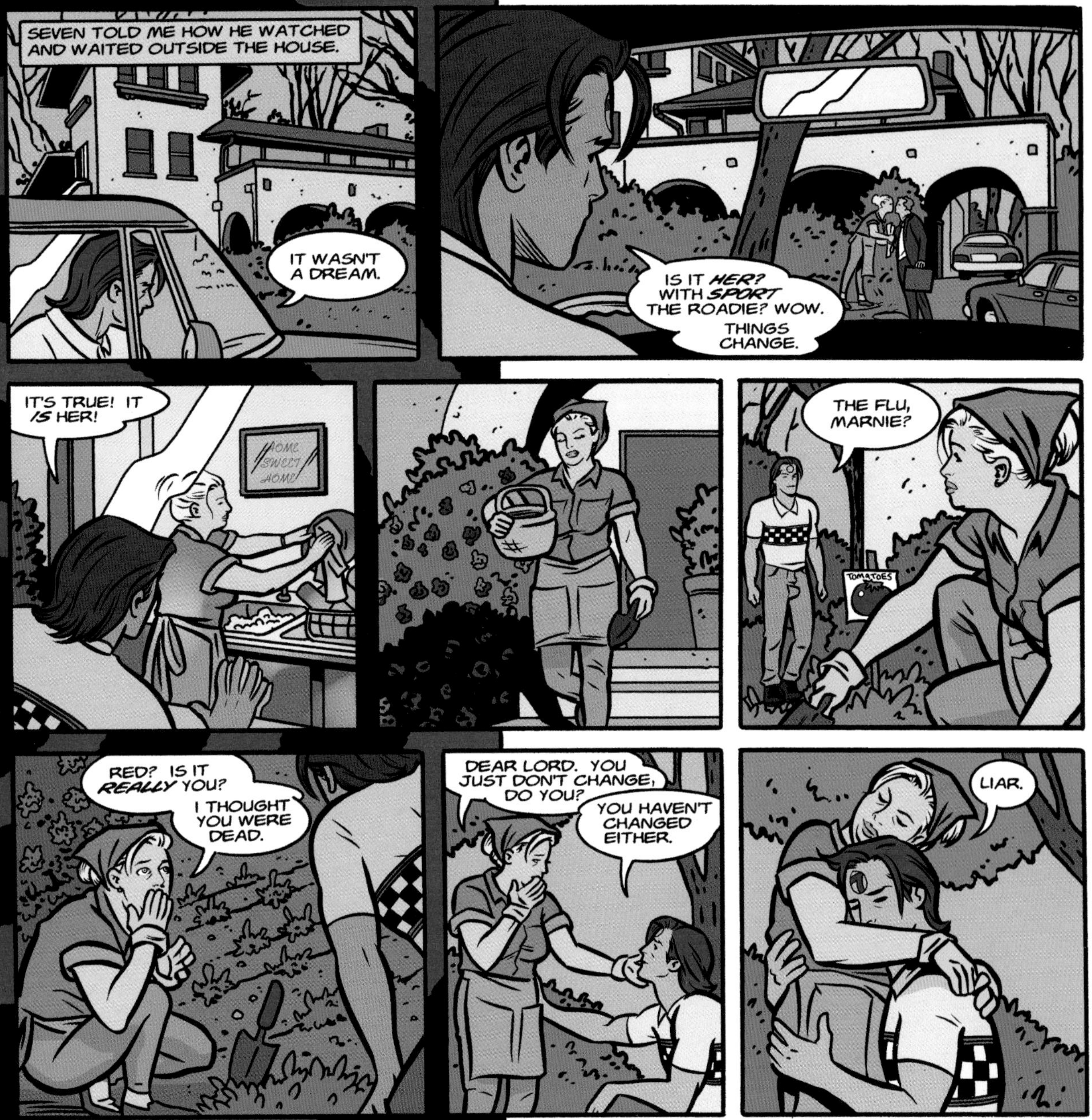
SEVEN TOLD ME HOW HE WATCHED AND WAITED OUTSIDE THE HOUSE.
IT WASN'T A DREAM.
IS IT *HER?* WITH *SPORT* THE ROADIE? WOW.
THINGS CHANGE.
IT'S TRUE! IT *IS* HER!
HOME SWEET HOME
THE FLU, MARNIE?
TOMATOES
RED? IS IT *REALLY* YOU?
I THOUGHT YOU WERE DEAD.
DEAR LORD. YOU JUST DON'T CHANGE, DO YOU?
YOU HAVEN'T CHANGED EITHER.
LIAR.

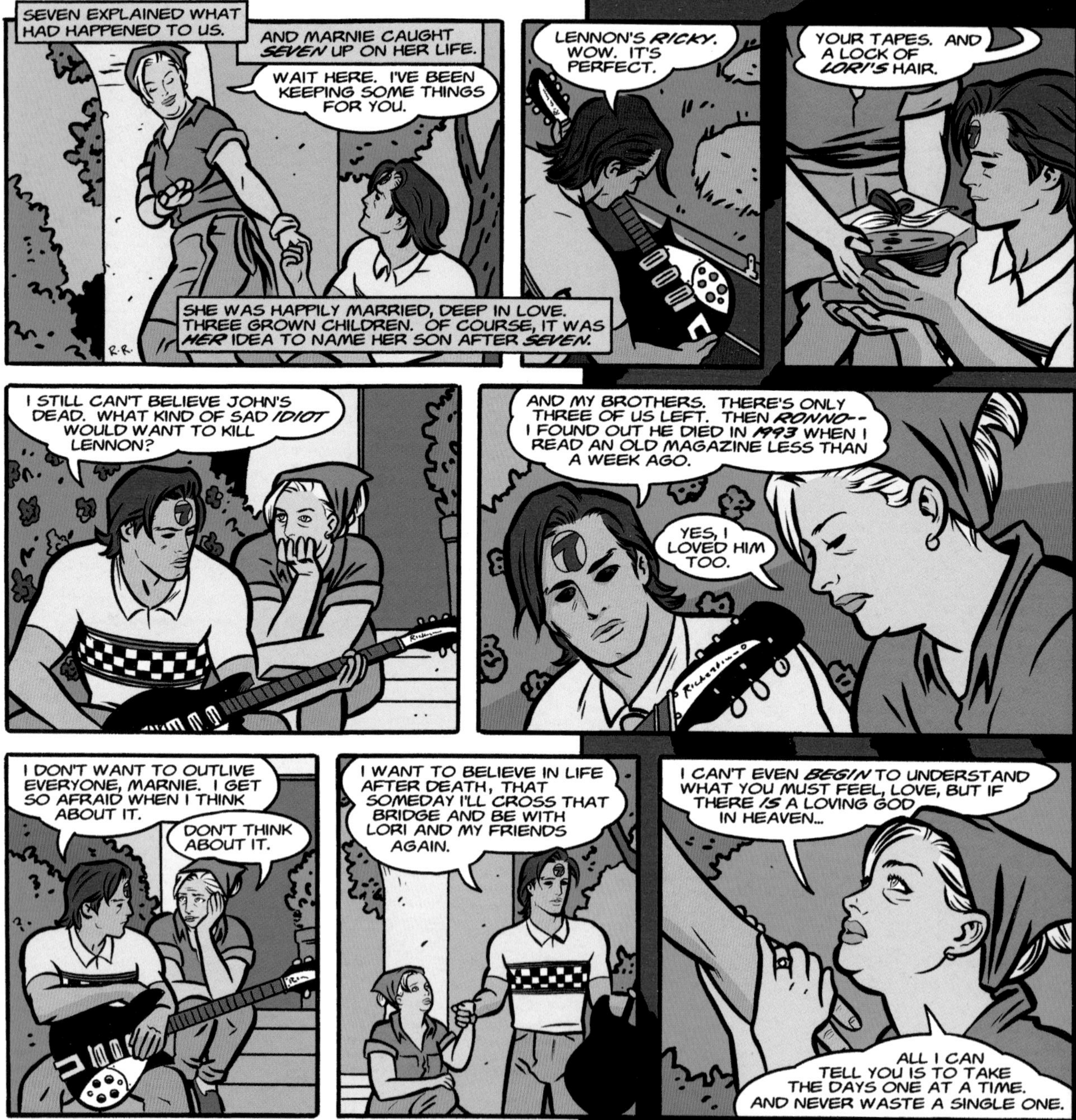

SEVEN EXPLAINED WHAT HAD HAPPENED TO US.
AND MARNIE CAUGHT SEVEN UP ON HER LIFE.
WAIT HERE. I'VE BEEN KEEPING SOME THINGS FOR YOU.
SHE WAS HAPPILY MARRIED, DEEP IN LOVE. THREE GROWN CHILDREN. OF COURSE, IT WAS HER IDEA TO NAME HER SON AFTER SEVEN.
R.R.
LENNON'S RICKY. WOW. IT'S PERFECT.
YOUR TAPES. AND A LOCK OF LORI'S HAIR.
I STILL CAN'T BELIEVE JOHN'S DEAD. WHAT KIND OF SAD IDIOT WOULD WANT TO KILL LENNON?
AND MY BROTHERS. THERE'S ONLY THREE OF US LEFT. THEN RONNO-- I FOUND OUT HE DIED IN 1993 WHEN I READ AN OLD MAGAZINE LESS THAN A WEEK AGO.
YES, I LOVED HIM TOO.
I DON'T WANT TO OUTLIVE EVERYONE, MARNIE. I GET SO AFRAID WHEN I THINK ABOUT IT.
DON'T THINK ABOUT IT.
I WANT TO BELIEVE IN LIFE AFTER DEATH, THAT SOMEDAY I'LL CROSS THAT BRIDGE AND BE WITH LORI AND MY FRIENDS AGAIN.
I CAN'T EVEN BEGIN TO UNDERSTAND WHAT YOU MUST FEEL, LOVE, BUT IF THERE IS A LOVING GOD IN HEAVEN...
ALL I CAN TELL YOU IS TO TAKE THE DAYS ONE AT A TIME. AND NEVER WASTE A SINGLE ONE.

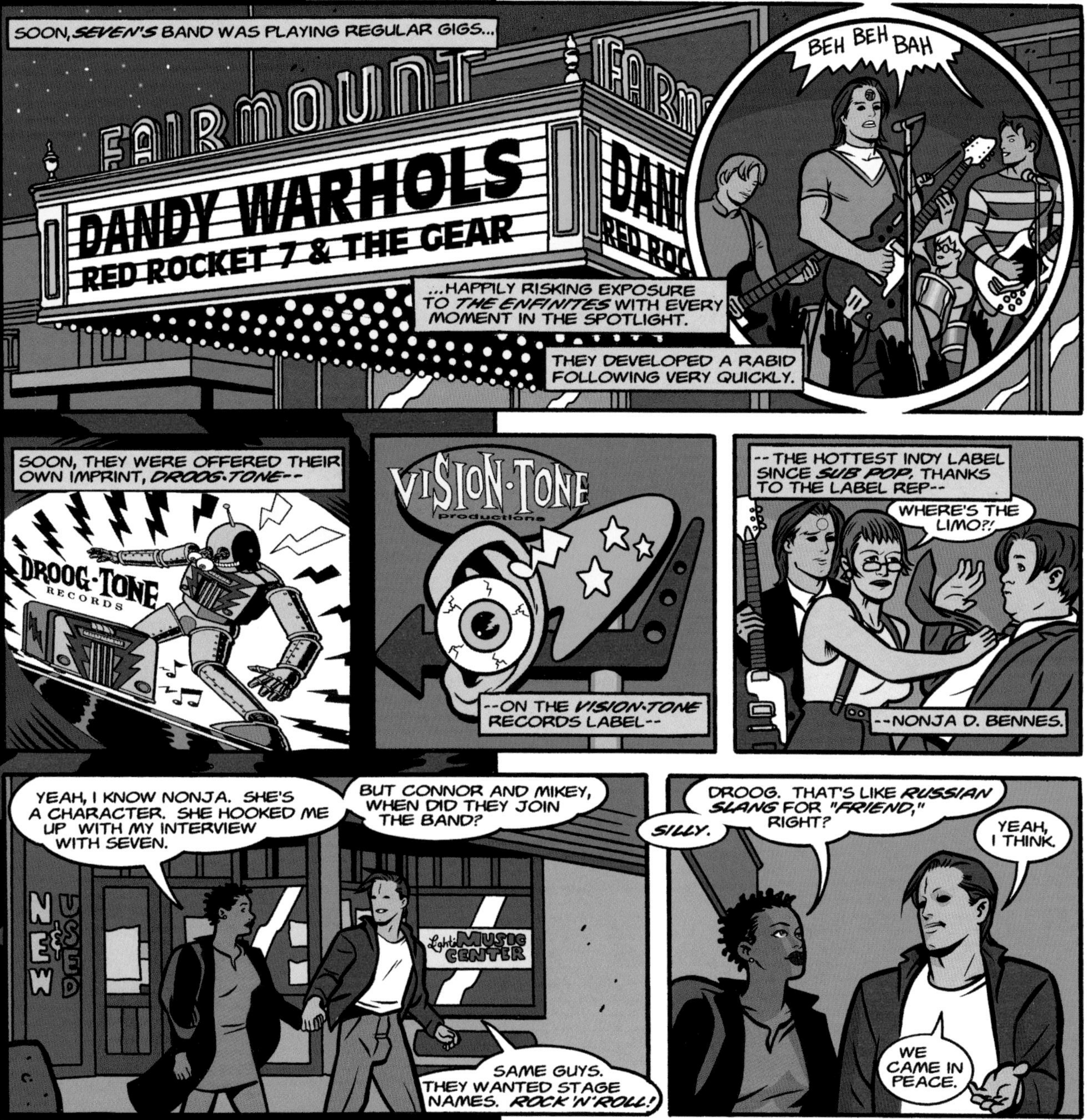
SOON, SEVEN'S BAND WAS PLAYING REGULAR GIGS...
FAIRMOUNT
DANDY WARHOLS
RED ROCKET 7 & THE GEAR
BEH BEH BAH
...HAPPILY RISKING EXPOSURE TO THE ENFINITES WITH EVERY MOMENT IN THE SPOTLIGHT.
THEY DEVELOPED A RABID FOLLOWING VERY QUICKLY.
SOON, THEY WERE OFFERED THEIR OWN IMPRINT, DROOG-TONE--
DROOG-TONE RECORDS
VISION-TONE productions
--ON THE VISION-TONE RECORDS LABEL--
--THE HOTTEST INDY LABEL SINCE SUB POP, THANKS TO THE LABEL REP--
WHERE'S THE LIMO?!
--NONJA D. BENNES.
YEAH, I KNOW NONJA. SHE'S A CHARACTER. SHE HOOKED ME UP WITH MY INTERVIEW WITH SEVEN.
BUT CONNOR AND MIKEY, WHEN DID THEY JOIN THE BAND?
NEW & USED
Light's MUSIC CENTER
SAME GUYS. THEY WANTED STAGE NAMES. ROCK 'N' ROLL!
SILLY.
DROOG. THAT'S LIKE RUSSIAN SLANG FOR "FRIEND," RIGHT?
YEAH, I THINK.
WE CAME IN PEACE.

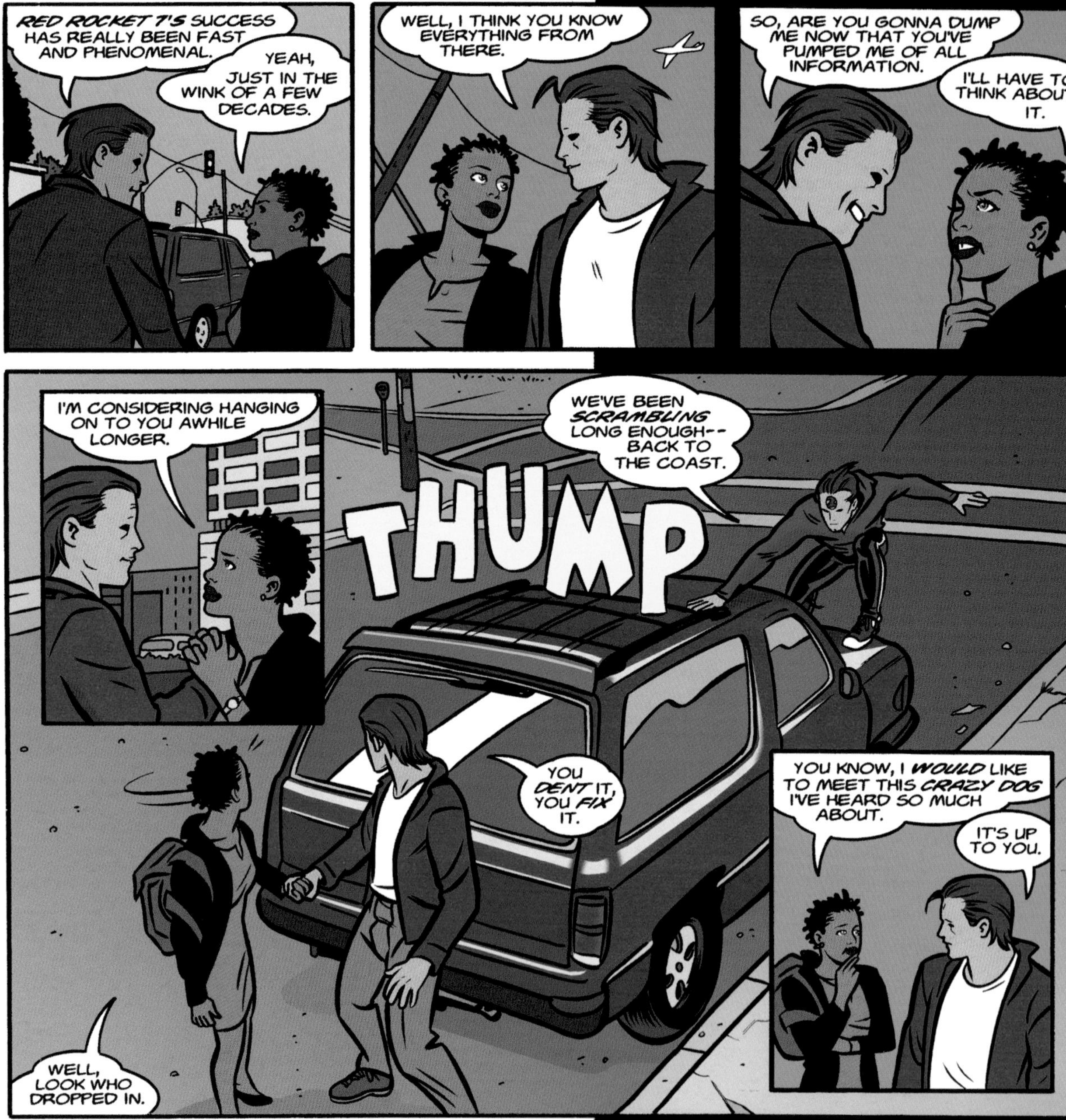

RED ROCKET 7'S SUCCESS HAS REALLY BEEN FAST AND PHENOMENAL.
YEAH, JUST IN THE WINK OF A FEW DECADES.
WELL, I THINK YOU KNOW EVERYTHING FROM THERE.
SO, ARE YOU GONNA DUMP ME NOW THAT YOU'VE PUMPED ME OF ALL INFORMATION.
I'LL HAVE TO THINK ABOUT IT.
I'M CONSIDERING HANGING ON TO YOU AWHILE LONGER.
WE'VE BEEN SCRAMBLING LONG ENOUGH-- BACK TO THE COAST.
THUMP
YOU DENT IT, YOU FIX IT.
WELL, LOOK WHO DROPPED IN.
YOU KNOW, I WOULD LIKE TO MEET THIS CRAZY DOG I'VE HEARD SO MUCH ABOUT.
IT'S UP TO YOU.

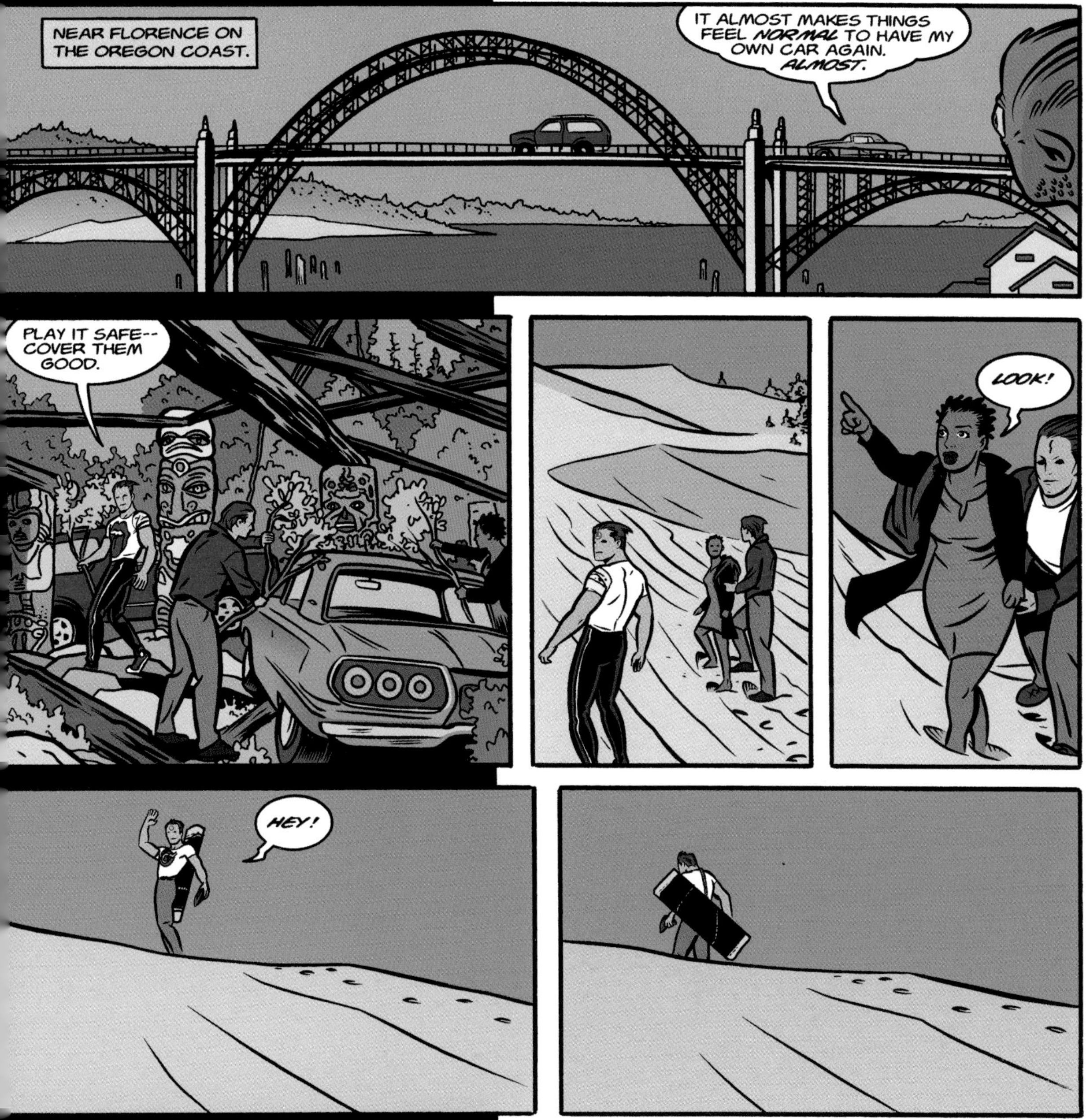
NEAR FLORENCE ON THE OREGON COAST.
IT ALMOST MAKES THINGS FEEL NORMAL TO HAVE MY OWN CAR AGAIN. ALMOST.
PLAY IT SAFE-- COVER THEM GOOD.
LOOK!
HEY!

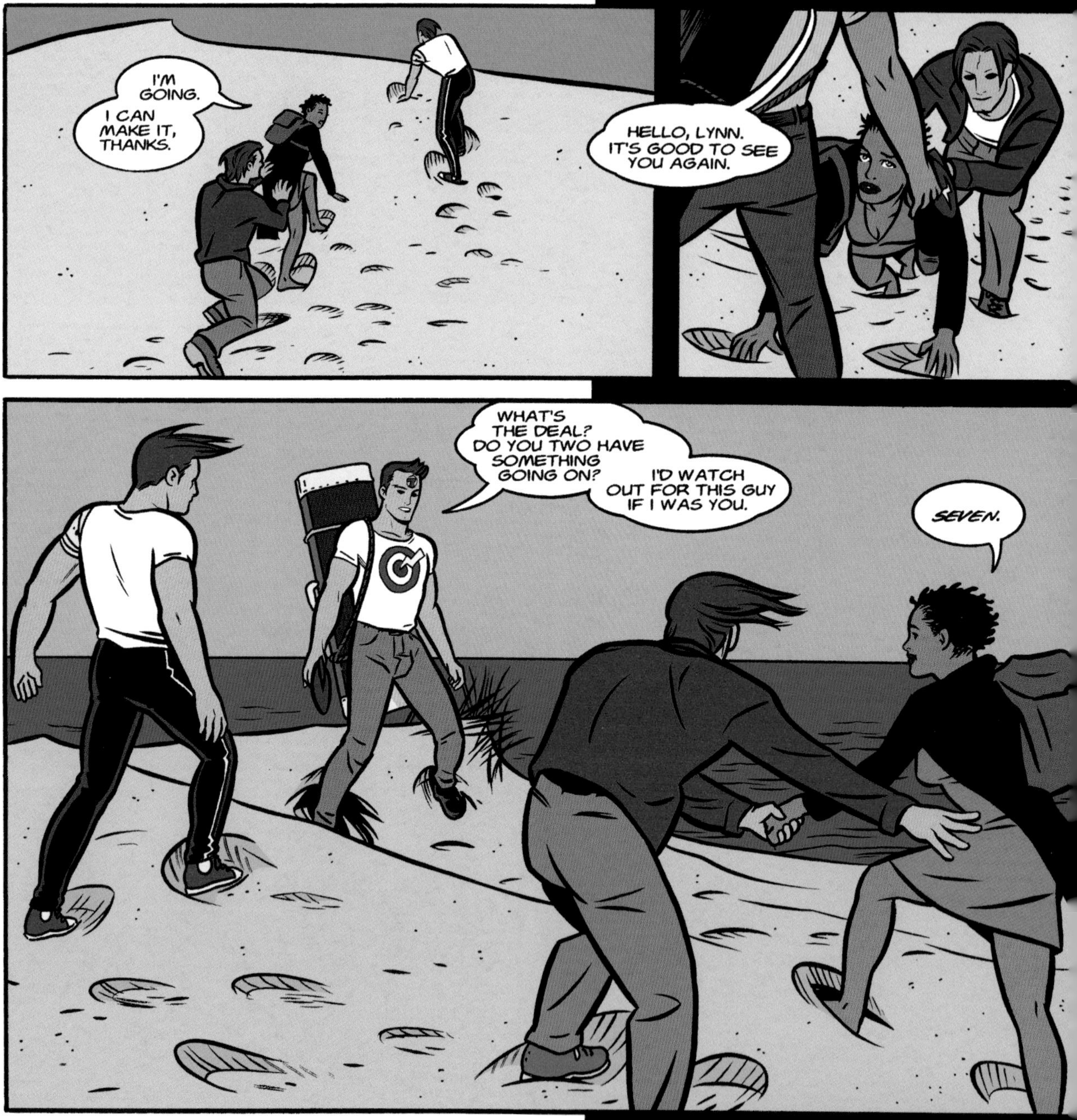
I'M GOING.
I CAN MAKE IT, THANKS.
HELLO, LYNN. IT'S GOOD TO SEE YOU AGAIN.
WHAT'S THE DEAL? DO YOU TWO HAVE SOMETHING GOING ON?
I'D WATCH OUT FOR THIS GUY IF I WAS YOU.
SEVEN.

NEXT: ASTROESQUE

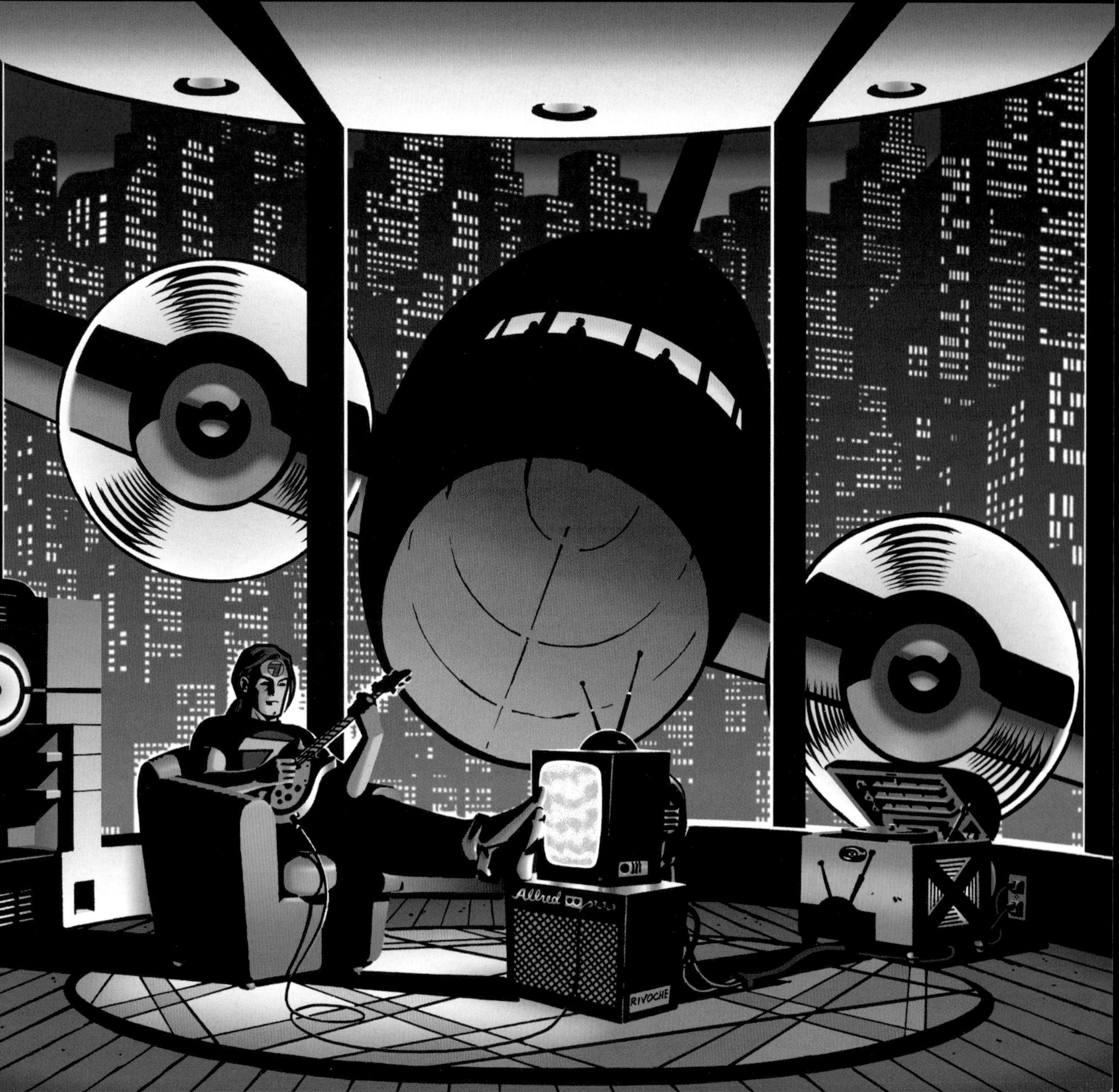
Allred
RIVOCHE

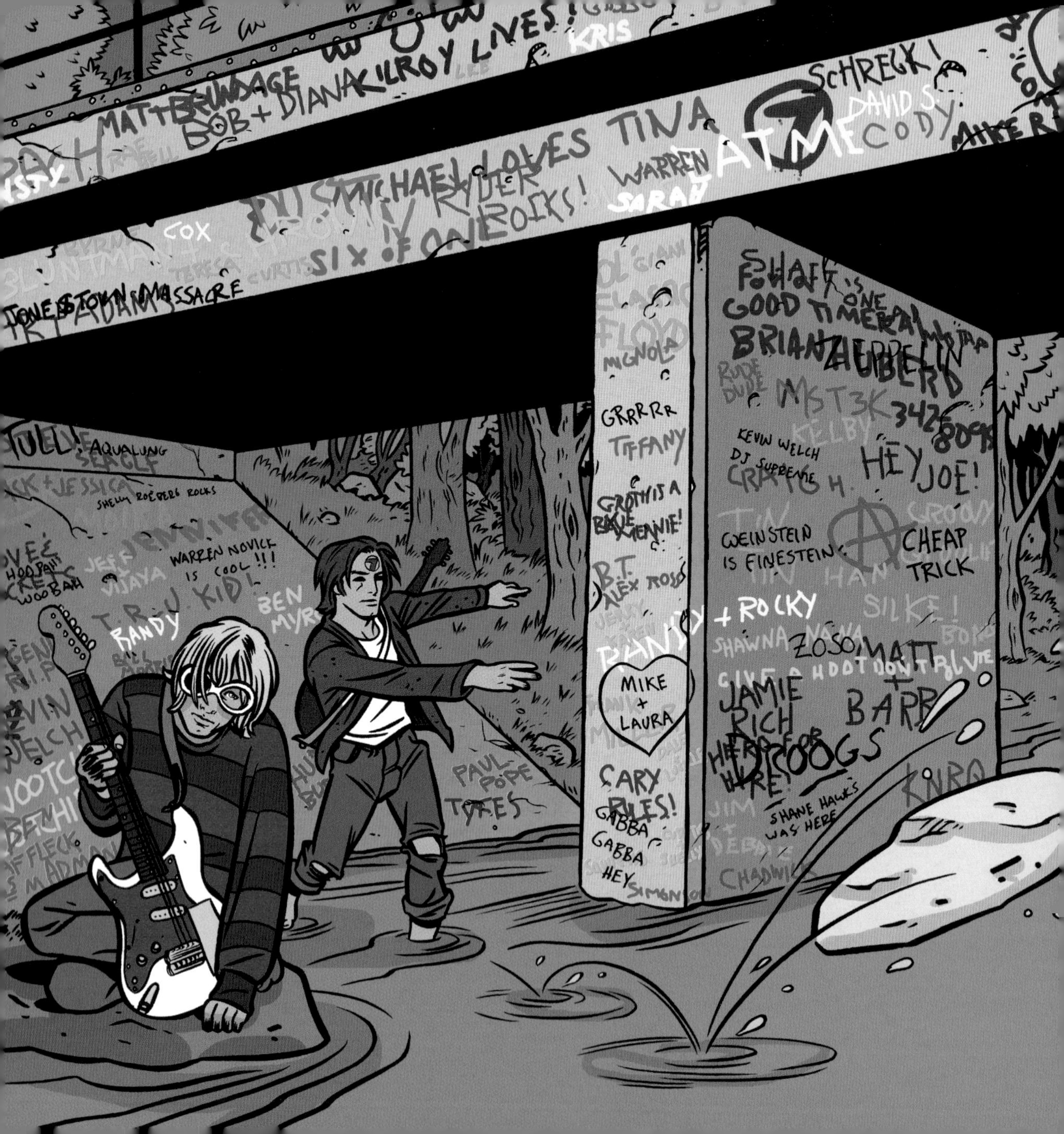

KILROY LIVES!
KRIS
MATT BRUNDAGE
BOB + DIANA
SCHRECK!
DAVID S.
TINA
ATME
CODY
MICHAEL LOVES TINA
WARREN
SARAH
ROCKS!
COX
SIX OF ONE
JONESTOWN MASSACRE
CURTIS
FLOYD
MIGNOLA
GOOD TIMES
BRIAN
ZEPPELIN
MST3K
KELBY
HEY JOE!
KEVIN WELCH
DJ SUPREME
GRRRRR
TIFFANY
WEINSTEIN IS FINESTEIN
CHEAP TRICK
B.T.
ALEX ROSS
+ ROCKY
SHAWNA
ZOSO
MATT + BARB
SILKE!
MIKE + LAURA
JAMIE RICH
DROOGS
SHANE HAWKS WAS HERE
CARY RULES!
GABBA GABBA HEY
CHADWICK
TULL!
AQUALUNG
SHELLY ROEBERG ROCKS
WARREN NOVICK IS COOL!!!
JEFF
VIJAYA
KID!
BEN
RANDY
PAUL POPE
TYRES

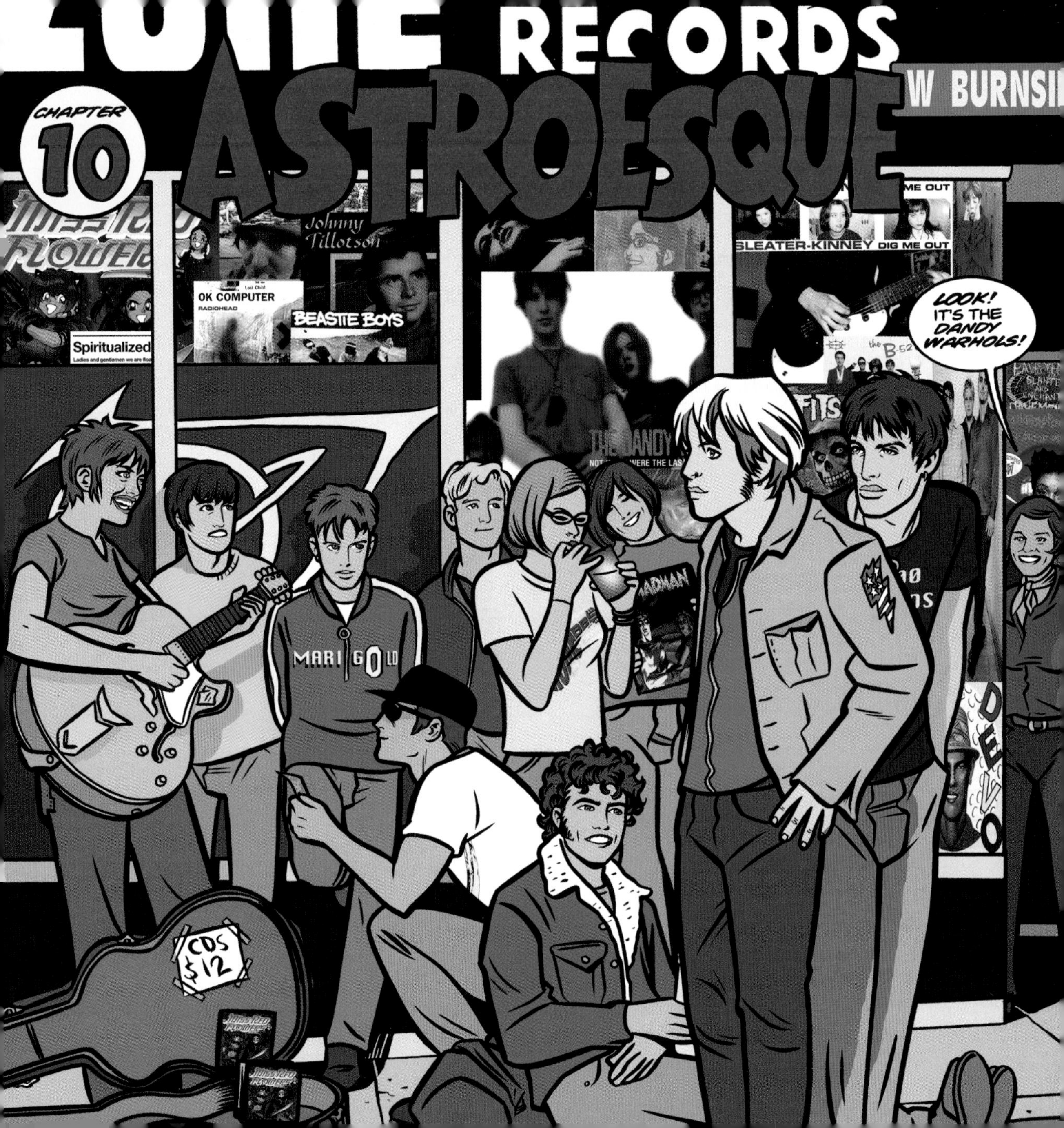
RECORDS
CHAPTER 10
ASTROESQUE
Johnny Tillotson
OK COMPUTER
RADIOHEAD
BEASTIE BOYS
Spiritualized
SLEATER-KINNEY DIG ME OUT
LOOK! IT'S THE DANDY WARHOLS!
MARIGOLD
CDS $12
DEVO

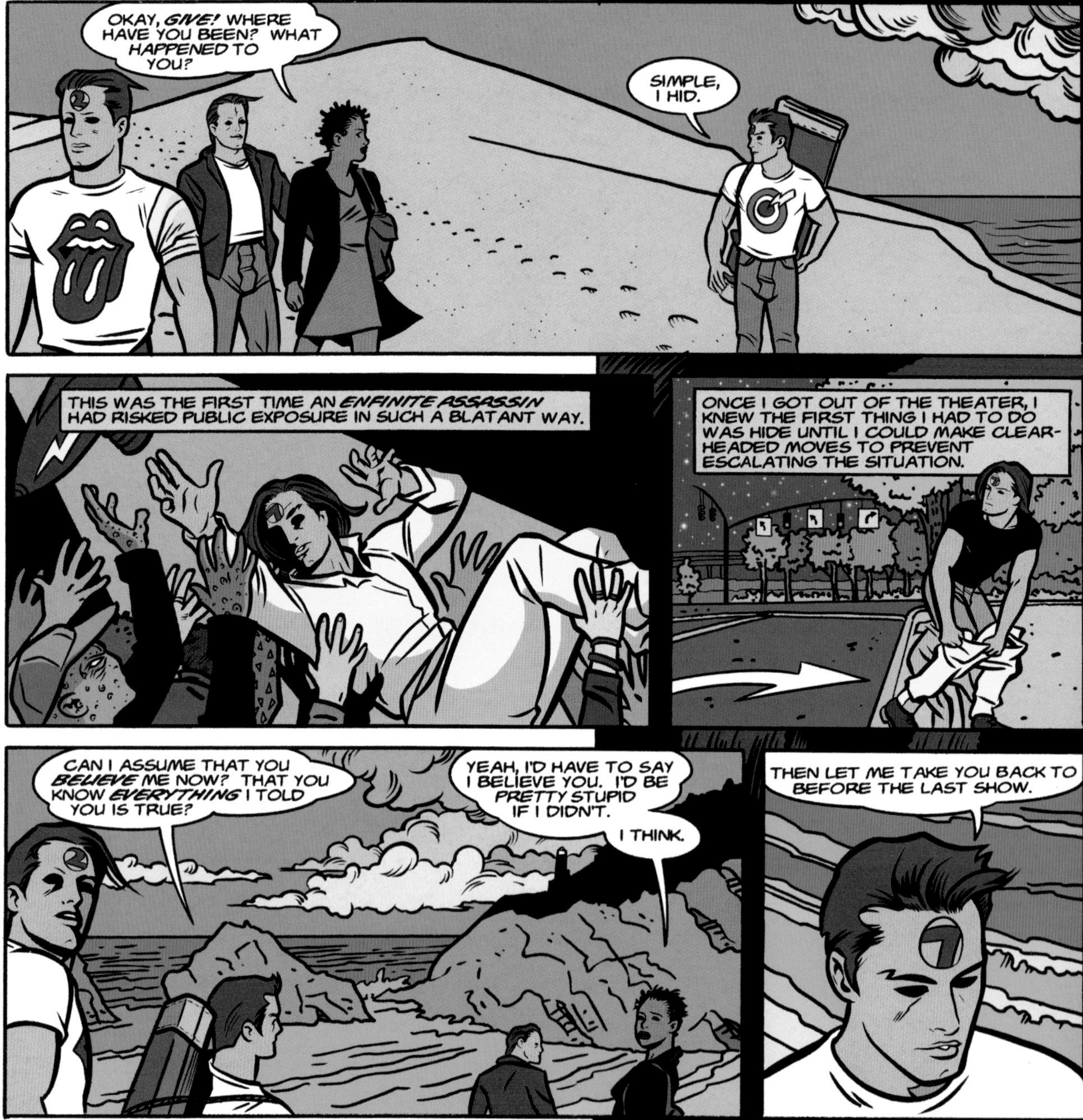
OKAY, GIVE! WHERE HAVE YOU BEEN? WHAT HAPPENED TO YOU?
SIMPLE, I HID.
THIS WAS THE FIRST TIME AN ENFINITE ASSASSIN HAD RISKED PUBLIC EXPOSURE IN SUCH A BLATANT WAY.
ONCE I GOT OUT OF THE THEATER, I KNEW THE FIRST THING I HAD TO DO WAS HIDE UNTIL I COULD MAKE CLEAR-HEADED MOVES TO PREVENT ESCALATING THE SITUATION.
CAN I ASSUME THAT YOU BELIEVE ME NOW? THAT YOU KNOW EVERYTHING I TOLD YOU IS TRUE?
YEAH, I'D HAVE TO SAY I BELIEVE YOU. I'D BE PRETTY STUPID IF I DIDN'T.
I THINK.
THEN LET ME TAKE YOU BACK TO BEFORE THE LAST SHOW.

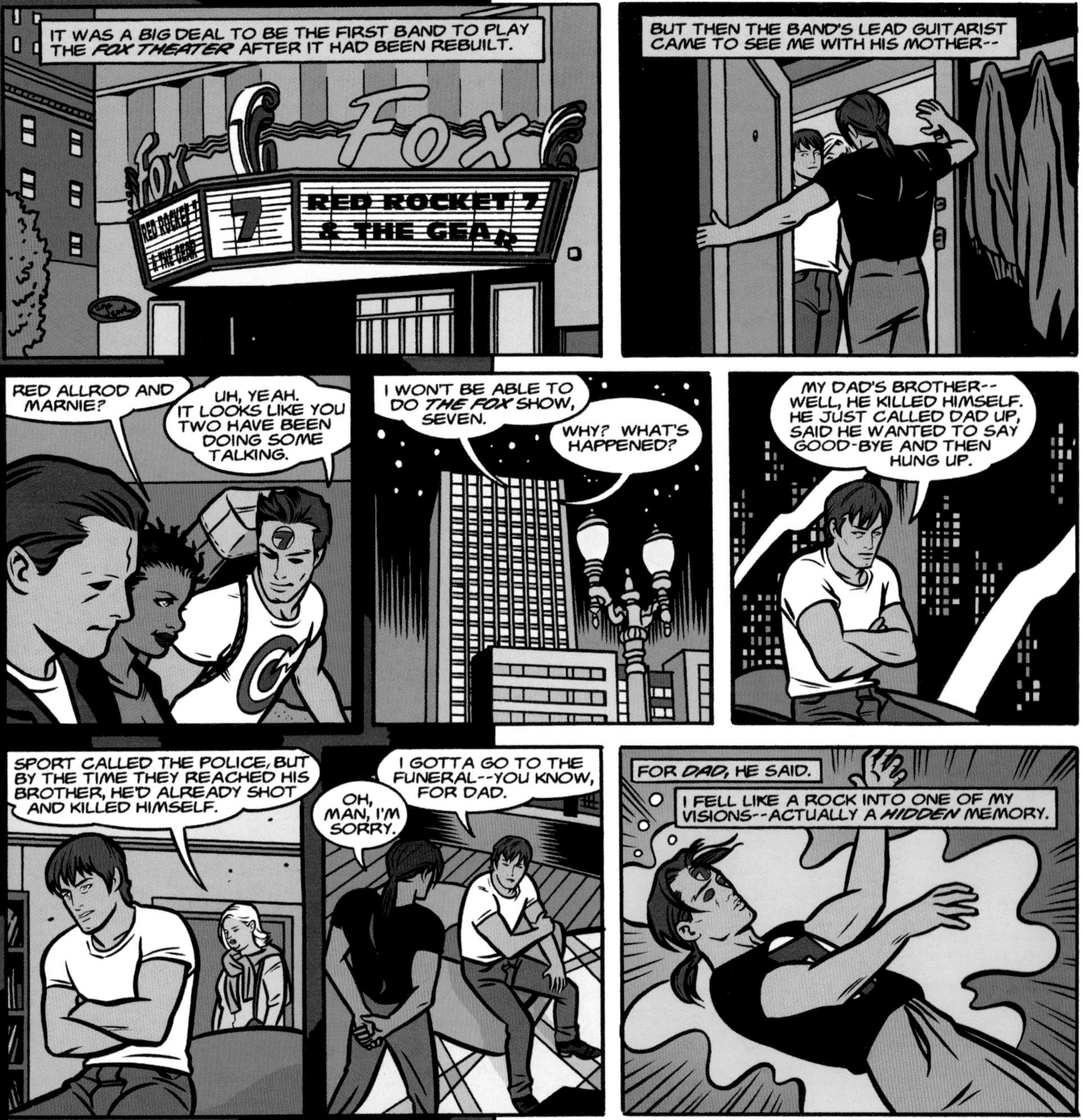
IT WAS A *BIG* DEAL TO BE THE FIRST BAND TO PLAY THE *FOX THEATER* AFTER IT HAD BEEN REBUILT.
FOX
RED ROCKET 7 & THE GEAR
7
RED ROCKET 7 & THE GEAR
BUT THEN THE BAND'S LEAD GUITARIST CAME TO SEE ME WITH HIS MOTHER--
RED ALLROD AND MARNIE?
UH, YEAH. IT LOOKS LIKE YOU TWO HAVE BEEN DOING SOME TALKING.
I WON'T BE ABLE TO DO *THE FOX* SHOW, SEVEN.
WHY? WHAT'S HAPPENED?
MY DAD'S BROTHER-- WELL, HE KILLED HIMSELF. HE JUST CALLED DAD UP, SAID HE WANTED TO SAY GOOD-BYE AND THEN HUNG UP.
SPORT CALLED THE POLICE, BUT BY THE TIME THEY REACHED HIS BROTHER, HE'D ALREADY SHOT AND KILLED HIMSELF.
I GOTTA GO TO THE FUNERAL--YOU KNOW, FOR DAD.
OH, MAN, I'M SORRY.
FOR *DAD*, HE SAID.
I FELL LIKE A ROCK INTO ONE OF MY VISIONS--ACTUALLY A *HIDDEN* MEMORY.

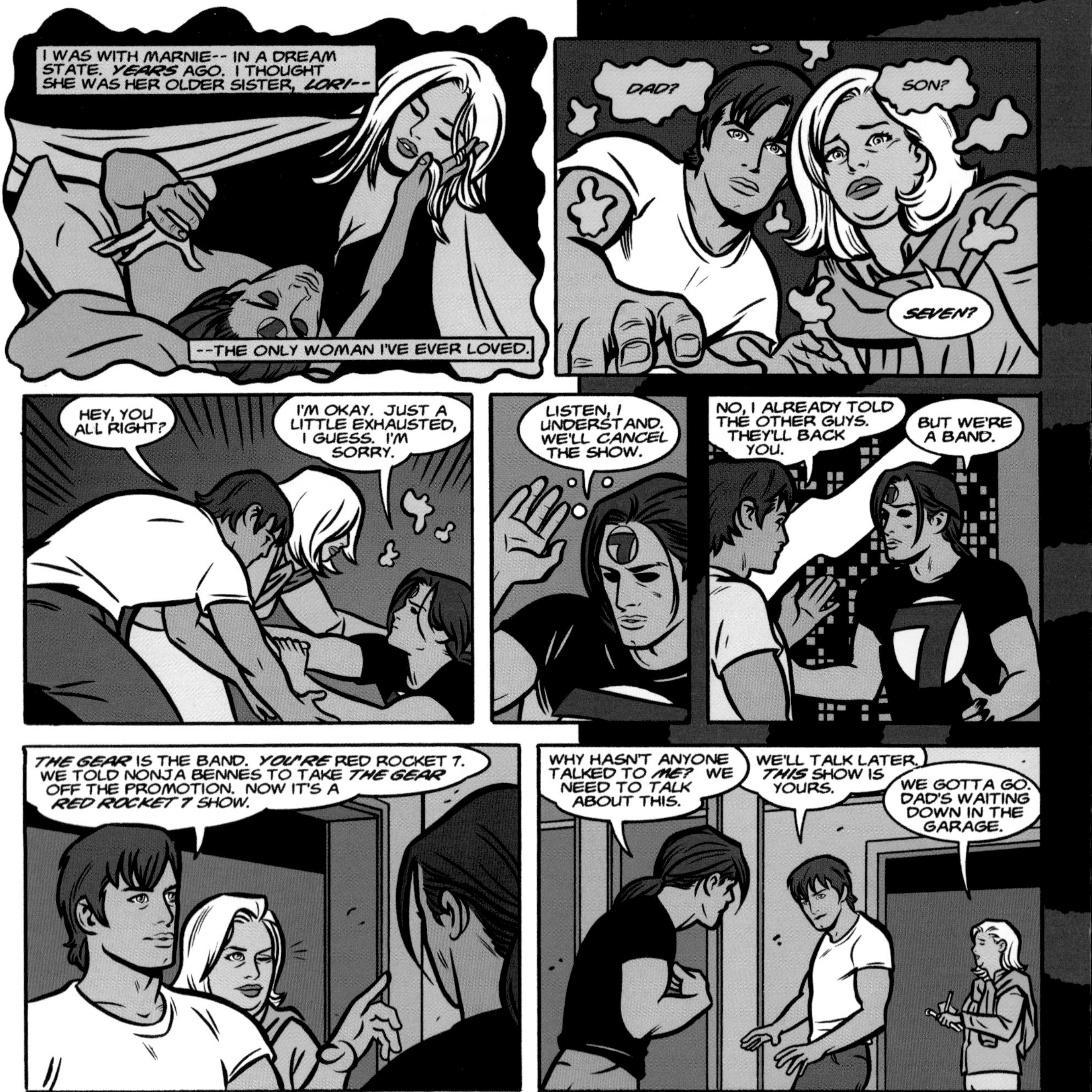
I WAS WITH MARNIE-- IN A DREAM STATE. YEARS AGO. I THOUGHT SHE WAS HER OLDER SISTER, LORI--
--THE ONLY WOMAN I'VE EVER LOVED.
DAD?
SON?
SEVEN?
HEY, YOU ALL RIGHT?
I'M OKAY. JUST A LITTLE EXHAUSTED, I GUESS. I'M SORRY.
LISTEN, I UNDERSTAND. WE'LL CANCEL THE SHOW.
NO, I ALREADY TOLD THE OTHER GUYS. THEY'LL BACK YOU.
BUT WE'RE A BAND.
THE GEAR IS THE BAND. YOU'RE RED ROCKET 7. WE TOLD NONJA BENNES TO TAKE THE GEAR OFF THE PROMOTION. NOW IT'S A RED ROCKET 7 SHOW.
WHY HASN'T ANYONE TALKED TO ME? WE NEED TO TALK ABOUT THIS.
WE'LL TALK LATER. THIS SHOW IS YOURS.
WE GOTTA GO. DAD'S WAITING DOWN IN THE GARAGE.

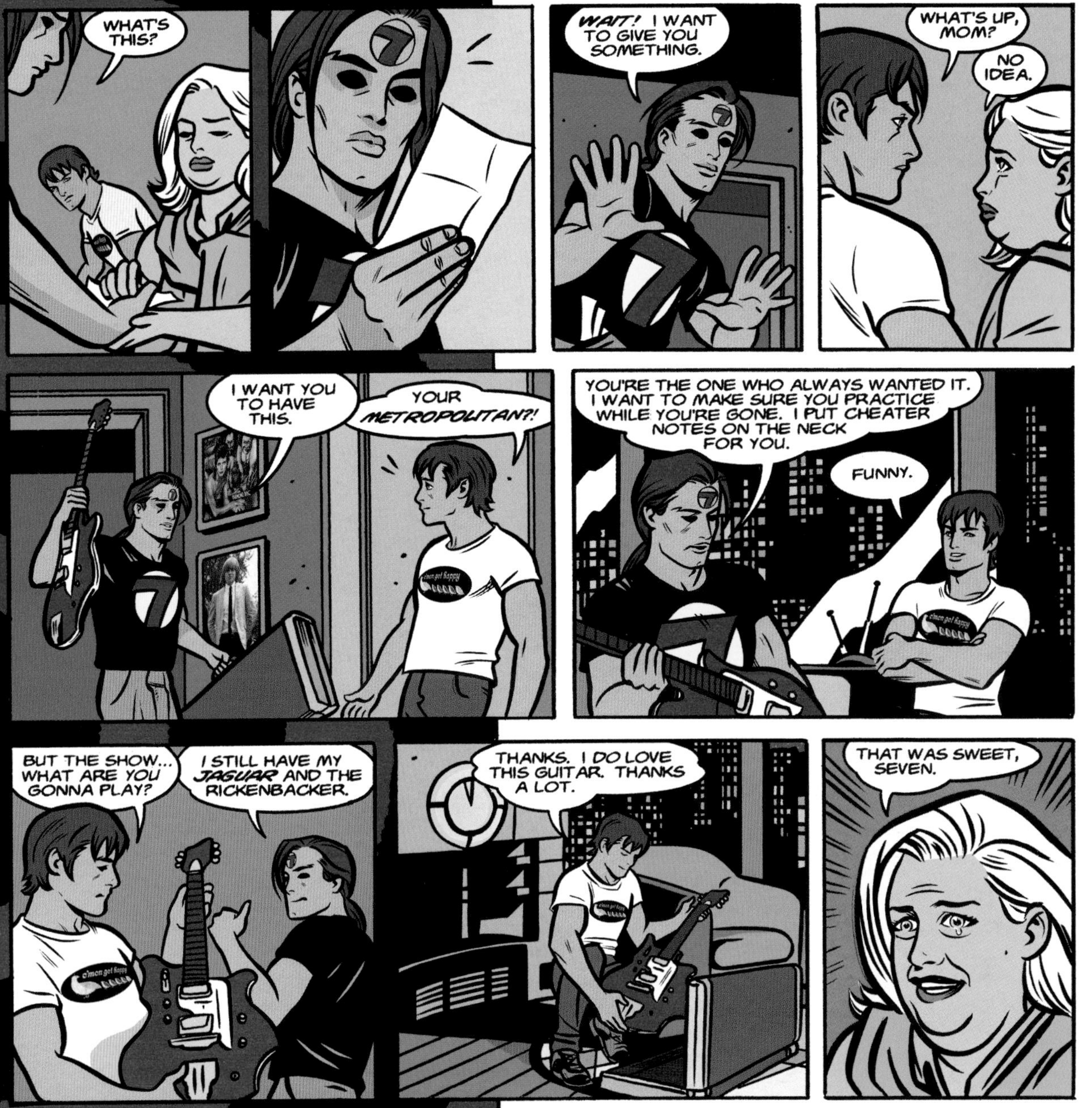
WHAT'S THIS?
WAIT! I WANT TO GIVE YOU SOMETHING.
WHAT'S UP, MOM?
NO IDEA.
I WANT YOU TO HAVE THIS.
YOUR METROPOLITAN?!
YOU'RE THE ONE WHO ALWAYS WANTED IT. I WANT TO MAKE SURE YOU PRACTICE WHILE YOU'RE GONE. I PUT CHEATER NOTES ON THE NECK FOR YOU.
FUNNY.
BUT THE SHOW... WHAT ARE YOU GONNA PLAY?
I STILL HAVE MY JAGUAR AND THE RICKENBACKER.
THANKS. I DO LOVE THIS GUITAR. THANKS A LOT.
THAT WAS SWEET, SEVEN.

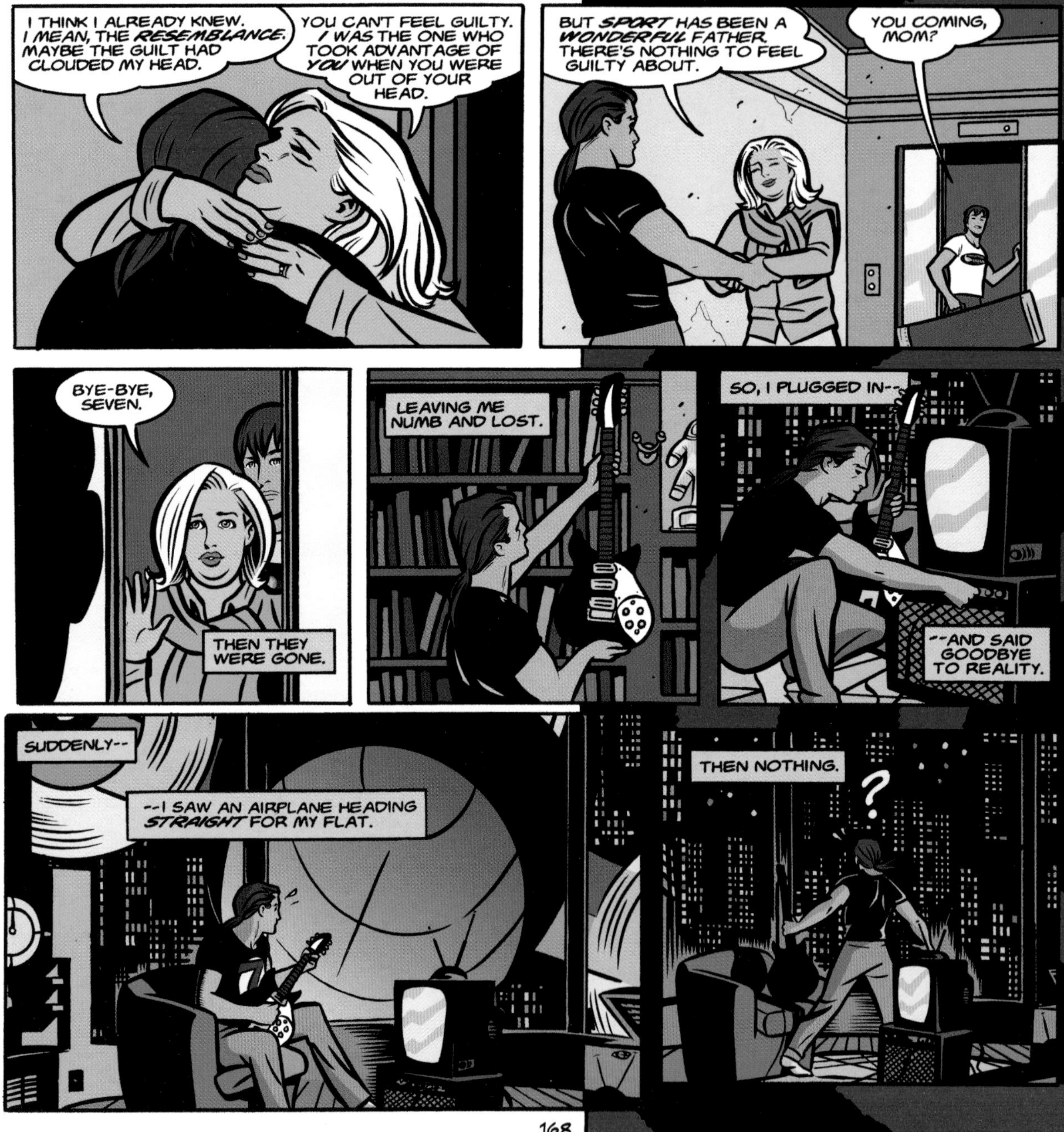
I THINK I ALREADY KNEW. I MEAN, THE RESEMBLANCE. MAYBE THE GUILT HAD CLOUDED MY HEAD.
YOU CAN'T FEEL GUILTY. I WAS THE ONE WHO TOOK ADVANTAGE OF YOU WHEN YOU WERE OUT OF YOUR HEAD.
BUT SPORT HAS BEEN A WONDERFUL FATHER. THERE'S NOTHING TO FEEL GUILTY ABOUT.
YOU COMING, MOM?
BYE-BYE, SEVEN.
THEN THEY WERE GONE.
LEAVING ME NUMB AND LOST.
SO, I PLUGGED IN--
--AND SAID GOODBYE TO REALITY.
SUDDENLY--
--I SAW AN AIRPLANE HEADING STRAIGHT FOR MY FLAT.
THEN NOTHING.
?

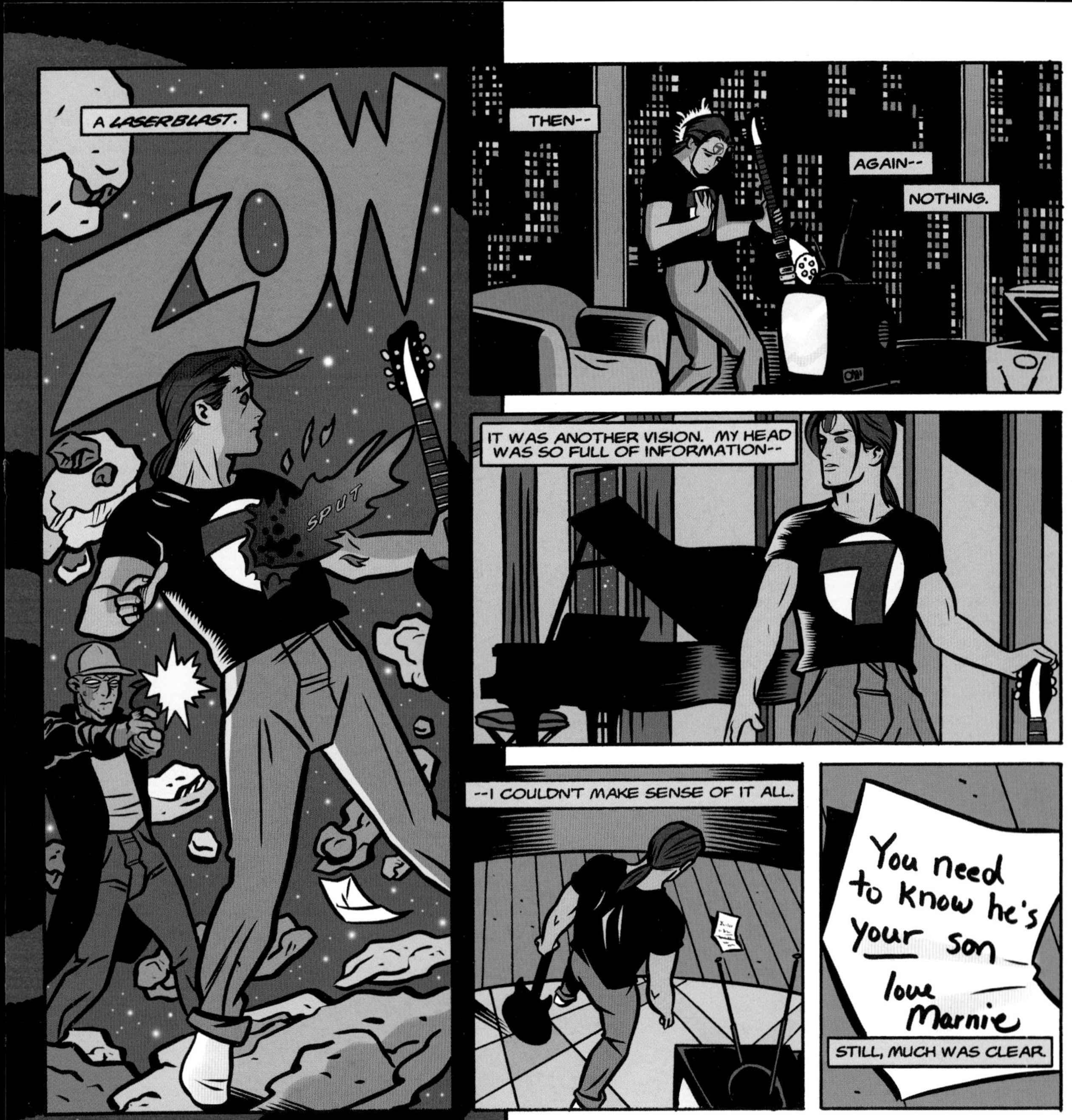
A LASERBLAST.
ZOW
SPUT
THEN--
AGAIN--
NOTHING.
IT WAS ANOTHER VISION. MY HEAD WAS SO FULL OF INFORMATION--
--I COULDN'T MAKE SENSE OF IT ALL.
You need to know he's your son
love Marnie
STILL, MUCH WAS CLEAR.

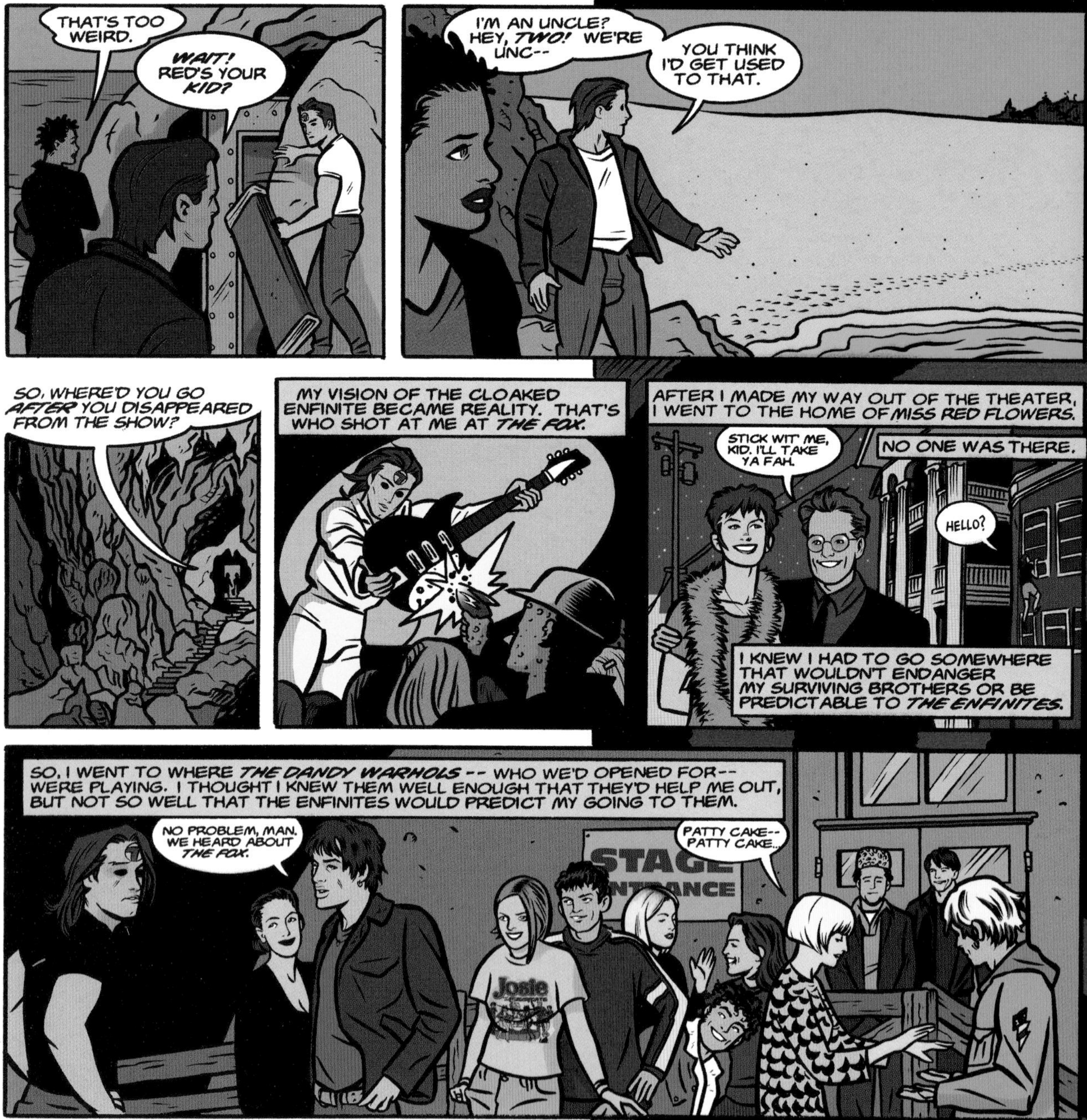
THAT'S TOO WEIRD.
WAIT! RED'S YOUR KID?
I'M AN UNCLE? HEY, TWO! WE'RE UNC--
YOU THINK I'D GET USED TO THAT.
SO, WHERE'D YOU GO AFTER YOU DISAPPEARED FROM THE SHOW?
MY VISION OF THE CLOAKED ENFINITE BECAME REALITY. THAT'S WHO SHOT AT ME AT THE FOX.
AFTER I MADE MY WAY OUT OF THE THEATER, I WENT TO THE HOME OF MISS RED FLOWERS.
STICK WIT' ME, KID. I'LL TAKE YA FAH.
NO ONE WAS THERE.
HELLO?
I KNEW I HAD TO GO SOMEWHERE THAT WOULDN'T ENDANGER MY SURVIVING BROTHERS OR BE PREDICTABLE TO THE ENFINITES.
SO, I WENT TO WHERE THE DANDY WARHOLS -- WHO WE'D OPENED FOR-- WERE PLAYING. I THOUGHT I KNEW THEM WELL ENOUGH THAT THEY'D HELP ME OUT, BUT NOT SO WELL THAT THE ENFINITES WOULD PREDICT MY GOING TO THEM.
NO PROBLEM, MAN. WE HEARD ABOUT THE FOX.
STAGE
PATTY CAKE-- PATTY CAKE...
Josie

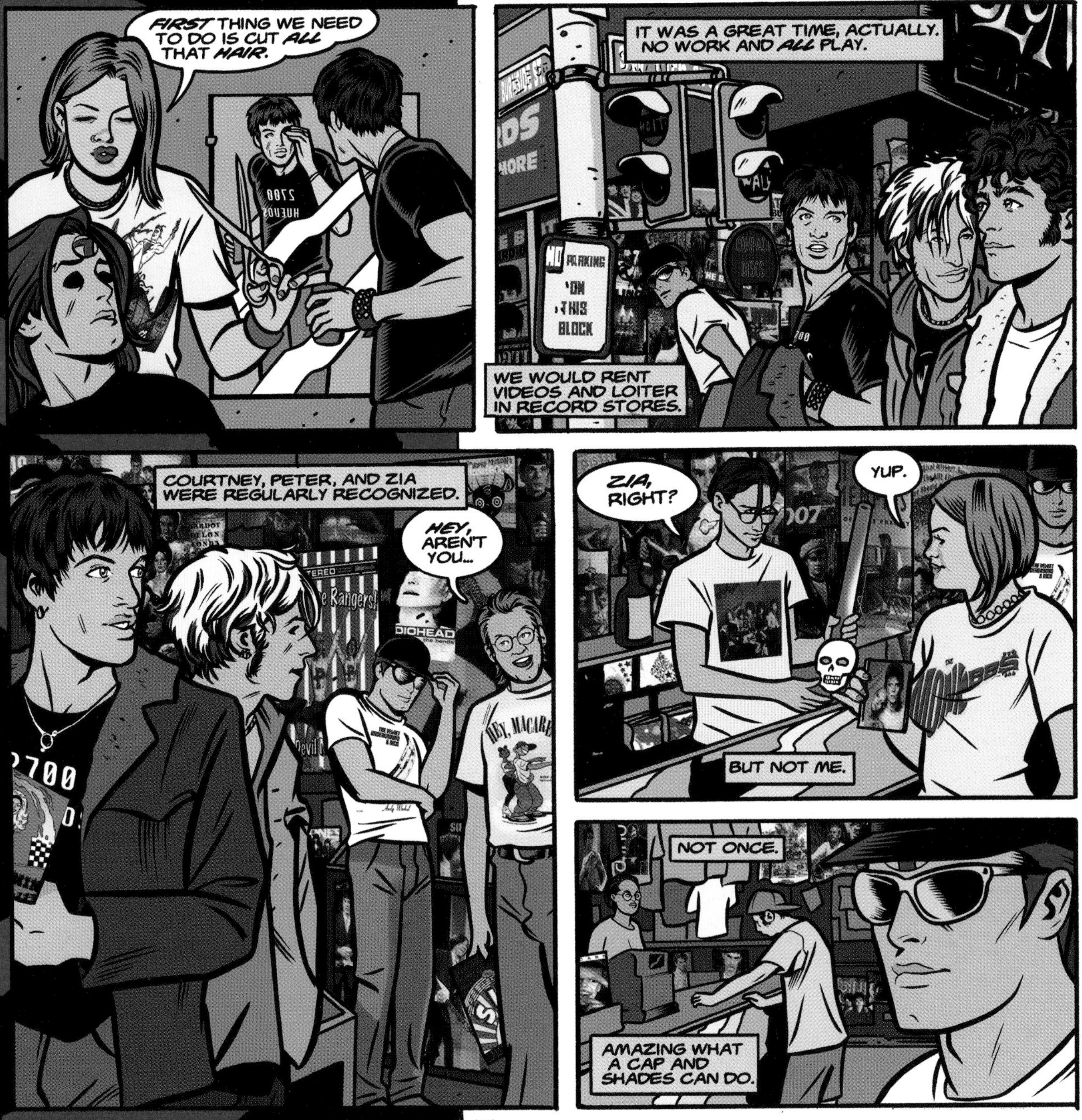
FIRST THING WE NEED TO DO IS CUT ALL THAT HAIR.
IT WAS A GREAT TIME, ACTUALLY. NO WORK AND ALL PLAY.
WE WOULD RENT VIDEOS AND LOITER IN RECORD STORES.
COURTNEY, PETER, AND ZIA WERE REGULARLY RECOGNIZED.
HEY, AREN'T YOU...
ZIA, RIGHT?
YUP.
BUT NOT ME.
NOT ONCE.
AMAZING WHAT A CAP AND SHADES CAN DO.

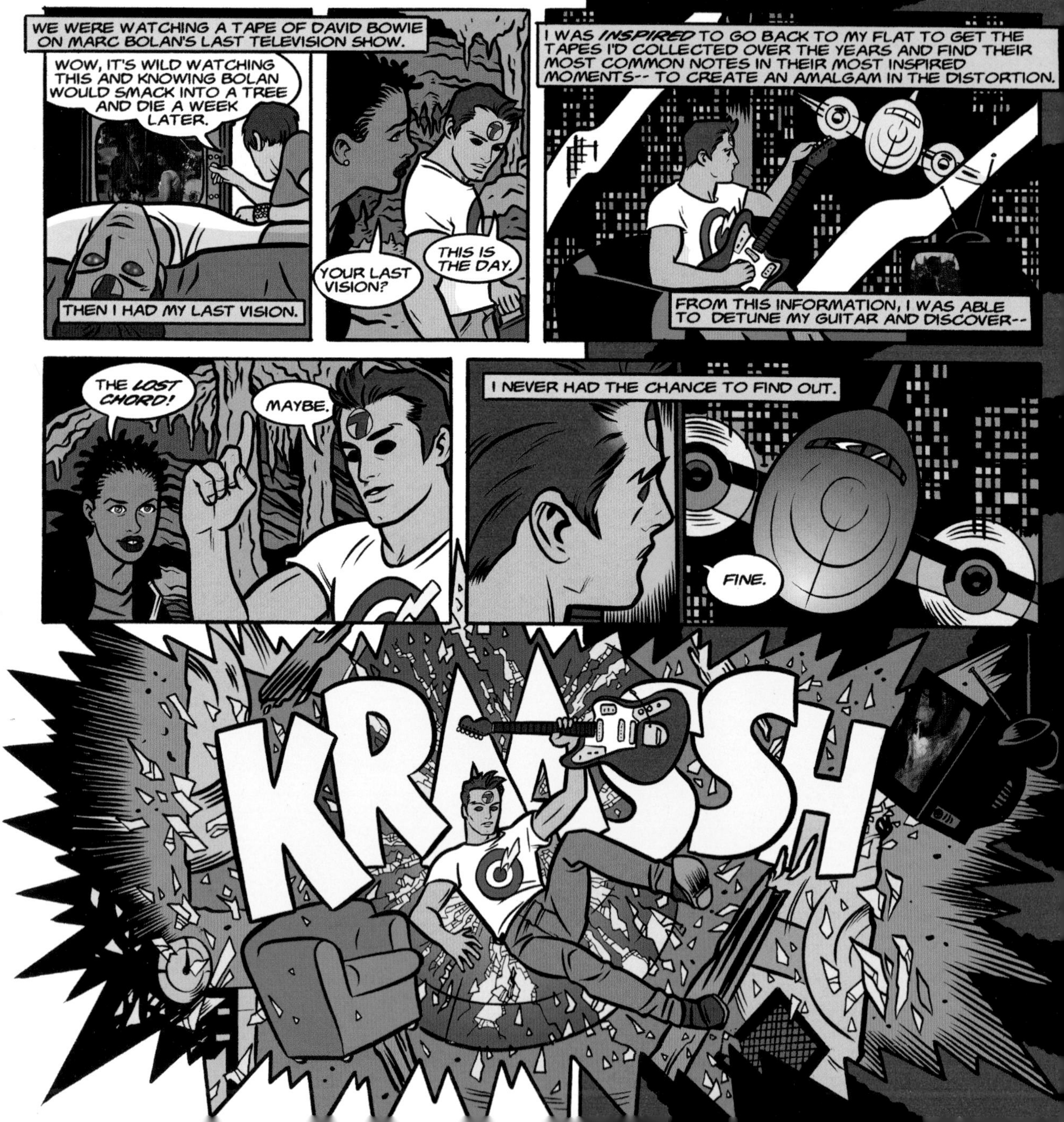

WE WERE WATCHING A TAPE OF DAVID BOWIE ON MARC BOLAN'S LAST TELEVISION SHOW.
WOW, IT'S WILD WATCHING THIS AND KNOWING BOLAN WOULD SMACK INTO A TREE AND DIE A WEEK LATER.
THEN I HAD MY LAST VISION.
YOUR LAST VISION?
THIS IS THE DAY.
I WAS INSPIRED TO GO BACK TO MY FLAT TO GET THE TAPES I'D COLLECTED OVER THE YEARS AND FIND THEIR MOST COMMON NOTES IN THEIR MOST INSPIRED MOMENTS-- TO CREATE AN AMALGAM IN THE DISTORTION.
FROM THIS INFORMATION, I WAS ABLE TO DETUNE MY GUITAR AND DISCOVER--
THE LOST CHORD!
MAYBE.
I NEVER HAD THE CHANCE TO FIND OUT.
FINE.
KRASSH

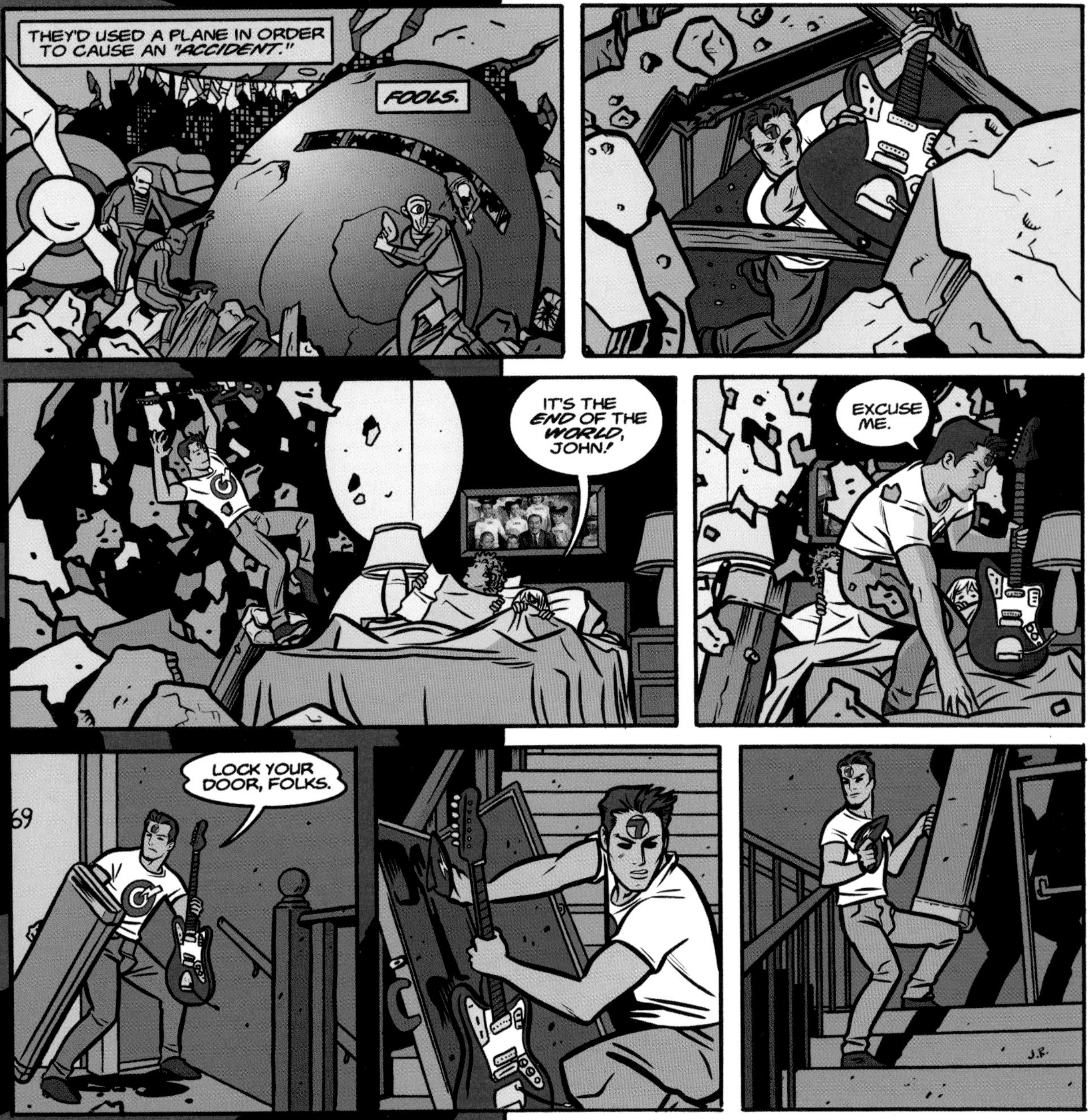
THEY'D USED A PLANE IN ORDER TO CAUSE AN "ACCIDENT."
FOOLS.
IT'S THE END OF THE WORLD, JOHN!
EXCUSE ME.
69
LOCK YOUR DOOR, FOLKS.
J.R.

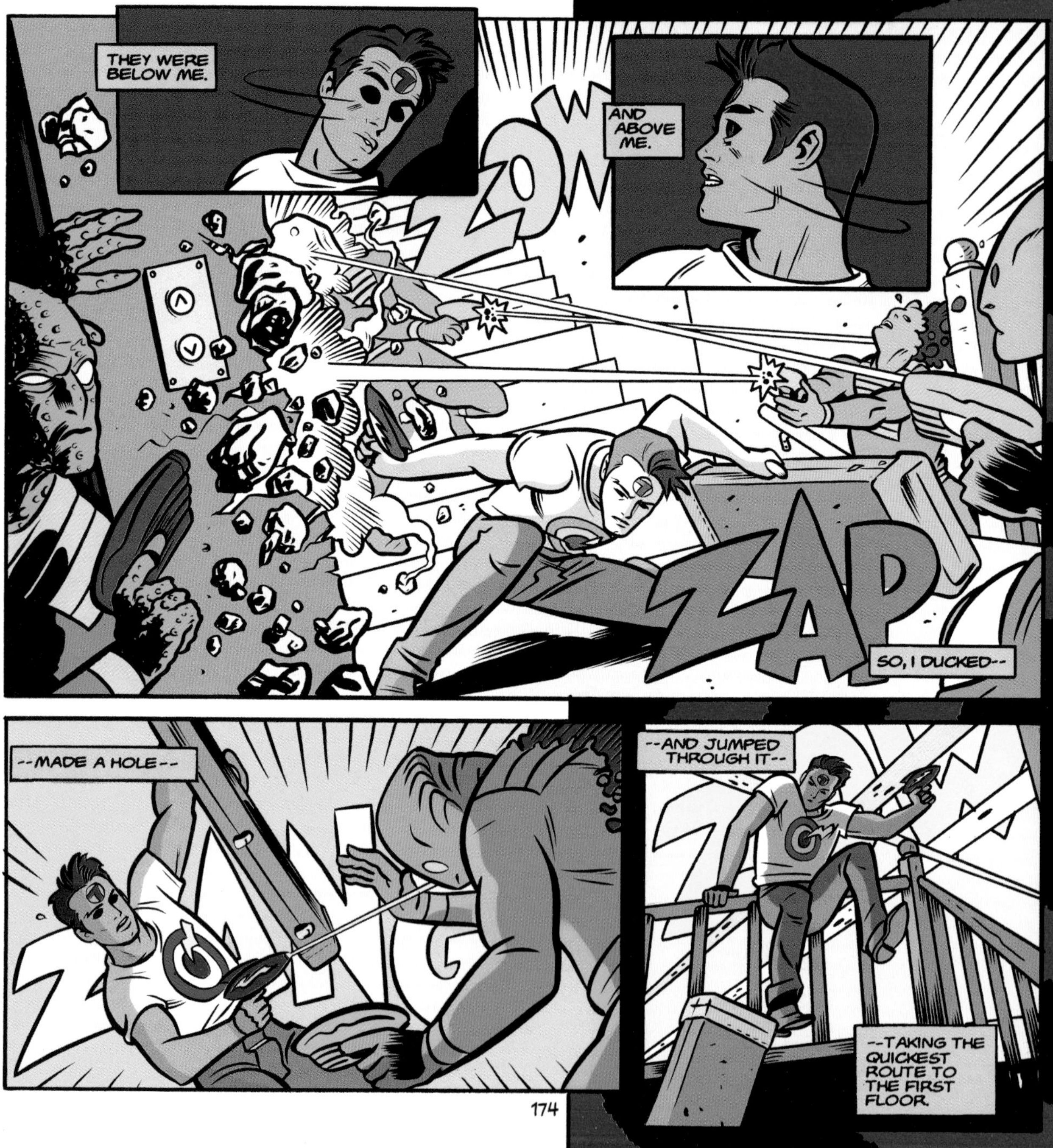
THEY WERE BELOW ME.
AND ABOVE ME.
ZOOM
ZAP
SO, I DUCKED--
--MADE A HOLE--
--AND JUMPED THROUGH IT--
--TAKING THE QUICKEST ROUTE TO THE FIRST FLOOR.

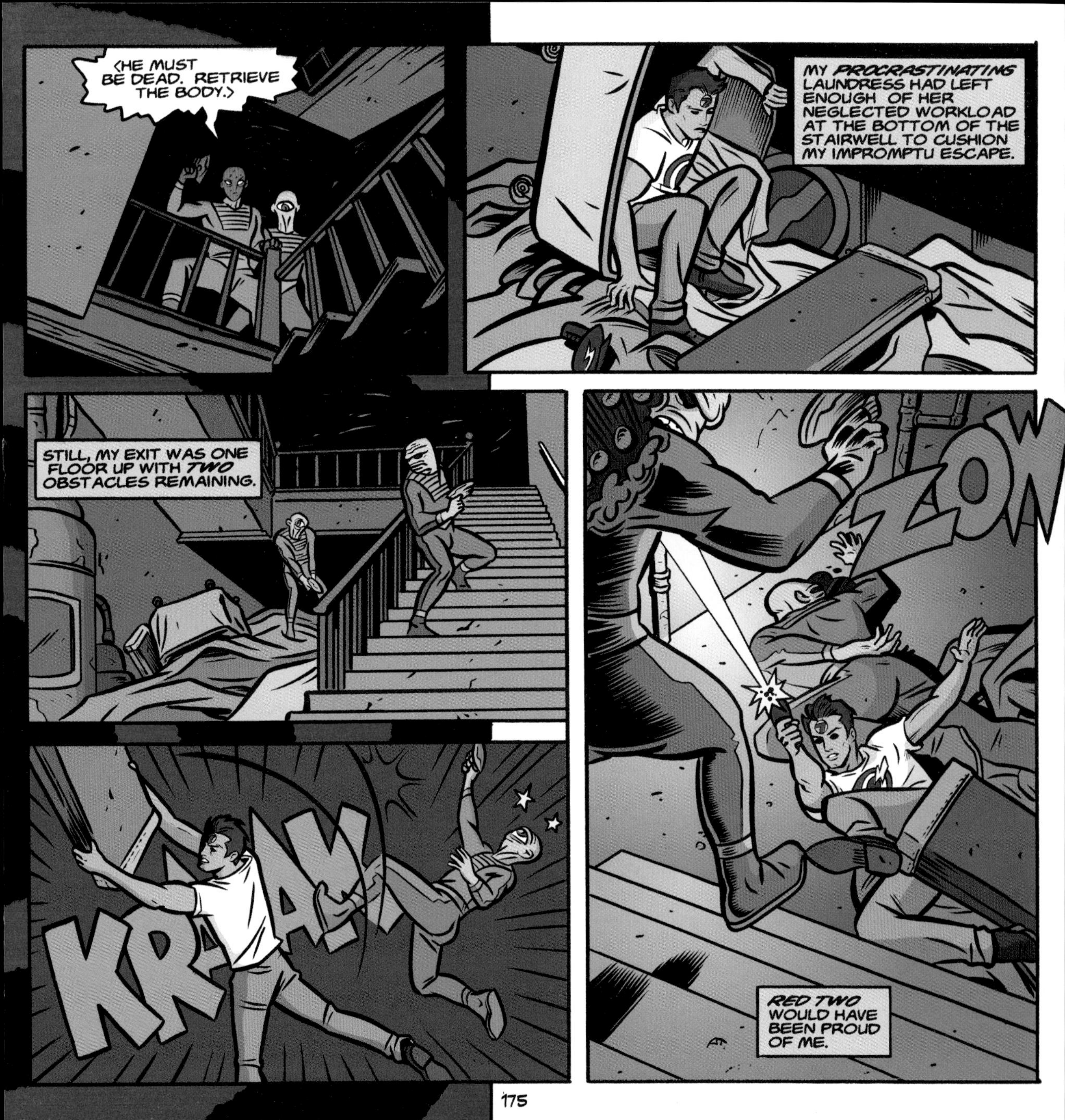

<HE MUST BE DEAD. RETRIEVE THE BODY.>
MY PROCRASTINATING LAUNDRESS HAD LEFT ENOUGH OF HER NEGLECTED WORKLOAD AT THE BOTTOM OF THE STAIRWELL TO CUSHION MY IMPROMPTU ESCAPE.
STILL, MY EXIT WAS ONE FLOOR UP WITH TWO OBSTACLES REMAINING.
KRAAM
ZZOW
RED TWO WOULD HAVE BEEN PROUD OF ME.

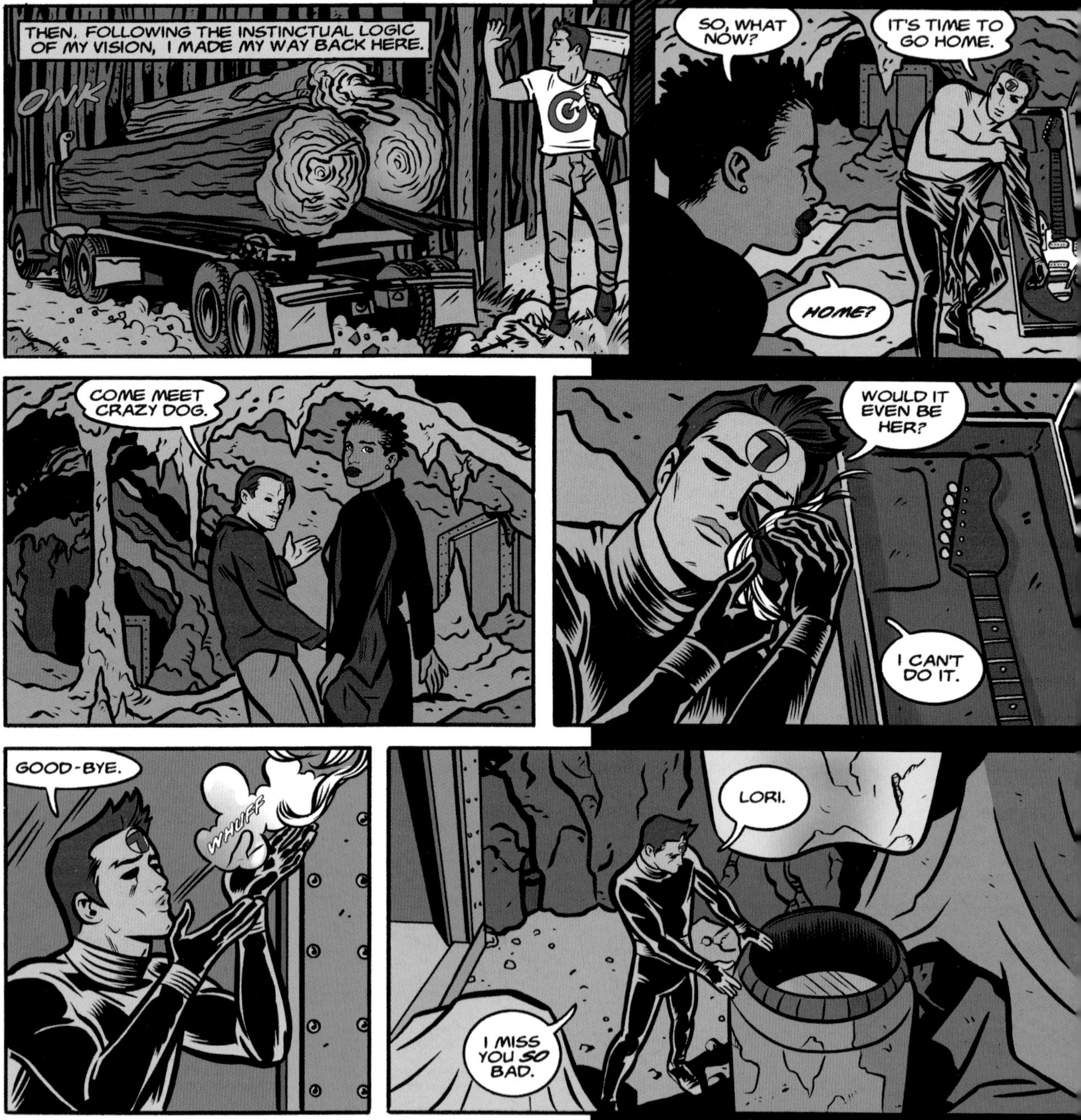
THEN, FOLLOWING THE INSTINCTUAL LOGIC OF MY VISION, I MADE MY WAY BACK HERE.
ONK
SO, WHAT NOW?
IT'S TIME TO GO HOME.
HOME?
COME MEET CRAZY DOG.
WOULD IT EVEN BE HER?
I CAN'T DO IT.
GOOD-BYE.
WHUFF
LORI.
I MISS YOU SO BAD.

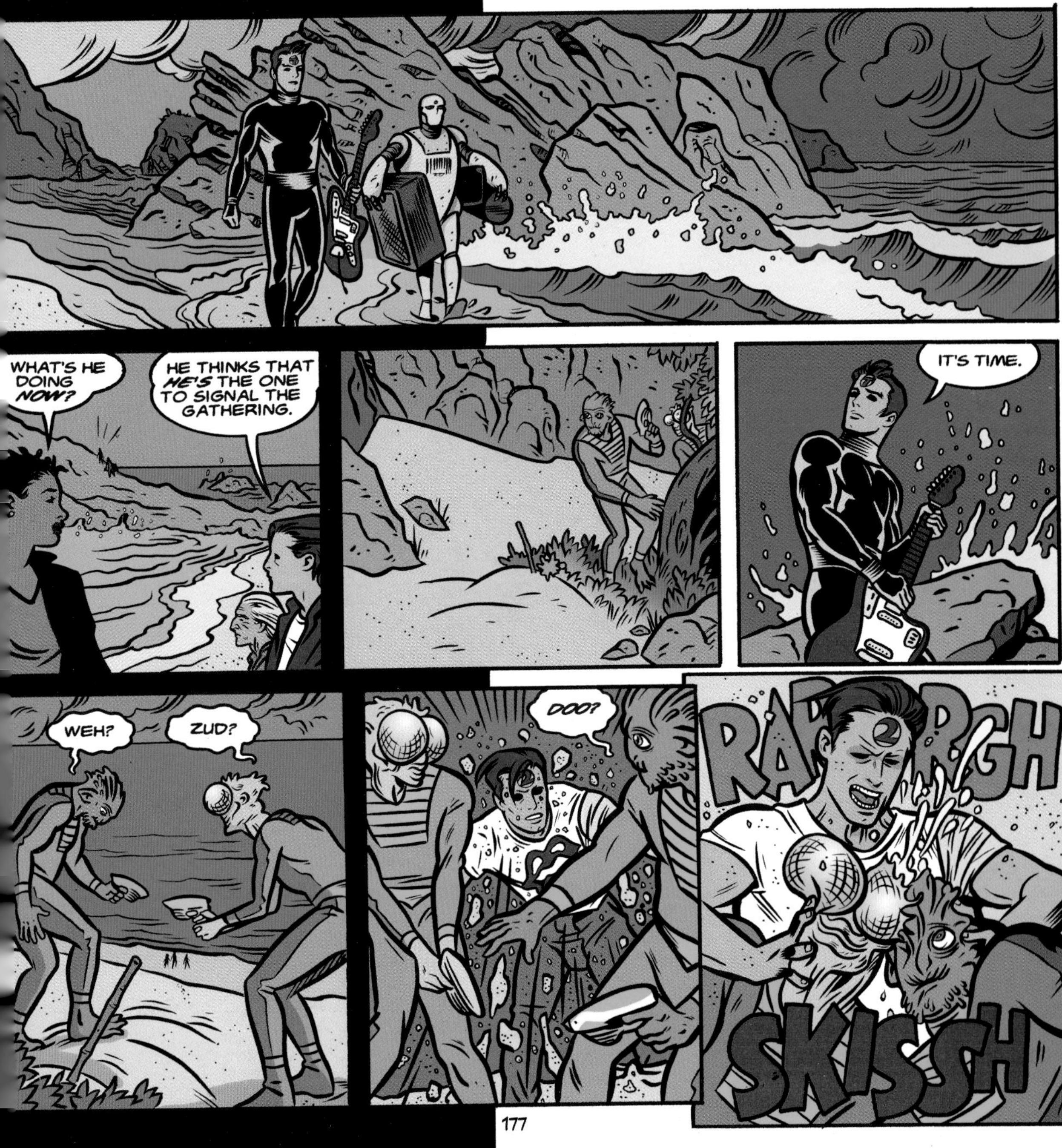

WHAT'S HE DOING *NOW?*
HE THINKS THAT *HE'S* THE ONE TO SIGNAL THE GATHERING.
IT'S TIME.
WEH?
ZUD?
DOO?
RAARGH
SKISSH

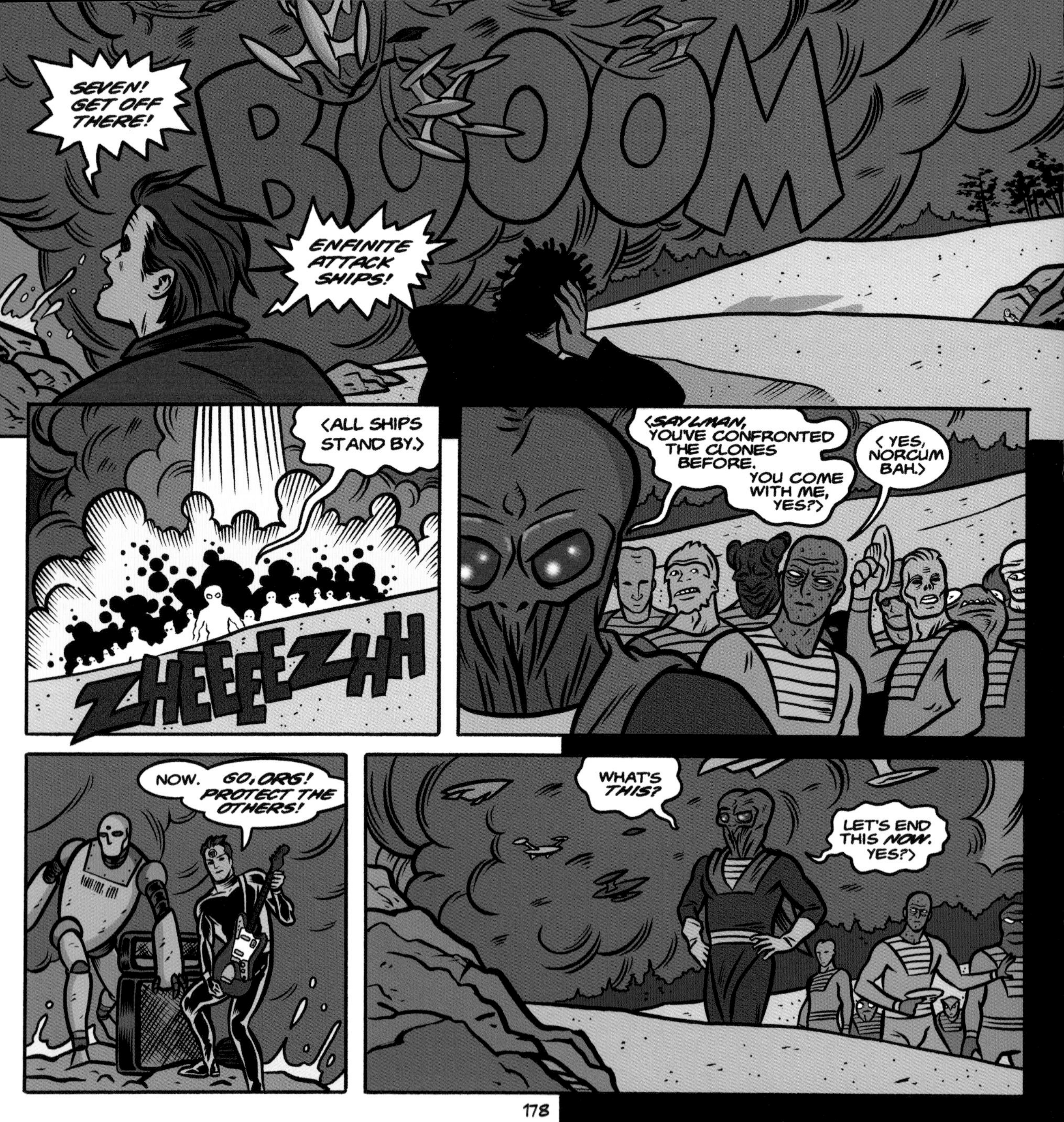
SEVEN! GET OFF THERE!
BOOOOM
ENFINITE ATTACK SHIPS!
<ALL SHIPS STAND BY.>
ZHEEEEZHH
<SAYLMAN, YOU'VE CONFRONTED THE CLONES BEFORE. YOU COME WITH ME, YES?>
< YES, NORCUM BAH.>
NOW. GO, ORG! PROTECT THE OTHERS!
WHAT'S THIS?
LET'S END THIS NOW. YES?>

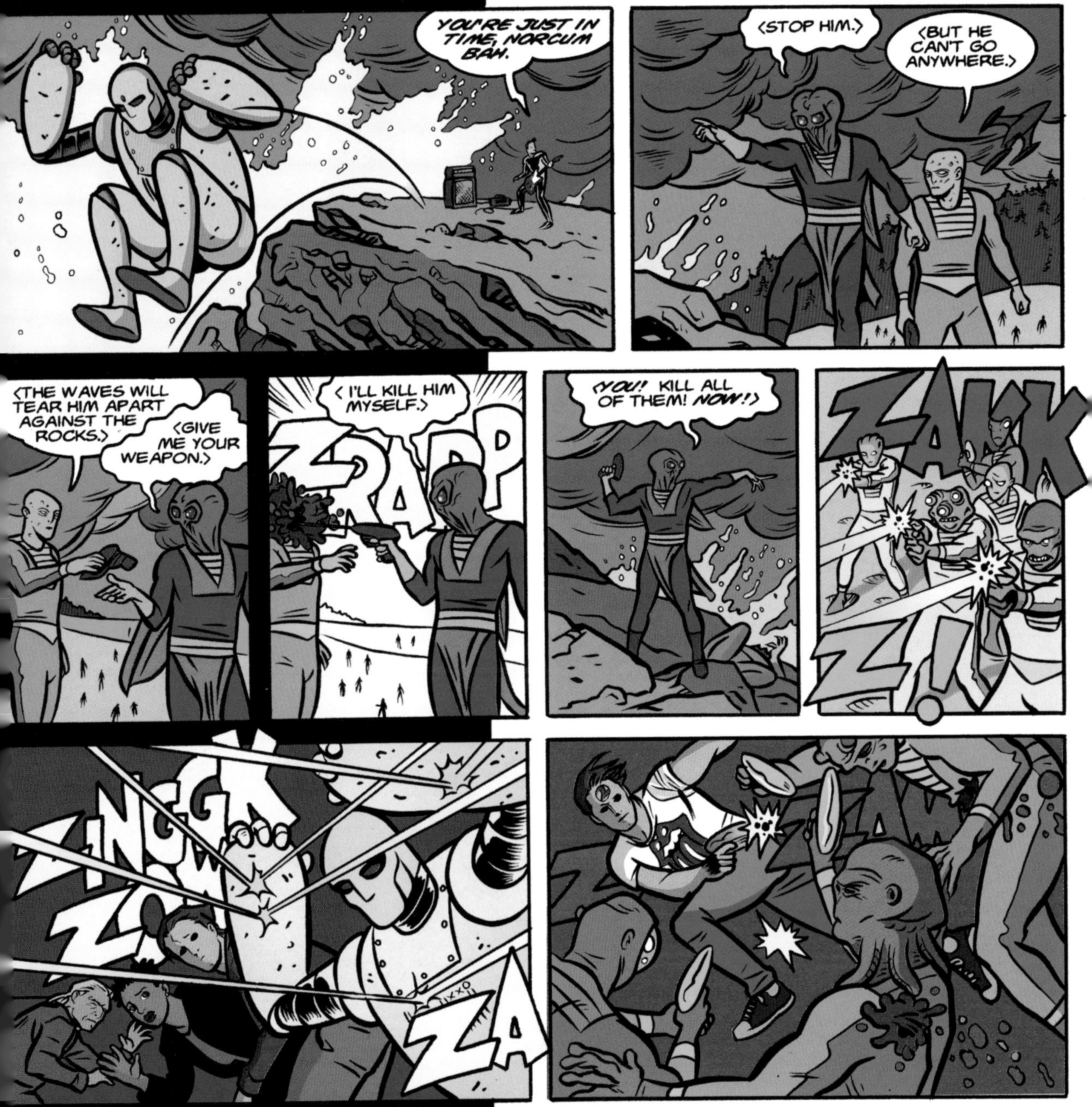
YOU'RE JUST IN TIME, NORCUM BAH.
<STOP HIM.>
<BUT HE CAN'T GO ANYWHERE.>
<THE WAVES WILL TEAR HIM APART AGAINST THE ROCKS.>
<GIVE ME YOUR WEAPON.>
< I'LL KILL HIM MYSELF.>
<YOU! KILL ALL OF THEM! NOW!>
ZA

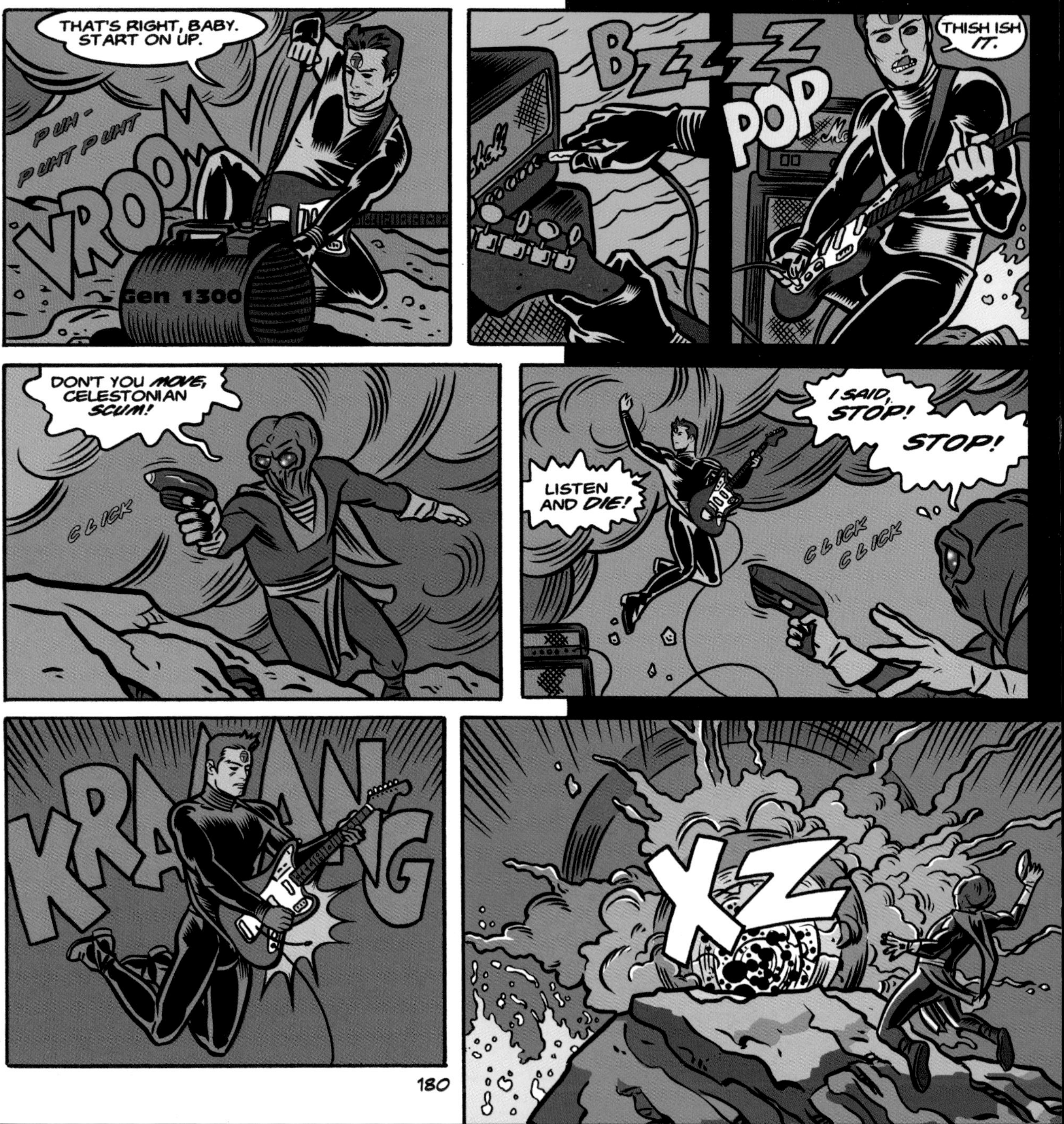
THAT'S RIGHT, BABY. START ON UP.
PUH-PUHT PUHT PUHT
VROOM
Gen 1300
BZZZZZ
POP
THISH ISH IT.
DON'T YOU MOVE, CELESTONIAN SCUM!
CLICK
I SAID, STOP!
STOP!
LISTEN AND DIE!
CLICK CLICK
KRAANG
XZ

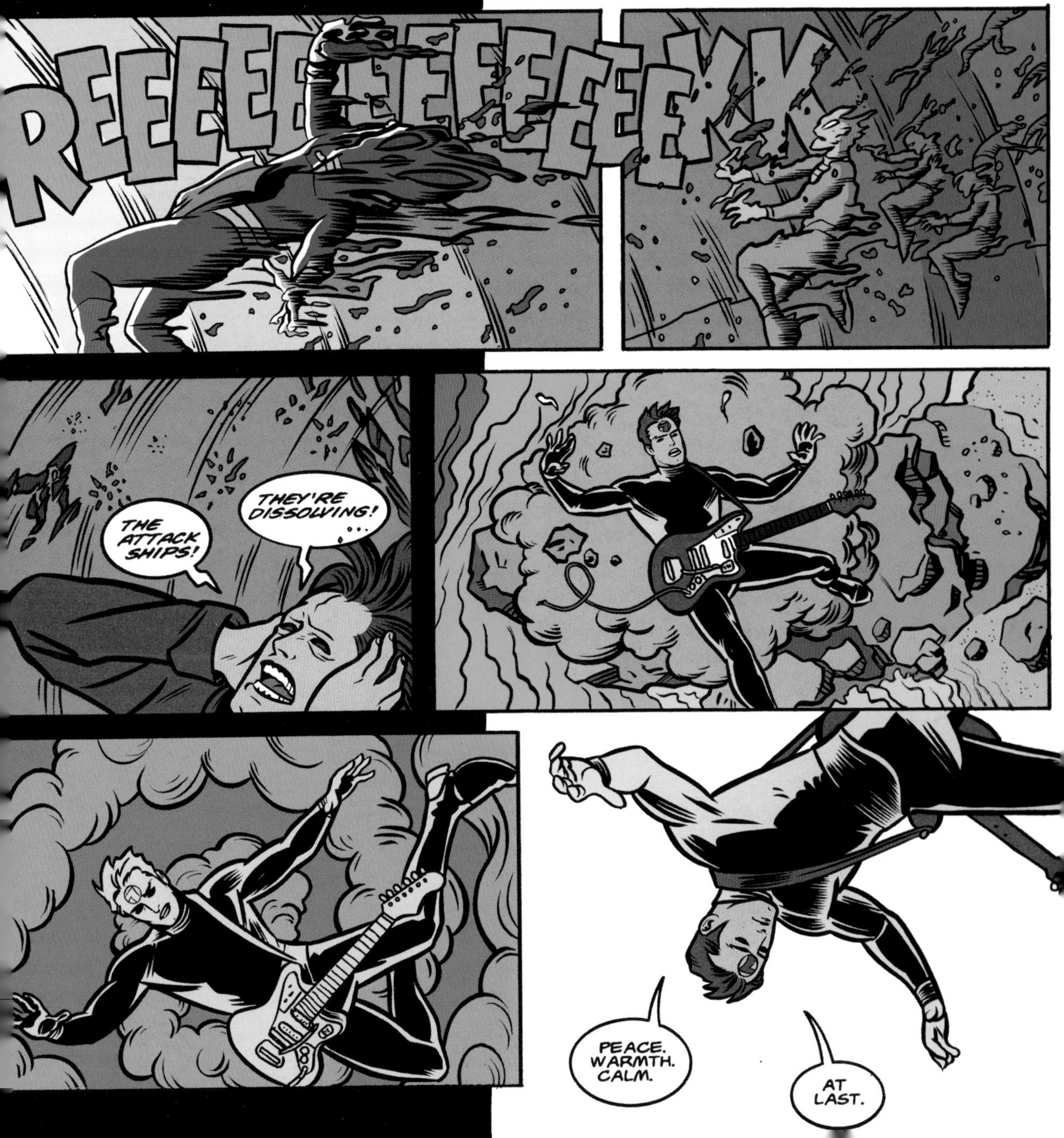
REEEEEEEEEEEEEEEEEEEEEEEEEEEEEEEKK
THE ATTACK SHIPS!
THEY'RE DISSOLVING!
PEACE. WARMTH. CALM.
AT LAST.

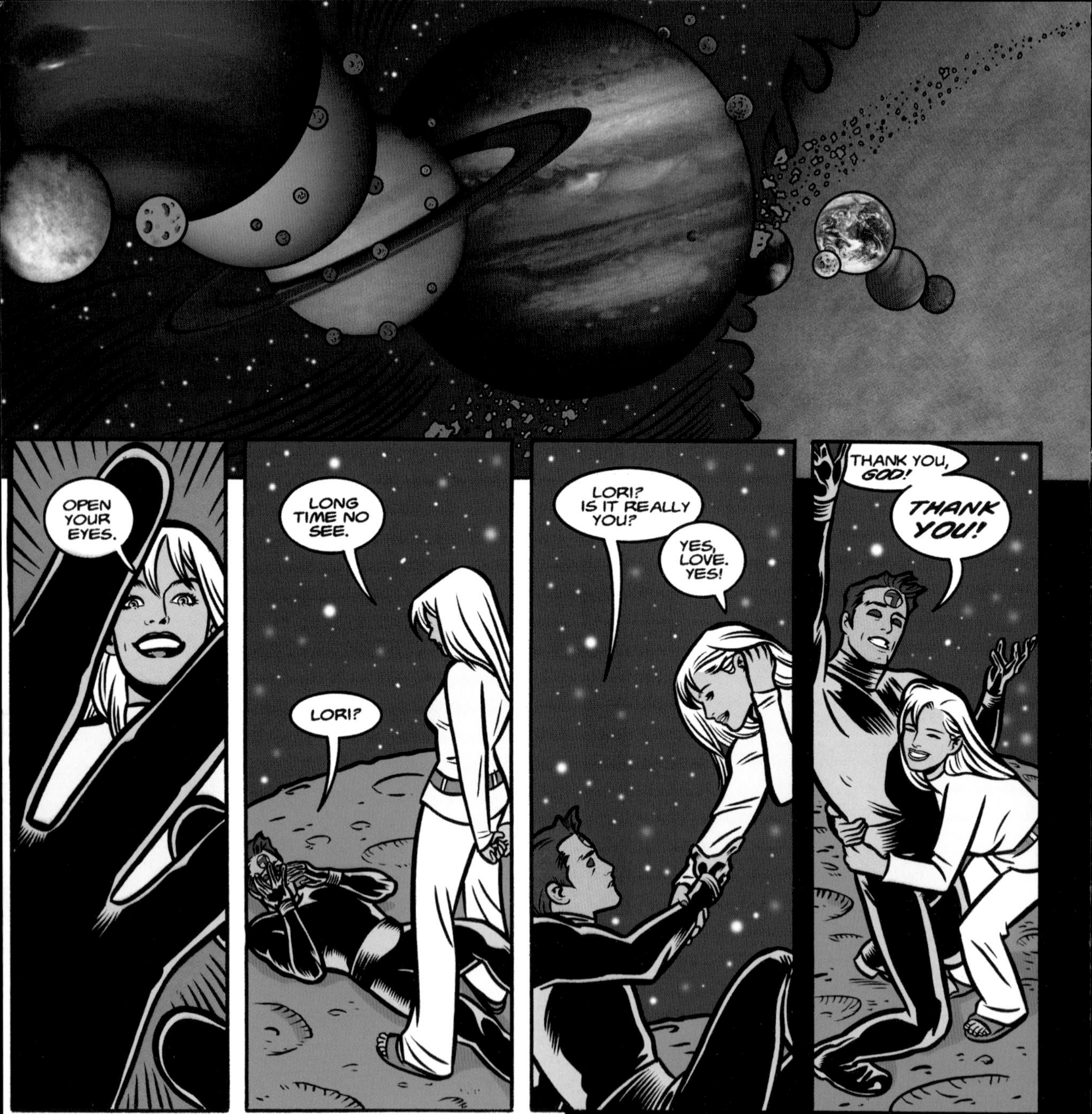
OPEN YOUR EYES.
LONG TIME NO SEE.
LORI?
LORI? IS IT REALLY YOU?
YES, LOVE. YES!
THANK YOU, GOD!
THANK YOU!

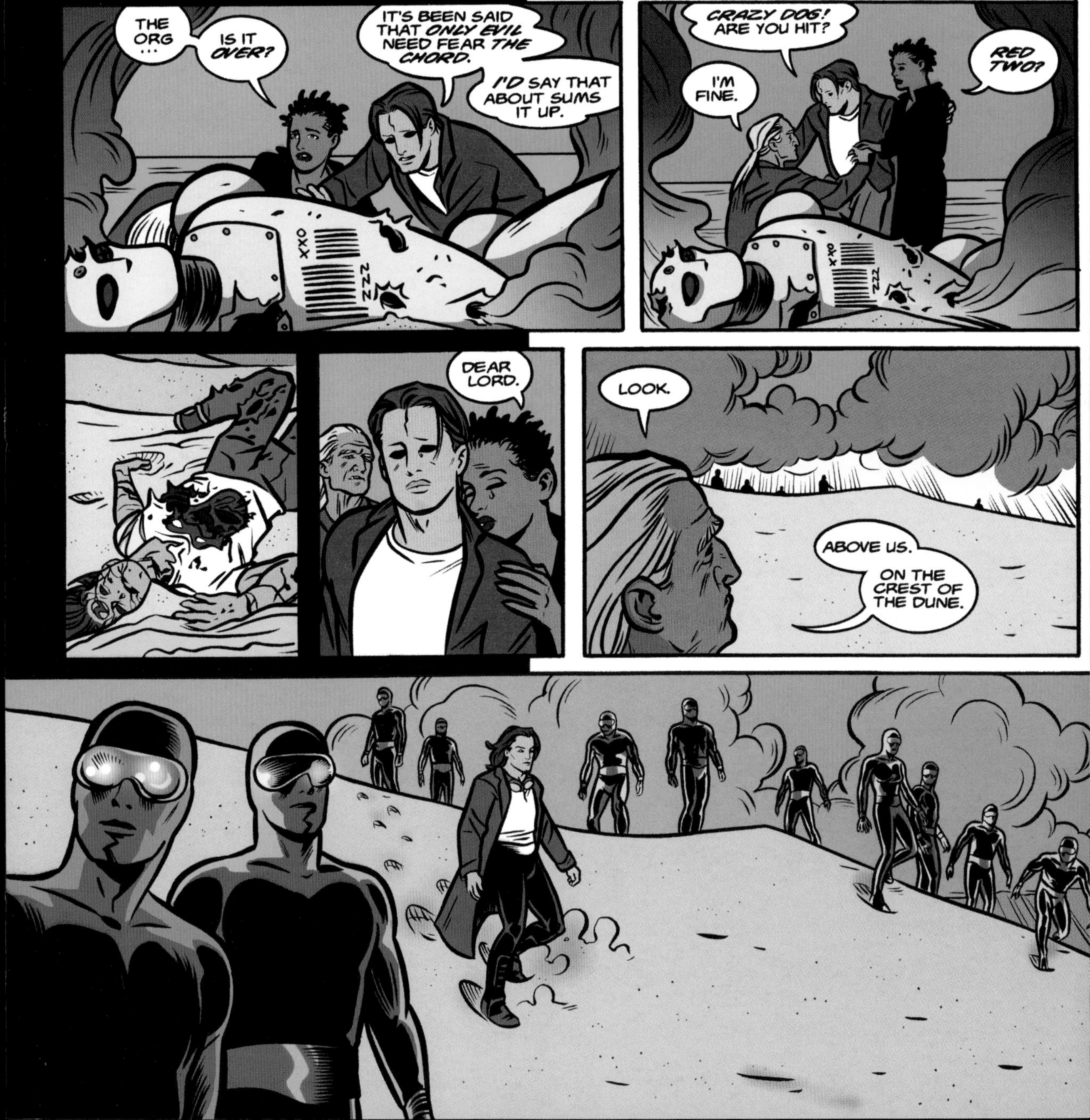
THE ORG ...
IS IT OVER?
IT'S BEEN SAID THAT ONLY EVIL NEED FEAR THE CHORD.
I'D SAY THAT ABOUT SUMS IT UP.
CRAZY DOG! ARE YOU HIT?
I'M FINE.
RED TWO?
DEAR LORD.
LOOK.
ABOVE US.
ON THE CREST OF THE DUNE.

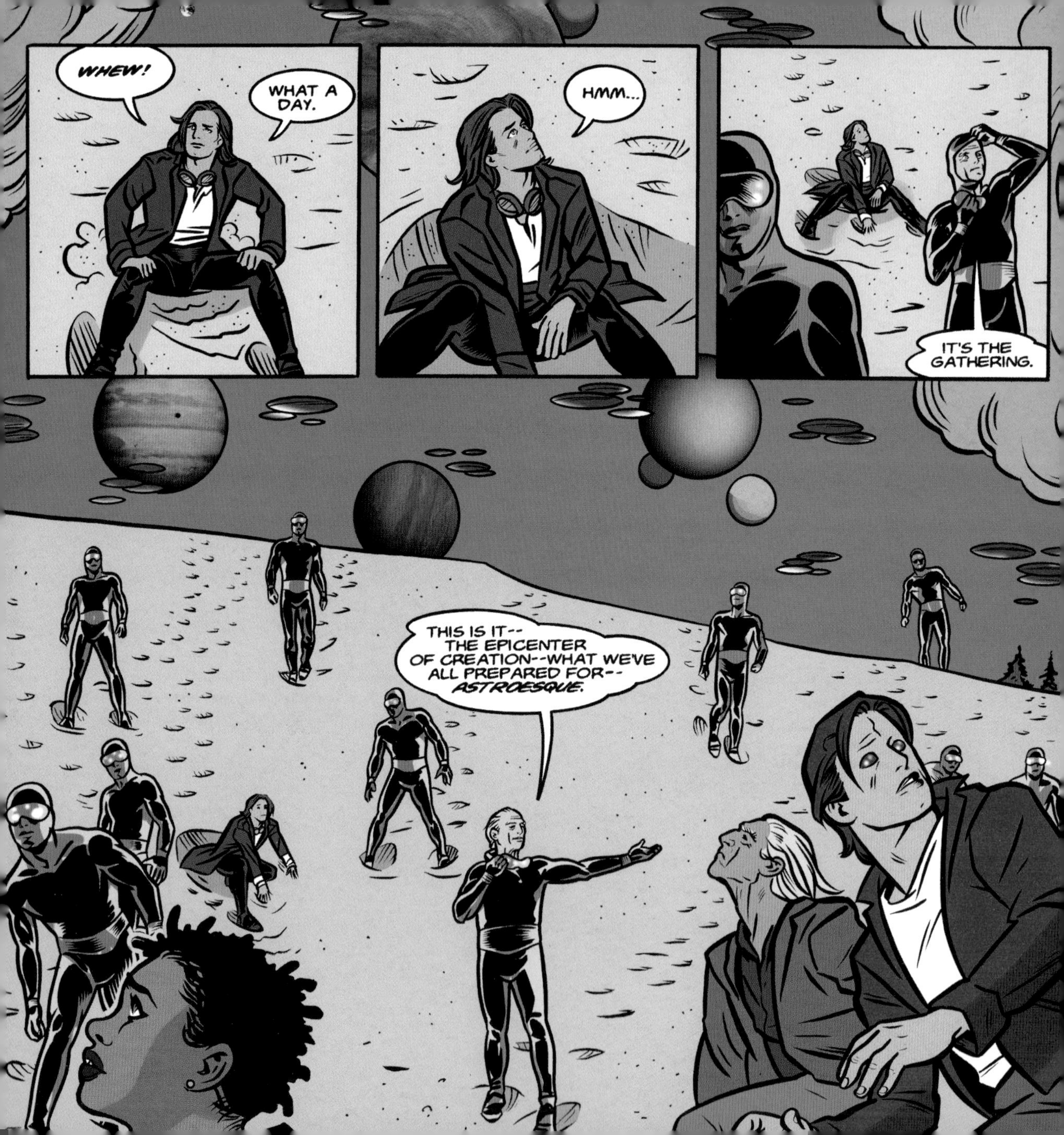
WHEW!
WHAT A DAY.
HMM...
IT'S THE GATHERING.
THIS IS IT-- THE EPICENTER OF CREATION--WHAT WE'VE ALL PREPARED FOR-- ASTROESQUE.

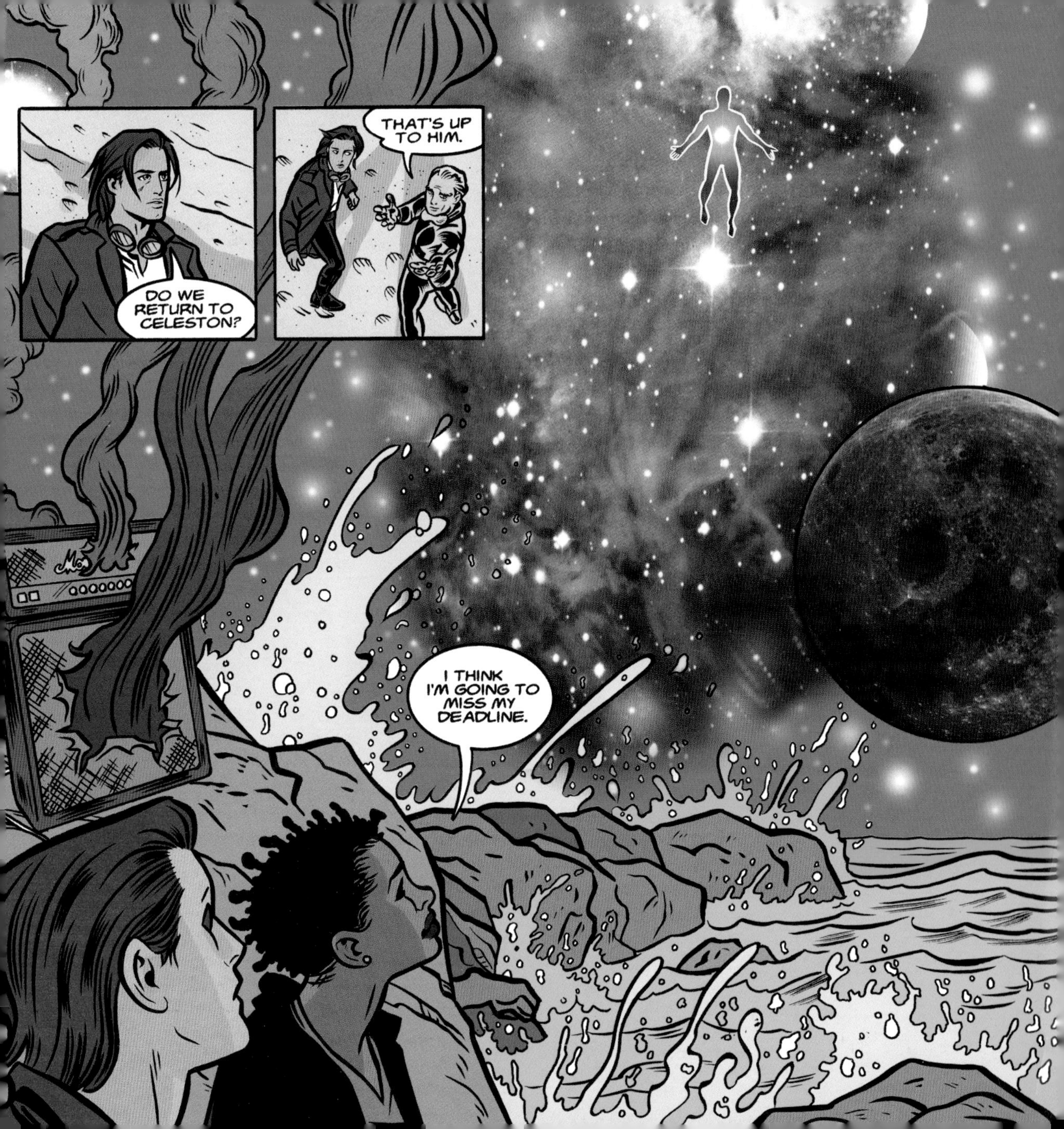
DO WE RETURN TO CELESTON?
THAT'S UP TO HIM.
I THINK I'M GOING TO MISS MY DEADLINE.

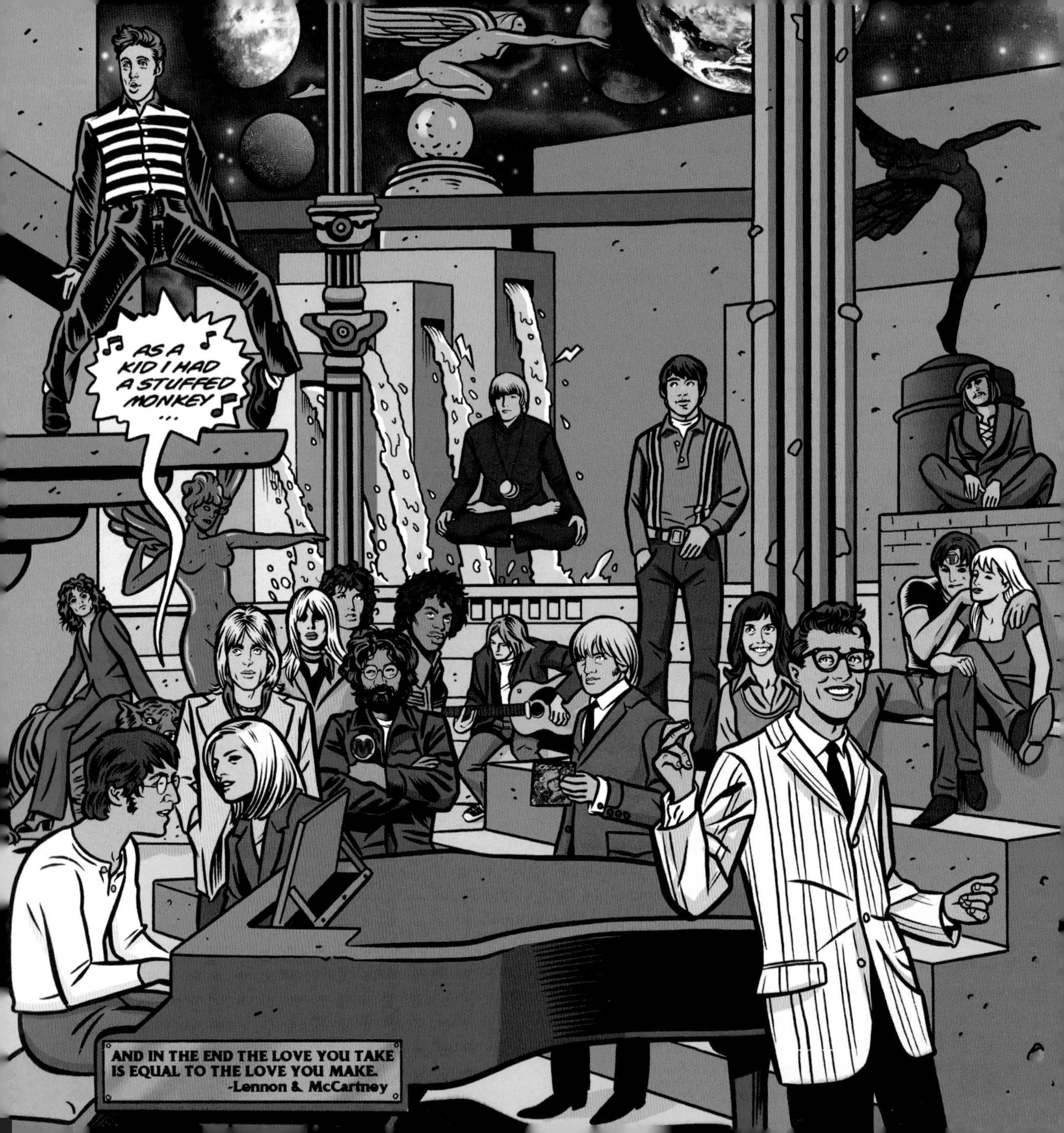
AS A KID I HAD A STUFFED MONKEY ...
AND IN THE END THE LOVE YOU TAKE IS EQUAL TO THE LOVE YOU MAKE.
-Lennon & McCartney

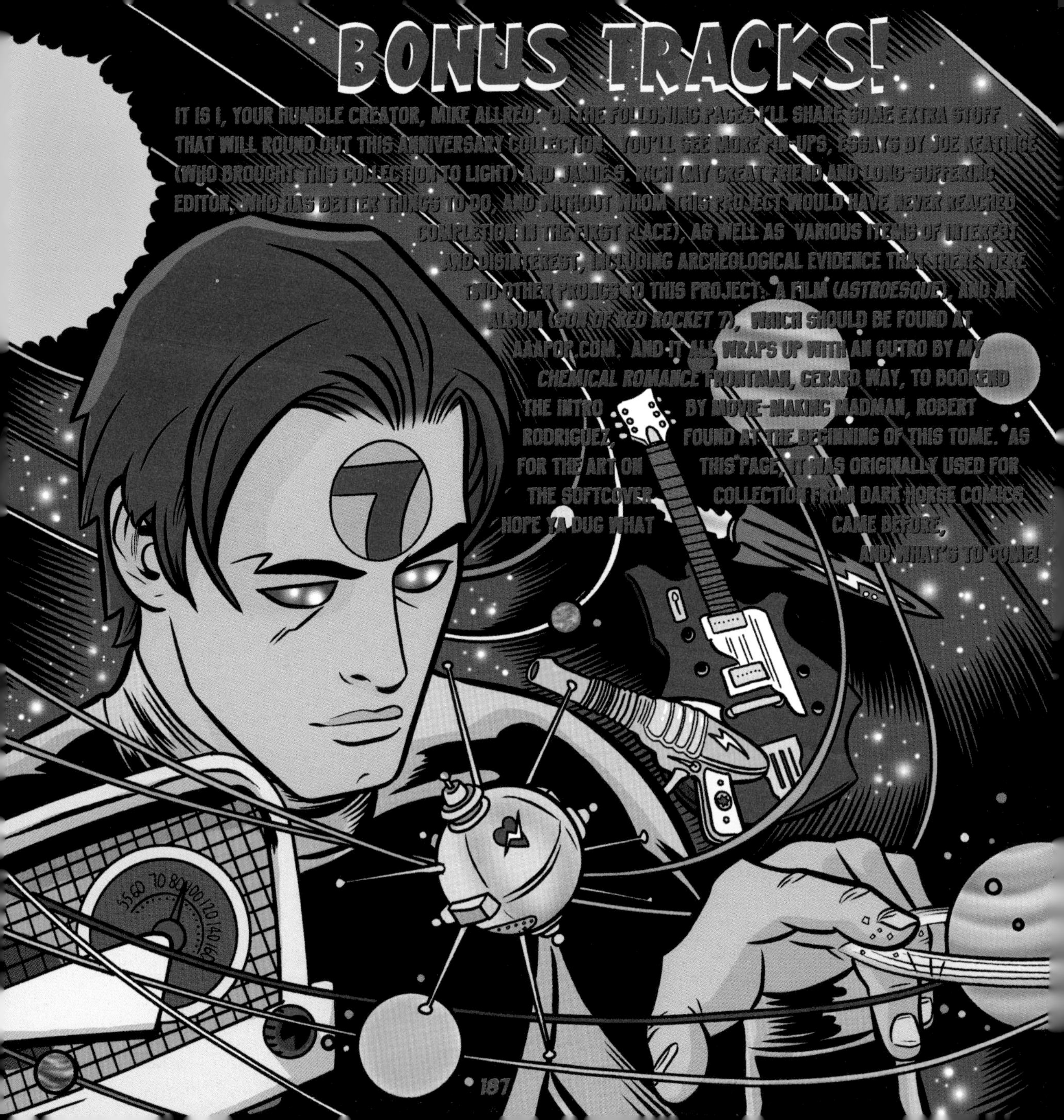

BONUS TRACKS!

IT IS I, YOUR HUMBLE CREATOR, MIKE ALLRED. ON THE FOLLOWING PAGES I'LL SHARE SOME EXTRA STUFF THAT WILL ROUND OUT THIS ANNIVERSARY COLLECTION. YOU'LL SEE MORE PIN-UPS, ESSAYS BY JOE KEATINGE (WHO BROUGHT THIS COLLECTION TO LIGHT) AND JAMIE S. RICH (MY GREAT FRIEND AND LONG-SUFFERING EDITOR, WHO HAS BETTER THINGS TO DO, AND WITHOUT WHOM THIS PROJECT WOULD HAVE NEVER REACHED COMPLETION IN THE FIRST PLACE), AS WELL AS VARIOUS ITEMS OF INTEREST AND DISINTEREST, INCLUDING ARCHEOLOGICAL EVIDENCE THAT THERE WERE TWO OTHER PRONGS TO THIS PROJECT: A FILM (*ASTROESQUE*), AND AN ALBUM (*SON OF RED ROCKET 7*), WHICH SHOULD BE FOUND AT AAAPOP.COM. AND IT ALL WRAPS UP WITH AN OUTRO BY *MY CHEMICAL ROMANCE* FRONTMAN, GERARD WAY, TO BOOKEND THE INTRO BY MOVIE-MAKING MADMAN, ROBERT RODRIGUEZ, FOUND AT THE BEGINNING OF THIS TOME. AS FOR THE ART ON THIS PAGE, IT WAS ORIGINALLY USED FOR THE SOFTCOVER COLLECTION FROM DARK HORSE COMICS. HOPE YA DUG WHAT CAME BEFORE, AND WHAT'S TO COME!

AFTERWORDS
DO YOU REMEMBER WHEN ROCK AND ROLL SAVED THE WORLD?
By Joe Keatinge

Ten years ago the embers of the early nineties boom were snuffed out by speculation and the comics industry's future grew quite bleak. Tired fans practically abandoned their stores as dreams of video games and the opposite sex danced in their heads. Great works such as *SIN CITY, STARMAN, EIGHTBALL, THE ACME NOVELTY LIBRARY* and many others were released with little acclaim outside of comics' inner circle.

The late nineties were a time when leaving a surefire hit for something untested and new was unheard of, but this didn't stop Mike Allred from taking a sabbatical on *MADMAN*. Mike had an all-new bag of tricks which had nothing to do with the denizens of Snap City.

RED ROCKET 7 was something truly new and different; 110% pure hi-fidelity science fiction.

Nowadays pursuing such a dream isn't considered so crazy, but this was a time before an ever growing number of musicians braved to play the visual instrument of graphic fiction. Music comics existed only on the fringe in titles such as Jamie Hewlett's *TANK GIRL*, Peter Bagge's *HATE* and Los Bros Hernandez's *LOVE & ROCKETS*. Taking them to the mainstream was Mike's dream.

His devotion paid off. One would be hard pressed to resist *RED ROCKET 7's* 10"x 10", record sized format, bound with staples and containing the very best of rock n'roll's history in seven, twenty four paged, sci-fi coated doses. It had everything you could hope for as robots, girls, guitars, aliens and ray guns rubbed elbows with John Lennon, Elvis Presley, Jimi Hendrix, David Bowie and, my personal favorite, The Dandy Warhols. Comics don't get much cooler than that.

RED ROCKET 7 not only gained a multitude of attention from the comics scene, but it infiltrated music magazines such as Alternative Press, Raygun, The Oregon Voice, The Face and Anodyne with article after article shocked by what this quirky mini-series accomplished.

This accomplishment could be enough for most, but not for Mike. Years before comics properly crossed over with movies, he expanded his vision far beyond the printed page with a self-made, indie feature prequel *ASTROESQUE* and *THE GEAR: SON OF RED ROCKET SEVEN*, a full LP which acted as a musical epilogue to the wake of RED ROCKET 7's musical utopia.

RED ROCKET 7 wasn't just another mini-series. It was a multi-media explosion aimed straight into your cerebral cortex, forever branding your brain with four-color images you'd never soon forget. The book solidified itself as part of mainstream pop culture, ten years before the rest of the medium thought to catch up.

RED ROCKET 7 still stands as a testament to everything comics are truly capable of. In an era when ideas fly by at a thousand miles an hour, it hasn't aged a bit and, if anything, holds its own against the volumes of comics it inspired. Creating such a long-lasting work isn't an easy feat.

Congratulations, Mike, for over a decade of saving the world from the dangerous forces of boring - one ripping panel at a time!

JOE KEATINGE is the PR & Marketing Coordinator for Image Comics, and co-editor of the graphic mix tape, POPGUN.

NOTES FROM THE EDITOR
SET THE CONTROLS FOR THE HEART OF THE PELVIS
By Jamie S. Rich

So, there I was, dressed in a silver sharkskin suit that fit like it was my own skin and wearing black lipstick some slightly under-twenty-one girl in the crowd had put on me as a thank you for buying candy-flavored drinks that we could share. We were right in front, just left of center, watching Blur headline in San Francisco. When Damon Albarn looked out at the front row, it was just a bunch of girls and then me, taller than the rest, shinier, a weird smile that was both light and dark. When "Girls & Boys" came on, was it any surprise I would be the one he'd choose to dance with, our arm movements locking in rhythm even with the space separating audience and performer between us? The girls who held the barrier with me were shooting daggers my way. They could not forgive this affront to their teen sexuality.

But I didn't care. It was 1997, and Jamie S. Rich was on top of the world.

I was twenty-five, and it wasn't uncommon for me to go up and down the coast from Oregon to California chasing Pulp or up through Seattle and into Canada to see Gene perform. I even jetted to New York City to see Suede, shouting my lungs out at Neil Codling and sneaking my way into the after party. It was the apex of Britpop in the 1990s, and though I lived in a virtual wasteland for that kind of music, I was wired in. I was even co-hosting a cable access television show called "@lright", a high-wire act we did every two weeks, hosting an hour of live television as an excuse to get free music and meet more bands. It was terrible to watch, I'm sure, but we were having fun.

There was one episode where Mike Allred came and hung out. He sat above the cameras, in the stair-ladder that was used to adjust the ceiling lights. I don't think he ever showed up on camera until the end, when we would dance to the latest import single under the closing credits, but my co-host kept mentioning him, referring to him as "Mike Alright". If I recall, he was there to see a concert with me after the broadcast. Probably the Dandy Warhols.

In addition to all of this, I was Mike's editor at Dark Horse Comics. I hadn't read *Madman* before arriving in Portland three years prior, but one of the first things I did as an editorial assistant at the Horse was to write half of the first set of Madman Bubblegum Cards. Mike liked what I did, and he asked that I do all fifty. When the second set came around, I was asked to do it again, but for this go-around, I'd do it on my own time and not on the clock. I actually got paid a writing fee! It was my first freelance writing gig.

Eventually, I became Mike's editor, seeing him through a couple of Madman crossover books before helping him initiate his newest project, his first major creation since the *Madman* book had become a huge hit. It was this wicked sci-fi epic, a sort of *Zelig* for the rock 'n' roll crowd, *Forbidden Planet* meets *A Hard Day's Night*, with, of course, echoes of *Performance* and *The Man Who Fell To Earth* and some obscure T. Rex TV show that only Mike ever heard of. It was called *Red Rocket 7*, and it was going to be seven issues and we wanted it to be 12" by 12" just like a vinyl record. I remember having to go into one of the bureaucratic budgeting meetings where some secret Masonic formula or other was used to decide what books would be a hit and which would fail. I had to look at the decision makers and explain to them why they should do this-- me, the goofy kid with anime bangs and eyeliner. The book got approved.

I doubt it was anything I did, though. Like I said, this was Mike's first post-Madman project, so it had to be a no-brainer, right? Sell it on that, and it's sold. I suppose it's indicative of what a hit *Madman Comics* was that Mike was able to get the company to pony up for an ambitious, three-pronged project that had come to him in a dream. In addition to this comic book series, there was a movie, *Astroesque*, that was already shot and ready to go, and eventually, there would be the musical album by The Gear, the backing band for Red Rocket 7. It's nuts to think about now, but we were doing it.

The *Red Rocket 7* period was an incredible time in my life. Like I said, I was twenty-five, and though I am not generally superstitious when it comes to age, I did recognize that I was at the cusp of something, some crossroad of life where I expected amazing things were going to happen for me-- or it could all fall to pieces. There was danger everywhere. Every good opportunity was also a chance for tremendous folly. It's a state of being I attempted to capture in my second novel, *The Everlasting*, published many years later. I'll leave it up to other twenty-five-year-olds to tell me if I got it right.

It was in this headspace that I rode along with Mike as he completed *Red Rocket 7*. Being his editor meant long conversations where we mainly talked about music and movies, my job really being to keep him creatively excited more than I needed to provide him with any artistic guidance. (My producer credit on the Gear record, *Son of Red Rocket 7*, amounted to the same thing; I was never even in Mike's home studio while he was recording.) His enthusiasm was so infectious, though, I think he probably was getting me fired up more than I was serving him. Sometimes Mike would drive up to Portland from Eugene, a trip of several hours, and we'd go on "research trips." More often than not, that meant traveling all over town to the different record shops looking for the vinyl copy of the Rolling Stones' *Their Satanic Majesties Request* with the 3-D cover. Occasionally, it meant real research, like heading over to Pioneer Square in downtown Portland to take reference photos for Rock 'n' Roll Heaven. Look at the last page of the book again. I'm actually Keith Moon. I stood in Mike's photos as size reference, and for the final piece, he turned me into Keith Moon. Freakin' Keith Moon, people! How rad is that?

It's not my only cameo in *Red Rocket 7*. I appear a couple of times as a background character, and I even get a line to say. No less than two of my girlfriends make appearances as well, which is kind of freaky to think about now. But then, the comic, particularly the last couple of issues, is full of Portland musical landmarks, from the now-defunct Ozone Records on Burnside to the local bands that Mike and I were digging at the time, some of which went on to great things (the Warhols) and some of whom faded (Marigold, anyone?). In its own way, *Red Rocket 7* became a snapshot of my life at the time.

But then things were about to get worse before they got better.

Our course was set, and everything seemed to be going right. The first issue came out, and the response was tremendous. We were hearing reports of how the odd size had worked in our favor, and some stores were racking the book in the prime spot by the cash register because the square size didn't fit in their rectangle racks. The reviews were positive, the fan response was good, we were on a high.

And then something happened before issue #2. All those things we had been hearing were so good were now being used as weapons to flog us for our hubris of daring to attempt such a different project. The record album size was a burden, no one wanted to stock it. Readers started to ask what had happened to Frank Einstein and complain that this wasn't *Madman*. Why wasn't Mike Allred doing more *Madman*? Dark Horse seemed to lose interest completely, biting their lips and just waiting it out. I tried to do some grassroots marketing, personally sending the comics to major magazines, but outside of a one-page profile in *Alternative Press*, got zero nibbles. The DH marketing department eventually apologized and said we'd get it back on the trade paperback, but I was gone by the time that came out, and I suspect without me there to hold some feet to the fire, the promise went unfulfilled. There were a few Eisner nominations: Best Limited Series, Best Covers, and Best Colorist for Laura Allred, in the summer of 1998, but we didn't win any of them, and shortly thereafter, *Red Rocket 7* almost completely vanished off the radar.

The commercial failure of the book was not my sole reason for leaving Dark Horse, but the general disregard I felt the book received was part of the larger problem that saw me seeking greener pastures. Oni Press was beckoning, as was my own writing career, and I heeded the call. This decision was another that would get worse before it got better, and then after a period of being very good, it got even worse, only for my life to eventually end up being the best it's ever been (a condition that has, thankfully, hung around). Mike and I have stuck it out through all of that. When he started to self-publish The Atomics, I was on board, we worked together at Oni, and now I am his editor at Image Comics. You can't pry us apart, even if both of us rarely leave our homes.

Things got better for *Red Rocket 7* over the years, too. Gradually, I began to notice a shift in opinion regarding the book. Sure, there were plenty who had never heard of it, but I never met anyone who out-and-out hated it. At Oni, I worked with a lot of young cartoonists. Almost all of them revered Mike, and quite a few of them would tell me how much they loved *Red Rocket 7*, even detailing the Herculean efforts they went through to get their hands on it. If memory serves, Steve Rolston, who drew *Queen & Country* for us before doing his own awesome *One Bad Day* graphic novel, was the first. His talking about it got other people to talk about it, and without either Mike or myself realizing it was happening, *Red Rocket 7* became a bona-fide, old-fashioned cult hit. So much so, that whenever the title was mentioned, or whenever the gajillionth reprint of *Madman: The Oddity Odyssey* would be released, someone would say, "Yeah, that's cool, but when are you going to reprint *Red Rocket 7*?"

Well, now you can all stop asking, because here it is. I suppose it's no longer underground anymore. Fans can start fighting over who was there first, who the real *Red Rocket 7* groupie is. Who among you will declare you knew of this comic back when it was cool, before it sold out to the man and all these poseurs jumped onboard?

Go ahead and boast all you want, suckers, because I have you beat. I was there way before all of you! That's right. That's me in the grainy video, down in the front row, wearing the silver suit, dancing with Mike Allred. I am Penny Lane, and he is a golden god.

It's 2008, and Jamie S. Rich is on top of the world.

J.S.R.
May 18, 2008
Achieved in the Valley of the Dolls

Jamie S. Rich is a writer of both comics and prose. Mike and Laura Allred drew the cover to his first book, *Cut My Hair*, back in 2000. Rich's most recent work includes the novel *Have You Seen the Horizon Lately?* and the comic books *Love the Way You Love* with artist Marc Ellerby and *12 Reasons Why I Love Her* with Jo'lle Jones. Rich and Jones will soon return with the hardboiled crime tale *You Have Killed Me*. Visit the author at www.confessions123.com to find out how that is going.

HAVEN'T YOU HEARD? MY NAME RHYMES WITH ELVIS?

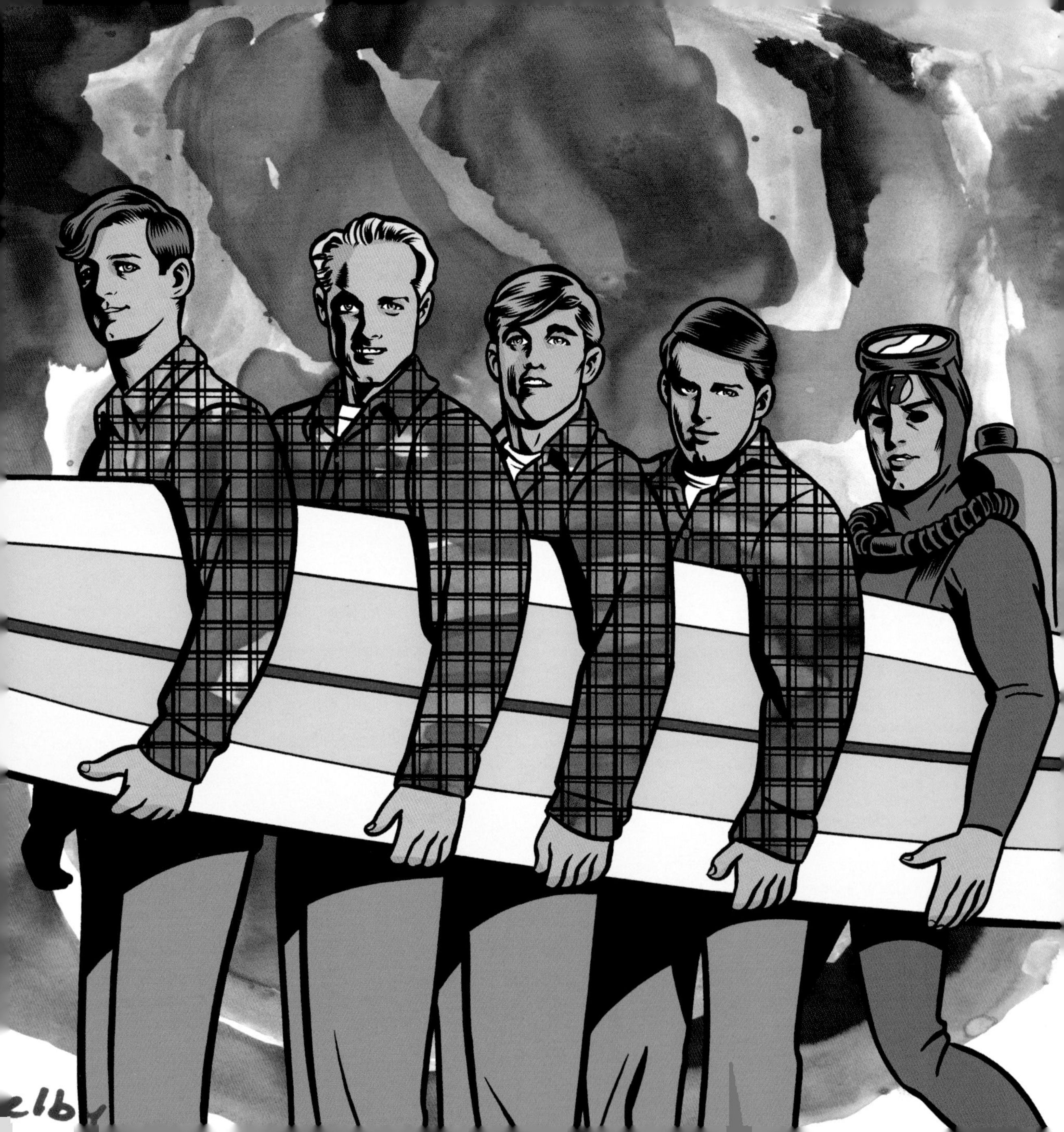

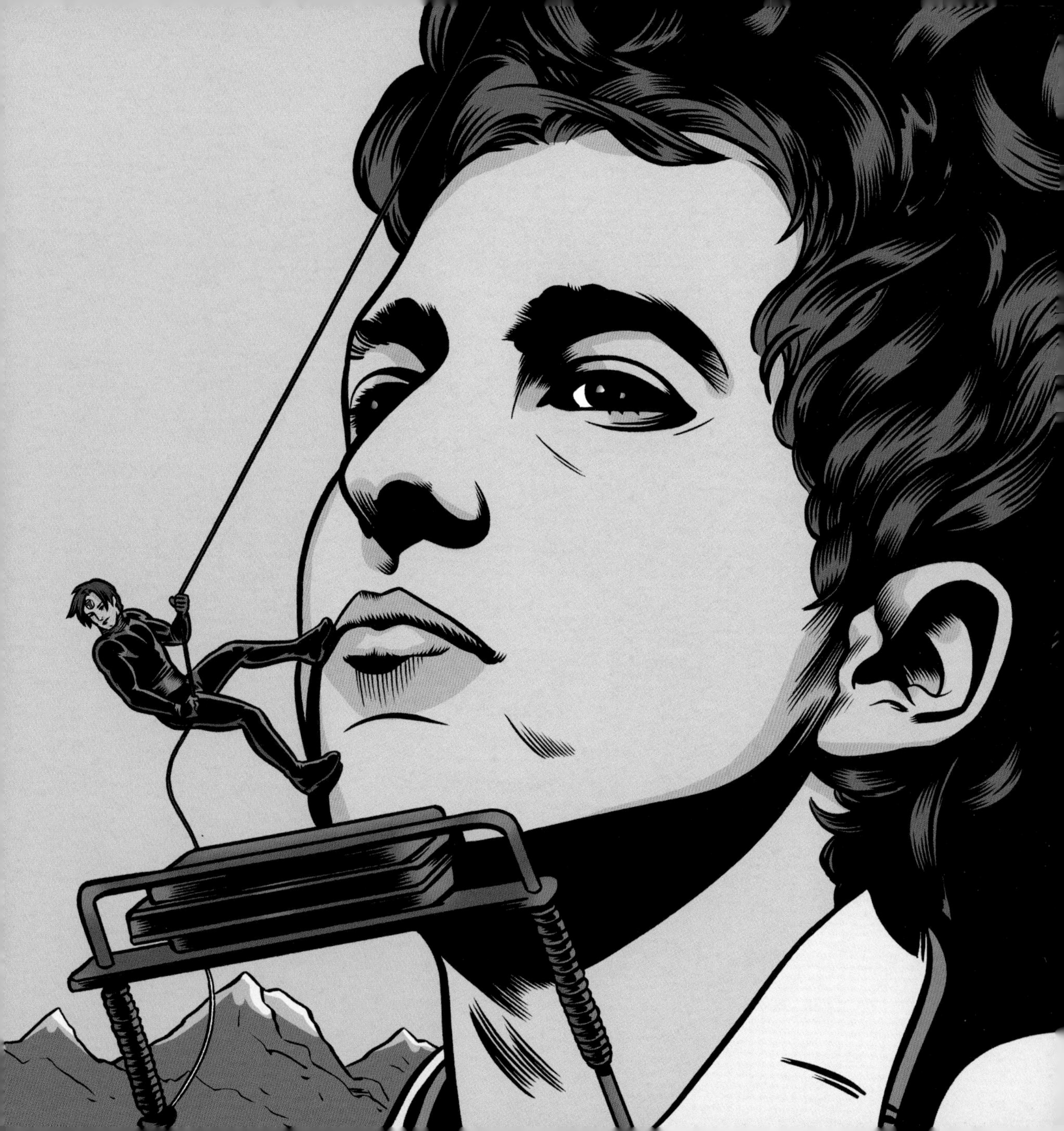

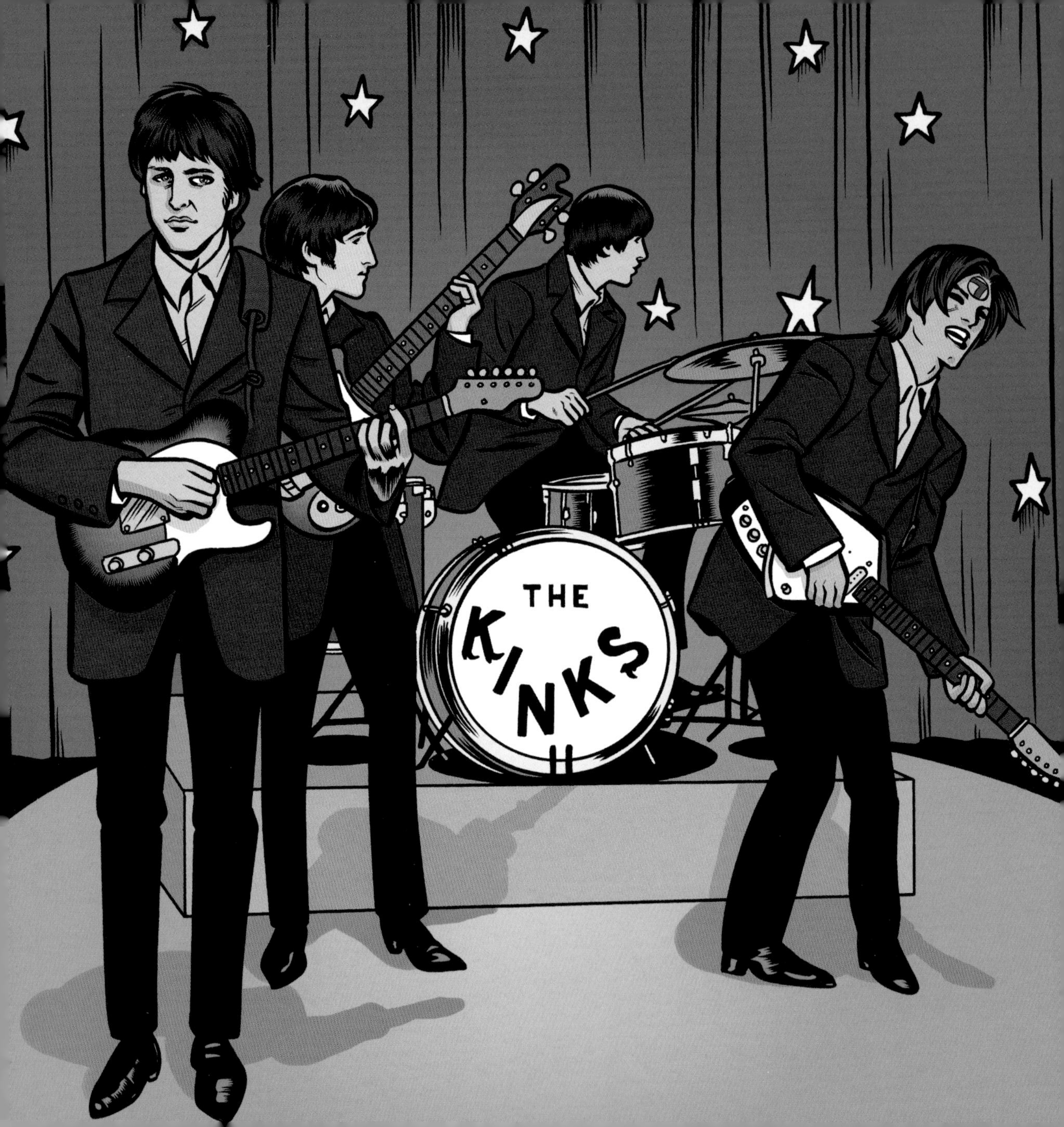
THE
KINKS

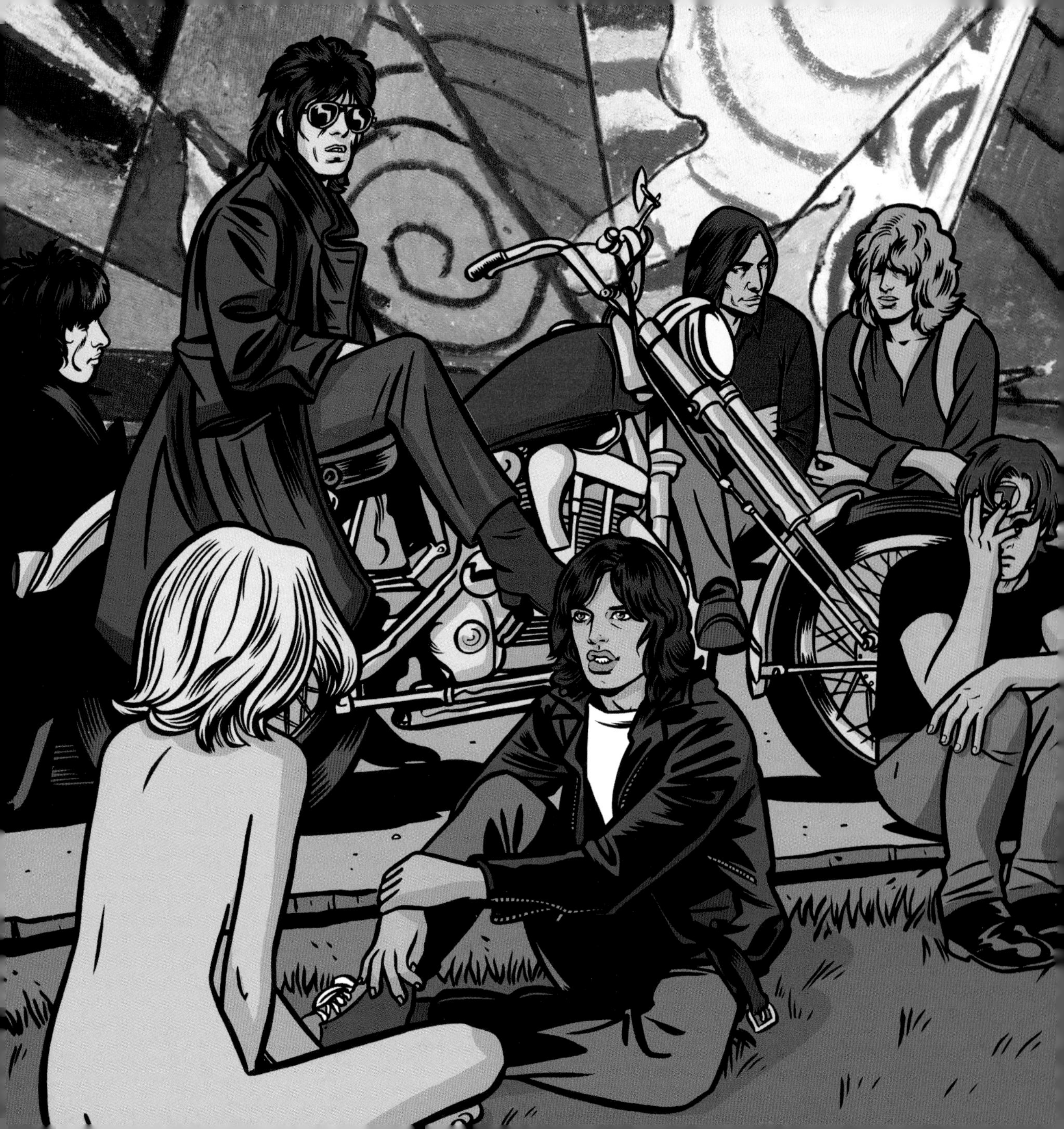

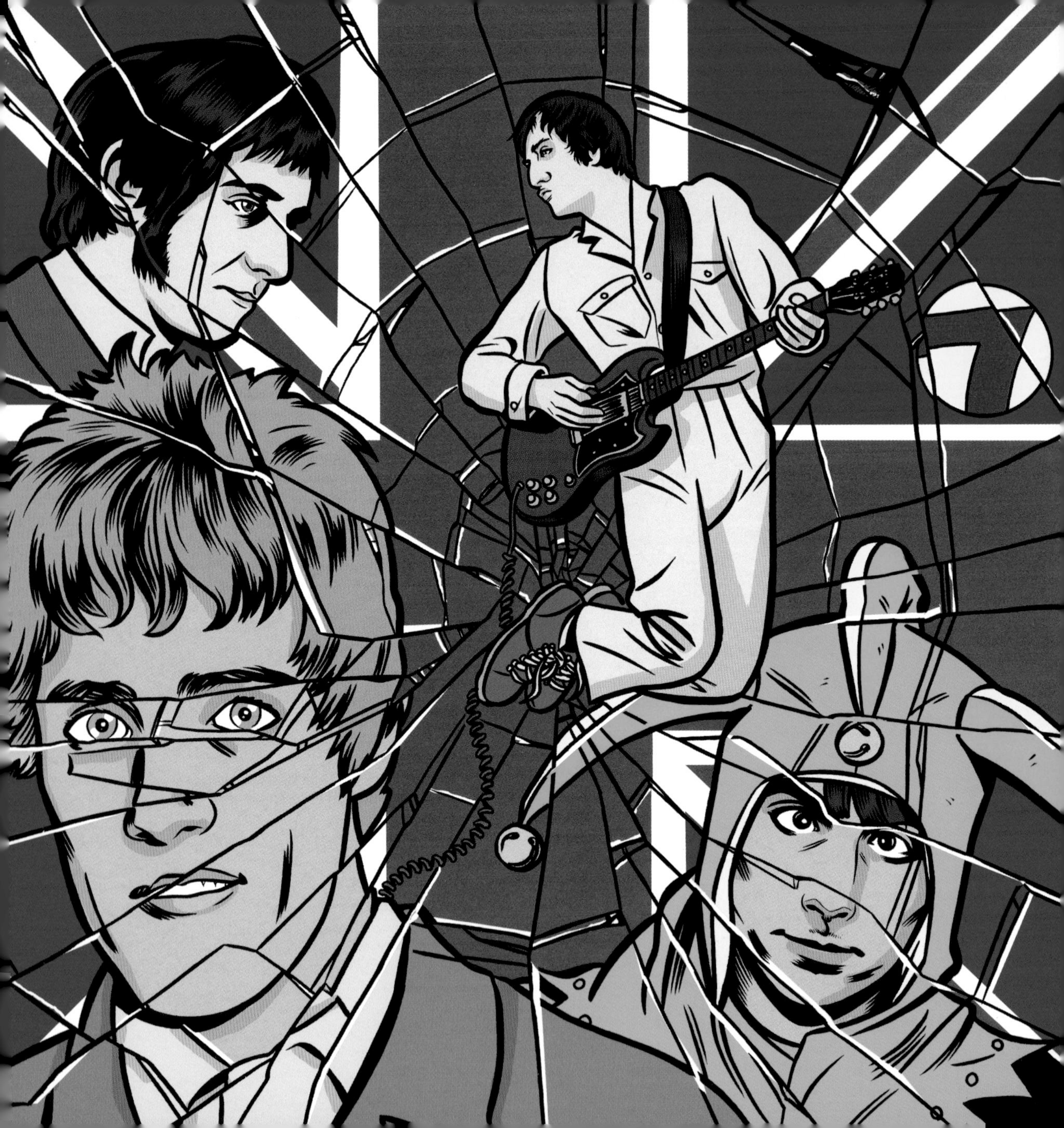

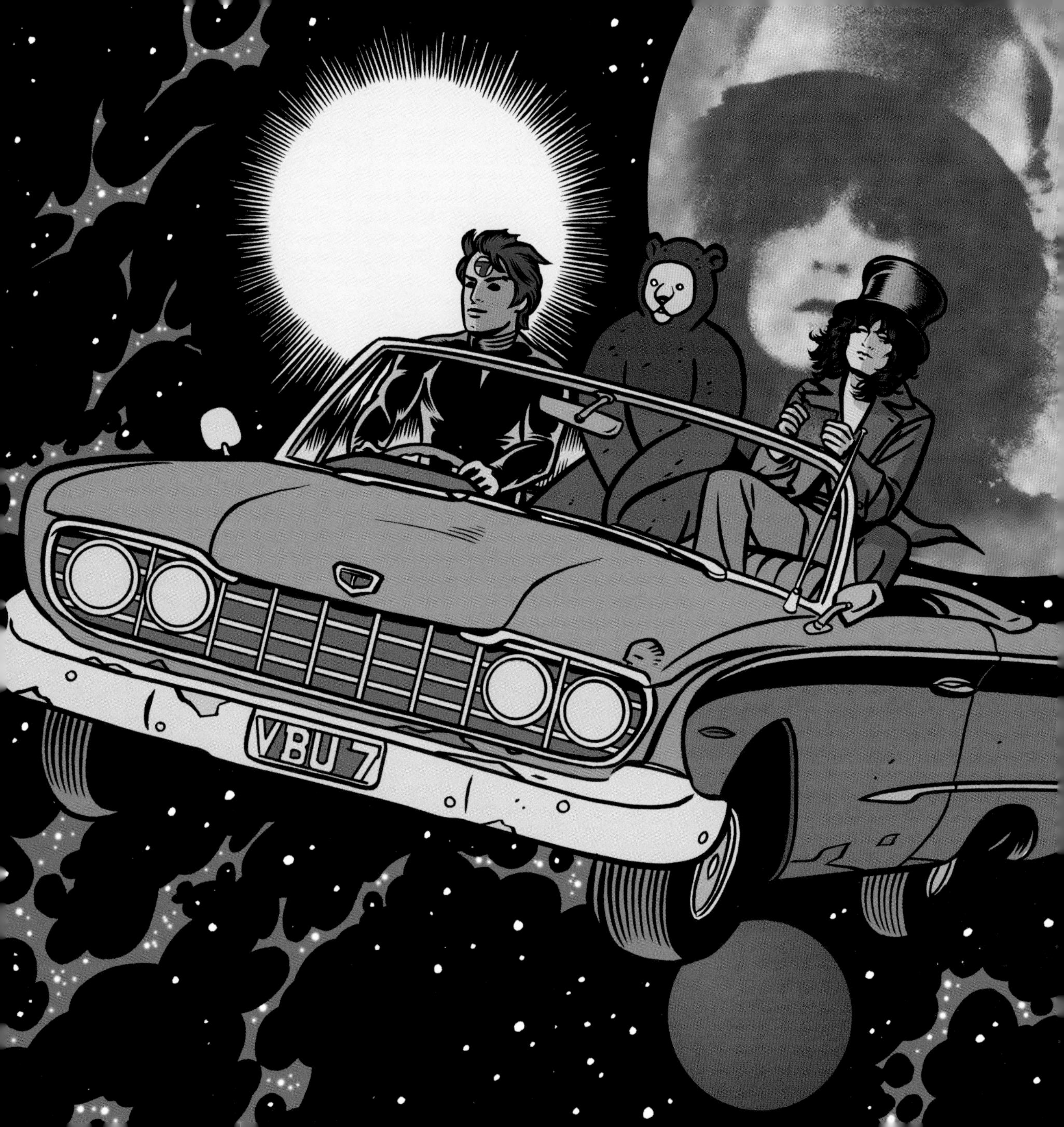
VBU 7

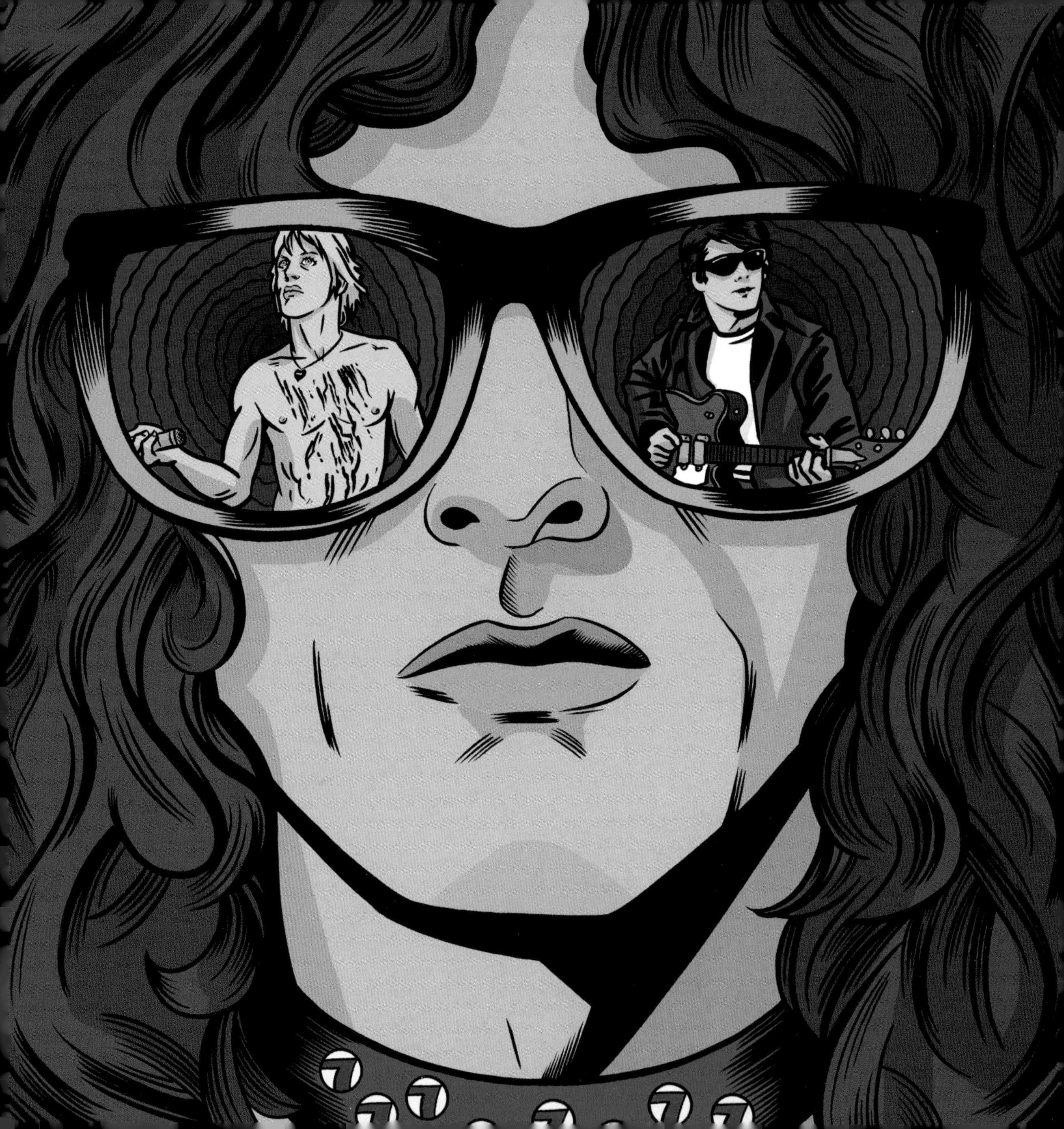

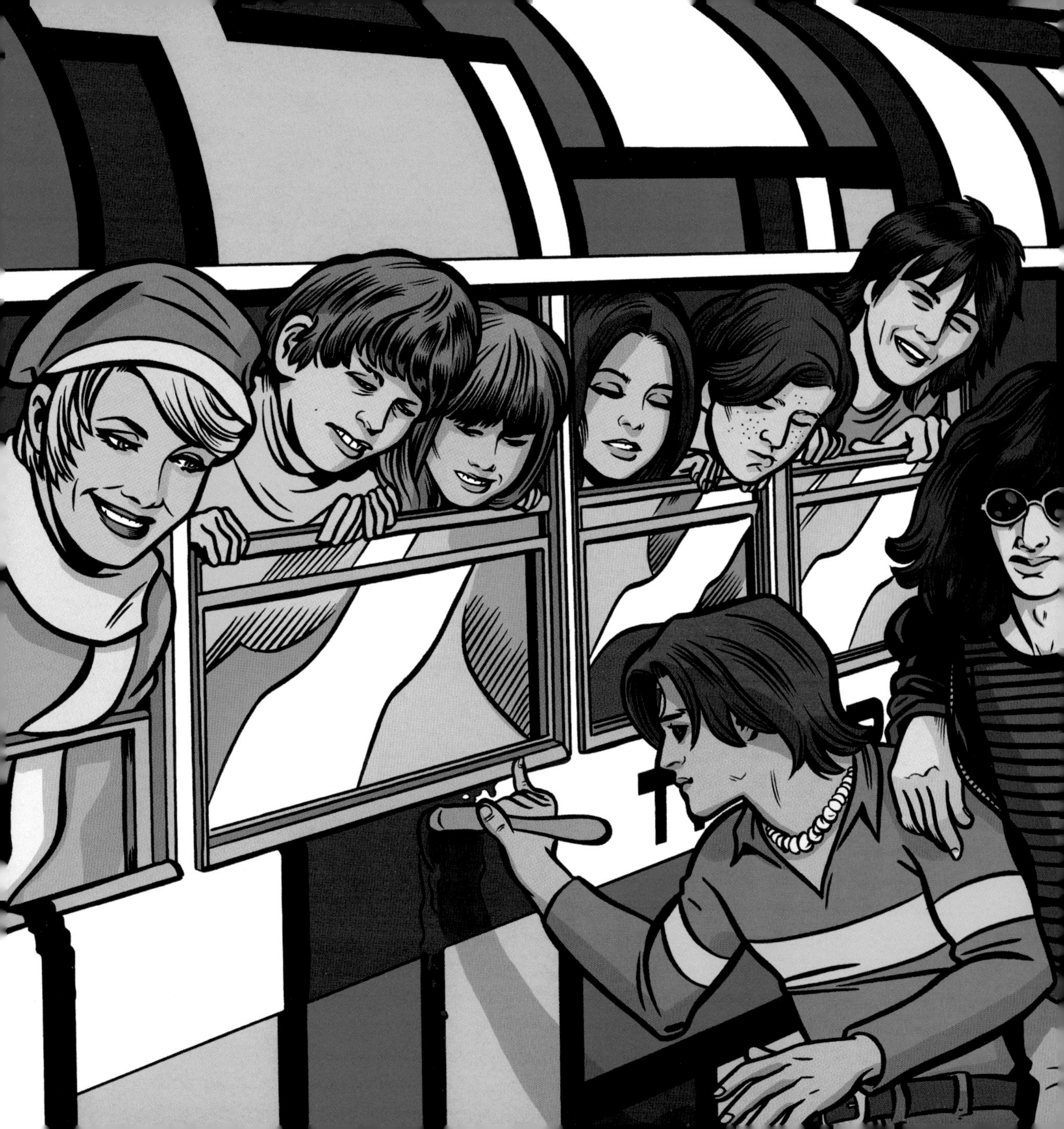

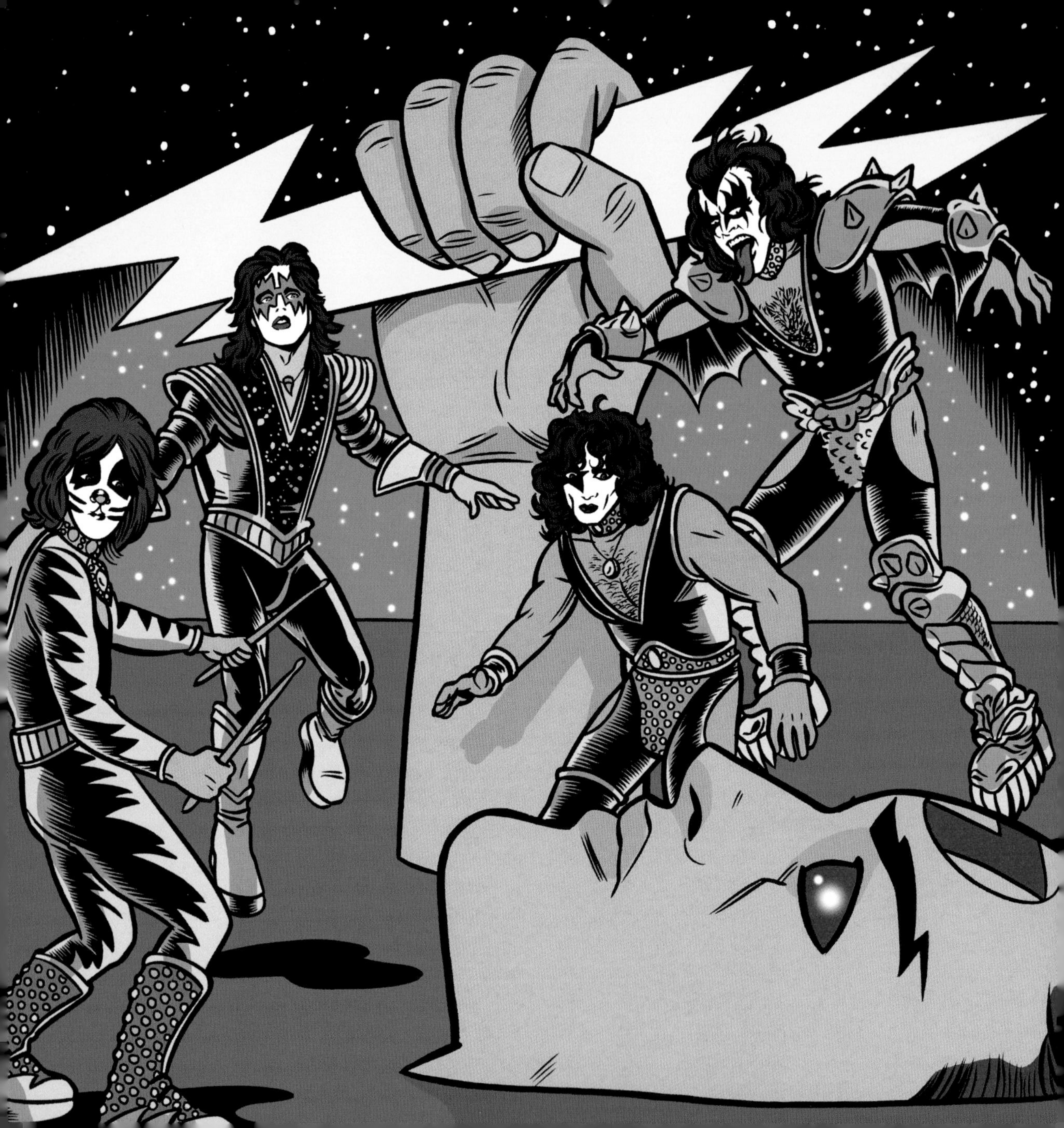

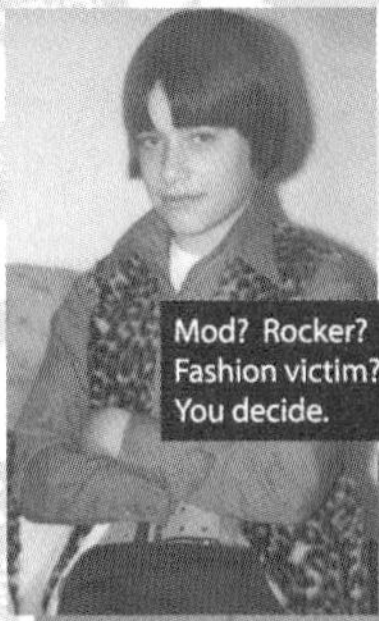

Mod? Rocker? Fashion victim? You decide.

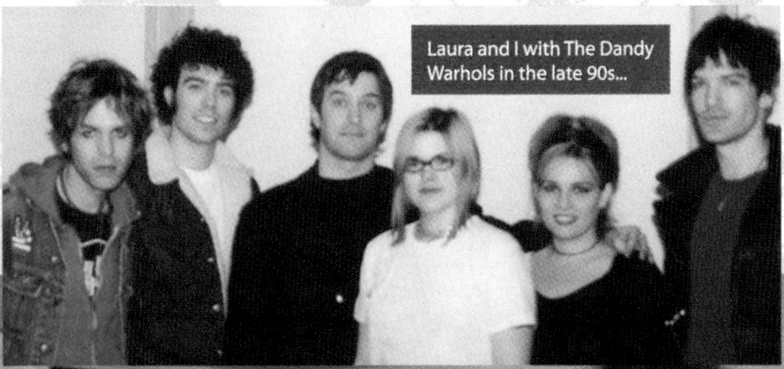

Laura and I with The Dandy Warhols in the late 90s...

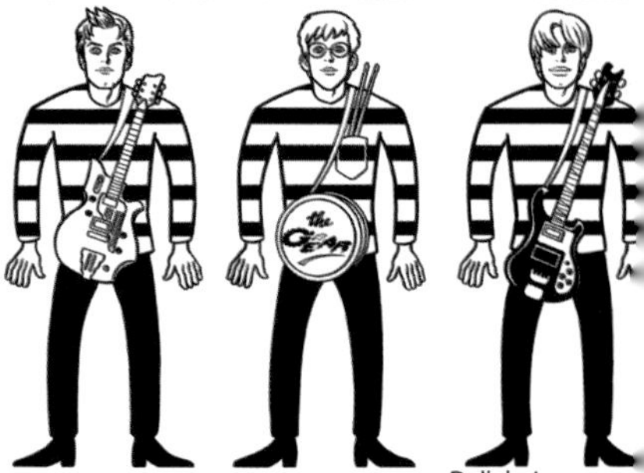

Doll designs (above) and a log design (below.

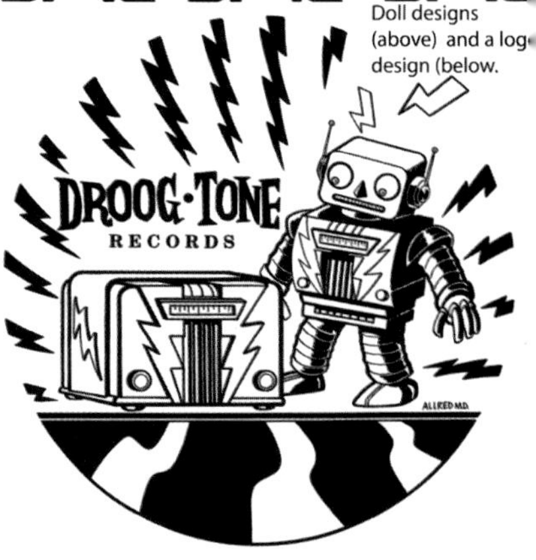
DROOG·TONE
RECORDS
ALLRED MD.

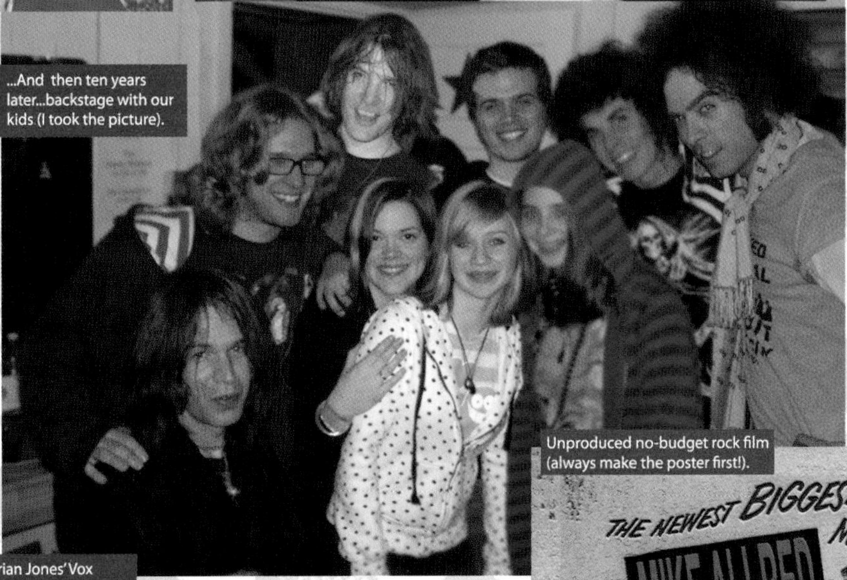

...And then ten years later...backstage with our kids (I took the picture).

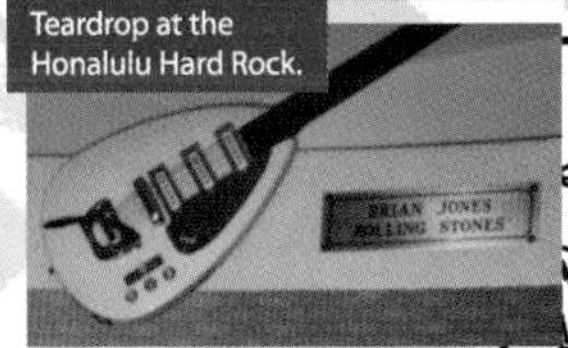
BRIAN JONES
ROLLING STONES

Brian Jones' Vox Teardrop at the Honalulu Hard Rock.

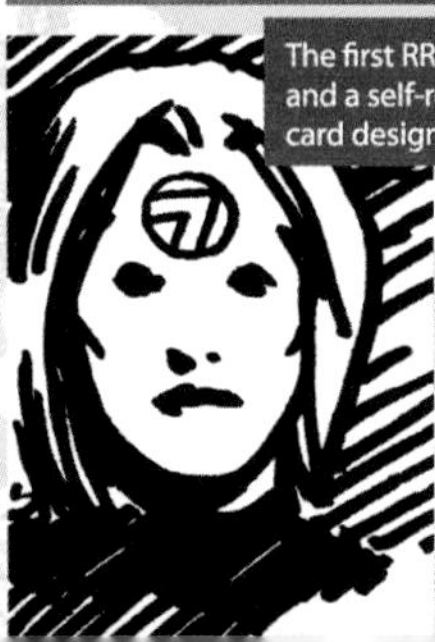

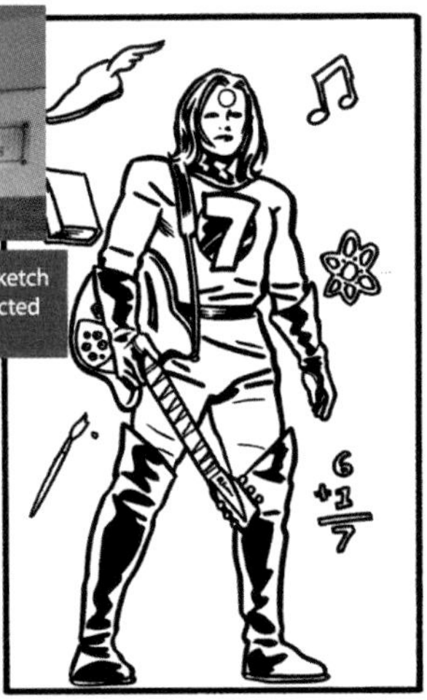

The first RR7 sketch and a self-rejected card design.

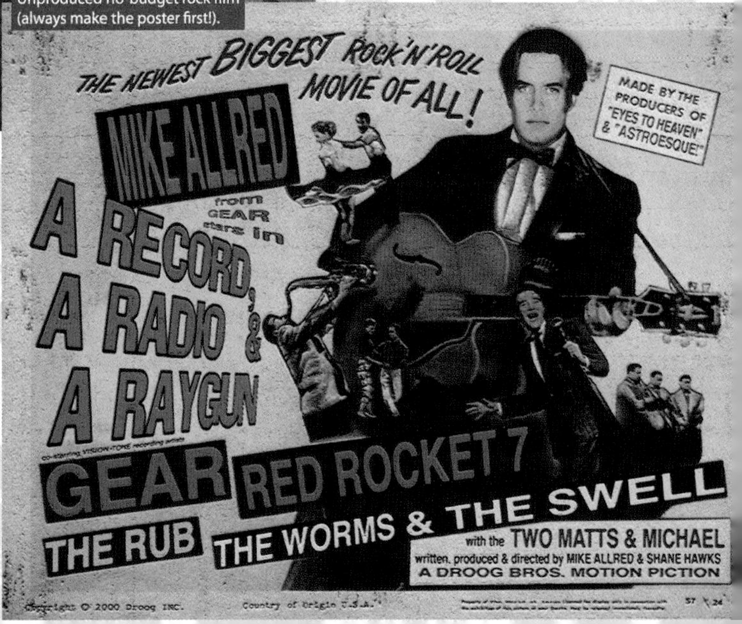
THE NEWEST BIGGEST ROCK'N'ROLL MOVIE OF ALL!
MADE BY THE PRODUCERS OF "EYES TO HEAVEN" & "ASTROESQUE"
MIKE ALLRED
from GEAR stars in
A RECORD, A RADIO & A RAYGUN
GEAR
RED ROCKET 7
THE RUB
THE WORMS & THE SWELL
with the TWO MATTS & MICHAEL
written, produced & directed by MIKE ALLRED & SHANE HAWKS
A DROOG BROS. MOTION PICTION
Copyright © 2000 Droog INC.
Country of Origin U.S.A.

Unproduced no-budget rock film (always make the poster first!).

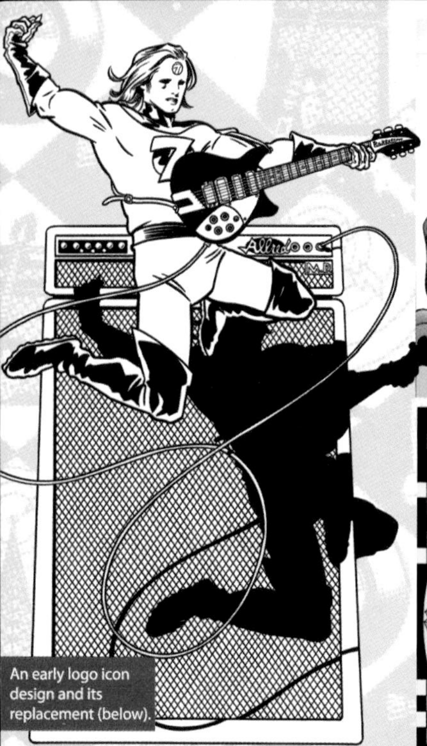

An early logo icon design and its replacement (below).

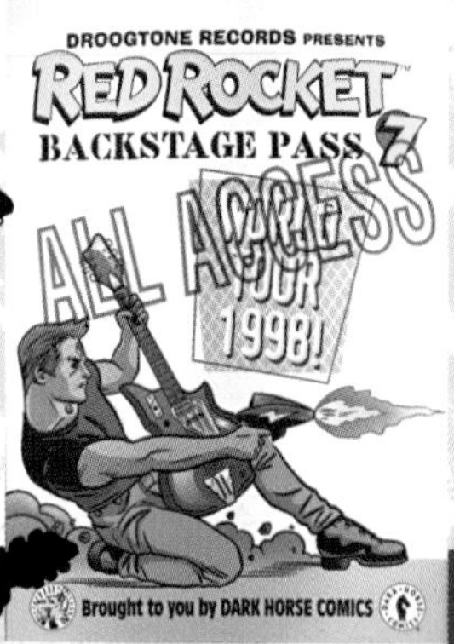
DROOGTONE RECORDS PRESENTS
RED ROCKET 7
BACKSTAGE PASS
ALL ACCESS
TOUR 1998!
Brought to you by DARK HORSE COMICS

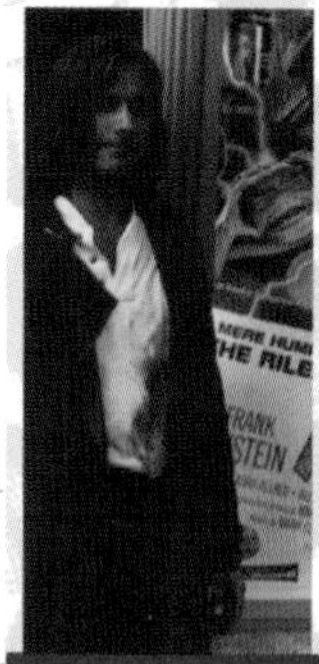

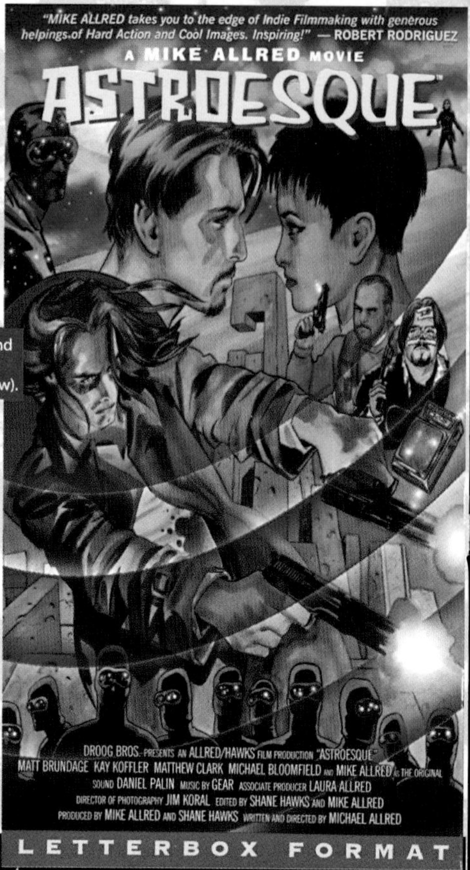
"MIKE ALLRED takes you to the edge of Indie Filmmaking with generous helpings of Hard Action and Cool Images. Inspiring!" — ROBERT RODRIGUEZ
A MIKE ALLRED MOVIE
ASTROESQUE
DROOG BROS. PRESENTS AN ALLRED/HAWKS FILM PRODUCTION "ASTROESQUE"
MATT BRUNDAGE KAY KOFFLER MATTHEW CLARK MICHAEL BLOOMFIELD AND MIKE ALLRED AS THE ORIGINAL
SOUND DANIEL PALIN MUSIC BY GEAR ASSOCIATE PRODUCER LAURA ALLRED
DIRECTOR OF PHOTOGRAPHY JIM KORAL EDITED BY SHANE HAWKS AND MIKE ALLRED
PRODUCED BY MIKE ALLRED AND SHANE HAWKS WRITTEN AND DIRECTED BY MICHAEL ALLRED
LETTERBOX FORMAT

Making Astroesque, and the video box. A 2000 tour shirt design (below).

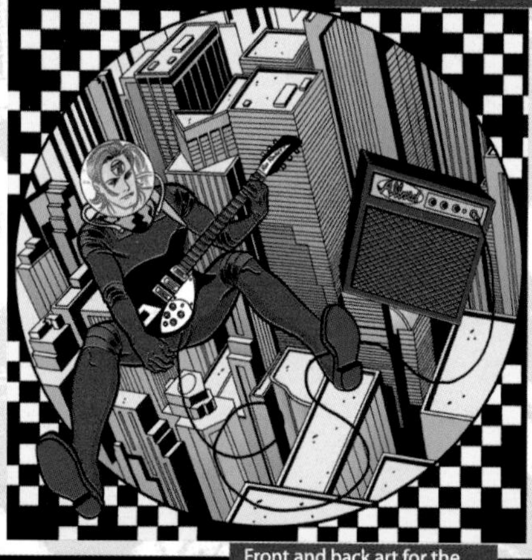

Front and back art for the (horribly mixed) Gear ep cd.

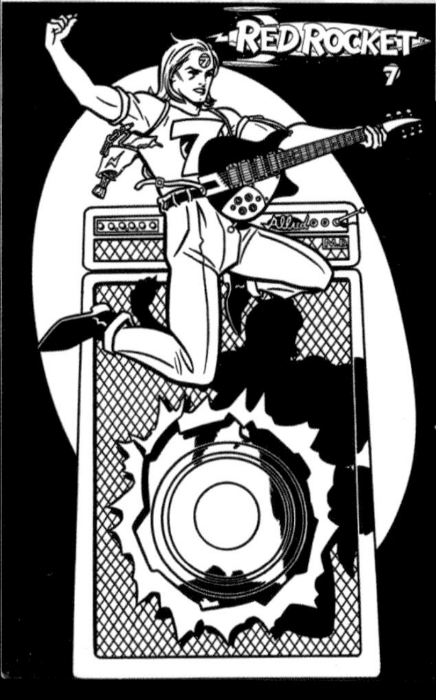
RED ROCKET 7

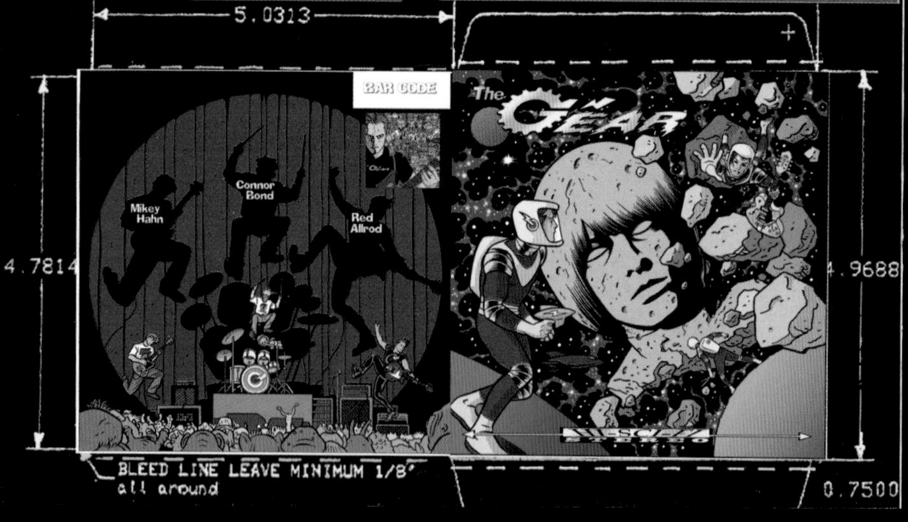
5.0313
BAR CODE
Mikey Hahn
Connor Bond
Red Allrod
The GEAR
4.7814
4.9688
BLEED LINE LEAVE MINIMUM 1/8"
all around
0.7500

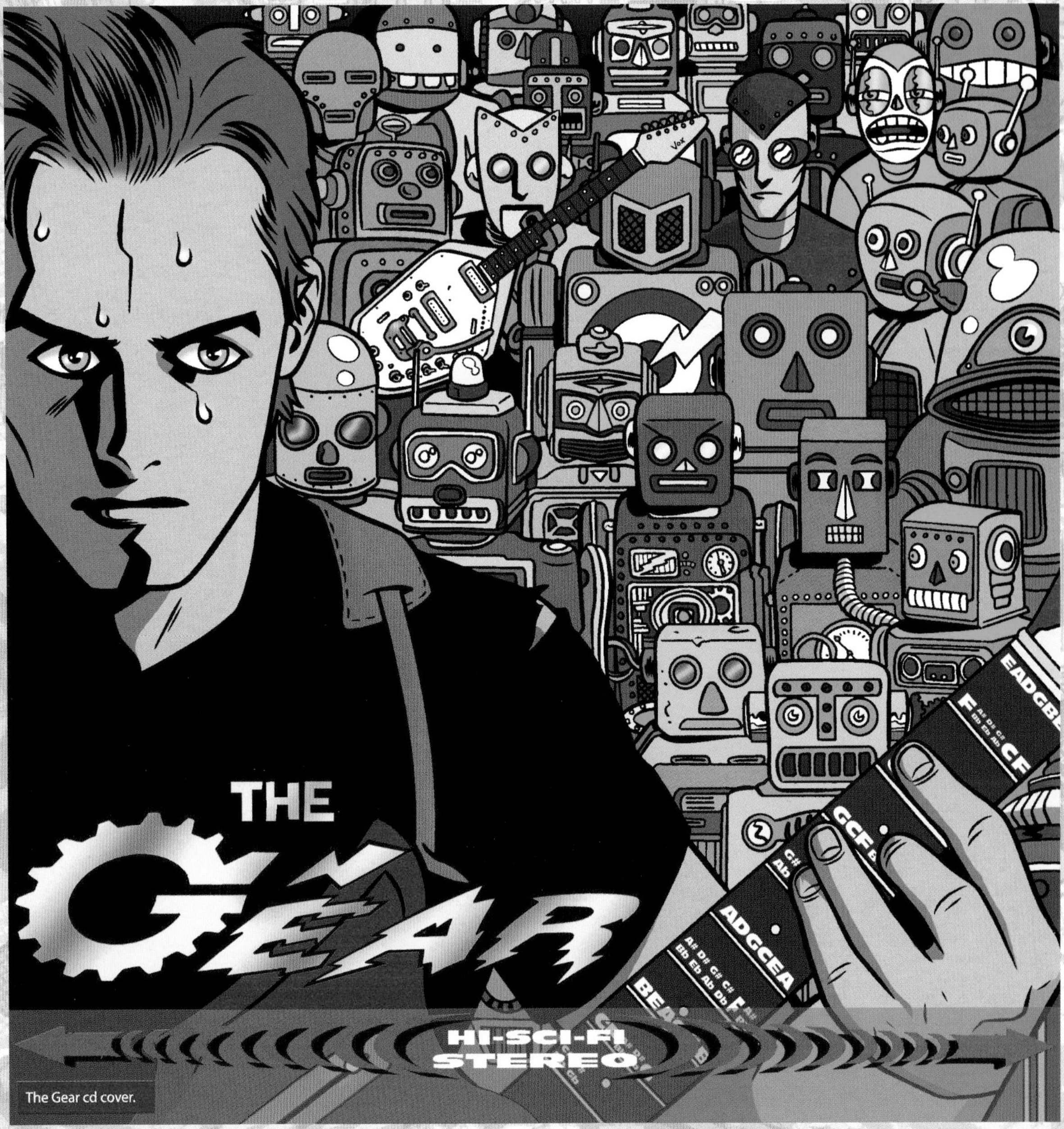
THE
GEAR
HI-SCI-FI
STEREO
ADGCEA

The Gear cd cover.

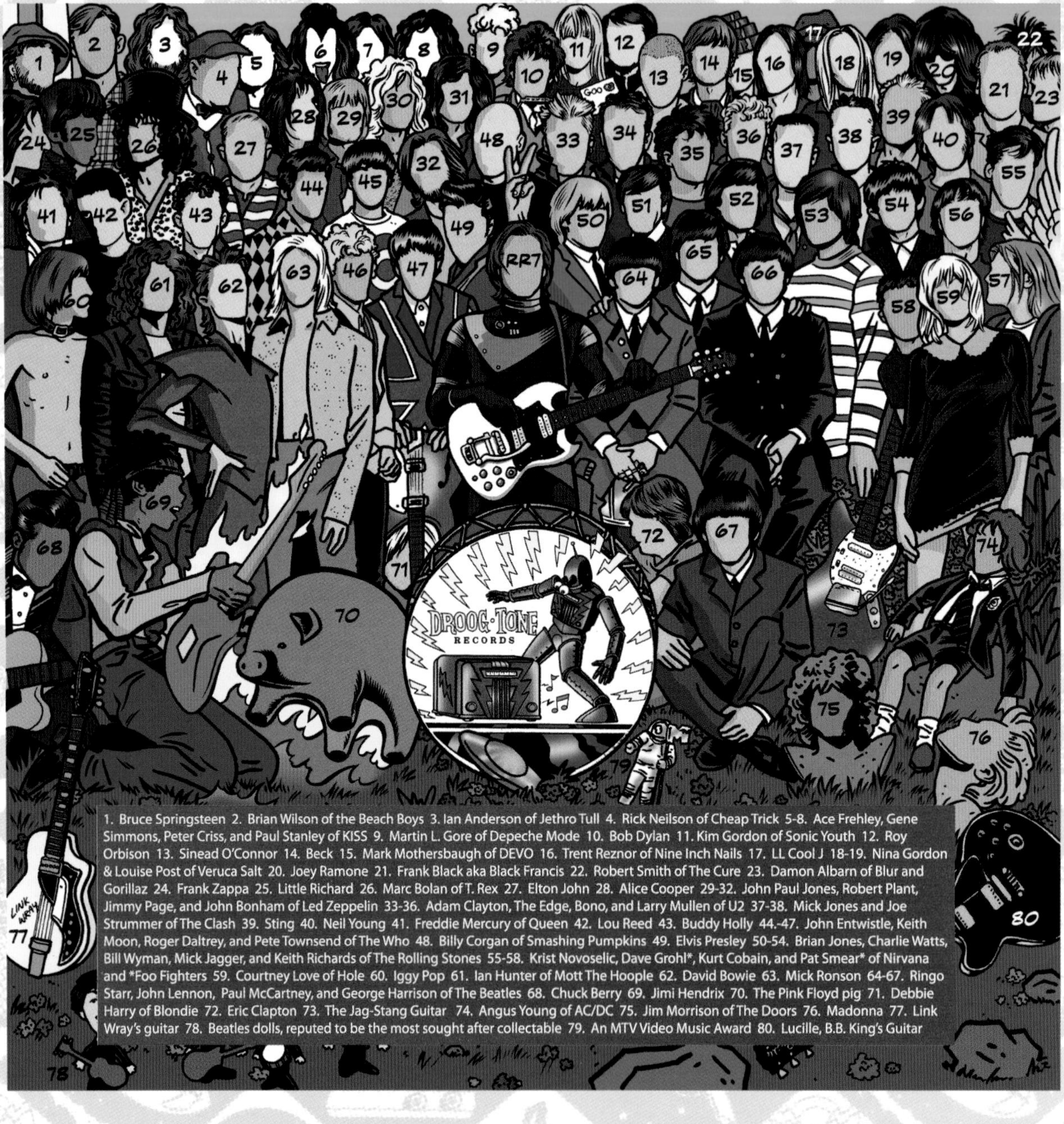
DROOG-TONE
RECORDS
LINK WRAY

1. Bruce Springsteen 2. Brian Wilson of the Beach Boys 3. Ian Anderson of Jethro Tull 4. Rick Neilson of Cheap Trick 5-8. Ace Frehley, Gene Simmons, Peter Criss, and Paul Stanley of KISS 9. Martin L. Gore of Depeche Mode 10. Bob Dylan 11. Kim Gordon of Sonic Youth 12. Roy Orbison 13. Sinead O'Connor 14. Beck 15. Mark Mothersbaugh of DEVO 16. Trent Reznor of Nine Inch Nails 17. LL Cool J 18-19. Nina Gordon & Louise Post of Veruca Salt 20. Joey Ramone 21. Frank Black aka Black Francis 22. Robert Smith of The Cure 23. Damon Albarn of Blur and Gorillaz 24. Frank Zappa 25. Little Richard 26. Marc Bolan of T. Rex 27. Elton John 28. Alice Cooper 29-32. John Paul Jones, Robert Plant, Jimmy Page, and John Bonham of Led Zeppelin 33-36. Adam Clayton, The Edge, Bono, and Larry Mullen of U2 37-38. Mick Jones and Joe Strummer of The Clash 39. Sting 40. Neil Young 41. Freddie Mercury of Queen 42. Lou Reed 43. Buddy Holly 44.-47. John Entwistle, Keith Moon, Roger Daltrey, and Pete Townsend of The Who 48. Billy Corgan of Smashing Pumpkins 49. Elvis Presley 50-54. Brian Jones, Charlie Watts, Bill Wyman, Mick Jagger, and Keith Richards of The Rolling Stones 55-58. Krist Novoselic, Dave Grohl*, Kurt Cobain, and Pat Smear* of Nirvana and *Foo Fighters 59. Courtney Love of Hole 60. Iggy Pop 61. Ian Hunter of Mott The Hoople 62. David Bowie 63. Mick Ronson 64-67. Ringo Starr, John Lennon, Paul McCartney, and George Harrison of The Beatles 68. Chuck Berry 69. Jimi Hendrix 70. The Pink Floyd pig 71. Debbie Harry of Blondie 72. Eric Clapton 73. The Jag-Stang Guitar 74. Angus Young of AC/DC 75. Jim Morrison of The Doors 76. Madonna 77. Link Wray's guitar 78. Beatles dolls, reputed to be the most sought after collectable 79. An MTV Video Music Award 80. Lucille, B.B. King's Guitar

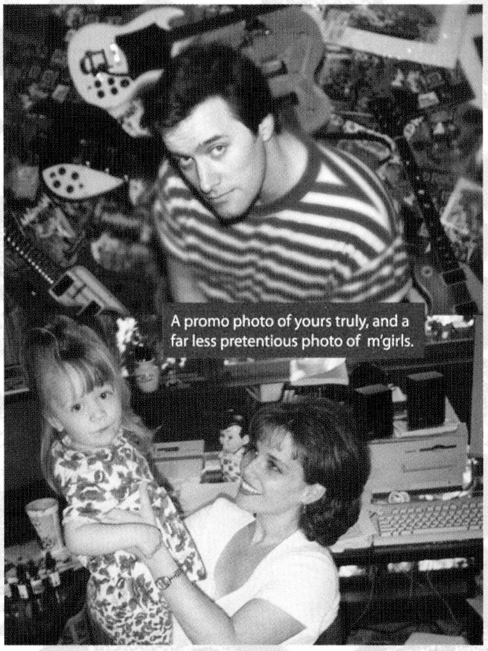

A promo photo of yours truly, and a far less pretentious photo of m'girls.

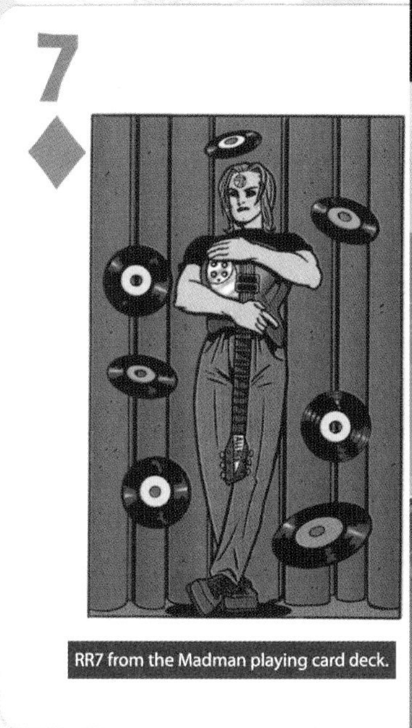
7

RR7 from the Madman playing card deck.

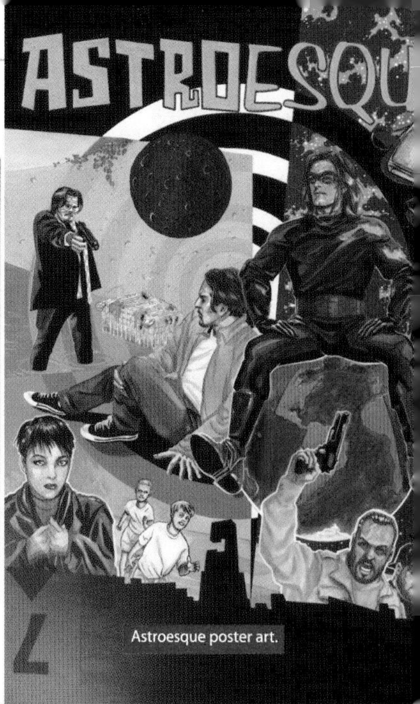

Astroesque poster art.

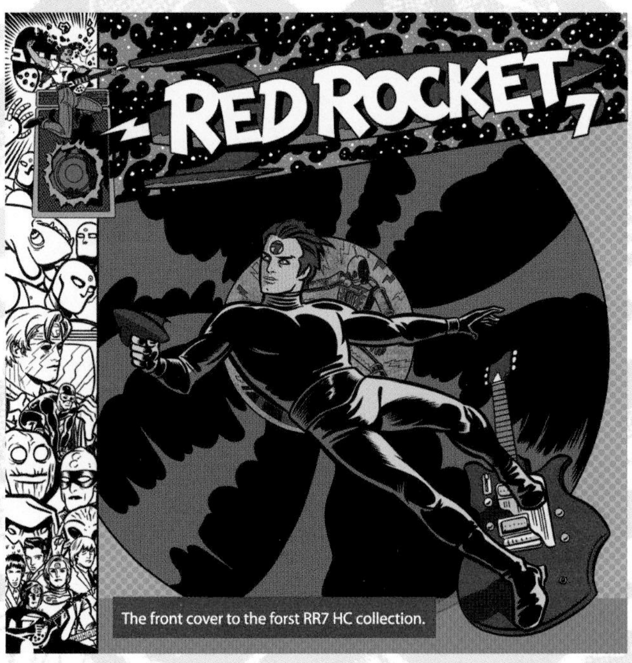
RED ROCKET 7

The front cover to the forst RR7 HC collection.

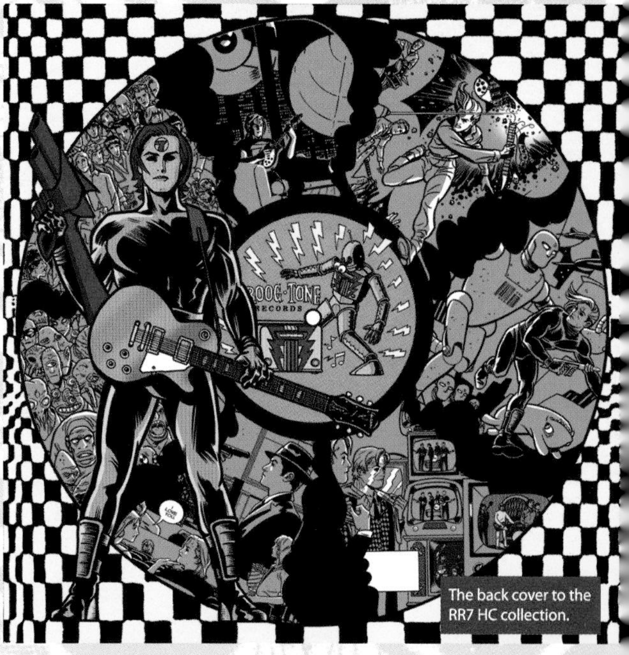

The back cover to the RR7 HC collection.

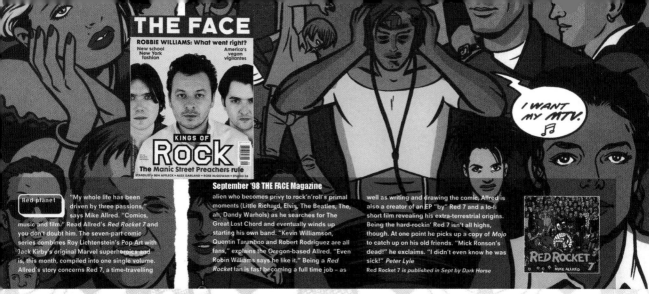

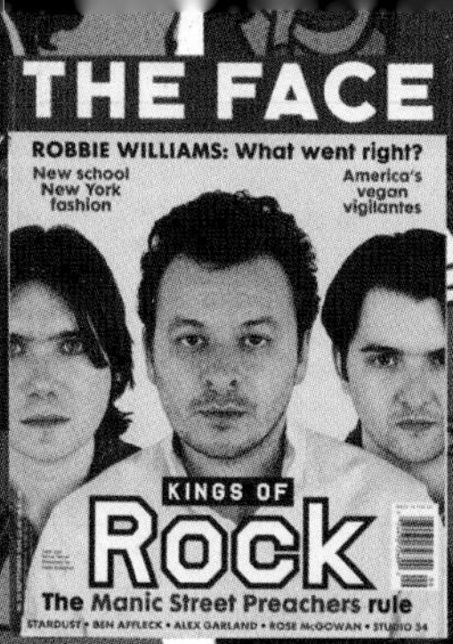
THE FACE
ROBBIE WILLIAMS: What went right?
New school New York fashion
America's vegan vigilantes
KINGS OF
Rock
The Manic Street Preachers rule
STARDUST • BEN AFFLECK • ALEX GARLAND • ROSE McGOWAN • STUDIO 54

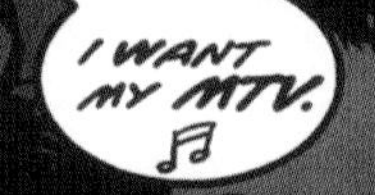
I WANT MY MTV.

September '98 THE FACE Magazine

Red planet "My whole life has been driven by three passions," says Mike Allred. "Comics, music and film." Read Allred's *Red Rocket 7* and you don't doubt him. The seven-part comic series combines Roy Lichtenstein's Pop Art with Jack Kirby's original Marvel superheroics and is, this month, compiled into one single volume. Allred's story concerns Red 7, a time-travelling alien who becomes privy to rock'n'roll's primal moments (Little Richard, Elvis, The Beatles, The, ah, Dandy Warhols) as he searches for The Great Lost Chord and eventually winds up starting his own band. "Kevin Williamson, Quentin Tarantino and Robert Rodriguez are all fans," explains the Oregon-based Allred. "Even Robin Williams says he like it." Being a *Red Rocket* fan is fast becoming a full time job – as well as writing and drawing the comic, Allred is also a creator of an EP "by" Red 7 and a lo-fi short film revealing his extra-terrestrial origins. Being the hard-rockin' Red 7 isn't all highs, though. At one point he picks up a copy of *Mojo* to catch up on his old friends. "Mick Ronson's dead!" he exclaims. "I didn't even know he was sick!" *Peter Lyle*

Red Rocket 7 *is published in Sept by Dark Horse*

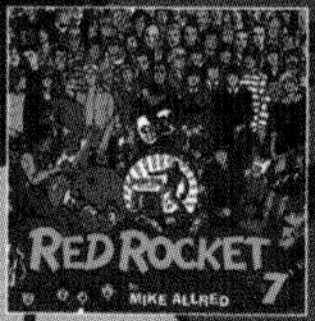
RED ROCKET 7
MIKE ALLRED

MUSIC-RELATED READING MATTER

From Elvis to the Beatles to David Bowie, Red Rocket 7 has been influencing rock history. His creator, Mike Allred, reveals the alien's origins to Dave Thompson.

A self-confessed pop-culture animal, Mike Allred is the author of *Red Rocket 7* (Dark Horse Comics Inc.), the monthly book that has, since last August, been detailing Red Rocket 7's remarkable career. Red is from outer space. He was cloned from an alien who reached earth in 1953 and, whether you know it or not, you've been listening to his music ever since. There's no shortage of sci-fi stuff going on in *RR7*, but there's also a highly personalized history of rock and roll through which the malevolent, green Enfinites pursue Red.

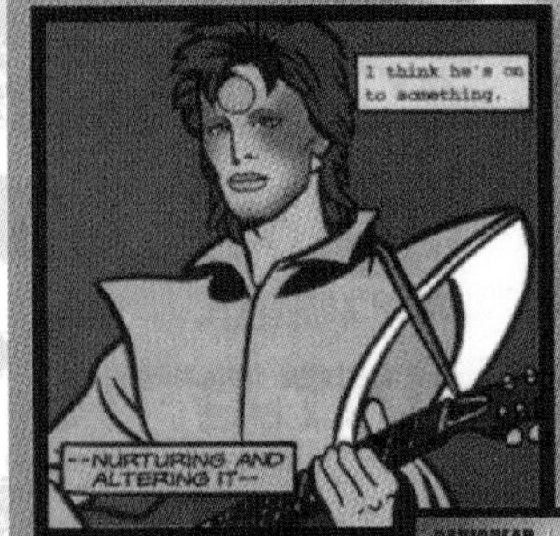
I think he's on to something.
--NURTURING AND ALTERING IT--

For anyone who has missed the story so far or forgotten how Red Rocket 7 taught Elvis all his moves and the Beatles all their chords, who maybe didn't know that Red was there when Brian Jones died (the Enfinites again), or that he was the inspiration for David Bowie's image, Allred should be familiar regardless. Creator of the *Madman* comics and a member of the band Gear, he is already one of the most high-profile names in the modern comicdom. And Allred freely admits that *Red Rocket 7* was spawned by a dream of pushing that profile even higher. Literally, a dream.

"In this dream," he recalls, "it was very clear to me how the world tied together, and it also became very clear to me how easy it is to take any creative project—even comics—and just do it, simply by removing barriers that initially seem impenetrable. So when I woke up, I was dead set on doing what I wanted, not waiting for any 'big break,' just getting on and doing it. And the fear of failure just evaporated. Suddenly, it became more important to me to simply create, rather than worry about how many people it would reach."

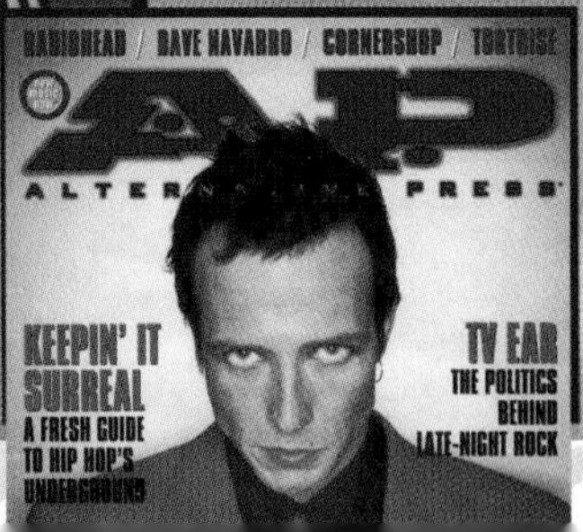
RADIOHEAD / DAVE NAVARRO / CORNERSHOP / TORTOISE
AP
ALTERNATIVE PRESS
KEEPIN' IT SURREAL
A FRESH GUIDE TO HIP HOP'S UNDERGROUND
TV EAR
THE POLITICS BEHIND LATE-NIGHT ROCK

What he created was the stuff of ultimate juvenile fantasy, gathering up everything that fascinated him as a child—sci-fi films and Bowie, horror stories and the Beatles—and then throwing it all together. Set to run over seven issues before reappearing in a collected edition, *Red Rocket 7* incorporates all those elements and more. The comic is fiction fired by cultural autobiography, a collusion that is only exacerbated by Allred's musical adventures: His aforementioned band, Gear, are just completing work on their debut album, titled—not at all coincidentally—*Red Rocket 7* and featuring several of the songs referenced in the comic as Red Rocket's own.

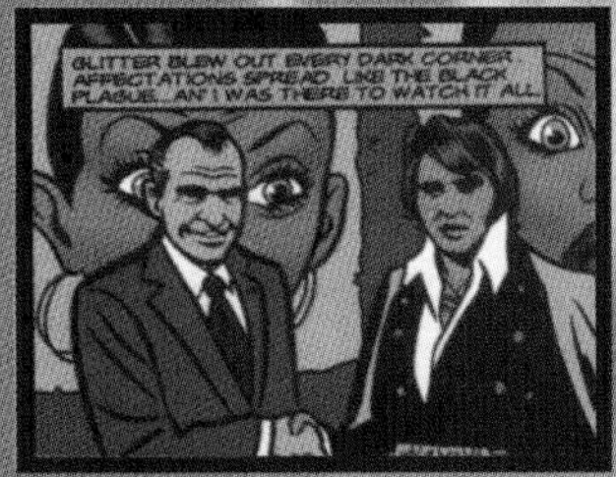
GLITTER BLEW OUT EVERY DARK CORNER. AFFECTATIONS SPREAD LIKE THE BLACK PLAGUE... AN' I WAS THERE TO WATCH IT ALL.

"It's a concept album in the same way David Bowie's *Ziggy Stardust* was," says Allred. "There's definitely some songs that tie in with the comic, but they stand on their own, as well."

The cross-marketing of a sci-fi comic and an accompanying record has been done before, most notably back in the mid-1970s when a crop of superstar session men got together to create *Flash Fearless Vs. The Zorg Women Of Tomorrow* (or some such nonsense—Alice Cooper was in on it, though). Like 99 percent of the record-buying public, Allred missed that one, but in any case he's confident that he has avoided the obvious pitfalls of such an endeavor. This time around, for instance, readers won't have to know the comic to make sense of the album—and vice versa.

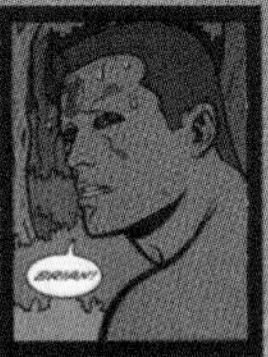

"We actually mapped out the things we didn't want to happen," he says, "and that scary comic-book elitism was one of them."

Thus, Allred's original idea of calling the group Red Rocket 7 was scrapped early on. Thus, too, Gear won't be appearing onstage in costume. And no one can blame them for that. The Enfinites are already blasting anyone and anything that comes too close to Red Rocket 7, and so far, Allred has managed to keep a couple of steps ahead of them. The last thing he needs is to start advertising his presence.

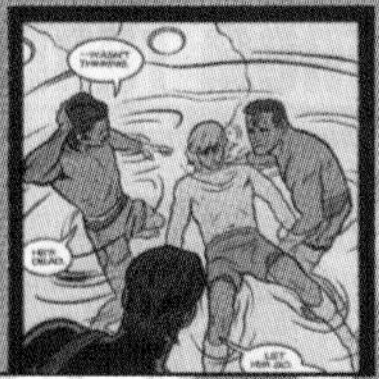

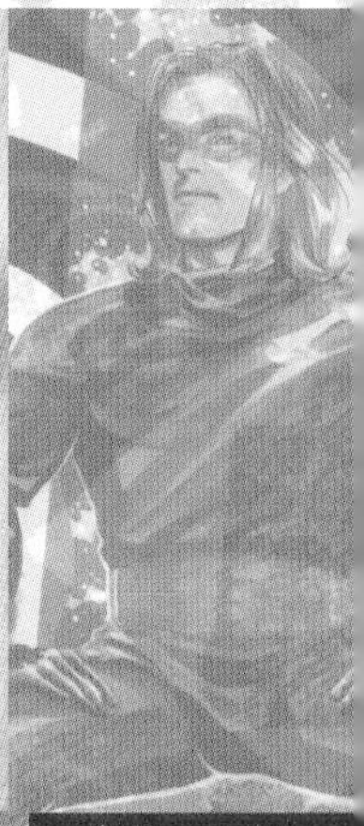

Articles in *The Face* magazine (above) and *Alternative Press* (below)

Sonic Boom

Nov '98 RAYGUN Magazine

Mike Allred's *Red Rocket 7* and the Pander Bros.' *Secret Broadcast* comics tap into the polysonic world of popular music

raygun

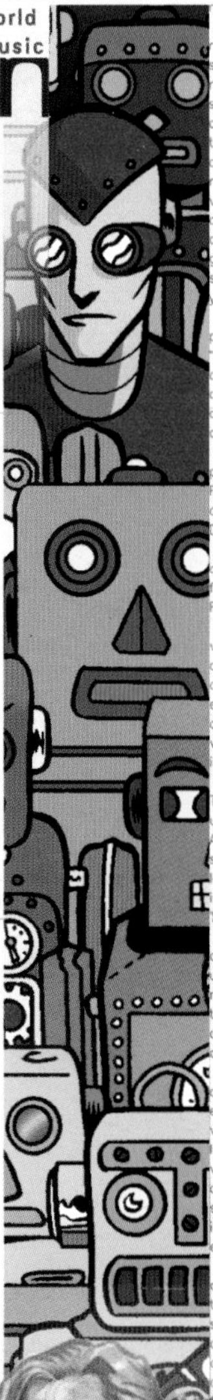

Over the years, comics and popular music have shared a long, healthy relationship with one another. The likes of KISS, the Rolling Stones, Public Enemy, Jimi Hendrix, Bob Marley, MC Hammer, Alice Cooper, and countless other sonic icons have all been rendered in glorious four color newsprint. But turning popular musical figures into comic book heroes is one thing. Creating original characters that interact in real (and surreal) musical environs is a totally different ballgame, and one that simultaneously elevates both the comic art form and the music which inspired it.

Two such artists working to creatively integrate the various arenas of popular music with the imaginative world of the comic book (and in the process create a new comic book/musical vocabulary) are Mike Allred and the Pander Bros. In both cases the artists are trying to lead people somewhere else, essentially redefining the potential of the comic book medium.

Allred, best known in comic circles for his delirious creation *Madman*, steps into the vast historical realm of popular music with *Red Rocket 7*, the story of an interstellar visitor (simply called 7 due to a bright red number seven emblazoned on his forehead) who spends several decades interacting with rock musicians, in the process, changing the course of rock 'n' roll history. Call it the Rock Musician Who Fell To Earth, if you will. And while the plot falls somewhere between *The Fugitive*, *Starman*, and *Help!* in reality the book is a magnum opus to popular music, with Allred presenting sly yet loving explanations of some of rock's greatest mysteries (In Allred's universe, original Stones guitarist Brian Jones drowns when he is accidentally pushed into a pool by 7 during a scuffle with rogue aliens; 7 also becomes the one who taught Elvis the pelvic thrust).

Allred's fascination with music is a long standing one. In fact, his first professional gig was as a disc jockey on KY-95 and KRSB in Roseburg, Oregon. Given his rock radio background, it's no wonder Allred has the protagonist of *Red Rocket 7* interacting with a bevy of pop music icons ranging from Little Richard to the Beatles, the Stones, Bowie, on through to newer acts like the Dandy Warhols, Nirvana, and so on. "I have a full appreciation and excitement for the great bands that came out of the British Invasion. The Yardbirds, the Kinks, I love the early Stones, the Beatles and their innovations, the Animals," remarks Allred. But reading *Red Rocket 7*, one easily picks up on the rock 'n' roll lineage as 7 travels through the decades interacting with the top acts of the day. In fact, the cover of issue №6 is a tribute to the Beatles' *Sgt. Pepper's* album cover, featuring likenesses of everyone from Sonic Youth and the Ramones to Bob Dylan, Neil Young, U2, and Smashing Pumpkins. "It's like a family tree [of rock music], which I traced," explains Allred. "You'll see a leap from the late '60s as the British Invasion died down, to the glam rock period with Bowie, T. Rex, Mott the Hoople. And from glam rock you find the roots of punk rock, and how that in turn became new wave. So you kind of have this history of rock 'n' roll—at least the music that interests me the most—threading through the back story of *Red Rocket 7*."

While the content of *Red Rocket 7* touches upon the allure of rock 'n' roll, the packaging itself is also a tribute to musical youth. The initial seven-issue run of the book (it has since been compiled into a graphic novel) eschewed the traditional 8 1/2" by 11" comic format in favor of a 10" square, paying tribute to the EP records of yesteryear. "I miss the record albums that you could open up, like the Who's *Quadrophenia*, where there would also be a book inside," Allred explains. "I miss the record album art form. Just being able to open something up and read liner notes from the band, or some really cool art designs that you can look at while you're listening to the album. Things like Zeppelin's *Physical Graffiti* or Bowie's *Diamond Dogs*, which created an atmosphere that went along with the album which you just don't get now. Just a lot of great graphics, and they were big, and it was as much fun to lay on your stomach and look at the interesting graphics and read all the lyrics while you were listening to the album."

But perhaps the boldest statement Allred makes is in the opening panels of issue №1, where 7, onstage before a sold-out crowd, remarks "I've heard the music labeled as avant pop. The music is always getting divided into genres and subgenres. Please ignore all that. Avant pop—alternative—call it what you want. To me, it's only rock 'n' roll." It's almost as if Allred, through the guise of 7, is railing against the growing commercial and corporate inundation of both radio and popular music.

While Allred's book captures the pure, raw essence of rock 'n' roll's past and present, as experienced through the eyes of a visiting alien, the Pander Bros.' *Secret Broadcast* project taps not only into the neon tribal aesthetic of the burgeoning US electronic movement and underground DJ culture, but also the ongoing exercise of pirate radio.

What's unique about *Secret Broadcast* is that it essentially began life as a CD and evolved into a comic almost as an afterthought. The initial idea for *Secret Broadcast* grew out of the previous project of Arnold and Jacob Pander, *Triple XXX*, and was envisioned as a soundtrack to that comic.

"When we were working on the *Triple XXX* project in Amsterdam, we were exposed to the whole pirate radio scene out there. And that was actually our first encounter with it," recalls Jacob. "This was back in '88 and '89, and the station was playing some of the first 'acid house,' really early techno stuff that we'd never heard before. And that had an impact on what we were doing already. That music became our soundtrack while we were drawing out there. So that has always been percolating in the back of our minds."

The basic premise of *Secret Broadcast* follows three protagonists—Toby, Carlos, and Gino—who operate their own pirate radio frequency under the call letters F.C.C.T., a rather sly stab at the governing body of American radio, the F.C.C., but at the same time a political and social statement about the continuing consolidation of commercial radio, the lack of creative programming on the dial, and the government's increasing control of the airwaves (i.e. radio today is fucked). *Pump Up The Volume*, this ain't.

Providing a direct link and adding an extra dimension to the story is the accompanying *Secret Broadcast* CD, which features a plethora of underground electronic music and is meant to be listened to while reading the book, thus creating the illusion that one is actually listening to pirate radio as the story unfolds. Ironically, the Panders enlisted the aid of several pirate radio operators during the creation of the project and have since worked on other projects with them.

"By having the project be linked to an actual act that's happening in the community, it gives the material an authenticity that isn't necessarily expressed literally," explains Arnold. "It gives it a sense of a real vibe which is happening around the country, and people reading the book and listening to the CD are getting to hear something that's going on in the world that they're possibly not aware of. And that is really what it's all about in terms of pop culture. Instilling that feeling that you're on to something that no one else knows about yet. So by virtue of getting involved with these people, Jacob and I wanted to make it a real experience and not just be a concept."

At the core of both *Red Rocket 7* and *Secret Broadcast* is not only the creators' love for the popular music spectrum, spanning rock 'n' roll on through digitized ambience, but also a desire to break down the barriers surrounding contemporary pop culture. Both Allred and the Panders are attempting to redefine our perceptions of what comics and music are all about. And through the merging of two distinctly American pop cultural art forms—rock 'n' roll and comic books—they have succeeded.

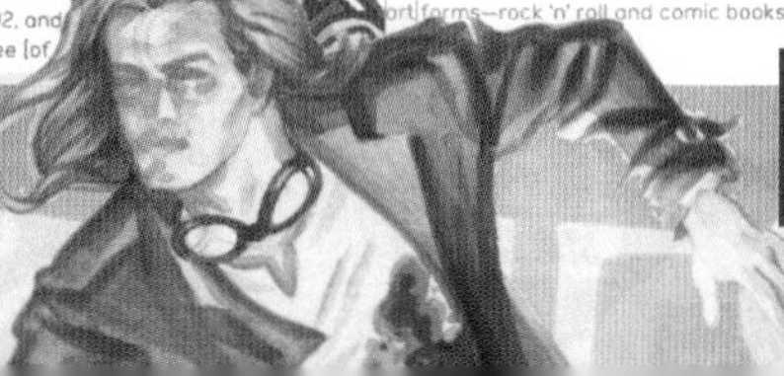

ILL LITERATURE

The rock-and-rolling comic-book adventurer Red Rocket 7 gets relaunched with an anthology and a companion CD.

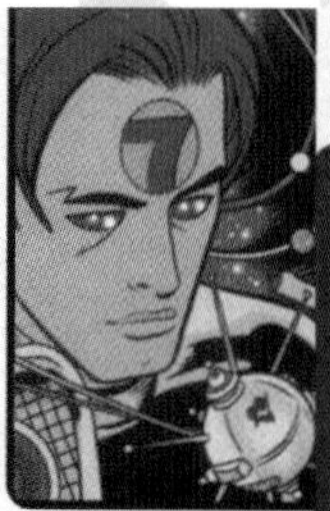

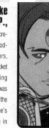

The last time Mike Allred visited A.P., he was full of threats. The creator of one of the greatest modern comic-book adventurers, the rock-and-rolling Red Rocket 7, Allred was just completing work on an RR7 album. He was also getting ready to publish the full adventures of everyone's favorite flame-haired alien in one book-length anthology.

A year later, and both phases of his master plan are complete. *Red Rocket 7* ($29.95, Dark Horse Comics) slams together all seven installments of the Red Rocket saga, tracking the space boy from his arrival on Earth in 1953 where he encounters a young Little Richard, and on through to another four decades of—well, basically, Red Rocket 7 hangs out with pop stars, and he gives them funny ideas. Would David Bowie have gone all glam and gay if Red Rocket 7 hadn't been around to help him think of it? Would the Rolling Stones have turned into demon-rocking bluesmen if Red Rocket 7 hadn't taken them down to the crossroads? Red Rocket knows all of rock's greats; one of Bowie's roadies even named his first-born after him. If this weren't a comic, it'd be one of the greatest stories in modern rock history. It is a comic, though, so we pretend instead.

Or do we? Released alongside the book, *Son Of Red Rocket 7* is the debut album by Allred's band the Gear. And while you can count on one hand the number of writers who've ever gotten a worthwhile musical idea into a listenable format, the Gear might well encourage you to grow another finger. Using the same types of psychedelic drones favored by the Dandy Warhols, the Brian Jonestown Massacre and almost anyone else who owns too many Velvet Underground records, the Gear are both a perfect accompaniment to *Red Rocket 7* and a great soundtrack. Seven songs at the end of the CD serve up *The Lost Red Rocket 7 Recordings*, tracks referenced throughout the comic but (obviously) unheard until now.

"The front of the disc is my real statement," Allred says of the album. "It's everything I love about music—the passion, the rhythm, the excitement. It's my tribute to my inspirations. The main thing I want to do is create the same type of joy that music created in me."

His art follows that same line of thought. Read through to the somewhat surprising conclusion of the Red Rocket 7 story, and a previously unpublished portrait gallery pays tribute of another sort to one of the most important rock-art books of the 1970s, Guy Peellaert's *Rock Dreams*. Criminally long out of print, *Rock Dreams* was a succession of paintings tracing the history of rock through image rather than events, and the results were disturbing, to say the least.

Allred's paintings, it must be said, do not have the same edge of incipient disaster that characterized *Rock Dreams*, but they probably weren't intended to. Rather, Allred captures the innocence of the scenes he describes: days when the Beach Boys really were surfboard-carrying All-American dream boats, and none of them was mad or dead or drunk; days when Marc Bolan really did fly through space in a sports car, with a teddy bear at his side; days when the Partridge Family really would have commissioned Red Rocket 7 and Joey Ramone to paint their bus for them.

It's a gentle nostalgia, as well as a pretty one, and even through the occasional outbreaks of violence that pock the Red Rocket 7 comic book, those qualities remain Allred's touchstone. Which is how it should be. *Red Rocket 7* is the story of Allred's dreams. Its success proves that a lot of other people share those dreams.

An article from *Raygun* magazine (above left) and another from *Alternative Press*(above right).

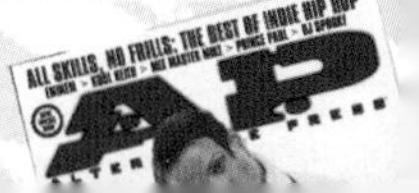

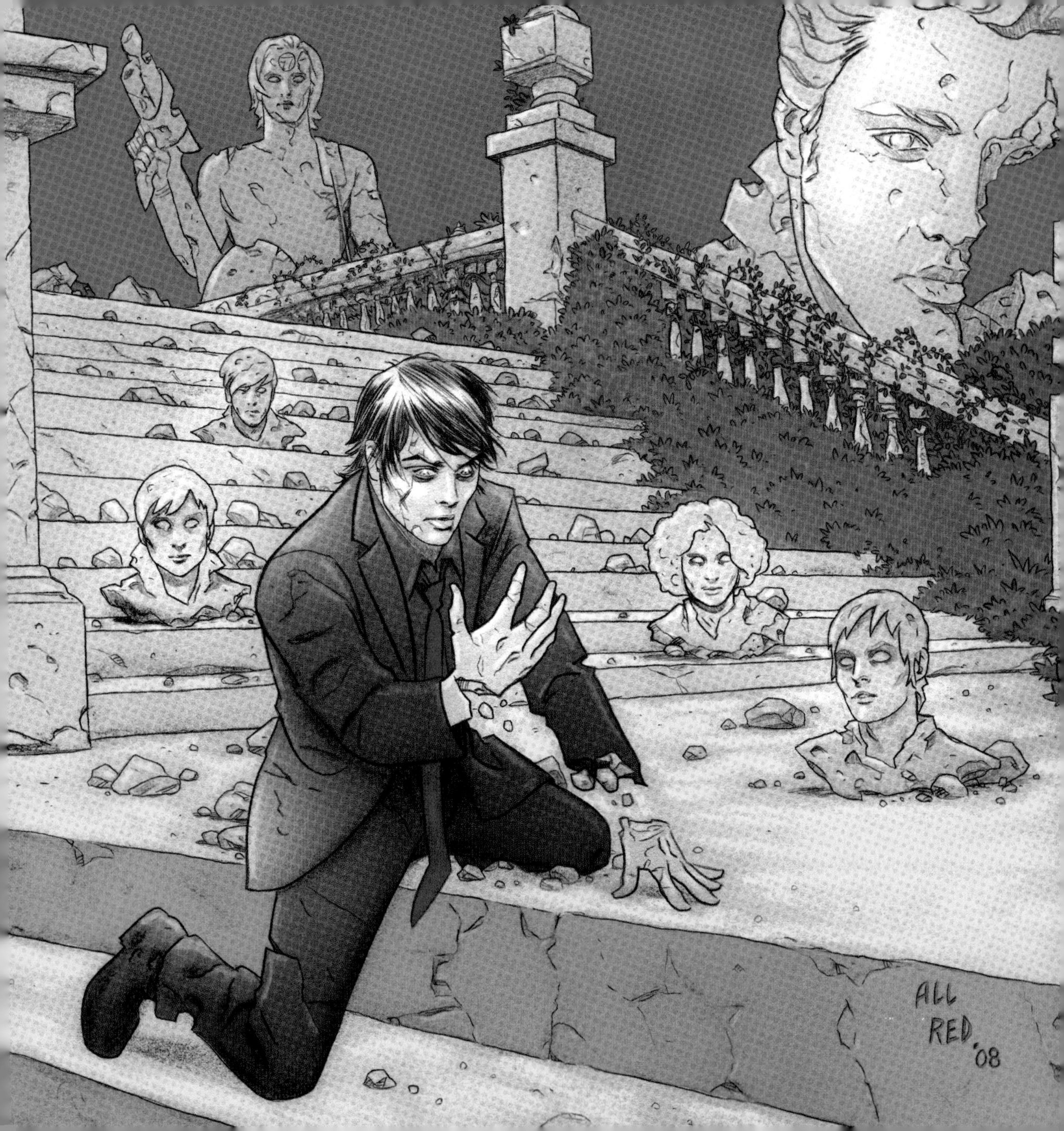
ALL
RED '08

O U T R O

By Gerard Way

Everyone wants to play guitar.

The thing is, until you plug it in for the first time you never know what you're capable of.

From the very first issue of *Madman* I was an instant fan…the carefree nature of the writing, the innocence of the lines on the page, the naivety of the hero, the risk in doing something new in a market full of cyborgs and metal bikinis— it was pure comics, pure ideas and pure love for the form.

Mike was plugging in.

He was doing it in a way that had never been done before, sticking that quarter-inch cable right into the brain of Jack Kirby, running it through a Vox AC30, patching into an Octivia, adding some wind-up teeth, sprinkling on some Pop-Rocks, and playing it right through the ink.

So when *Red Rocket 7* came out I rushed to the comic shop, obviously, because it involved my two favorite things— music and comics, or more importantly—music and Mike Allred.

Not only was it written and drawn by my new favorite artist, and wonderfully colored in Lichtenstein-Technicolor by Laura Allred, but it had Fender Jaguars. Jaguars with matching headstocks, nods to *Sgt. Pepper's*, and of course— ray-guns.

I expected something amazing. What I didn't expect to read was such an outstanding and surreal love-letter to the world of music. All of it's villains and heroes, it's spacemen and lunatics- and it wasn't elitist, it didn't exclude. It had everyone from Little Richard to Noel Gallagher and so much more than that—it contained a story of taking the big risk, and putting something out there in the universe.

The moment you decide to start a band, put a pen to paper, direct a film, or type a story, you are displaying yourself for the world to judge, love, or condemn, and in most cases, both. For *Red Rocket 7*, Mike did all four—starting The Gear, filming *Astroesque*, writing and drawing the comic. It is a complete vision, an ambitious expression never attempted to this extent in comics, and an utter triumph.

This is *Red Rocket 7*, plugged in. And it's louder than it was in '97.

Cue the house lights.

-Gerard Way,
Los Angeles, California
July 2008

Gerard Way is the lead singer for a nifty little band called MY CHEMICAL ROMANCE,
and is the creator/writer for the Eisner award-winning comic book, *THE UMBRELLA ACADEMY*.

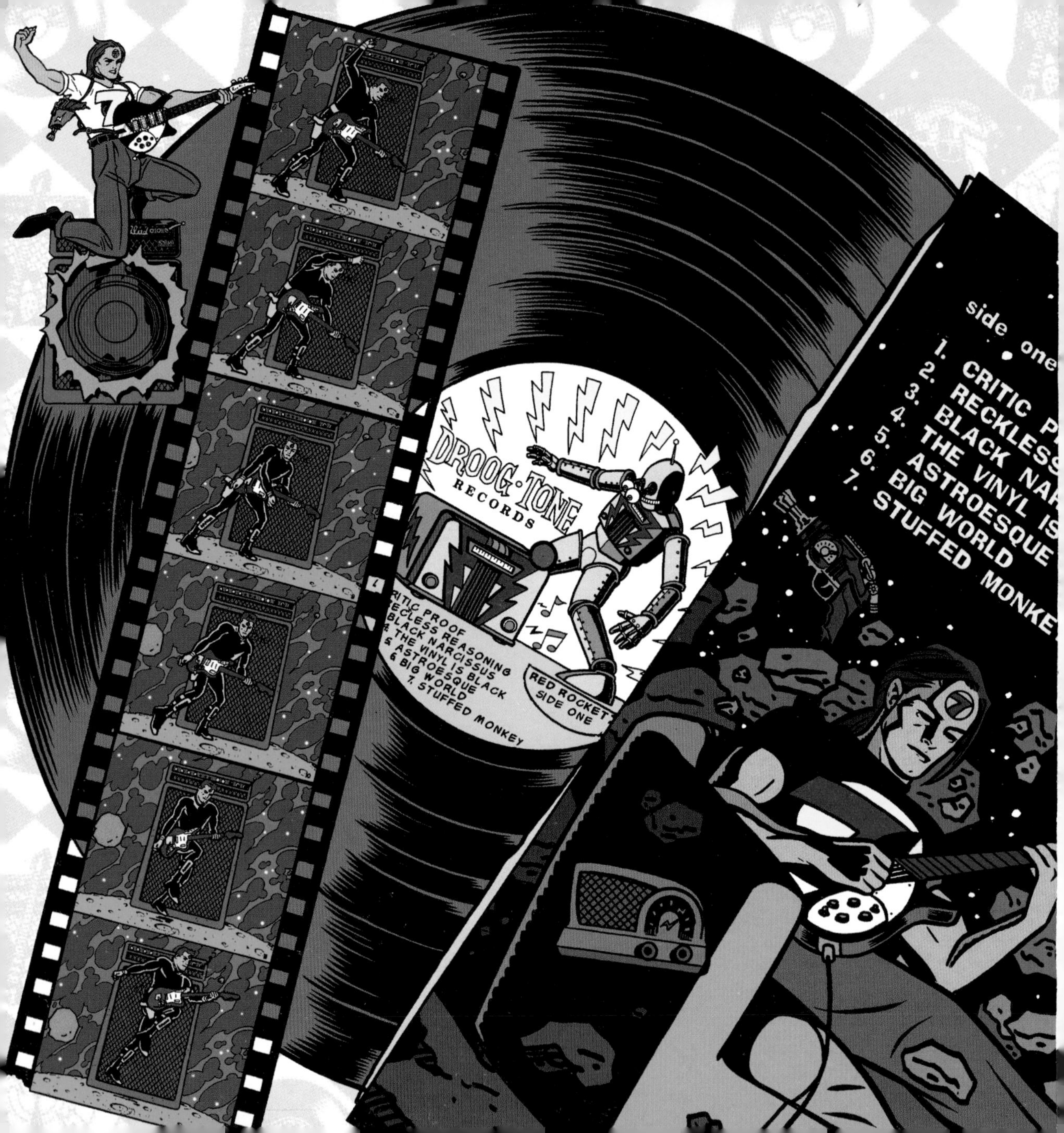

DROOG-TONE
RECORDS
RITIC PROOF
ECLESS REASONING
BLACK NARCISSUS
4. THE VINYL IS BLACK
5 ASTROESQUE
6 BIG WORLD
7. STUFFED MONKEY
RED ROCKET 7
SIDE ONE
side one
1. CRITIC P
2. RECKLESS
3. BLACK NA
4. THE VINYL IS
5. ASTROESQUE
6. BIG WORLD
7. STUFFED MONKE